*Routledge Revivals*

# Combating Terrorism

Terrorism suffers the fate of many issues receiving wide media coverage: it is much discussed but little understood. First published in 1990, this book develops a clear conceptual framework which will enable the reader to come to a better assessment of the exact extent and nature of the threat posed by terrorism and of the measures appropriate to combating it. With numerous case studies including the British in Northern Ireland and the Americans in the Middle East, the author gives a comparative survey of counter-terrorism in the United States, the United Kingdom, and Canada.

# Combating Terrorism

## G. Davidson Smith

Routledge
Taylor & Francis Group

First published in 1990
by Routledge

This edition first published in 2011 by Routledge
2 Park Square, Milton Park, Abingdon, Oxon, OX14 4RN

Simultaneously published in the USA and Canada
by Routledge
270 Madison Avenue, New York, NY 10016

*Routledge is an imprint of the Taylor & Francis Group, an informa business*

**Publisher's Note**
The publisher has gone to great lengths to ensure the quality of this reprint but
points out that some imperfections in the original copies may be apparent.

**Disclaimer**
The publisher has made every effort to trace copyright holders and welcomes
correspondence from those they have been unable to contact.

A Library of Congress record exists under LC Control Number: 89010970

ISBN 13: 978-0-415-61530-3 (hbk)
ISBN 13: 978-0-415-61531-0 (pbk)

# Combating Terrorism

G. Davidson Smith

London and New York

First published 1990
by Routledge
11 New Fetter Lane, London EC4P 4EE

Simultaneously published in the USA and Canada
by Routledge
a division of Routledge, Chapman and Hall, Inc.
29 West 35th Street, New York, NY10001

© 1990 G. Davidson Smith

Typeset by LaserScript Limited, Mitcham, Surrey
Printed and bound in Great Britain by Mackays of Chatham PLC, Kent

*British Library Cataloguing in Publication Data*

Smith, G. Davidson, *1934-*
Combating terrorism.
1. Terrorism. Policies of governments
I. Title
322.4'2

ISBN 0-415-03067-6

*Library of Congress Cataloging in Publication Data*

Smith, G. Davidson, 1934-
Combating terrorism / G. Davidson Smith.
p. cm.
Includes bibliographical references.
ISBN 0-415-03067-6
1. Terrorism – Prevention. I. Title.
HV6431.S64 1990
363.3'2 – dc20                                      89-10970
                                                         CIP

# Contents

*Contents*

# Figures

# Preface

On 9 December 1955, a serious outbreak of rioting occurred in the city of Montreal, Québec, Canada. The circumstances involved approximately 1,500 university students who halted urban public transportation for a period of six hours. A seemingly minor government decision to increase the price of transit fares (from three tickets for thirty cents, to two tickets for twenty-five cents) allegedly prompted the disturbance. During the ensuing violence, 172 trams and 52 buses were heavily damaged, some by fire, and 114 persons were arrested.

Sporadic renewals of unrest continued in the downtown area for two days, requiring the deployment of 500 policemen to restore order. The situation eventually demanded that Mayor Jean Drapeau issue an edict banning all demonstrations. But the sight of that huge metropolis virtually brought to a standstill by mindless destruction employed in an attempt to alter government policy by means of intimidation created a lasting impression.

From that beginning has followed a continuing fascination with politically motivated violence. I have witnessed the growth of modern terrorism at close quarters, first in my own country and later at various times and places around the world. The experiences have reinforced my opinion that senior decision-makers in government, as well as those charged with operational response, must recognize the need for sound counter-terrorism policies and policy measures. It is my hope that this volume will be of some assistance to those charged with policy development and the implementation of policy.

My deep appreciation is extended to Professor Paul Wilkinson, who has been my mentor and guide; to my wife, Martha, who continues to be my source of motivation, support, and encouragement; and to Marie Dionne and Patricia Rutt for their hard work and generous concern.

# Abbreviations

| | |
|---|---|
| EOKA | Ethniki Organosis Kypriakou Agoniston (Cyprus) |
| EPA | Northern Ireland (Emergency Provisions) Act (UK) |
| ERT | Emergency Response Team (Canada) |
| ETA | Euskadi ta Askatasuna, or Basque Fatherland and Liberty Movement (Spain) |
| ETO | European Theatre of Operations |
| FAA | Federal Aviation Administration (USA) |
| FALN | Armed Forces of National Liberation (USA–Puerto Rico) |
| FBI | Federal Bureau of Investigation (USA) |
| FCO | Foreign and Commonwealth Office (UK) |
| FEMA | Federal Emergency Measures Agency (USA) |
| FISA | Foreign Intelligence Surveillance Act (USA) |
| FLN | Front de Liberation National (Algeria) |
| FLQ | Front de Liberation du Québec (Canada) |
| FP-25 | Popular Forces of April 25 (Portugal) |
| GAO | General Accounting Office (USA) |
| GCHQ | Government Communications Headquarters (UK) |
| GOC | General Officer Commanding |
| GRAPO | Grupo Revolucionario Antifascista Primero de Octubre (Spain) |
| GSG-9 | Grenzshutzgruppe 9, special unit of the Federal Border Guard (West Germany) |
| IAC | Intelligence Advisory Committee |
| ICAO | International Civil Aviation Organization |
| ICSI | Interdepartmental Committee on Security and Intelligence (Canada) |
| IG/T | Interdepartmental Group on Terrorism (USA) |
| INLA | Irish National Liberation Army (Eire & UK) |
| IRA | Irish Republican Army, also know as the OIRA or 'Officials' (Eire & UK) |
| IS | Internal Security |
| JCAG | Justice Commandos of the Armenian Genocide |
| JIC | Joint Intelligence Committee (UK) |
| JIO | Joint Intelligence Organization (UK) |
| JRA | Japanese Red Army |
| KKK | Ku Klux Klan (USA & Canada) |
| M/CTP | Office for Counter Terrorism and Emergency Planning (USA) |
| MI-5 | Security Service (UK) |
| MI-6 | Secret Intelligence Service (UK) |
| MIS | Ministerial steering committee on intelligence (UK) |
| MoD | Ministry of Defence (UK) |
| MOU | Memorandum of Understanding |
| MP | Military Police, or Member of Parliament |

| | |
|---|---|
| NATO | North Atlantic Treaty Organization |
| NEST | Nuclear Emergency Search Team (USA) |
| NIO | Northern Ireland Office (UK) |
| NORAID | Irish Northern Aid Committee. US-based group with the declared purpose of providing funds for relief of families deprived of wage-earners because of the struggle against Britain. Alleged to be a source of funding for terrorist operations of PIRA. |
| NSC | National Security Council (USA) |
| NSDD | National Security Decision Directive (USA) |
| OAS | Organization of American States |
| October Crisis | Period of national emergency declared by Canadian Government, including proclamation of the War Measures Act, which commenced in October 1970, and was a result of terrorist activities of the FLQ. |
| OD | Foreign Affairs, Defence and Northern Ireland Committee (UK) |
| ORAE | Operational Research and Analysis Establishment (Canada) |
| PCO | Privy Council Office (Canada) |
| PFLP | Popular Front for the Liberation of Palestine |
| PIRA | Provisional Irish Republican Army, also known as the 'Provos' or 'Provisionals' (Eire & UK) |
| PLO | Palestinian Liberation Organization |
| PRM | Presidential Review Memorandum (USA) |
| PSB | Police and Security Branch (Canada) |
| PTA | Prevention of Terrorism (Temporary Provisions) Act (UK) |
| RAF | Royal Air Force (UK) |
| RCMP | Royal Canadian Mounted Police |
| RDPG | Royalty and Diplomatic Protection Group of the Metropolitan Police (UK) |
| REC | Regional Emergencies Committees (UK) |
| RM | Royal Marines (UK) |
| RN | Royal Navy (UK) |
| RPG-7 | Rocket-Propelled Grenade-7 (Soviet bloc weapon) |
| RUC | Royal Ulster Constabulary (UK) |
| SAC | Security Advisory Committee (Canada) |
| SACHR | Standing Advisory Committee on Human Rights (UK) |
| SAS | Special Air Service Regiment (UK) |
| SCC | Special Coordination Committee (USA) |
| S/CT | Office of Ambassador-at-large for Counter-Terrorism (USA) |
| SDLP | Social Democratic and Labour Party (UK) |

| | |
|---|---|
| SEAL | US Navy Sea, Air, Land teams; a branch of US Special Forces |
| SERT | Special Emergency Response Team (Canada) |
| Sinn Fein | Political wing of the IRA; a similar organization exists for PIRA, known as Provisional Sinn Fein (Eire & UK) |
| SNLA | Scottish National Liberation Army (UK) |
| SOF | Special Operations Forces (USA) |
| SPARG | Security Planning and Research Group (Canada) |
| Spetsnaz | Special commando forces of the Soviet Union |
| SPG | Special Patrol Group (UK) |
| Summit | Canada, USA, UK, Japan, West Germany, France, and |
| Seven | Italy; grouping originally convened to discuss economic co-operation |
| SWAT | Special Weapons and Tactics team |
| SWP | Socialist Workers Party (UK) |
| T-8 | Metropolitan Police protective advisory unit (UK) |
| TA | Territorial Army (UK) |
| TAOR | Tactical Area of Responsibility |
| TIGER | Terrorist Intelligence Gathering, Evaluation and Review (UK) |
| Trevi | International Counter-terrorism Group |
| TSWG | Technical Support Working Group (USA) |
| Tupameros | Uruguayan terrorist group |
| TWA | Trans World Airlines (USA) |
| UDA | Ulster Defence Association (UK) |
| UDR | Ulster Defence Regiment (UK) |
| UFF | Ulster Freedom Fighters (UK) |
| UN | United Nations |
| USCG | United States Coast Guard |
| UVF | Ulster Volunteer Force (UK) |
| WGT | Working Group on Terrorism (USA) |

Chapter one

# The threat

## Introduction

The phenomenon of terrorism has demanded increasing scrutiny over the past two decades. Terrorism has become a central and controversial issue of world-wide attention – a subject of analysis and debate not only by members of the military and law-enforcement communities, but also by government officials and academics alike.

Terrorism's current influence on the mechanics of civilization has been sufficient to earn egregious labelling as 'the greatest evil of our age, a more serious threat to our culture and survival than the possibility of nuclear war, or even the rapid depletion of the planet's natural resources'.[1] Such dangerously exaggerated expressions of judgement serve to confuse and obscure basic realities. Noted international authority, Professor Paul Wilkinson, makes it plain that 'generalizations and evaluations covering the whole field of modern terrorism should be treated with considerable reserve'.[2] Perhaps of greater significance, he sounds a percipient warning with the corollary: 'Over-simplified analysis of the phenomena tends to induce simplistic and dangerous proposals for panaceas.'[3]

Terrorism is not a phenomenon unique to the modern era. Viewed from a historical perspective, examples of terrorist behaviour are abundant. The Book of Exodus, for instance, describes seven plagues visited upon ancient Egypt to secure the release of the tribes of Israel. The Jewish Zealots conducted a campaign of terror against the Romans in the first century A.D.; a Shi'ia Muslim sect known as the Assassins gave literal meaning to that word in the eleventh century by systematically murdering 'those in positions of leadership and influence ... achieving political aims through the power of intimidation'.[4]

The Jacobin Reign of Terror in France during the revolutionary period of the 1790s is frequently cited in reference to the origin of terrorism as a political concept. Similarly, the anarchist Narodnya Volya's determined use of violence in their efforts to topple the Russian tsars

1

through the latter half of the nineteenth century is given credence as an antecedent of modern terrorism. Also worthy of mention are the activities of the Croatian–Serbian terrorist group, the 'Black Hand', who were responsible for the assassination of Archduke Ferdinand at Sarajevo in 1914, an act which triggered the First World War.

But the terrorism of today is not simply a product of history, although past and present events continue to play a dominant role. Rather, the very nature of modern civilization has largely promoted a recrudescence of terrorism as a political tool. Dramatic strides in technological innovation, sharply defined international power blocs, and the striving for influence in developing nations, as well as religious, ethnic, and cultural discord, have all made contributions to the current growth of terrorism. Nor does contemporary terrorist activity present an awesome threat, defying comprehension in terms of genesis and response. An accurate understanding of terrorism is obtainable through precise assessment in a given context. The assessment, however, must include the complexities of motivation, organization, methodology, and desired goals. It is through a serious appraisal of those factors that the threat may be better understood and more effectively countered.

A correct perspective of the threat, therefore, must take into account the following characteristics associated with terrorism: (1) contemporary historical evolution; (2) motivational underpinnings; (3) aims and strategies; (4) organizational infrastructure; (5) features of modern civilization which encourage use; and (6) current and future implications for society. These aspects are the subject of examination in the remainder of this chapter.

Terrorism, as opposed to other forms of violence, is the systematically applied threat or use of illegitimate force with the designed intent of achieving a goal by means of such a method of coercion. It is violence used as a policy; it is fear or terror engendered on an organized basis. Eckstein and Aron, among other authorities, agree that terrorism is inherently indiscriminate in the strategy of its use.[5] Terrorism has many applications, including purely criminal purposes; it is politically motivated terrorism, however, which is of major concern in the modern context.

From the standpoint of the practicalities of response, identification of the motivation underlying acts of terrorism offers more benefit than a pedantic attempt at definition of the phenomenon. A number of reasons support that opinion, such as the feasibility of developing appropriate policies of response, recognition of likely targets of terrorist interest, aggregation and assignment of suitable protective resources, as well as other measures which must be implemented, not the least of which being the nature of publicity to be devoted to the problem. An examination of the following two examples will help to illustrate this contention:

(a) Late on the evening of 9 December 1984, Iranian security forces managed to board a hijacked Kuwaiti airliner at Tehran airport; the Iranians overpowered the hijackers and released the hostages, who included two American citizens.[6]

(b) The *Daily Telegraph* of the following day, aside from publicizing the Tehran incident, contained a small news report of poisoned turkey warnings issued by members of the UK-based Animal Liberation Front (ALF).[7]

Disparate incidents in themselves, one quite obviously fraught with international implications and with lives immediately at risk, and the other purely domestic and questionable in its real threat to human life. Nonetheless, the deadly hijacking affair and the irresponsible consumer scare share a common bond as examples of politically motivated terrorism. Both events represent violence, or the threat of violence, used as a policy with the aim of achieving a political goal by means of coercion. The hijackers sought the release of persons convicted of terrorist crimes in Kuwait; in the case of the ALF, the activity was part of a continuing campaign seeking to change government legislation in Britain pertaining to the use of animals for scientific purposes.

While both incidents represent terrorism, they are each deserving of a different response. Fundamental as it may appear on the basis of the two examples, such a reality does not always obtain. Over-reaction, over-expenditure of resources, excessive publicity, and draconian legislation (or weakness and under-reaction) on the part of government or the public is not uncommon. Such circumstances often result from a misconception of the animating nature or source of a terrorist threat.

General George Grivas's oft-quoted remark concerning the operational employment of the British Army on Cyprus as 'a sledge-hammer used to crack a nut'[8] in the battle against EOKA brings home the point. Failure to understand the 'driving-force', or motivation, behind terrorist activity is often conducive to an under- or overestimation of the threat which, in turn, may foster an incorrect level or type of response. In real terms, for instance, the British Government's extensive and increasingly sophisticated reaction to PIRA attacks is properly different from that required to cope with current levels of the ALF threat.

Motivational basis, therefore, is examined first in assessing the nature of the threat presented by the phenomenon of terrorism. Included within the context is brief reference to the contemporary historical development of terrorist activity, because in many cases the two aspects are rooted together.

## Motivation

The collapse of colonial empires following the outcome of the Second World War, coupled with the subsequent rise of nationalism and the emergence of Third World nations, played a significant role in the modern evolution of terrorism. Terrorist behaviour quickly surfaced in the actions of 'national liberation' movements and the guerrilla warfare which erupted in locales such as Indo-China; there, first between the French and the Viet Minh forces, and later between the Viet Cong and the combination of indigenous Vietnamese and 'Free World' forces.

Terrorism was the technique adopted by the Irgun Zvai Leumi and the Stern Gang in their efforts to oust the British from Palestine. The military, the nationalists, and the extreme right 'colons' employed terrorism in the Algerian war; the communists espoused the tactic in Malaya, as did the Mau-Mau in Kenya, and Grivas and EOKA made good use of it on Cyprus. Castro introduced the method to Cuba in his battle against Batista, and the Doukhobors toyed fitfully and ineffectually with the concept in Canada.

Prior to the mid-1960s, terrorist activity could be feasibly described as relatively localized in scale and intensity, being generally confined within specific countries or narrowly limited to certain regions as a consequence of cross-border intrusions. In the wake of the 1967 Arab–Israeli war, however, a new dimension became evident when the PLO began international reprisal attacks against Israeli targets in foreign states. Terrorism began to change in character from what had been previously viewed as something of a domestic problem to that of a threat having major international proportions.

Athens air terminal was the scene of a PFLP assault on an El Al airliner in December 1968. The action was promptly revenged two days later by an Israeli commando raid on Beirut airport, causing an estimated $43 million damage to parked aircraft. The two incidents represented a foretaste of the deadly spiral of strike and counter-strike which still continues.

Closely aligned to movements with nationalist aspirations, separatist and irredentist groups have formed a conspicuous part of the international terrorist membership. Some groups, as in the case of the FLQ in Canada, succumbed in the face of determined governmental opposition; others, such as ETA in Spain, continue to survive despite strenuous efforts by security forces to suppress them. One variety of this category, unable to surface within their homelands, has transported terrorism to other nations where its chosen targets are diplomatic or exile communities. Two Armenian organizations, ASALA and JCAG, whose origins can be traced to Lebanon and the civil war of 1975–6, typify that development.

Racial, ethnic, and religious frictions have been another source of militancy in which terrorism has featured in attempts to secure particular goals. Historically, terrorism used in this context has been principally domestic in nature, typical of groups such as the Ku Klux Klan in the USA, and more recently the activities of the Black Liberation Army, Posse Comitatus, and the Jewish Defence League. An alarming international character has evolved, however, in the resurgence of Muslim fundamentalism emanating from the seizure of power in Iran by the Ayatolla Khomeini and his supporters. Suicide bombing attacks mounted by fanatical Shi'ias have markedly raised the threshold of danger, especially to western interests.

In parallel with all of the foregoing has been a growth in the use of terrorism by radical ideological movements. The Charles Martel Club of France, the Black Order of Italy, the Angry Brigade of England, and the Communist Combatant Cells of Belgium are illustrative of the broad spectrum from the far Right through fascism and anarchism to the far Left. More widely publicized, of course, have been the activities of the Red Army Faction of Germany and the Red Brigades of Italy.

Of late, an offshoot has appeared in the use of terrorist-type tactics to highlight the objectives associated with environmental protection, pollution, nuclear proliferation, and even the rapid advance of modern technology. Examples of the trend are found in the bombing by Direct Action in Canada of a firm engaged in the manufacture of parts for cruise missiles, the attacks by a Swiss ecology group against military training areas in that European nation, assaults upon computer firms by Action Directe in France, and the placing of bombs in the vicinity of nuclear reactor sites in West Germany.[9] Animal-rights activists in Britain and anti-abortionists in the USA have also demonstrated a willingness to resort to terrorist methods in attempts to draw attention to their aims.

In March 1973, a 298-ton coastal vessel, the *Claudia*, was intercepted off Ireland with a cargo of arms supplied by Libya and intended for the IRA. On the basis of involvement in logistical support of terrorist groups, as well as by giving refuge to fugitive terrorists and establishing terrorist training camps, Libya and several other 'rogue' nations have been seen to epitomize another modern evolution of terrorism: state sponsorship.

State terrorism, *per se*, is not a novel form of behaviour and has been a practice over the centuries in many countries. Colonel Gaddafi, for example, has been guilty of its application in his pursuit of dissidents both domestically and internationally. He is not unique in the latter activity; Stalin had his agents follow Trotsky to Mexico for the purpose of assassination. Gaddafi, however, took the matter a step further by giving practical and vocal support to an international range of terrorist groups almost on a random basis. While Gaddafi's reasons have not always been clear, some motivation may have been correctly determined by Robert Fisk: 'The nature of the struggle seems to be of less importance than the fact that it exists ....'[10]

On review, the post-Second World War experience of terrorism lends itself to the development of a typology based on motivation, as depicted in Figure 1. Categorization of terrorist activity in this manner is helpful in assisting us to determine the nature of the threat and the response which the threat demands. As discussed later, the typology alone does not suffice for policy analysis, but is part of the overall framework which contributes to that function.

*Figure 1* Terrorist motivations[*]

| | Type | Motivation |
|---|---|---|
| 1. | Nationalist–separatist–irredentist | Self-determination based on the unification, separation, or return of territory governed by another nationality; has ethnic overtones. |
| 2. | Issue | Militant protest to remedy perceived grievances or wrongs, such as government legislation. |
| 3. | Ideological | Pursuit of radical ideals of the Right or Left, such as fascism, anarchism, nihilism. |
| 4. | Exile | Opposition to prevailing situation in homeland |
| 5. | State and state-sponsored | Enforcement and oppression, or surrogate or open conflict. |
| 6. | Religious | Conflict of fundamental beliefs or doctrines. |

[*] See also Paul Wilkinson *Terrorism and the Liberal State* (2nd edition, London: The Macmillan Press Ltd., 1986)

The figure in itself is not sufficient explanation of the individual divisions; following paragraphs provide a more detailed explication of each category. But first, a note of caution: use of the typology for threat analysis and determination of response must be associated with consideration of other factors. Those factors, which include terrorist aims and strategies, organizational infrastructure, methodology, and current technology receive attention in later sections of this chapter. The typology merely offers a neat and systematic means of classifying terrorist groups according to motivation, from which position further close examination may be conducted.

### Nationalist–separatist–irredentist

A significant proportion of contemporary terrorist motivation springs from the desire for self-determination on the part of a minority ethnic or cultural element of a national population. Generally this nationalist spirit includes a wish to separate a portion of territory from the current hegemony, and frequently the rationale is based upon irredentist claims. Very few examples exist which do not incorporate at least two of these stimuli.

The FLQ in Canada was a classic example of nationalism combined with separatism and, looking back beyond 1759, an irredentist derivation was arguably present. Basque terrorism in Spain has foundations in nationalism and separatism, as does that of the Tamils in Sri Lanka, the Kashmiris in India, and the Kurds in the Middle East. Both the Croat and Armenian terrorist groups embody all three motivations in the claims for an independent statehood based upon historical derivation.

### Issue

The use of terrorist tactics by previously moderate protest groups is a relatively new departure, although it is gradually becoming more prevalent. Tactical 'successes' achieved by prominent terrorist groups (e.g. PLO, PIRA) in respect to ransoms paid, prisoners released, or the garnering of widespread publicity have engendered emulation by animal-rights activists, ecologists, and others of a similar ilk. Issue-group militancy usually stems from a wish to rectify a supposed grievance or wrong which is generally attributed to governmental action or inaction.

Several dangers are inherent in the use of terrorism by issue-motivated organizations, not the least of which is the possibility of an escalation of attacks to a level which threatens lives. The Animal Liberation Front in Great Britain has warned that its members 'may arm' themselves, and the group has used dangerous contaminants when adulterating consumer products in shops.[11] Anti-abortionist attacks in the USA have recently altered in character from bombings conducted 'under the cover of darkness during times when there was some hope that no one would be hurt' to use of mail bombs and an explosion 'in mid-afternoon, with clinic patients and staff on the premises'.[12]

Resort to violence by issue groups has some basis in frustration over the inability to achieve sought-after goals, a circumstance which could lead to an increased level of attacks and greater dangers. The latter might result from inexperience, an error of judgement, or the reality of confrontation with opponents. A tendency toward the formation of vigilante groups to fend off the protesters' assaults is a worrying development in both the USA and Great Britain. (Vigilantism is not confined to issue groups; this type of reaction can be mounted against other types of terrorists, e.g. racial, religious and ethnic.) Of equal concern is the possible enactment of draconian government legislation designed to protect against militants, but which actually creates inroads on human rights.

## *Ideological*

Long associated with the reality of politically motivated violence, ideological doctrines form the backdrop of a marked proportion of terrorist groups. It is important to recognize from the outset that terrorism related to ideology, however, is not merely the purview of the Left of the political spectrum. Anarchists, nihilists, fascists, and neo-Nazis spread the use of terrorism across to the far Right. Generally, nonetheless, it is the extremist militant representatives of the various colourings who advocate and/or indulge in terrorist behaviour.

Terrorism based upon ideology is exemplified by the activities of the Baader–Meinhof Gang and the Revolutionary Cells of West Germany, the Red Brigades and the Black Order in Italy, FP-25 in Portugal, and GRAPO in Spain. While the aforementioned groups openly proclaim their ideological motivation, such is not always the situation. Ideology is sometimes blurred purposely by terrorists to encourage recruitment or to avoid alienating a base of support. The PIRA, for instance, who claim nationalist inspiration, down-play any reference to acknowledged leftist leanings when publicizing their cause in the USA for fear of disrupting their considerable American constituency.

Similarly, issue groups are a favourite target of extremists of both the Left and Right and are regularly infiltrated by ideologists who seek to use such 'innocent' movements for their own purposes. Animal-rights organizations in Great Britain are known to contain anarchists in their membership; Ronnie Lee, a spokesman for the Animal Liberation Front, is a self-confessed anarchist and former member of the Troops Out of Ireland movement. It is necessary, therefore, to examine the literature of a movement carefully, and particularly the writings of the leadership, to assess the motivational foundation correctly.

## *Exile*

As the term implies, groups of this nature reside elsewhere than their homeland through personal choice or eviction. Exile groups often have a nationalist–separatist–irredentist motivation and an ideological basis, as well as the parallel desire to oust a regime in their established national home. The previously mentioned Armenian terrorist organizations, ASALA and JCAG, are respectively left and right in political affiliation.

Currently, serious friction between Sikh inhabitants of the State of Punjab and the central Indian government has been the cause of the formation of Sikh exile groups. A tragic consequence was the destruction of an Air India jet off the coast of Ireland, with the loss of over 300 lives, in June 1985. The device responsible for the incident was allegedly planted by Sikhs living in the Canadian expatriate community; and a similar outrage was foiled a year later when Canadian police arrested five Sikhs living in the Montreal area who were plotting to place a bomb on board a jet at Kennedy airport in New York. During the previous month, Sikh extremists shot and seriously wounded a moderate Sikh legislator who was on a visit to Canada's west coast.

A feature of exile-based terrorist activity is the conduct of attacks against members of the diplomatic or business communities. In the case of irredentist movements, such as the Croats and Armenians, the assaults are against representatives of the ethnic groups held responsible for the exile's grievances, e.g. Yugoslavs and Turks respectively. Exile terrorists, however, also employ violence against fellow countrymen who are part of, or support, a national regime opposed by the exiles. Libyan diplomats, for instance, have been victims of anti-Gaddafi exile militants.

In a similar manner, exile groups have threatened or attacked representatives of governments or businesses having a relationship with the offending state. The Pilatus aircraft factory in Switzerland was sabotaged because it manufactured aircraft used in counter-insurgency roles in Guatemala. The African National Congress (ANC) issued a pointed warning to Canadians in 1983 in regard to the potential dangers of doing business with the Republic of South Africa.

### State and state-sponsored

Terrorism practised by the ruling or governing powers of a state has been mentioned earlier. Control or repression is the purpose and, generally, the activity is confined within the national borders of the state. Idi Amin's regime in Uganda and 'Papa Doc' Duvalier's despotism in Haiti were based on state terrorism, as was Adolph Hitler's Third Reich. Not infrequently, in the case of Gaddafi's Libya or Khomeini's Iran, for instance, the state will attack exile dissidents in an attempt to suppress opposition.

State sponsorship of terrorism is a worrisome trend which has emerged more openly over the past decade. The term 'surrogate warfare' is one consequence and refers to support of terrorist groups by one state to promote its aims in relation to another state. The method has particular attraction in the modern world where declared conflict carries the possibility of nuclear involvement, especially if a connection with superpower rivalry exists.

While Gaddafi and Libya have been singled out as a prominent example of state-sponsored terrorism, other nations such as Syria, Iran, South Yemen, North Korea, and Bulgaria have also been accused of similar indulgence. South Yemen has long been the location of training camps for an international range of terrorist groups which includes ASALA, the Baader–Meinhof Gang, PIRA, and the PLO. Bulgarian influence was seen in the attempt to assassinate the Pope in 1981, Syria has been implicated in various actions of which the 1985 Rome–Vienna airport attacks are a part, and North Korea was responsible for a 1983 bombing incident in Burma which killed seventeen South Koreans. A North Korean agent also confessed to involvement in the 1987 bombing of a South Korean airliner destroyed over Burma with a loss of 115 lives.

Equally as reprehensible as the provision of arms, equipment, training, and finances through state support of terrorist groups has been the abuse of diplomatic privileges by the participating nations. Acting in the guise of legitimate diplomats, intelligence agents of the involved states have advised upon and directed terrorist activity in foreign countries. The sanctity of the diplomatic pouch, a means understood to be reserved for the secure transfer of legitimate items, has been frequently abused by the shipment of terrorist equipment. The weapons used in the shooting which erupted from the Libyan People's Bureau in St James's Square in 1984 were undoubtedly transported into and out of Great Britain in such a manner.

## Religious fanaticism

Not unlike state terrorism, religious fanaticism has been a source of terrorist motivation over the centuries. The cult of the Assassins had its foundations in a fanatical Muslim religious controversy which has resurfaced with particular intensity in Iran since the overthrow of the Shah in 1979. While more a case of pure religious bigotry, the fulminations of Ian Paisley often contain a current of religious fanaticism which acts as an encouragement for sectarian violence in Northern Ireland.

The suicide bombing attacks by Shi'ia terrorists in Lebanon, although not properly representative of Muslim theology, do underline the extent to which religious fervour may be manipulated for political purposes. Similar religious motivation prompted the murder of President Anwar Sadat of Egypt in 1981, as well as being responsible for the seizure of the Grand Mosque of Mecca in 1979 by activists who accused the Saudi Princes of being unfit to guard the Holy Cities. The Muslim Brotherhood continues to pose a troublesome threat to stability within Egypt and the Sudan.

Religious fanaticism has contributed to the formation of exile terrorist groups, as in the case of the Sikhs in Canada and Great Britain. Religious underpinnings, however, have also been evident in extremist ideological movements; groups such as The Aryan Nations, The Order, and The Covenant, The Sword and the Arm of the Lord typify right-wing terrorist activity in the USA. Terrorism associated with a combined religious-ethnic stimulus has been another area of growth in the United States and is claimed to have had some influence on the actions of the Jewish Defence League.

Classification of terrorist motivation has the advantage of establishing a perspective which assists the determination of a suitable response. By identifying the nature of the threat, it becomes easier to select appropriate policies, allocate correct deterrent and/or suppressive resources, and deliver adequate publicity to the threat and the response. But reference to the typology is not a complete solution; the aims and strategies of terrorist activity, combined with an understanding of terrorist infrastructure, must be explored to appreciate the scope of threat presented.

## Aims and strategies

The comment has often been voiced that terrorism represents mindless, senseless, purposeless, indiscriminate, and unpredictable violence. Except in the circumstance of a true psychopath, such conditions do not obtain; and even in the twisted mind of a lunatic like Jack the Ripper, some reason or motive probably existed. Rather, the very fact that terrorism seems to embody those characteristics of irrationality provides a source of its effect and a purpose for its use: the creation of fear.

Beyond terrorism's use to create fear and apprehension, it serves other more substantive ends. The following paragraphs offer a survey of some of those roles.

### Publicity

Perhaps, almost more than anything else, terrorists seek publicity: 'the propaganda of the deed'.[13] The FLQ demanded that the Canadian government publish and broadcast the group's manifesto as one condition for the release of James Cross. Ernest Evans cites the 1944 assassination of Lord Moyne in Cairo and the 1975 bombing of the Fraunces Tavern in New York City as two examples of terrorist acts committed for the purpose of publicity.[14] The former was intended to draw world attention to the situation of the Jews under the British mandate in Palestine, and the latter was seen as a means to achieve prominence for the Puerto Rican independence movement.

Publicity is more than simply an aim which terrorist groups seek to achieve. Publicity may be sought in an effort to prompt a reaction, gain a concession, encourage political or diplomatic support, or for purposes of recruiting or obtaining logistic assistance. In fact, publicity plays a part in most of the aims and strategies pursued by terrorists.

### Over-reaction by government

Many terrorist groups endeavour to prompt a draconian response from those in a position of authority. A rationale is the hope that such over-reaction will engender public support for the terrorists and eventually cause the populace to rise in revolt. Carlos Marighella emphasized this aspect in his *Minimanual of the Urban Guerrilla*.[15] The Tupamaros had such an aim partly in mind when they kidnapped the British ambassador, Sir Geoffrey Jackson, in Uruguay. Unfortunately for that latter nation, the terrorists did succeed to a degree; the democracy which once flourished in Uruguay was replaced by a military dictatorship in the process of defeating the Tupamaros.

### Loss of public confidence

Hand-in-hand with a seeking of over-reaction are attempts to undermine public confidence in government, expose apparent weaknesses, and demonstrate the righteousness of the terrorist cause. The PLO attack on the Israeli school at Ma'alot succeeded in the first two aspects – many Israeli officials were publicly abused in the aftermath in the belief that the government was not providing adequate security.[16]

The PIRA have made no secret of their efforts to convince the British public that the policies of Westminster are wrong; by attacks on British soldiers, PIRA has hoped that the public would call for a withdrawal of troops from Ulster. Conversely, terrorists will make use of this strategy when the authorities appear to be gaining the upper hand; Armenian terrorists attempted to bomb an Air Canada installation in Los Angeles following the arrest of several members of the group in Toronto.[17]

### Destabilization

The aim of terrorist attacks is frequently directed toward keeping the authorities and the security forces off balance. Menachim Begin admitted that such was one goal of the Irgun's attacks against British forces in Palestine. In a wider sense, the strategy may simply be to keep the pot boiling, as in the current Middle East conflict where Arab extremists strive to defeat the peace moves of moderates or to provoke Israeli retaliation.

## Coercion

Terrorist acts may serve the purpose of subduing opposition at home or abroad, as with Gaddafi's hit-squads of 1980, whose intent was the smashing of exile opposition. Similarly, Armenian terrorists hope to coerce the Turkish Government to admit to alleged acts of genocide during the First World War, and Sikh groups have turned to terrorism with the aim of convincing the Indian Government to grant concessions in the Punjab.

## Discipline

Terrorism is one means by which terrorist groups intimidate and discipline their own members, or maintain support in a community. The activities of PIRA in Northern Ireland provide ample evidence of this combined aim and strategy. The practice of knee-capping is one method of instilling discipline, the outright murder of alleged informers (male or female) is another.[18] Such atrocities make it an extremely difficult task for security forces to gain much-needed intelligence of terrorist activities or organization.

## Logistics

Terrorism is a costly business, requiring extensive logistical resources and back-up. Consequently, terrorists must often resort to purely criminal acts to acquire the funds, equipment, or other needs for the conduct of their campaign. The FLQ carried out a number of bank robberies in the Montreal area during the 1960s, and several members were arrested in a foiled attempt to steal weapons from a gun shop in the city. In a like manner, links have been established with state sponsors (e.g. Libya and PIRA) for logistic purposes, although the relationship has little, if any, further connotations.

## Extortion

Not unlike attempts at coercion, such moves seek to extort a concession or a response favouring the terrorists. One of the purposes behind the hijacking of a Lufthansa airliner in 1977, an incident which was ended by the surgical intervention of West German elite forces at Mogadishu, was the extortion of an agreement from the Bonn government for the release of imprisoned Red Army members. In a like manner, the FLQ sought the release of 'twenty-three political prisoners' held in Quebec jails and a cash payment of $500,000, as well as an aircraft to fly the terrorists to Cuba.[19]

### Legislative

Generally, issue groups pursue aims and strategies designed to influence government legislation; their purpose is to obtain the passage, modification, or rescinding of laws or regulations in conformance with their aims. Terrorist violence, however, is also associated with legislation intended to thwart terrorism, as in the case of the Prevention of Terrorism Act (PTA) and the Northern Ireland (Emergency Provisions) Act (EPA) in the United Kingdom. Arguably, similar actions have been taken by Loyalist factions in Ulster who oppose the Anglo-Irish Agreement.

### Cost in lives and property

In simple terms, such terrorist activity is conducted in an effort to make 'the costs ... too high to be worthwhile'.[20] It is a variation of coercion and the attempt to undermine public confidence. The Irgun and the Stern Gang pursued the policy in Palestine, as did Grivas and EOKA on Cyprus. The fact that the strategy did seem to have a measure of success in those situations, however, was more a matter of the circumstances of the time rather than the actual effect of the terrorist actions.

The PIRA in Northern Ireland continues to follow this strategy as a principal policy manoeuvre. In recent years they have concentrated many of their attacks on the police and the Ulster Defence Regiment (UDR) in the hope of lowering security-force morale and reducing recruitment. In conjunction, PIRA have carried out destructive attacks on police stations and barracks. PIRA follows its raids with threats against contractors and construction workers, aiming to reduce police/UDR influence in the surrounding area by eliminating tangible proof of security-force presence and obstructing its replacement.

While the immediate aims and strategies associated with terrorist groups are usually apparent on the surface, it is prudent to look beyond the obvious. Terrorists may have both short- and long-term goals as the basis of their actions. The December 1983 PIRA bombing of Harrods in London's Knightsbridge district was intended to disrupt the holiday shopping period. The attack was also part of PIRA's longer-range policy aimed at convincing the British public of the futility of the Loyalist cause in Ulster and the risks involved in the continuing support of the Province by the British Government.

One of the reasons for the Rome–Vienna airport massacres was an attempt to discourage immigration to Israel via those two points of departure; in fact, the attacks had an aim of dampening enthusiasm for emigration to Israel in its entirety. Similarly, the suicide bombings against the Multinational Force in Beirut were designed to lessen western public support for the continued presence of the Force and to bring about its withdrawal, thereby restricting western policy options in the Middle East conflict.

Motivation, aims, and strategies provide an insight into the genesis and reasons for terrorist behaviour. The systemology of terrorist groups, the organizational infrastructure, offers a further understanding from the operational standpoint.

## Infrastructure

Critical to the successful organization and functioning of a terrorist group, as with any directed activity, is leadership. It is not necessary to belabour this point; plentiful examples are available of the roles played by terrorist leaders such as Michael Collins, Menachim Begin, George Grivas, Carlos, Abu Nidal, Andreas Baader, Ulrike Meinhof, and Che Guevara, to name but a few. Effective leadership provides the personal motivation, initiative, direction, and inspiration within a terrorist organization.

Conversely, terrorist leaders are often jealous of their position, and do not encourage delegation of authority and responsibility through fear of creating rivals. For that reason, they place the group in danger of extinction in the event of their capture, or else promote schisms and the development of splinter groups. The PLO is one example of leadership differences and rivalries which have led to the formation of conflicting sub-groups.

Knowledge of a terrorist leader's background, habits, traits, and ideals can be of much benefit to policy planners and security forces as a means of anticipating terrorist actions. Nonetheless, the elimination of a leader does not necessarily bring about the collapse of a group; the Red Army Faction in West Germany still clings to the writings and examples set by Baader and Meinhof. Similarly, the *Minimanual* of Marighella and the theories of Guevara retain credibility amongst some extremist militants.

Previous mention has been made of the need for an adequate logistical base for the conduct of terrorist activity. Weapons, explosives, and other technical equipment are often obtained by thefts or the capture of security-force stocks, but large supplies and sophisticated items must generally be obtained by purchase. Funding, therefore, becomes a problem and looms as a serious matter just for the expense involved in daily living. PIRA, for example, must pay 'benefits' to the families of its imprisoned members as well as salaries to its active duty personnel.

To finance operations, terrorists resort to bank robberies, kidnap and ransom, and protection rackets which are becoming increasingly more elaborate. In Northern Ireland, a semi-legitimate involvement has appeared in the form of the 'Black Taxis' which operate in Belfast and Londonderry, allegedly under the aegis of both Republican and Loyalist organizations. Much contention centres on the purpose of monies raised by the NORAID sponsorship in the USA as well.

In a paper delivered at the 1986 International Academic Conference on Terrorism, James Adams provided a valuable insight on the modern financing of terrorist activity.[21] As well as exploding some myths about the extent of state sponsorship associated with the Soviet Union and Libya, he attributed the survival of some terrorist groups to a consequence of good financial planning. 'The reason is that they were better capitalists.'[22] They were able 'to see that good financial planning means having enough cash to buy and keep support, to pay for arms and to build a propaganda base among the people the organization claims to represent'.[23]

A new and dangerous turn of events has been evidence of terrorist association with the narcotics world, a circumstance which has occasioned the term narco-terrorism. Increasing concern has arisen in the USA over links between terrorist organizations and international drug traffickers. Major involvement has been noted in Latin America, Jamaica, Mexico, and Burma, with 'part of the profits of the illicit narcotics trade ... being channelled to groups that are using the money to wage politically motivated struggles ...'.[24] In some locations the terrorist groups have provided protection to the narcotics smugglers in return for arms, ammunition, equipment, and funding.

From the organizational standpoint, the fundamental structure of most terrorist groups is based on the cell system: that is, individual aggregations of from three to seven persons known only to each other or to the cell leader by whom they were originally recruited. The purpose of such isolation is to prevent infiltration by the security forces or, in the event of a member being captured, the exposure of the entire terrorist organization. The cell system became very popular with the FLN in Algeria when the French Army was successful in widely identifying the membership of terrorist groups based upon a more formal military pattern. The PIRA restructured itself in a similar manner in 1977 in an effort to overcome British penetration of its organizational structure.[25]

While the cell system does provide reasonable security, it can have the disadvantage of inhibiting a rapid passage of information. Messages must be delivered by means of a 'dead-drop' or only through one person in each cell, although the telephone or coded speech on citizens'-band radio transmitters helps to alleviate the difficulty.

Within a terrorist group, tasks and responsibilities are often allocated by specialization; for instance, certain individuals specialize in bomb-making, others in sniping or assassination or the theft of vehicles and equipment, while some merely serve as observers or 'runners'. Following the 1984 murder of Mary Travers and the attempted assassination of her father, Magistrate Tom Travers, in Belfast, the weapons used were strapped under the skirt of a female accomplice whose only task was to transport the revolvers from the scene.[26]

The establishment of linkages between terrorist groups has not been a major characteristic over the past two decades. Relationships have been known on a co-operative basis, PIRA and ETA being one example in terms of putative exchanges of 'firearms and technical (explosives) expertise'.[27] The Japanese Red Army conducted the Lod Airport attack in support of Palestinian conflict with the Israelis, but generally the associations have been tenuous and confined to passage of information or identifying sources of weapons and other equipment.

Concern has grown, however, over evidence of a closer degree of union amongst left-wing European extremists during a series of bombings and assassinations in the years 1984–5. A link was proclaimed in public statements between Action Directe in France and the Red Army in Germany, with suggestions of a wider association with FP-25 in Portugal and the Communist Combatant Cells in Belgium.[28] In this particular series of events, the target of attack was the NATO infrastructure, which provided a common point of interest for the individual groups. But, generally, terrorist groups do not share the same aim and may not have a similar motivational base, so that co-operation is not an advantage, and reasons of security may inhibit any consideration of a wider relationship.

Some authoritative sources claim that terrorism is a highly overrated threat, and that as 'a serious, direct threat to modern society, terrorism in general has been remarkably unsuccessful'.[29] Yet in one respect, if the fall in transatlantic tourism reflected the effect that the Rome and Vienna airport outrages had on Americans' willingness to vacation in Europe, terrorist philosophy does work. The 40 per cent drop in airline passengers flying from the United States to Europe was not the only consequence. Other ramifications affecting domestic economies ensued, plus the ill will that terrorism aroused, perfectly served the purpose of dividing friend from friend and undermining the confidence in the power of states to preserve the decencies of life.

Terrorism, however, becomes a more distinct threat when it is used as part of a system of insurrection. The previously mentioned linkage between groups does represent a danger, but terrorism linked to the wings of a formalized insurgent movement constitutes a greater peril. Diagramatically, this circumstance is presented in Figure 2.

*Figure 2* Model insurgent movement[*]

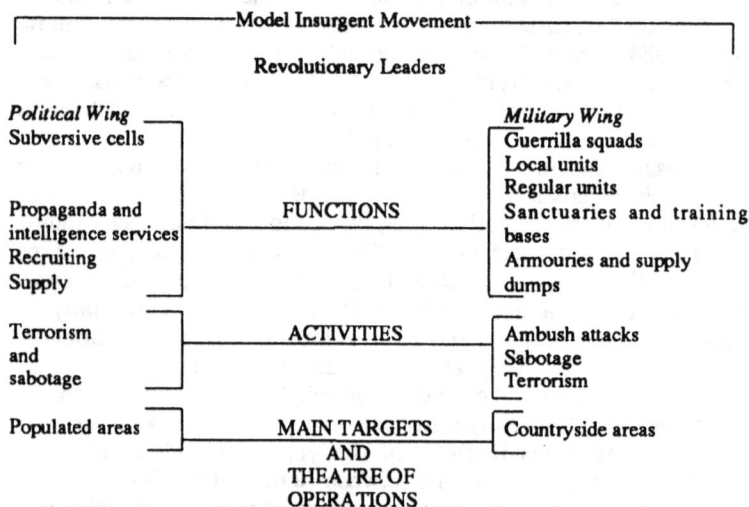

| Model Insurgent Movement | | |
|---|---|---|
| | Revolutionary Leaders | |
| *Political Wing*<br>Subversive cells | | *Military Wing*<br>Guerrilla squads<br>Local units<br>Regular units |
| Propaganda and<br>intelligence services<br>Recruiting<br>Supply | FUNCTIONS | Sanctuaries and training<br>bases<br>Armouries and supply<br>dumps |
| Terrorism<br>and<br>sabotage | ACTIVITIES | Ambush attacks<br>Sabotage<br>Terrorism |
| Populated areas | MAIN TARGETS<br>AND<br>THEATRE OF<br>OPERATIONS | Countryside areas |

[*] See Sir Robert Thompson, *Defeating Communist Insurgency* (London: Chatto & Windus, 1974), p. 33. See also Bard E. O'Neil, William R. Heaton and Donald J. Alberts (eds), *Insurgency in the Modern World* (Boulder: Westview Press, 1980); Douglas S. Blaufarb, *The Counterinsurgency Era: U.S. Doctrine and Performance* (London: The Free Press, Collier-Macmillan, 1977).

The revolutionary leadership of such an insurgent movement provides the core, the directing and motivating mechanism, for the two operative wings. The political wing provides the 'legitimate front' of the movement and is principally concerned with subversive agitprop, or agitation propaganda. The military wing has the responsibility for the obviously more open and armed activities of insurrection. In a well-controlled and well-organized movement, the two wings work in close harmony and with specifically related objectives, as well as providing mutual support.

For ease of explanation, the model depicts the two wings as being associated with urban or highly populated areas and with the countryside, respectively. Both wings, nonetheless, can function in either locale and most certainly the political wing would be operative across the spectrum. The establishment of subversive cells, the use of agitprop, and the recruiting of members would occur in the countryside as well as in the cities. The Viet Cong used this method to gain and secure control of large areas of the countryside in South Viet Nam. Similarly, the PIRA has used its active duty (or 'military') personnel to maintain its sway in Republican sectors of Belfast and Londonderry by means of violent intimidation coupled with the less threatening actions of its political wing.

Ambush attacks, terrorism, and guerrilla-type operations in the countryside provide a valuable source of propaganda for the political agitators in the populated areas. (In the rural areas, however, the more important tasks are the elimination of village leaders and the coercion of the population.) In return, the urban centres are a source of supply of medicines, food, equipment, funding, and valuable intelligence for the military wing. In conjunction, terrorist activities in the urban areas tend to concentrate the attention of the authorities and security forces, forcing the diversion of suppressive resources and creating the impression of a much more serious and widespread insurrection than may well be the reality.

Following the model through to its extremes, as the insurrection gains in size and strength, the military elements gradually formalize into 'main force' units and adopt the appearance of a 'regular army'. In such a manner, and by association with the apparently legitimate political front, the insurrection becomes a recognized uprising which may result in the overthrow of the government in power.

An interesting illustration of this concept is available in Louis Fournier's account of the FLQ in Canada. In his opening chapter, Fournier describes the intentions of the original organizers of the group: 'The FLQ would become the radical wing of the national liberation of Quebec.'[30] Later pages offer close to a mirror image of the model shown in Figure 2, as follows:

> Two main networks, which were to stay in touch with each other, soon made their appearance: the Armée de liberation du Québec (ALQ), which introduced itself as the military branch of the FLQ ... and the network based on the FLQ's 'official' newspaper La Cognée, which constituted the political branch of the movement.[31]

It is unlikely that advanced nations in the western world would be subject to a threat of the magnitude or sophistication depicted by the model. Yet feelings ran high in Canada during the FLQ campaign, and mishandling on the part of the Canadian government, or better leadership of the militants, might have prompted other developments. Wilkinson, however, identifies the real threat as existing elsewhere: '... the greatest danger to democratic societies from terrorism in the long term does not stem from internal violence, but from growing instability in the Third World'.[32] Wilkinson emphasizes that the increased incidence and lethality of terrorism in those nations is a condition which they are inherently ill-prepared to counter.

'And since 1945 revolutionary take-overs in Asia, Latin America and Africa have tended to bring to power Marxist-style regimes ...'[33] whose policies are antithetical to western interests. Similarly, such regimes export their philosophies, and the resulting conflicts hold the potential of elevating to large-scale confrontations. It is such implications, and the features of modern civilization which encourage and facilitate the use of terrorism, that are next the subject of attention.

### Factors and implications

Modern communications have provided the terrorist with almost instantaneous access to a worldwide audience. Media response has elevated acts of terrorism to a type of theatre watched on television by millions of people around the globe. Perhaps the most memorable, or infamous, example occurred at Munich on 5 September 1972, when Palestinian 'Black September' terrorists invaded the living quarters of the Israeli Olympic Team. Since that occasion, not only television, but also radio, newspapers, and journals have devoted extensive coverage to terrorism to the point of controversy.

It is widely accepted that media coverage is a significant aim of terrorist strategy; 'terrorists want a lot of people watching, not a lot of people dead',[34] is an oft-quoted truism. (But if public notice can only be obtained by killing a lot of people, many groups are happy to oblige.) Conflicting with the wisdom of down-playing terrorist spectaculars is the media contention of the 'people's right to know' and the vital importance of a free press in open societies. These concerns, and the complex problems they raise, were sufficient to promote two major conferences in the USA during the 1970s, as well as a comprehensive study sponsored by the Dutch State University in 1980.[35] Notwithstanding, the subject remained under contentious discussion at the International Academic Conference on Terrorism at Aberdeen University in 1986.

Correspondingly, media coverage of a disturbance in Belfast, Northern Ireland, involving the 1984 visit of NORAID spokesman Martin Galvin, brought bitter recriminations from public figures in the Province. The two main Unionist political parties 'exceptionally, buried their differences to recall the Northern Ireland Assembly in special session ... and condemned press and television reporting of the mayhem'.[36] In different circumstances, the media coverage of the TWA hijacking in June 1985 was described as 'terrorvision'.[37]

Exceptional advances in modern technology have materially facilitated the growth and spread of terrorism, and will continue to do so with the advent of improvements in communications, weapons, transportation, electronics, and explosives. Ease of international travel offers global mobility to terrorists; the ready availability of a variety of weapons, explosives, and other munitions, and the new vulnerabilities of a society increasingly dependent on complex systems and other fragile technology combine to make terrorism an attractive means of political expression.

Miniaturized electronic components, radio-controlled detonating devices, plastic explosives, compact high-powered automatic small-arms, and infra-red and heat-seeking missiles that fit easily into a suitcase are just a small sample of the technology and armoury available to terrorists. The imagination and ingenuity of both terrorists and security forces largely dictate constraints to employment of such a potential arsenal of destruction. One example of the implicit dangers was the need to fit special anti-missile protection to the aircraft used by HM Queen Elizabeth II of Great Britain during her travel to and from Jordan in 1984.[38]

Once the purview of the mad bomber or anarchist, explosives have now become standard and sophisticated equipment in terrorism's inventory. Even the assassin is no longer restricted to the gun or the knife, as witness the murder of Lord Louis Mountbatten on 27 August 1979. More alarming are the avenues open in regard to the use of nuclear, chemical, and bacteriological agents for terrorist purposes, where even a hoax produces disproportional results. The reliance of modern civilization on computerization has created another rich vein for terrorist activities, forcing computer-dependent industries to expend huge sums in protective effort.

Both government and business have had to face soaring expense in the provision of greatly improved comprehensive physical security measures. The 23 October 1983 suicide attack that killed 241 US Marines in Beirut, Lebanon, probably produced the most profound fillip for increased protective infrastructure, especially by American government agencies at home and abroad. Concrete barriers, strengthened fencing and gates, bullet-proof glass enclosures, wider use of surveillance devices, and guard patrols rapidly became evident at military and diplomatic installations in the aftermath.

Corporate interest has been more subtle, but perhaps more readily aware of the threats posed by terrorism. Once almost unheard of, insurance premiums paid in 1983 to cover US firms against losses from kidnapping, extortion, and physical violence were estimated at some 80 million dollars. Boom times have resulted for scores of private protection firms created to help business cope with security threats. A prominent example is Control Risks Limited of London, whose staff provide a fascinating cross-section of academics, former intelligence agents, ex-military personnel, and retired members of the famed Special Air Service (SAS). An April 1986 article in the *Wall Street Journal* mentions that 'in the wake of recent events a wide range of companies has sprung up offering advice, training, personnel and equipment aimed at helping businesses protect their interests'.[39]

Callers were once admitted to the sacrosanct corporate headquarters of the Dow Chemical Company in Midland, Michigan, merely by stating their name and business to a receptionist in the lobby. Now, heavy glass panels and sliding security doors, electronically controlled, prevent access for employees and others until positive identification has been produced, and visitors must generally await an escort. The ever-polite doorman at a London West End residence of diplomatic families has been replaced by remote-controlled doors and individual miniature television screens installed in each flat for the purpose of monitoring access to the building.

Patterns of daily living have altered dramatically to accommodate precautions designed to thwart opportunities for terrorist actions. Perhaps the most obvious manifestations are the elaborate security procedures which passengers undergo prior to boarding aircraft at airline terminals. First introduced by the USA in 1973 in response to a spate of aircraft hijackings, they have become so standard and routine that the majority of today's travellers barely pay heed to them. In fact, in certain parts of the world passengers might well refuse to board a commercial airliner if not subjected to a security examination.

Application of airport controls has not been universally rigorous, however, so that terrorists have continued to manage to evade detection on occasion and to succeed in their attempts to seize aircraft or to place explosive devices on board. The destruction of the Air India flight off the coast of Ireland in June 1985, and the bombing of a TWA 727 jet over the Mediterranean in April, 1986, are but two examples of failures in screening procedures or use of inadequately sophisticated detection equipment.[40] Following the October 1985 'seajacking' of the Italian cruise liner *Achille Lauro*, a similar focus has been placed on the need for stricter methods of examining passengers and luggage before the boarding of vessels.[41]

Military and law-enforcement bodies have had seriously to rethink their roles and to adapt new methods to counter terrorist violence. The experience of the British Army and the Royal Ulster Constabulary (RUC), for instance, is a vivid illustration of the need for flexibility combined with co-operation and an ever-alert attitude. Even before British troops became involved with Aid to Civil Power duties in Ulster in 1969, an inherent requirement existed *inter alia* for a better common military-police appreciation of individual responsibilities, command and control arrangements, policies, and long-range goals. Military and

RUC training, equipments, procedures, and tactics have undergone constant reappraisal in the face of continually changing terrorist operations. Terrorists, contrary to some opinion, often display a high degree of cunning and ingenuity which must be matched by the security forces.

A number of countries have developed specialized elite counter-terrorist security forces, with many of the groups becoming well known as a result of their exploits. For the most part, the origins of such units lie in regular military or paramilitary organizations from which elements have been detached to perform the unique duties. Possibly the more familiar examples are the British Special Air Service (SAS) and the West German *Grenzschutzgruppe 9* (GSG-9), the former renowned for its splendid resolution of the Iranian Embassy seizure in London and the latter for its successful rescue of a hijacked Lufthansa aircraft at Mogadishu. 'Recognized more for its stunning accomplishment at Entebbe than by its name, is the Israeli General Intelligence and Reconnaissance Unit 269, which has been a forerunner in the field of anti-terrorist commandos.'[42]

The incidence of terrorism has demanded other changes, particularly in the realms of government policy, administration, and legislation. Notable in that regard have been the Prevention of Terrorism Act and the Northern Ireland (Emergency Provisions) Act, which are acts passed by the British Parliament primarily to counter terrorism on the part of the IRA and PIRA. The Canadian Government found it necessary to resort to the extraordinary peacetime use of the War Measures Act in 1970 as a means of response to the bombing, kidnapping, and murder carried out by the FLQ.

In the USA, dramatic moves have occurred during the 1980s decade. Triggered to a large degree by tragic events in the Middle East which began with the Iranian Hostage Crisis, legislation now permits greater sanctions against terrorist behaviour to include rewards for information and apprehension of those persons involved, as well as 'both federal investigative and prosecutive jurisdictions'[43] on a global basis. The recognized need for improved intelligence resources to combat terrorism eventually brought about a relaxation of the restrictive Levi Guidelines imposed on the activities of the FBI in the aftermath of the Watergate scandal.

The US Government (and the Canadian Government, also) has established agencies within federal departments for the purpose of counter-terrorism research, analysis and policy development, and the control and co-ordination of response measures. Linked to the development has been allocation of responsibility for the education and training of diplomats and overseas personnel in regard to the threat of terrorism and the necessary security precautions to be taken. The Canadian Department of External Affairs provides a small handbook,

*Tips on Terrorism*, containing security suggestions for Canadian business people travelling or working abroad.

The fear of terrorist attacks in the USA increased to such an extent that by 1983 the Washington, DC area was described as having a 'fortress mentality'.[44] While significant improvements to the security of government premises and facilities were clearly visible, the most publicized and controversial action undertaken to date by the US Government occurred on the night of 14 April 1986, when American aircraft from bases in Great Britain and from aircraft carriers in the Mediterranean Sea bombed targets in Libya as an act of retaliation for Gaddafi's acts of state-sponsored terrorism.

International fora have been the scene of repeated calls for joint co-operation and sanctions aimed at combating terrorism. Major endeavours to achieve collaboration at the UN have consistently foundered on the problem of definition, but some gradual advances have been realized as in the Convention on the Prevention and Punishment of Crimes Against Internationally Protected Persons. In a like manner, three Conventions drawn up under the auspices of the International Civil Aviation Organization (ICAO) have been of value: Tokyo, 1963; The Hague, 1970; and, Montreal, 1971 (See Chapter Two, note 150).

Notwithstanding, a more effective route towards co-operative response has been demonstrated through bilateral agreements between states. Sometimes these have been arranged 'between states of completely opposed ideological colour',[45] such as the Anti-Hijack Pact between the USA and Cuba of 1973. Similarly, improvements have been achieved in police co-operation and the sharing of intelligence by administrative innovation, such as the Trevi system. (See Chapter Two, note 155).

Complementing these graduated progressive efforts, the Bonn, Venice, Ottawa, London, and Tokyo Declarations resulting from the economic summit meetings of the seven leading industrial nations have furthered accord in combating the threat. The 1986 Tokyo Summit was deemed a major success, but a Canadian representative warned that 'It remains to be seen whether we can translate these fine-sounding words into actual deeds.'[46] Mutual agreement has been difficult to obtain, as evidenced by the reactions of France and Eire to the 1976 European Convention on Terrorism and their reservations on political asylum.[47] The now trite phrase, 'one person's terrorist is another person's freedom-fighter' bedevils attempts at consensus.

Shadowing developments overall have been the repercussions of East–West superpower rivalries, closely associated with competition amongst the Third World nations. Claire Sterling implied that much of the current terrorist phenomenon was the consequence of a managed and manipulated conspiracy on the part of the Soviet Union.[48] The contention does contain an element of validity in the sense that the Soviets are known to maintain training bases and to provide a range of support, especially small arms, for groups of 'freedom fighters' around the world. But the 'giant conspiracy' theory lacks solid evidence or foundation; the Soviets, as do other nations, pursue their policy aims by a variety of means and methods.

The Soviet appreciation of the value and utility of terrorism cannot be overlooked, however. A recent NATO Fellowship Report, aside from alluding to the obvious overt Soviet array of military force, identified two other dangers:

(a) The psychological threat, 'which is aimed at terrifying, deceiving, demoralizing, dividing ... disarming and neutralizing the West'.
(b) The covert threat, including 'support for subversive, terrorist and protest groups ... Turkey was brought to the brink of chaos in the early 1980s by a massive terrorist attack masterminded, controlled and supplied by the Soviets'.[49]

Taken in conjunction with the Soviet development of 'spetsnaz'[50] forces, the 1984–5 attacks on the NATO infrastructure by left-wing terrorist groups produced considerable unease.

Martha Crenshaw has pointed at the utility of terrorism: 'One reason for the prevalence of ... terrorism in the modern world is its effectiveness as a strategy in which the benefits often exceed the costs to the insurgent organization.'[51] Underscoring the publicity and resource factors, she continues, 'Compared with other methods of violent resistance, the cost of terrorism is low.'[52] It is, therefore, easy to accept that 'terrorism is the weapon of the weak'.[53] It is also possible, nonetheless, to recognize that terrorism may be the weapon of the too strong who seek to exert their influence and to achieve their ends by encouraging the weak.

In late 1984 to early 1985, sixty bombing attacks occurred in Europe over a three-month period; Europe has been the scene of 40 per cent of international terrorist incidents over the past five years. Not surprisingly, statistics have shown a growth rate of 10 to 15 per cent in international terrorist incidents and a figure of 30 per cent when domestic attacks are added.[54] During 1985, there was a record high of 782 international incidents, not including hoaxes, threats, or other dubious incidents. The figure dropped to 774 in 1986, but

(the) decline is deceptive without looking behind the figures. The difference between 1985 and 1986 represents one incident – 329 deaths from the Air India bombing. Moreover, 1986 could have included as many as 800 more deaths if several attempted aircraft bombings had succeeded.[55]

The cost in lives and in property destroyed by terrorist atrocities has been considerable, despite disclaimers that the loss of life is proportionally minor when compared to other statistical evidence. Northern Ireland provides a case in point, where more than 2,600 lives have been lost in the conflict since 1969 and over 20,000 persons have been injured. Translated into terms of the US population, the figures represent '276,000 deaths and over 1 million injured'.[56] From a Canadian perspective, the 'equivalent loss of life in Canada, with a population 17 times larger than that of Ulster, would be 45,730'.[57]

> It is estimated that 75% of the loss of growth in Ulster ... over the past 13 years was attributable to violence. This produced a total cost over the period of £3.4 billion. (Adding indirect exchequer spending, for instance on security, the total soared to £1 billion annually.)[58]

Terrorism has been variously described as 'war without limits',[59] 'surrogate war',[60] and 'the form of warfare for our time'.[61] Admiral James D. Watkins, former Chief of US Naval Operations, said that terrorism is 'an already declared war'.[62] In real terms, an ominous 'trend in the 1980s has been the rise in indiscriminate attacks, such as setting off bombs aboard airliners, in terminals ...'.[63] Equally disturbing in portent, especially for those who advocate a response tailored to the rule of law, has been the implementation of the threatened US policy of retaliation. The Reagan administration warned of the possibility of similar action should terrorist attacks continue, and suggestions were voiced about unleashing CIA resources in covert war against terrorism, as well as the rescinding of the ban on assassination.[64]

Under such circumstances it is well to heed the commentary of Wilkinson once again:

> Terrorism is certainly an evil, but it is by no means the worst evil. It pales into insignificance when one compares it with the lethality and destructiveness of a major civil or international war. Those who have the responsibility for determining the response of Western governments to international terrorism must be aware of those pitfalls and risks.... If powerful Western states disregard the inhibitions of international law and use means against terrorism which are totally disproportionate to the threat, they will risk increasing the very anarchy in which terrorists flourish.[65]

Chapter two

# General policy

## Introduction

The major theme of this volume involves government *policies* associated with response to terrorism, a statement which prompts the question: what is meant by government *policy*? The answer requires brief elaboration, although most people would demonstrate a broad understanding in the sense of policy being a government's perceived position or approach in relation to a given situation or set of circumstances. For instance, former US Vice-President George Bush made it clear that 'the [American] Government's policy in combatting terrorism would remain one in which there was a willingness to retaliate...'.[1]

## Characteristics of policy

Christopher Hewitt, in his study of the effectiveness of certain anti-terrorist policies, writes of 'macro' and 'micro' policy.[2] Hewitt cites emergency legislation and the use of security forces as examples of the former; the liberal-democratic policy of adherence to the rule of law would also fall within that category. In other words, macro policy is one which has a wide application and a general dimension. The British Government's traditional policy of maintaining an unarmed police force in Great Britain would equate, too, although representing a course of *inaction*. Micro policy, on the other hand, is suggestive of a more narrow involvement, such as hostage negotiations and surveillance techniques. Micro policy encompasses individual circumstances, means, and methods. The Canadian Government's decision to allocate responsibility to the Royal Canadian Mounted Police (RCMP) for the development of a national hostage rescue team is an example of a micro policy emanating from the macro policy of use of security forces in response to terrorism.

Policy obviously generates policy. The British policy decision to arm some members of the police who patrol certain major airports, e.g.

Heathrow, involved a host of related policies. A policy was required for the type of weapon to be issued, and another was necessary for the conditions under which the weapon could be used. Those demands were not merely the stuff of regulations, but were based upon serious consideration of alternatives in conjunction with the policy of rule of law, the historical policy of British policing, and the government's policy of resolve in the face of the threat of terrorism. Policy is not always openly declared or recognized formally. For years the Canadian Government refrained from officially stating in a public document that it would not pay ransoms to terrorists, but historically that principle formed part of the Canadian response to terrorism. Similarly, the British Government generally followed a no-concessions approach over the past sixteen years which was accepted as policy without the reality of an official announcement.

Richard Rose has said of policy that it 'can refer to a set of expectations and intentions, or to a series of actions and their consequences, or to all of those together'.[3] British security policy in Northern Ireland has the intention of restoring 'effective and impartial application of the law',[4] as well as the expectation of establishing conditions which do not require a military presence to enforce the law. Consequently, the police in that embattled province have not only been returned to a position of dominance *vis-à-vis* security responsibility, but have also been given very considerable material support to assist them. One result has been the ability of the British Government to pursue the attendant policy of reducing the numbers of troops in Northern Ireland.

Policy not only generates policy, but it also generates policy measures. The distinction is often finely drawn, and frequently the two may appear to represent one and the same thing. The West German GSG-9 is a measure resulting from that nation's policy to provide a security unit for 'the carrying out of police missions of special significance'.[5] Organizational behaviour, infrastructure, and resources, therefore, may be seen to represent both policy and policy measures. With regard to terrorism, the fact that a government does, or does not, manifest a response may well originate in a perception of the threat. Recourse to perception of the threat, however, is *per se* a demonstration of policy and from which other policy and/or policy measures may or may not follow. The outcome, nonetheless, will undoubtedly also mirror experience, level of concern and determination, and constitutional factors among other influences.

Policy measures, like policy itself, may take two major forms. Policy, and the measures which flow from it, may be direct or indirect in nature. (The terms active and passive may also be used and do apply; but to avoid confusion over definition of passive, as denoting submission and lack of action, the words direct and indirect were preferred.) One example of direct policy is the US Government's opposition to terrorism in all its forms; a direct measure resulting from that policy is the decision to pay rewards for information about terrorist operations. The Canadian Government's use of its military resources to protect the 1976 Olympic Games from terrorist attack involved both a direct policy and a direct measure. Indirect policies or measures are inherently more difficult to identify and may often arguably appear to be direct, or may seem to take that form in their implementation. Immigration procedures and customs controls, while demonstrably direct in their application, frequently reflect an indirect policy or measure in response to the threat of terrorism. (Except in the United Kingdom, where certain immigration and customs measures are a direct part of direct counter-terrorism policy.)

Risking accusations of digression into debate over policy-science theory, it must be acknowledged that government policy and policy measures are not developed in isolation. Richard Simeon has correctly observed that 'bureaucratic agencies are central elements in the policy-making process, and no study of policy could ignore them'.[6] Graham Allison, in his major case-study *Essence of Decision*, explored the 'bureaucratic politics' hypothesis as one example of such influence.[7] Nonetheless, as Simeon continues, 'bureaucrats and politicians operate within a broader ... framework, defined by such factors as prevailing ideologies, assumptions and values, structures of power and influence, patterns of conflict and division...'.[8] Simeon recognizes that policy is more than *just* the result of the influence of bureaucracy and politics despite their key roles in government circles. Policy also reflects the influence of external factors such as environment, history, culture, economic conditions, pressure groups, media orientation, and ideas. Moreover, policy can be seen as a function of cause and effect, as in the case of policy in response to terrorism. Figure 3 and the accompanying explanation provide an elaboration.

Fundamentally, the diagram depicts terrorism as a *Threat* (1) from which a *Perception* (2) develops, eventually impacting upon the *Decision-making machinery* (3). (For the purpose at hand, the latter is assumed to represent government.) The *Decision-making machinery* responds by initiating *Policy* (4) and directing its translation into policy *Measures* (5), which are then subject to *Implementation* (6). *Implementation* creates a reaction in the *Threat*, causing the cycle to begin once again. It can be seen that the directional arrows are two-headed, indicating both a clockwise and a counter-clockwise flow of activity. The counter-clockwise flow relates to the motivational impacts, as previously described. The opposite flow represents the learning process, or experience, gained throughout the operation of the cycle. Terrorist use of highly sophisticated explosives and detonators, for example, would demand the implementation of new measures of response, calling for new policy and new policy decisions. Those activities may also result in a changed perception of the threat, which could have an effect upon the attitude of the terrorists.

*Figure 3* Envelope of Influences: environment, institutions, values, ideas, history, and so on.

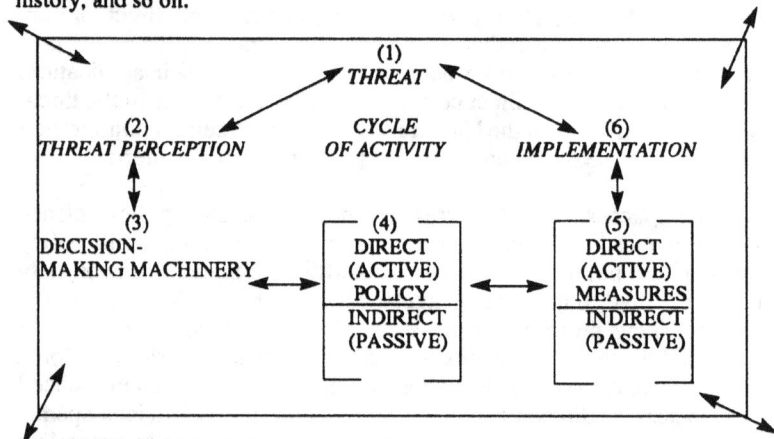

To avoid lengthy discussion, the example has been portrayed and explained in very simple terms and without reference to major internal influences, actions, or inactions. For instance, implications related to the magnitude or precise nature of the threat are omitted, as are the complexities of achieving agreement on policy, inter-departmental frictions or wrangling over 'turf', and problems of the availability and type of resources associated with implementation. With regard to clockwise repetition of the cycle, however, inaction at stage (3) could prompt greater or lesser action at stage (1). Similarly, actions taken at stages (3) through (6) could promote a reaction at stage (1) which would result in either a change in stage (2), causing a modification to the nature and extent of activity in the remaining stages, or no change and a continuance of the status quo.

Surrounding the basic *Cycle of activity* is the *Envelope of influences*, comprised of the many variables mentioned earlier, e.g. environment, history, culture, values, precedents, demography, regionalization, ideology, power structure, institutions, pressure groups, and so on. The *Envelope* can be seen to impact upon each of the six components of the *Cycle*, creating obvious or subtle, and/or significant or minor effects throughout. In return, the actions of the *Cycle* can have an impact on components of the *Envelope*; extreme behaviour or misconduct on the part of security forces could bring about an adverse reaction from pressure groups, or terrorist atrocities could stimulate increased pressures for government response.

Thus, the *Threat* itself is subject to external modifying influences, as well as to any internal pressures generated by stages (2) through (6). Initially, for instance, a terrorist presence may originate and grow, or fail to germinate and mature, as a consequence of the *Envelope*. Should a presence develop and become sufficient to stimulate stage (2), the terrorists then may also face the reactions of the *Decision-making machinery* in making an assessment of stage (2), and deciding upon steps to be taken in the remaining stages, (4), (5) and (6). But the *Decision-making machinery* in making an assessment at stage (2), and deciding upon steps to be taken in the remaining stages, also responds under the influence of the *Envelope*. *Policy*, policy *Measures*, and *Implementation* benefit or suffer in a like manner. Therefore, while all of the components of the *Cycle* are influenced by their internal interactions, they are influenced as well in varying degrees by the *Envelope* factors.

No attempt has been made to weight the individual influences, or to assign a place of prominence to either the internal or the external relationships. The purpose of the diagram, and the concept, is to illustrate that policy is the outcome of a wide variety of inputs, and that the translation of policy into measures and implementation is similarly affected. The concept is intended as an explanatory backdrop to the policies and policy measures examined in this and following chapters, and to assist with an understanding of the complexities of policy development and direction. For example, shortly after his inauguration in 1981, President Reagan warned terrorists that 'our policy will be one of swift and effective retribution'.[9] Yet by the end of that year, 'observers were dismayed to find that little in the way of substantive policy dealing with terrorism had emerged'.[10] Both the internal constraints (in part involving uncertainty within the *Decision-making machinery*), and the external influences of the *Envelope* (in part the outcome of pressures of the American democratic system and heritage) had combined to inhibit progress.

In summary, government policy is fundamentally an aim, intention, or expectation which may be expressed in a variety of ways and means. Such policy may be broad and general, or narrow and specific, and may generate other policy or policy measures. It is not necessarily open and declared, but may be the consequence of convention or values established over a period of time. Organizational behaviour, resources, and capabilities may alone or severally manifest government policy, as well as representing extensions of policy in the form of policy measures. Policy and policy measures are more than just a sum of their parts, however, being influenced by a wide range of internal and external variables. This brief analysis of policy characteristics affords entry into discussion of the main theme. Within that theme, the nature of government systems will be among variables selected for examination as sources of influence on the development and implementation of policy and policy measures. First to be considered, however, is the place of history.

### Historical dimension

Kelly and Mitchell have pointed to the 'myth of the peaceable kingdom' and the assumption 'that Canadians have traditionally been, and remain a thoroughly non-violent people'.[11] In reality 'there has been significantly more internal conflict in the past than most of us are aware of'.[12] It is a blissful ignorance which partially stems from comparison with more dramatic and better publicized events in the USA, and combining to enhance the error of perception have been the smaller quantity and lower intensity of civil strife to be found in Canada's history than in that of the nation's large southern neighbour.

Conflict and violence *have* marked the birth and development of Canada as a nation. Looking back to the nineteenth century, Canada's record includes the 1837–8 Papineau and Mackenzie-inspired rebellions in Lower and Upper Canada, the Red River Rising of 1869–70, and the Northwest Rebellion of 1885. Paradoxically, as in many of the country's violent interludes, the events actually helped to strengthen national bonds. The Red River and Northwest convulsions, for instance, spurred construction of a transcontinental railway linking the east and west coasts of Canada. (Transportation problems associated with moving security forces to cope with the Red River unrest provided one catalyst for a decision largely vindicated fifteen years later by the need again to move troops and police in the face of Louis Riel's second insurrection.)

Three major incidents of violence in Canada stand forth within the first half of the twentieth century: the Quebec City riots of 1918, the Winnipeg general strike of 1919, and the Regina riot of 1935, to which might well be added mention of the Halifax riot 'celebrating' the end of the Second World War. Of a more contemporary nature, 'available data indicate that there were ... some 24 anti-government demonstrations, 19 riots, 1 political strike, 10 pro-government demonstrations, 92 armed attacks, and 8 conflict-related deaths'[13] in Canada over the period from 1955 to 1965. Examples of vicious, labour-related violence were apparent in the 1974 rampage at the James Bay hydroelectric project and the 1977 shooting of eight strikers at the Robin Hood Flour Mills in Montreal.

The foregoing attests to the validity of the myth theory and illustrates that violence, political or otherwise, has not been a stranger to Canadian history, culture, and institutions. Notwithstanding, Canada 'has never [known] a crisis regarding recognized authority as in some countries where civil wars or other traumatic national events presaged a drastic change in both politics and, eventually, government'.[14] Because of that background, and because 'There has been little political violence in Canada in the twentieth century',[15] the politically motivated terrorism of the FLQ came as a stunning shock and surprise to most Canadians.

It may reasonably be argued that Canada was first among the three predominantly English-speaking NATO nations to have experienced what can be described as the modern paradigm of politically motivated violence, or terrorism. The FLQ made its initial public appearance on the night of 7 March 1963, with incendiary-bomb attacks against militia armouries in the city of Montreal. 'For the next ten years, wave after wave of political violence [turned] Quebec into one of the hot-spots of North America ... climaxed by a double kidnapping and the "execution" of one of the hostages taken by the FLQ during the October Crisis of 1970.'[16] Despite the polemical tone of Louis Fournier's statement, his quotation serves to reflect Canada's early encounter with contemporary political terrorism. Through most of the 1960s, of the three referenced liberal democracies, only Canada faced the embarrassment of 'a revolutionary movement made up of volunteers ready to die for the cause',[17] with sabotage a major plank in its platform and political and economic independence as its aim. The FLQ demonstrated a continuity which pre empts 1968 as the year generally accepted as the datum point of current global terrorist activity.

The emergence of the FLQ was an outgrowth of the *Envelope*, the conditions, constraints, and influences which had created pressure upon one major segment of Canadian society. Isolated to a marked degree within the province of Quebec, many Francophone Canadians feared and resented what they saw as threats to their culture and heritage. Economically they felt themselves to be the have-nots who had been abused and exploited by Anglo-American colonialism. Independence was the foundation of the rallying cry, an idea which gained credence and impetus from the examples of Algeria and Cuba. Ideology, however, although having a place among the intellectual founders and within the conceptual framework of FLQ doctrine, was not the main attraction. Separation and independence for Quebec were the primary focal points of interest which invited support for the movement. Before its conclusion at the turn of the decade, the FLQ affair, although principally domestic in nature, included international aspects which stretched beyond merely the seizure of a British diplomat and the eventual sanctuary of his abductors in a foreign country. Implications of external state sponsorship were involved, as well as links with foreign terrorist groups, in terms of training, material, and moral support. Only the absence of the hijacking and destruction of an aircraft differentiated the context from a litany of current terrorist operations.

Attempts to revive the movement in the years immediately following 1970 were unsuccessful, and any semblance of protest associated with FLQ inspiration was quickly investigated by security agencies. As late as 1984, the appointment of a former member of the FLQ to a post in the Quebec Government 'caused a public outcry'.[18] The concept of separatism and independence for the province did not die, however, albeit the separatist Parti Qubecois (PQ) was voted out of office in 1985, and abandoned separation in its platform. A new political movement, Ressemblement democratique pour l'independence, was formed by disgruntled former members of the PQ who stated an intention to 'maintain independence as a political goal...'.[19]

The decisive (and to some observers, draconian) response of the Canadian Government, as embodied in the October Crisis, shattered the FLQ in 1970–1. But although the experience of 1963-71 led to some changes in the Federal Government's security and intelligence infrastructure, the dynamics of the FLQ's operations did not engender a wider perspective of the threat of terrorism. Canada continued to regard itself as the 'peaceable kingdom', and its leading role as a peacekeeper in the United Nations discouraged domestic speculation concerning the nation's attractiveness as a target of terrorist interest. Canada's generally low profile in world affairs, and (akin to the United States) physical separation from principal regions of terrorist activity (e.g. Europe and the Middle East) also contributed to a rather smug sense of well-being.

But the threat could not be entirely ignored, and responsibility for the security of participants in the 1976 Olympics served to promote a degree of Canadian awareness and response expertise. Similarly, the need to protect high-ranking delegates to the 1981 economic summit in Ottawa brought about another surge of recognition and temporary preparedness. It was not, however, until a series of events which began in 1982 that Canadians once again turned their attention more directly to the dangers of terrorism. In that year, ASALA's attempted assassination of a Turkish diplomat in Ottawa, and the later assassination of his military attach colleague (claimed by JCAG), and terrorist bombings in western and central Canada by a group known as Direct Action, stirred serious concerns. Debate over a proposed government bill to create a new national security service (whose purview would include terrorism), terrorist actions in other parts of the world which could not go unheeded, and Canadian participation in the London Summit declaration of 1984 helped to maintain the sensitivity. The March 1985 attack on the Turkish Embassy in Ottawa by Armenian terrorists, followed three months later by alleged Sikh terrorist involvement in bombs placed on airliners in

Canada, provided a continuing stimulus, as well as warning of external influences exerted on the ethnic communities which form a significant element of the Canadian population.

From a position of splendid isolation and overweening confidence generated by the outcome of the October Crisis, Canada has gradually moved to a reawakening: the 'menace of terrorism must be fought'.[20] In March 1986, the Canadian Government, after prolonged internal review, announced the decision to form a national Special Emergency Response Team (SERT). SERT was described as a resource for hostage situations 'where ... the authorities have no choice but rescue by armed assault'.[21] In combination with other moves designed to counter terrorism (discussed later in this and following chapters), the acceptance of a need for SERT has suggested a more realistic current perception of the threat on the part of Canadians than was fundamentally the case in the past and even at the height of the FLQ operations.

'If the United States is to achieve a more effective structure of deterrence against ... terrorism, then it must begin by realizing that its own national experience has been a poor guide to the problem....'[22] Ernest Evans's statement is accurate in its reference to the historical character of domestic political violence in the USA. Americans, for all their professed love of 'The Right to Bear Arms', have steadfastly displayed a preference for the ballot-box rather than the bullet. Unlike Canadians, however, Americans are accustomed to violence. Tradition and current levels of violent crime in the two nations bear witness to that reality. But not unlike Canada a 'striking fact about American history is that there are few or no instances of groups out of power attempting to achieve ... violent social change by means of insurrection, guerrilla war, coup d'etat or terrorism'.[23] Domestic political conflicts in the USA have generally been attempts to maintain the status quo of any given time. As Evans explains, even the American Revolution and the Civil War were fought more for protecting established conditions than for instituting 'a new social order'.[24]

Domestic political terrorism is not a stranger to the American scene, nevertheless, and without need to mention incidents of the past two decades. The 1859 Harper's Ferry raid by John Brown has been described as 'one of the first confrontations between U.S. Armed Forces and modern terrorism in the continental United States'.[25] In the aftermath of the Civil War, the Ku Klux Klan acquired an infamous reputation for its practice of politically motivated terrorist behaviour. New York's prestigious financial district was the site of a terrorist bombing in 1920 which took the lives of thirty-four people, injured over 200 others, and caused more than $2 million of property damage. Foreshadowing current accusations of Soviet complicity in acts of terrorism, the US Attorney General at the time proclaimed the incident to be a communist plot. But early US domestic experience with political terrorism was essentially spasmodic and localized, lacking a desire to change the system of government. Quoting Walter Laqueur, 'terrorism in the United States was limited in scope and purpose; there was no intention of overthrowing the government, killing political leadership or changing the political system'.[26] With certain specific exceptions, (e.g. excluding groups such as 'The Order', discussed later) Laqueur's reference to events prior to the middle of the twentieth century continues to apply, and especially when comparing the recent history of terrorism in the United States, Canada, and the United Kingdom.

Political violence was virtually non-existent in the United Kingdom during the 1960s, although the situation was to change in the decade which followed. The 1960s, however, were unsettled years for the USA and Canada, but the unrest differed markedly in style and proclaimed goals. Civil-rights campaigning by the Black community was the central issue of confrontation in the United States, joined later by militant activism in support of the anti-war movement, whereas separatist-inspired outbursts by the FLQ brought violence to the normally placid Canadian environment. Of greater significance was the fact that terrorism was a declared policy of the Canadian dissidents, while individual acts of terror were more properly the norm in the USA. The pressures of the American *Envelope* were not those which initiated terrorist behaviour in Canada or which were to encourage the renewal of IRA violence in the United Kingdom. Despite shared circumstances of abused minorities, the three nations did not face identical challenges to governmental authority and sovereignty. Discounting incipient Puerto Rican nationalism, political violence in the USA was not characterized by attempts to overthrow the government or by actions of separatist or irredentist movements. Even when the Weathermen faction made its appearance, the leadership failed to project a coherent aim, other than a blending of anarchist-nihilist rhetoric.

The American experience of the 1960s and early 1970s might justifiably be described as a period of serious civil disobedience rather than anything more extreme or sinister. Structured acts of terrorism were not manifest, certainly not as witnessed in Quebec or later in Ulster. American civil-rights disturbances generally took the form of street marches, demonstrations, sit-ins, and several destructive racial riots which mainly affected the urban ghettos inhabited by the demon-strators themselves. Campus violence was similarly confined largely to college and university premises; but other than espousing a common anti-war theme, the eruptions were not typified by a clearly defined and articulated political ideology. In looking at the 1970s 'decade of the terrorist', James B. Motley has offered four reasons why terrorism in America did not reach the tragic levels of other countries. Motley cited the nature of US society and government, or the 'safety valves', as factors which eased pressures and precluded the need for a resort to terrorist strategies and tactics. Notwithstanding, his comments included a warning that conditions might change, and the 'fusing of the criminal, racist and the ideological zealot could prove to be a dangerous combination to the nation's stability...'.[27] The activities of a domestic group calling itself 'The Order' are indicative of such a trend. The organization signed a 'declaration of war' against the United States in 1984, and proclaimed itself to be 'anti-black, anti-semitic ... dedicated to the overthrow of the United States and Canadian governments'.[28]

Motley also underlined the value of publicity, without which terrorism appears as nothing more than a localized criminal act. He maintained that 'few terrorist incidents in the United States have qualified as national media events',[29] partly because terrorist violence has not been particularly lethal in America. In keeping with that observation, he noted that the 'high level of violent crime in the United States overshadows the comparatively low level of terrorist violence. Domestic terrorist incidents ... hardly seem significant or frightening to the American public.'[30] A fourth claim that 'foreign terrorists have rarely operated on American soil' may not stand the test of time.[31] Suggestions have been made by the FBI that dangerous links exist between domestic groups in the USA and foreign organizations overseas.[32] Unquestionably in the past it has been easier and more productive for outsiders to strike at the wide range of attractive US targets in Europe, the Middle East, Asia, and Latin America. A tightening of physical security measures in those areas, plus terrorist pressure upon ethnic communities in America, could generate a future increase of foreign-initiated incidents on the US mainland.

Merged with the US historical genesis has been the American obsession with terrorism as a common crime. The assassinations of Martin Luther King and Robert Kennedy presaged a growth of domestic and international terrorism within the American context. Those two misfortunes, however, were seen as individual criminal acts, not as advents of a new phenomenon. Statisticians and law-enforcement agencies have long battled over what represents a simple criminal act versus a terrorist incident. Psychotic terror, as practised by the Manson Family, and politically motivated bombings of the FALN have been treated alike by police under the rubric of crime. As late as 1976, the *Disorders and Terrorism* report of the National Advisory Committee on Criminal Justice Standards and Goals had a crime-oriented approach to the problem of terrorism.[33] In short, terrorism as a political tool has not played a major part in the domestic historical American experience. Consequently, the nation has been slow to accept terrorism as a real threat to political stability and national security. Nurtured by a history which did not reflect political change based upon extremist behaviour, it has been difficult for US citizens and government officials to comprehend the reality of terrorism 'as a strategy for achieving political goals'.[34]

Many observers tend to excuse the American bafflement in coping with terrorism on the basis of the nation's historical evolution and the lack of experience with the phenomenon. In doing so, however, they overlook American extra-territorial familiarity with terrorism which actually had beginnings in early US history. In a more proximate identification, Edward Mickolus's chronology of international incidents mentions over forty representative events involving American citizens and facilities just during the twenty years from 1947 to 1967.[35] Generally so quick to grasp the essence of new ideas, Americans (like Canadians) have not been alert to distant warnings about the threat of terrorism. Admittedly, a large proportion of early terrorist attacks against overseas US targets were blurred by the influence of surrounding issues or were subsumed under the image of widespread anti-Americanism. Nonetheless, over the years Americans have not only been the victims but also close witnesses of terrorism in many countries and should have been able to reap the benefits of such knowledge.

One US Army officer has taken the example of the Barbary Pirates as an early American experience with terrorism. Writing in *Joint Perspectives*, he likened the conflict in the Mediterranean at the turn of the nineteenth century to that of the Iranian crisis endured by America 180 years later.[36] In 1904 a similar event in Tangier prompted then President Theodore Roosevelt's famous statement, 'Perdicaris alive or Raisuli dead.' Perhaps somewhat tongue-in-cheek, Roosevelt's attitude at that time has been termed the model for policy in use by recent Federal administrations. (The incident might also serve to demonstrate the value of international co-operation in the struggle against terrorism: US and British ships provided a show of force in an effort to secure the release of hostages held by Raisuli.) American experience with the Moros in the Philippines, while more in the nature of guerrilla warfare, provided another introduction to terrorism, and particularly of a type analogous with contemporary Shi'ite suicide attacks in the Middle East. Perhaps closer to present-day events were a number of kidnappings and hostage-takings which took place in Mexico in the 1920s, as well as bombings in Mexico and Cuba in the 1930s. All of those examples involved American personnel and installations, both commercial and diplomatic. A foretaste of the future was provided by two particular incidents in the 1930s: an American police official was assassinated by nationalists in Puerto Rico, and the US consul general was murdered in Beirut, Lebanon.

The post-Second World War decades through the 1960s presented

Americans, and the world, with abundant evidence of terrorism used to foster political aims. Insurgencies in Palestine, Greece, North Viet Nam (Indo-China), Algeria, Cuba, and Cyprus all contained examples and lessons about terrorist activity. Granted, the aura of guerrilla war was present in most cases, but terrorism formed a distinctive pattern within the operations and especially so in Palestine, Algeria, and Cyprus. American observers were on the scene during all those occasions, certainly as members of the military or the diplomatic corps. Some advantage did obtain: use of helicopters to good effect by US Armed Forces in Viet Nam was an outcome of French experience in Algeria.

Raoul Castro provided the US and the Canadian governments with a foretaste of the future when he seized citizens of both nations as hostages in Cuba in 1958. Despite US Secretary of State Dulles's claim that the United States would never yield to blackmail, the US did negotiate with the Cubans and acceded to some demands which included a temporary halt of bombing raids by Batista's air force. Five years later in Caracas, Venezuela, the US Army attaché and deputy chief of the US military mission were kidnapped and then released when the Venezuelan Government freed seventy political prisoners. Like the Cuban incident, such occasions have been the source of criticism pointing at a lack of consistency in US counter-terrorism policy. It is also known that some large US-based corporations have paid blackmail demands to terrorists, but have suppressed acknowledgement of their actions to avoid adverse publicity or possible encouragement of similar threats.

How much the Americans learned from the backyard experience of neighbouring Canada during the FLQ crisis is difficult to judge accurately. Certainly the FBI had a marginal involvement, and the problems of the lengthy undefended border were highlighted when a female FLQ sympathizer was apprehended after transporting explosives to the United States to assist a Black terrorist group with an attempt to blow up the Liberty Bell. (From the author's personal experience, the US military viewed the situation as another counter-guerrilla action and was undoubtedly confirmed in that opinion when the Canadian Forces were committed during the October Crisis of 1970.) Ultimately the United States was to receive its own particular baptism of fire through the years of the Viet Nam war. While essentially a military venture, many Americans from all walks of life spent time 'in-country' through the 1960s and 1970s and not all of them as members of the US Armed Forces. Diplomats, teachers, politicians, civilian contractors and businessmen, missionaries, and a host of others were subjected to the impact of Viet Cong terrorism. Several major incidents involved US diplomats and intelligence personnel, the 1968 Tet attack on the American embassy in Saigon being perhaps the most notable. Security measures, then as now, were often deplorably after the fact in design and implementation, but that original need should not have gone uncorrected in similar situations elsewhere (e.g. Beirut) fifteen years later.

Canadians, as well, warrant criticism for an ostrich-like attitude towards overseas terrorist events from the standpoint of acknowledging the growing threat and the requirement to introduce protective measures. Canadian observers, both diplomatic and military, were present in many of the same locations as their American counterparts. As mentioned earlier, however, Canadians have indulged themselves in the notion that their frequent position as intermediaries, or their distance (both literally and figuratively) from sources of terrorist conflict, would absolve them from any involvement. Canadian reaction and response to terrorism, like that of the US, has been a function of perception of the threat and a belief that 'it could not happen to us'.

Judged on the basis of US domestic history and the absence of home-grown terrorist activism, it is possible to appreciate some of the initial confusion surrounding American perceptions of terrorism. Attacks by militant factions overseas have been deprecated as anti-Americanism or communist plots. Compounding that opinion has been the vision of the United States as a giant world power possessing immense and sophisticated resources, making it immune to terrorist assaults. Valuable experience gained by US personnel in many parts of the world has been ignored or misinterpreted, sometimes purposely to serve political, diplomatic, or bureaucratic interests. These conditions have not altered dramatically and continue to produce controversy in the development of US counter-terrorism policy. One example of such circumstances was a statement made to the House of Representatives Foreign Affairs Committee as late as March 1985 by Robert B. Oakley, director of the United States anti-terrorism programme. Oakley revealed that 'his office [was] disorganized and probably could not respond quickly to attacks on American embassies'.[37] He admitted 'that we haven't been able to get our act together'.[38] Various reasons (examined later) contributed to Oakley's dilemma, including the historical lack of national experience, but certainly a lack of experience gained outside the continental USA could not serve as an excuse.

Undoubtedly, however, the years from late 1979 through the 1980s decade reflect the greatest impact upon America in regard to modern terrorism. Terrorist activity associated with the Viet Nam war was dismissed as a function of guerrilla warfare; in conjunction, the public, government, and military chose to blot out memories of the unpopular conflict as much as possible. Recognition was given to terrorist atrocities of the 1970s and some effort was expended to provide a response, but the threat was overseas and was overshadowed by major domestic political problems in the USA. Not until the 444 days of the

Iranian hostage crisis did American interest focus sharply on the threat of terrorism. From the conclusion of that traumatic event, US installations, citizens, and influence increasingly became principal targets of terrorist attack in foreign countries. The Iranian incident shook American complacency and wounded the nation's pride to the point where Ronald Reagan's promises to take positive action against terrorism virtually assured him of election to the presidency, especially when compared to Carter's seeming ineffectiveness. But Reagan's expressed determination did not prevent a string of terrorist atrocities in the years following his 1981 inauguration, and which saw him fumbling for a response much in the manner of his predecessor. Suicide attacks upon US Marines and American diplomatic premises in Beirut, attacks upon US personnel and facilities in Europe, aircraft hijackings involving US citizens (one of which in Beirut rivalled the Iranian embassy take-over in terms of publicity), and the seizure of an Italian cruise liner during which an elderly American cripple was murdered, were part of a long list of terrorist crimes directed toward America and Americans.

Anger, frustration, and the perceived need for a forceful reply to terrorism which would demonstrate American determination and proclaimed policy of retaliation finally encouraged a major decision to use American military resources as an instrument of counter-terrorism. In April 1986, US aircraft bombed targets in Libya in answer to evidence that the Libyan leader, Colonel Gaddafi, was guilty of state-sponsored terrorist attacks against Americans. The action evoked much controversy around the world, although generally applauded in the United States, and raised questions about future American behaviour. Disputatious though the event may have been, it did much to assuage Americans' injured pride. The attack also signalled to a considerable extent the degree to which American perception of the threat had altered over the years.

Writing in the introduction to *British Perspectives on Terrorism*, Paul Wilkinson states, in part, 'that Great Britain has enjoyed freedom from major internal strife and violence for over one hundred and fifty years...'.[39] Richard Clutterbuck echoes that comment in the opening pages of *Britain in Agony*: 'We do have an unrivalled record of non-violence in our society ... [it is] nearly 300 years since we had a violent or unconstitutional change in our system of government.'[40] T.A. Critchley begins *The Conquest of Violence* with a quotation from *The Times* by a *Washington Post* correspondent, 'British experience in building a non-violent relatively gentle society seems of paramount importance to a world beset by police brutality and student nihilism.'[41] The accuracy of these observations is undisputed. It is ironical, however, that each can be found in a volume written at a time when the United Kingdom was on the verge of experiencing, or had been subjected to, the trauma of terrorist violence. To be fair, with the exception of a minor campaign by the Angry Brigade in the early 1970s, and relatively small-scale activities of animal-rights groups, the violence has not originated in Great Britain. The majority of contemporary incidents has been a consequence of the Northern Ireland conflict which erupted in 1969, coupled with the spread of international terrorism.

The United Kingdom does have an early history of violence associated with the unification of the nation, although that tendency abated in the wake of the seventeenth century civil war and virtually came to an end with the failure of the Jacobite rebellion in 1745. This is not to say that Great Britain has been free of turbulence from that time. A number of major riots and minor uprisings took place through the eighteenth and nineteenth centuries, some associated with religion (Gordon Riots, 1780), and some with the Industrial Revolution (Luddites, 1811–13), or impatience with modest attempts at reform (Chartists, 1838-48). Critchley describes the 'lesser struggle' during the years from the 1850s to the First World War when clashes and riots over the right to demonstrate, to march in procession, and demands for female suffrage occurred, as well as the mushrooming of labour unrest at the end of the first decade of the twentieth century.[42]

For all these ripples, Great Britain settled comfortably into the lengthy Victorian era with Parliament meeting the challenges by compromise and tolerance, confident of its sovereignty. Despite the existence of a standing army dating from Cromwellian times, it was the unarmed police formed by Sir Robert Peel in the 1830s who gradually came to the fore as the representatives of law and order. Over a period of forty years from 1869, the military was called out on merely twenty-four occasions, and only twice was the order to fire given. In Canada during the same span, troops were called upon double that number of times for strike-breaking duties alone.

The First World War brought a halt, temporarily, to the industrial strife that burgeoned in 1911–12. The nation, and the Empire, rallied to face the threat to Europe when patriotism transcended all other issues. For a brief year following the 1918 Armistice, labour violence flared anew, climaxed by the August 1919 riots in Liverpool, and then dissipated. '[T]he half century after 1919 has been a relatively tranquil period ...'[43] – tranquil, that is, until the resurgence of labour confrontations and the intrusion of politically motivated terrorism which have marred the past two decades.

> The ... United Kingdom [has] largely been concerned, historically, at least, with only spasmodic outbreaks of terrorism, associated with the problems of Ireland and the British connection.

Nevertheless, the United Kingdom, like all Western states, is now open to the growth of international terrorism.[44]

Richard Thackrah would be rather more accurate if he were to say Great Britain instead of United Kingdom; it is the former, not the latter, which has had minimal experience with terrorism.

Thackrah *is* correct in his allusion to the Irish dimension. It was a Fenian group who, 100 years ago, exploded two dynamite charges simultaneously at Westminster Hall and the House of Commons. It was Fenian activism that led to the formation of the Special Branch in 1883. It was the IRA Council that 'decided to declare war on Britain'[45] in January 1938 in an act that initiated a terrorist campaign in England which in the space of a year and a half resulted in at least 128 outrages, killing six people and injuring over 100. And it was the strife associated with the Civil Rights Campaign in Northern Ireland in 1969 that eventually brought terrorist brutality to Great Britain in the form of the IRA/PIRA and INLA bombings and shootings over the past fifteen years.

During those same fifteen years, Great Britain also felt the shock of international terrorist attacks. As early as 1970, the PFLP attempted to hijack an El Al airliner which had just taken off from London airport, and one of the conspirators, Leila Khaled, was taken into custody by British authorities. In the years immediately following, attempts were made successively on the lives of the Jordanian ambassador and a businessman who supported Israeli interests, and a letter-bomb campaign killed a member of the Israeli embassy in London. More sensational and horrific incidents were represented by the 1980 seizure of the Iranian embassy and the 1982 shooting of the Israeli ambassador. It was during 1980 that Gaddafi launched his 'hit-teams' in an effort to suppress the activities of Libyan dissidents, many of whom resided in Great Britain. Despite the success of British law-enforcement agencies in apprehending some of Gaddafi's agents, it did not dissuade further Libyan efforts which ultimately led to the 1984 St James's Square incident and the death of a female officer of London's Metropolitan Police. Libyans have not been alone in deserving of responsibility for recent international terrorism in England. A Kashmiri group kidnapped the assistant commissioner of the Indian consulate in Birmingham in 1984 in an attempt to halt the execution of a terrorist in New Delhi, subsequently murdering the diplomat when their demands were not met. In January 1986, a leading moderate of the London Sikh community was assassinated as a protest against moves to bring about a peaceful resolution of conflict in the Punjab.

London, as with Paris, Rome, and Vienna, continues to be a focal point for international terrorist activity because of its position as a major centre of international affairs. The presence of a large international diplomatic representation, as well as numerous expatriate communities, offers terrorist groups a lucrative range of targets. Consequently, a casual visitor to the London metropolitan area might be led to believe that Great Britain suffers a much greater incidence of terrorism than is actually the fact. Diplomatic premises have taken on more obvious physical protection, signs warn of the dangers of unattended packages, security vehicles periodically rush through the streets with sirens wailing, and armed police officers are plainly in evidence at Heathrow airport. Yet the nation's capital does not exhibit the almost frantic range of highly visible protective measures as are witnessed in Washington, DC. Similarly, within and without London, the British mainland and its residents maintain a relaxed, unperturbed demeanour, typified by an insistence upon the policy of an unarmed police force. Indeed, government decisions to equip some law-enforcement personnel with weapons for special purposes (e.g. protection of international air terminals) has met with registered public dismay and criticism.

One reason for such an attitude is the aforementioned dearth of experience with political violence for more than two generations. It is quite feasible to extend that back through Critchley's 'lesser struggle' to encompass Wilkinson's 'one hundred and fifty years'. Putting aside the actions of the Irish terrorists, monstrous as they have been, and those of an international nature, 'there has been no parallel to the Red Army Faction, the Red Brigades, the Japanese Red Army, or even the American Weathermen'.[46]

British experience with terrorism is not wanting, however, but the majority of it has not been gained at home in the mother country of Great Britain. Some early lessons were taught across the sea in Ireland at the end of the First World War, during the battle for independence led by Collins, De Valera, and others. (Unhappily, many of those teachings went unheeded or were forgotten, especially the value of intelligence infrastructure, and had to be relearned after 1969.) Rather, it was following the Second World War that the British received their major schooling in the phenomenon of terrorism. The venue for this tutored knowledge would be known in the American vernacular as 'the school of hard knocks'. More precisely it was located in what remained of the British Empire. Hardly had peace been declared than troubles erupted in Palestine, with growing terrorism on the part of the Irgun Zvai Leumi and the Stern Gang. Conflict in that British Mandate was followed during ensuing years by similar outbreaks in Malaya, Kenya, Cyprus, Aden, and Rhodesia. Few people at the time, nonetheless, correctly judged or recognized the nature of the violence or were able to foresee its future influence.

The 'students' who learned the most about terrorism in those years were primarily members of the British Armed Forces, who had to bear the brunt of dissident confrontations. Among their number were observant soldiers like General Sir Frank Kitson, who not only assimilated what was taught by terrorist activists, but was capable of translating that knowledge into widely published books on the subject. The British Army, in particular, became recognized in military circles around the world as a leading authority on counter-insurgency warfare – a form of conflict which almost invariably embraced terrorist tactics. But a dangerous theme pervaded much of the training and formal education associated with the experience and the lessons learned. The perception focused on counter-insurgency and 'low-intensity warfare' conducted on a foreign soil. The problem of the military performing a suppressive role in direct confrontation with the civilian population of its own homeland was not seriously considered. Thus, while valuable expertise was gained by active duty overseas, a fundamental weakness melded into thinking and doctrine: the concepts were not designed for use in the United Kingdom.

This state of affairs existed in Northern Ireland from the beginning of the serious rioting in Belfast and Londonderry in 1969. Desmond Hamill provided illustrations when describing the first use of troops in Belfast, emphasizing that little had been done about the suggestion to deploy the Army: 'So that the Army knew nothing of the rigid sectarian geography of the city with its myriad little side streets ... [and] certainly no maps had been produced.'[47] The memories of 1919–21 had faded; it did not seem possible that British troops would be required for internal security duties within the United Kingdom. Admittedly, the Troubles of 1969 came as something of a surprise even to those intimately connected with the province. Confrontations had occurred during the previous year as the Civil Rights Movement gained its momentum; but, as expressed in *The Economist*, 'it [was] embarrassing that so few papers in England ... paid much attention to what [was] going on in an integral part of this country'.[48] The small flames that appeared at Burntollet Bridge in January 1969 quickly grew into 'The Rage of Ulster' by April, blossomed in July and were out of control by mid-August.

Granted, the IRA was not any better prepared initially for the conflict than were the police or the army. The 'Northern Campaign' of 1956–62 had been a disaster for the Republican group, who dumped all arms and materials and withdrew all full-time active volunteers in February of the final year. In fact, during the 1969–70 period, the IRA earned the censorious nickname of 'I Ran Away' because of its inability to provide support to Catholic enclaves in Belfast and Londonderry. Recovery, however, was not long in materializing and especially so once the 'Provisionals' undertook the leading role in opposition to the security forces.

The speed with which the situation deteriorated in Ulster and the magnitude of the problem caught the British Government off guard. From the moment when Michael Collins had 'signed [his] own death warrant'[49] in 1921, the Province had almost been a law unto itself. Treated with benign neglect by Westminster, with its own parliament at Stormont, Northern Ireland seemed farther from Great Britain than the few miles across the Irish Sea. At the time when the Troubles broke out in 1969, the principal officer concerned with Northern Ireland at the Home Office in London had 'other duties [which] included responsibility for collecting dog licences throughout the United Kingdom'.[50]

'John Bull's other Island [had] experienced a whole series of bloody conflicts ... from the Wolfe Tone Rebellion to the Irish independence struggle of 1919–21',[51] so that rumbles from Ulster in the mid-1960s had not drawn much attention. Even 'Paisley's tub-thumping and his success in attracting and rousing crowds',[52] or the activities of the UVF in 1966, failed to arouse much interest. Northern Ireland had been relatively quiet from 1921, with the Protestant majority apparently well able to control the Catholic minority in their midst. It seemed unlikely that anything to the contrary could occur; and should the unthinkable arise, the British Army hovered in the background to put matters right again. But the circumstances had changed over the preceding half-century, and the pressures of the *Envelope* were different. The Catholic minority was larger, more vociferous, and more determined and desperate. The Civil Rights Movement had succeeded in drawing world-wide attention, with television cameras a means of delivering instant and graphic publicity on a continuous basis. Daily coverage of the violence in Northern Ireland shocked viewers throughout the United Kingdom, as well as stirring material support for the nationalist cause from the large expatriate Irish community in the United States. The bankrupt policies of Stormont, despite Terrence O'Neill's attempts at reform, showed starkly against efforts to improve the status of minorities in other nations.

The police in Ulster were quickly overwhelmed by the scale and intensity of the violence. Exhausted, demoralized and quite unable to cope in terms of manpower, equipment, training, attitude, or policies, they could do little except withdraw to their barricaded station-houses. In response to a request for Military Aid to the Civil Power, the British Government dispatched military reinforcements in an attempt to restore a state of law and order. The initial appearance of the soldiery was sufficient to gain a breathing space, but the atmosphere of calm was not to be long-lasting. The Army was trained and equipped to fight counter-insurgency battles in foreign countries, not unrest and terrorism emanating from citizens of the United Kingdom. The faces yelling insults from behind barricades or the figures hurling dangerous objects from roof-tops were those of fellow countrymen. The Army suddenly had a lot of new learning to do, many new tactics to develop and much new equipment to obtain. The police in Northern Ireland virtually had to be rebuilt from scratch.

The British have a traditional reputation for muddling through. Response to the events of 1969 did not bring about a hasty, ill-conceived over-reaction on the part of the British Government. More than two years passed before the parliament at Stormont was dissolved and direct rule was imposed from Westminster, a period of time devoted to allowing Northern Ireland to seek its own solutions. On the British mainland, anti-terrorist legislation in response to the violence was not passed until 1974 in the aftermath of several especially brutal PIRA bombings in England. Similarly, the threat of both Irish and international terrorism has brought about the gradual introduction of protective measures by the British police, most notably on the part of the London Metropolitan force. The Brighton hotel bombing of 1984, however, demonstrated that the approach to counter-terrorism has not been uniform throughout the nation.

Culpable or not in terms of neglect, since 1969 the United Kingdom has had to contend with severe domestic terrorism in one area of the British Isles. The conflict has spilled over to mainland Britain, to be joined by the reality of international terrorism. The British Government and people have had to face the violence with marginal domestic experience of it over the past fifty years, and with the resources of an unarmed police (excluding Northern Ireland) and an army trained to fight overseas. It is a nation selfishly proud of its personal liberties and freedoms, and historically opposed to intrusive restraints. The response to the violence has drawn both world acclaim and criticism, but the response has also reflected a serious perception of terrorism's threat to stability and law and order.

The United Kingdom, Canada, and the United States have a shared modern experience of domestic and international terrorism. That experience is neither identical in character or intensity, nor has it evoked precisely identical response. In part, the history of violence in each nation has contributed to the nature of the response; in part, the circumstances of each situation have influenced the reaction. The experience has, nevertheless, demanded that each nation develop and pursue counter-terrorism policy as one consequence of the threat.

## Philosophy of use of force

Before moving to an examination of policy development, policy, and policy measures, reference must be made to a characteristic philosophy

47

of law enforcement in all three nations. It will be seen to be founded upon certain basic principles which, in turn, guide the formation and implementation of counter-terrorism policy. These are: the supremacy of the rule of law, civilian control by the democratically elected constitutional government, and the use of minimum force to preserve internal order and security.

'The second major foundation of any liberal state is the supremacy of its rule of law.'[53] Wilkinson cogently argues this principle in the opening chapters of *Terrorism and the Liberal State*, quoting, in one instance, a famous passage from Locke's *Second Treatise on Civil Government*:

> in all states of created beings, capable of laws, where there is no law there is no freedom. For liberty is to be free from restraint and violence from others; which cannot be where there is no law; and is not, as we are told, a liberty for every man to do as he lists.[54]

It is the rule of law which forms the basis of the freedom and liberty that are the constitutional rights of citizens in Canada, the United States, and the United Kingdom. It is 'one rule for rich and poor, for the favourite at Court, and for the countryman at plough',[55] and for those who break the law, and for those who administer the law.

The rule of law, however, is inadequate without controls. Wilkinson refers to the place of an independent judiciary as a means 'of guarding against breaches of the constitution by the legislative and executive departments'.[56] It is a task which has traditionally been fulfilled by the courts of all three nations. But control must extend even further, and incorporate the influence of the people's democratically expressed will. That influence is manifested by the actions of the government, elected in accordance with principles of the nation's constitution. The people freely elect the government, giving the government a mandate to legislate and supervise laws which the people deem appropriate. The government's task, as well, is to ensure that the laws are administered in a fair, sound, and equitable manner. Thus, control is exercised through the mandate of the people, the legislation and supervision of the government, and the oversight of the independent judiciary.

The enforcement and administration of the law is essentially the job of the judiciary and the police in Canada, the United States, and the United Kingdom. The police forces are guided by the principle of *minimum force* in the conduct of their duties. The use of minimum force is reflected by the reliance placed upon standard law-enforcement bodies as the first line, and major elements of response to terrorist activities. Despite the availability of military resources, it is the police who bear the initial brunt of confrontation with terrorists and, to the greatest extent possible, continue to oppose them through protective and investigative services. Military resources are used in a back-up role on extreme occasions when police become over stretched or lack technical expertise (e.g. bomb disposal); but the military is regarded as an adjunct, not as a primary source of response capability, and always under firm control of the civil authority. The military concept of *maximum force* is resisted in the three nations, and is employed only as a last resort in a grave emergency.

Unlike many European and most Soviet bloc countries, the police in Canada, the USA, and the United Kingdom are not centralized entities. Rather, they are pluralistic in form and structure, as described in detail in Chapter Four. Consequently, they do not lend themselves to the concept of a 'Third Force' which is specially organized and equipped to cope with civil unrest, riots, and major civil disobedience. Under such conditions, if the police are overwhelmed, it is the military that provides support in a very specific and circumscribed manner. Again, that activity and the special police–military relationships are given careful attention in Chapter Four.

## Policy development

It would be incorrect to assert that the FLQ represented Canada's first and only encounter with political terrorism during the 1960s. A year prior to the FLQ's 'explosive' appearance in Montreal, the Doukhobor 'Sons of Freedom' sect dynamited an electrical power pylon in British Columbia, through the years 1966–8, Cuban, Yugoslav, and Croatian expatriate groups carried out several terrorist bombings in Canada. Such activities aside, the FLQ remained the primary threat and concern, as well as presenting an archetypal example of modern terrorist activity. Canada's early and serious encounter with terrorism through the medium of the FLQ, and the October Crisis in particular, had significant and long-lasting effects. Those effects were both positive and negative in nature and impact. They are best illustrated by reference to two major principles which underlie and guide Canadian counter terrorism policy: (1) adherence to the rule of law; and (2) perception of the threat. With no intention of disrespect or facetiousness, 'upon these commandments lie all the law [of] the prophets'.[57]

Canada's position in relation to the rule of law is not difficult to understand; it is a principle inherent within the make-up of Canadian history, culture, ideology, and institutions. Canada is a liberal-democratic nation, with a government based upon the British parliamentary system, and a written Constitution which contains a Charter of Rights and Freedoms guaranteeing fundamental protection for those who legally reside within the scope of national sovereignty. Examples of Canada's attitude in support of that principle *vis-à-vis* terrorism are available in statements delivered by Canadian delegates at the United Nations.[58] Canada has been quick to endorse international agreements and conventions whose intent incorporates the legal contravention of terrorist actions, and the nation has also established bilateral treaties in an effort to stimulate wider co-operation. Pursuit of that aim was displayed at the Bonn, Venice, Ottawa, London, Tokyo, and Toronto Economic Summit meetings, and the Canadian Government has expressed similar views to the Organization of American States (OAS). (Various international agreements and conventions mentioned hereafter in this Chapter are described in the additional notes to Chapter Two.)

Controversial though it may have been in some aspects, Canada's handling of the October Crisis, and reactions in the aftermath, underscore the place of rule of law as a cardinal principle of Canadian counter-terrorism policy. The various tiers of government functioned within the bounds of duly enacted legislation, and correct relationships were maintained between the security forces, especially in regard to the military and the police. Accusations of over-zealous or illegal behaviour on the part of some law-enforcement personnel were subject to investigation and official government inquiries in the years following. Concern for the observance of legal and constitutional rights also had a prominent role in arguments surrounding the need for the new Canadian Security Intelligence Service (CSIS).

From the standpoint of perception of the threat, however, Canadian policy development has been somewhat ambivalent. Canadians have been lulled into a false sense of security, and a portion of the responsibility for such an attitude must be laid at the doorstep of Canadian experience with the FLQ. Canada has been applauded for the firm and expeditious manner in which it dealt with that terrorist threat; little argument can be voiced in disagreement or to detract from the successful outcome. But that period was fundamentally a nascent phase of terrorism's current evolution; the weapons, technology, organization, training, range of support, and practical knowledge which are now available to terrorists were not part of the FLQ's inventory. The FLQ was a parochial expression of dissent, commanding rather marginal allegiance among the population of Quebec. The group was small, fragmented, lacking in truly dynamic leadership, and it was deprecated by many prominent Francophone politicians who did not favour violence as the means to achieve the dream of a separated and independent Quebec. The movement made many errors; perhaps its most damaging mistake was the murder of a Quebec Government minister, Mr Pierre Laporte, which horrified Canadians of all ethnic derivations.

The Government of Canada, on the other hand, was able to move from a position of strength to combat the FLQ threat. The authorities, to use military parlance, could afford to 'concentrate their forces' and to apply them to one geographical region of the country. The FLQ was swamped by the security resources arrayed against it, and had, as well, alienated the 'sea' in which it had to swim if it were to survive. Canadians have tended to ignore the possibility of an opposite scenario involving terrorist activities, one creating demands for the dispersion of security forces across the nation. While an eventual outcome of such a situation might not differ from that of 1970–1, the time required to achieve success and the related costs would undoubtedly be many times greater. In fairness, a lack of preparedness and the commission of errors by the security forces during the October Crisis did prompt subsequent Federal government action and steps were taken to remedy some of the faults, as described later in this chapter. The relative ease, speed, and success associated with security operations during the October Crisis, however, together with related factors, have had the effect of lessening the perception of terrorism as a threat for Canada and Canadians.

It is accurate to state that Canadians have largely escaped the tragedies of domestic and international terrorism which have erupted with such frequency and intensity around the globe since 1968. Excepting the FLQ adventure, Canada has not been subjected to the spate of politically motivated hijackings, kidnappings, and hostage incidents that have plagued Europe and the Middle East, and which have induced stress within the United Kingdom and the USA as well. To emphasize the point, both the 1976 Olympic Games held in Montreal and the 1981 meeting of heads of government at the Western Economics Summit convened at Montebello, outside Ottawa, passed without the intrusion of terrorist activity. Indeed, during the 1987–8 period, Canada was successively the venue of four major international events which took place without incident: the Francophone Summit (Quebec City); the Commonwealth Heads of Government Meeting [CHOGM] (Vancouver); the Winter Olympics (Calgary); and the Economic Summit (Toronto).

Physical environment and location have played a large part in keeping Canada outside the focus of terrorist attention, as has the nation's relatively low profile in world affairs during the past twenty years. With few notable exceptions (e.g. Turkish and Cuban diplomats), tempting targets have not been present to invite terrorist attacks. On the rare occasions when obvious attractions did exist, as in the case of the Montreal Olympics, the visit of the Pope or CHOGM, security precautions were so intense and comprehensive that they precluded the likelihood of an actual attack. Noteworthy, too, was the fact that at those times the groups having the most sophisticated ability to implement a threat (e.g. the PLO) were not in a position to do so.

Quoting from Prime Minister Trudeau's national broadcast on 16

October 1970, announcing the unprecedented use of The War Measures Act in peace time: 'Canadians have always assumed that [terrorism] could not happen here'.[59] That assumption has prevailed to a disproportionate degree within Canada, even to the time of the March 1985 assault on the Turkish embassy in Ottawa. On the occasion of that incident, a Canadian official decried any potential for terrorist development in Canada. 'After all,' he maintained, 'people emigrate to Canada because it is a peaceful nation and they would not have any interest in conducting violent acts or attempting to upset the status quo.'[60]

The combination of such circumstances makes it possible to appreciate the sense of complacency and confidence which have marked Canada's response to the threat of terrorism. That is not to say that Canada has failed to regard terrorism in a serious manner; to make such a claim would be invidious. The Canadian view was clearly enunciated by Mr Trudeau in 1970 when he explained that the use of The War Measures Act was 'to deal effectively with the nebulous yet dangerous challenge to society represented by the terrorist organizations'.[61] Former Minister of External Affairs, Mitchell Sharp, told the 1972 General Assembly of the United Nations that 'we must strongly condemn all acts of international terrorism, direct or indirect...'.[62] The Report of the McDonald Commission, published in 1981, identified three basic categories of threat to Canada's security against which protection was needed. The second of those listed was terrorism.[63] In 1986, a Special Senate Committee on Terrorism and the Public Safety was convened to report on 'matters relating to terrorism as a real or potential threat to Canada and to Canadians'.[64] Among other findings, the Committee concluded that 'international terrorism presents a major challenge to Canada, to Canadian policy, to intelligence and to law enforcement, currently and for the foreseeable future'.[65] In the wake of the Report, the Federal Government formed an interdepartmental Counter-Terrorism Task Force to examine contingency planning and crisis management in Canada.

Notwithstanding, the failure to adopt a long-term perspective, or to heed the lessons of other nations, coupled with fading memories of the tension-filled days of 1970, have inhibited urgency in the development of Canadian counter-terrorism policy or measures. A low perception of the threat has not inspired the need for greater action, and expediency and pressure for financial economies have often taken priority. The use of commercial security firms to provide protection for diplomatic premises, for instance, while economical in terms of police resources, was inadequate and had unfortunate results.[66] The much-delayed (and controversial, in this author's opinion) introduction of SERT offers another illustration, and reflects the general Canadian attitude towards terrorism since the ending of the October Crisis.

Much criticism has been levelled at US policy-makers because of what have been seen as inconsistencies, blunders, and errors in attempts to come to grips with the response to terrorism. Robert W. Taylor said that 'one could effectively argue that the United States never had an organizational policy toward terrorism'.[67] His references to kidnapping and hostage incidents in which pressure was applied to accede to the terrorists' demands (e.g. the 1969 abduction of the US ambassador to Brazil) were especially pointed. Taylor compared that event to the subsequent seizures of Dan Mitrione in Uruguay and the US Embassy in Khartoum, when 'no concessions' was the rule and the Americans were killed by their captors. He further alluded to the bargaining conducted to free the Tehran hostages, as opposed to the hard line taken in the Dozier incident.[68] Taylor's critiques are valid, but need to be balanced against circumstances. It must be recognized that as a major world power, the US has been a particularly tempting target for terrorist attacks, made even more feasible by the nation's desire to maintain its democratic image and its reluctance to dispense with the open posture of its missions abroad. Also, through to the end of the 1970s, the United States did not appreciate the growing potential of terrorism as an instrument of political blackmail. Somewhat like Canada, the perception of the threat was low. It is of considerable additional significance that government in the USA is encumbered by a federal structure in which both politics and the bureaucracy have an immense influence.

President Nixon came to power at the time when terrorism was beginning to emerge as a tactic of politically motivated dissent and militancy. Nixon's immediate concerns were the Viet Nam war and rising US public opposition to a continued American presence in the conflict. Preoccupation with events in the Far East, combined with domestic unrest, produced a not unreasonable uncertainty in policy response to terrorism. To his credit, Nixon did take practical steps to suppress the rash of skyjacking which had reached a high point in 1969, especially in regard to Cuba-bound seizures. A bi-lateral treaty was concluded with the Castro government in the early 1970s, electronic inspections were later introduced at airports, and sky-marshalls were placed aboard aircraft. It was not until the horrors of Munich and Lod, however, that the Nixon administration was convinced of the need for 'the most effective means to prevent terrorism here and abroad'.[69]

The means chosen to implement reaction was the high-level Cabinet Committee to Combat Terrorism, which met only once and was abolished by President Carter in 1977. Despite its 'singular' meeting, the Committee did establish a Working Group which provided a forum and point of reference for several years. Another outcome was a principle of counter-terrorism policy that has generally been followed since that time: no concessions, in conjunction with a refusal to negotiate with blackmailers. The workings of the Cabinet Committee and its subordinate group were overtaken by the events of the Watergate scandal and, to a degree, by President Carter's human-rights policies. Carter did direct a reorganization of the US terrorism response infrastructure, but it was not until the Iranian Crisis that his administration became more aware of the dangerous influence of terrorism on a global scale. Ronald Reagan was able to grandstand on the Carter failures to deal effectively with terrorism, promising a new and energetic US attack on the phenomenon. But, much to his chagrin, Reagan did not find the path any easier to tread.

Lack of consistent direction and concern with terrorism has not been merely a function of presidential failings. White House aides and advisors have not proved to be fully cognizant of the problem, particularly during the Carter era. Secretary of State Kissinger has been accused of having more interest in the policies of *détente*, and the political ramifications of that undertaking, than in curbing terrorist activity. Congress, too, showed itself to be predisposed towards placing constraints on the intelligence community and presidential powers rather than considering the long-range effects which might result. Definition, always a nuisance, continues to plague the implementation of constructive measures, as evidenced by President Reagan's difficulties in obtaining passage of legislation because of contention over defining terrorism and terrorists.

Within the various government agencies, friction has proved to be a significant stumbling-block to the development of a co-ordinated counter-terrorism policy. Bureaucratic in-fighting and 'turf' problems have dogged the efforts undertaken to produce a systematic organiz-ation, and, as yet, 'no single agency or official is in overall command'.[70] Bickering has not eased among the various agencies, some of which claim that the FBI, the department responsible for domestic counter-terrorist operations, does not take the matter seriously. The FBI, in response, points to data illustrating a number of successful investig-ations and prosecutions of terrorist groups in the United States. The military, by its own admission, did not begin to regard terrorism as a threat until the late 1970s, and then only in response to attacks upon its facilities and in accordance with presidential direction.

While the Reagan administration's proposals have had some success in obtaining congressional approval, the more so in the light of terrorist atrocities in the Middle East and Latin America, civil-rights agitators have opposed many of the moves. Concern over intelligence functions has continued to be apparent in regard to measures involving computer databanks and the infiltration of clandestine organizations by law-enforcement personnel. Other pressure groups, such as the large Irish–American lobby, generate well-publicized obstructions to measures (e.g. US–UK Extradition Treaty) which might prove unfavourable to their cause. Action of the latter sort has been a particular hindrance to development of American programmes of assistance to law-enforcement agencies in other nations. In the Irish case, as in others, it has prevented the supply of modern weapons and equipment to police forces on the basis that the items would be used to suppress minorities, e.g. by the Royal Ulster Constabulary (RUC).

Congressional and pressure-group influence during the aftermath of the Nixon resignation impacted severely upon the American intelligence community. Undoubtedly some positive and much-needed supervisory and control measures did result, and were welcomed by experienced members of agencies such as the CIA. The overall consequences were not altogether healthy, however, creating morale problems and the loss of valuable government employees, as well as the destruction of records and data collected over years of investigation and research. Consensus among security specialists indicates that the larger problem has been the resulting break-down of trust that existed between US and foreign intelligence services. Beginning with concerns over inroads on the confidentiality of exchanges of information, sources, and so on, though congressional oversight, legislation modifying the Freedom of Information Act has further undermined that relationship. Foreign intelligence services fear that their investigations of terrorist and criminal activities might be compromised by sharing information in the USA. In conjunction, the Privacy Act weakened information-gathering on the part of law-enforcement agencies in the United States by restricting the records that may be maintained on an individual citizen.

In accordance with the fundamental democratic ideal and constitutional principles, the US response to terrorism has its foundations in the rule of law. For the most part, the American government has endeavoured to combat terrorism through recognized legal methods and sanctions. The afore-mentioned bilateral agreement with Cuba is one example; the agreement has continued to operate in principle, despite a formal denunciation by Castro in 1975 because of an alleged US violation. An early attempt at international co-operation was initiated in 1972 at the United Nations by then-Secretary of State William Rogers. That effort to achieve a Convention for the Prevention and Punishment of Certain Acts of International Terrorism subsequently foundered on the inability to obtain consensus on the definition of terrorism and its causes. Nonetheless, the United States has been a prominent advocate and supporter of the three major international conventions against aircraft hijacking and sabotage, as well as a leading proponent of co-operation against terrorism through the medium of the Summit Seven meetings.

Excepting what was a hostage rescue attempt in 1980, until 1985 the United States resisted the temptation to employ its military resources in response to terrorist provocations overseas. In October of that year, however, American fighter aircraft intercepted an Egyptian commercial airliner over the Mediterranean and forced it to land at an Italian air base. The purpose of the action was to apprehend terrorists alleged to be responsible for the hijacking of a cruise liner and the murder of an American passenger. Arguments flow over the legitimacy of the military intervention; while it had merit in its intent, it must be regarded as questionable in terms of international law, as well as setting a dangerous precedent and example for other nations. Five months later American military forces responded again to terrorist activities, on that occasion in retaliation for state-sponsored attacks originated by Libya. President Reagan had promised to follow such a policy, although opposed by some members of his administration and frustrated by circumstances which were not conducive to military operations. The use of military force was a major departure in American policy of response to terrorism. It was a move which also illustrated a substantial change in perception of the threat over the years from 1968.

The development of British policy in response to terrorism has been rather more steady than that of Canada or the United States. Canada felt the shock of terrorism in 1969–70, reacted, and then tended to lapse into a sense of immunity until the 1980s when terrorist violence prompted a gradual renewal of alertness. The United States, awakened to the threat in the early 1970s, was distracted by more pressing issues until the end of the decade, and then faced a rapid escalation of terrorist onslaughts. The United Kingdom began the 1970s with growing terrorist experience in Northern Ireland that eventually spread its influence to Great Britain and, while progressively reduced in scale, did not cease. Various other factors have also promoted a more constant awareness in Britain of the dangers of terrorism than has been the case in either Canada or the USA.

British policy development in response to the threat has a three-legged foundation, beginning with post-Second World War experience overseas. Locations such as Palestine, Malaya, Kenya, Cyprus, and Aden provided an introduction to violent civil unrest involving the use of terrorist tactics. It was the military, in particular, who first learned to contend with terrorism in those locales. The character, techniques, and equipment of the response, however, were not altogether suitable for use in the United Kingdom. Interrogation methods, for instance, were described as 'Techniques [that] would offend against English law'[71] when it was discovered that they had been used in Northern Ireland during the 1971 internment procedures. That is not to say that early British policy condoned extremes, as occurred with the French in Algeria. Arrest, interrogation, and detention of suspected terrorists had been subjected to parliamentary scrutiny in 1966, and a revised Joint Directive on Military Interrogation was issued. But even that modified form of response to terrorism was not deemed acceptable within the United Kingdom. Many sound lessons had been assimilated during overseas duty, yet a grave oversight was included: a failure to appreciate that such policies and measures were not necessarily appropriate for circumstances at home.

Similarly, in domestic situations of civil unrest which exceeded the resources of the police, British policy has traditionally relied upon use of the military. Historical precedent is well established, although in Great Britain troops have not performed the task since 1919. It has been natural, therefore, to include military aid to the civil power as a response to large-scale rioting and violence. Law and order, however, remain primarily matters for the police; any use of troops is expected to cease immediately upon restoration of an atmosphere of normalcy and stability. The idea of committing military forces over a very lengthy period of time, as has been the situation in Ulster, was not contemplated.

The second leg is represented by the particularly vicious nationalist–separatist–sectarian conflict in Northern Ireland. Terrorism, more virulent and sophisticated than previously encountered in colonial struggles, has been a feature of the years of turbulence from 1969. The violence has not been confined to Ulster, but has spilled over to affect security in Great Britain and Eire, as well. The result has been a two-pronged requirement: (1) to provide security in Great Britain with the least possible disturbance to the population; and (2) to provide the means to return a state of normalcy to the Province of Ulster.

The final leg has grown out of the need to combat international terrorism. Great Britain's island status is of little significance in an age when Amsterdam's Schipol airport is barely an hour's travel from Heathrow. Customs and immigration controls hold little fear for terrorists sponsored by rogue states who abuse the privileges of the diplomatic bag to deliver weapons, explosives, and passports for use in assassination attacks. Protection of diplomats and their official residences demands different policies in the face of threats by extremists with suicidal religious beliefs or by militants determined to pursue their causes wherever the opportunity permits.

While Great Britain has been largely 'free of indigenous neo-Marxist and nihilist terrorism',[72] it has encountered militancy in the form of the Angry Brigade and sporadic campaigns by Welsh and Scottish nationalists. Over the period from the mid-1970s, activism on the part of the animal-rights movement has increased and has incorporated terrorist behaviour. The relatively low level of the violence has not been sufficient to create a fourth leg of experience for Britain, but it has demanded attention by the government and the law-enforcement agencies. A need has been created for the consideration of appropriate policies and measures of response which must not lend encouragement to terrorist claims of 'government oppression' in such matters.

'There is a very strong temptation in dealing ... with terrorism ... to act outside the law.... If the government does not adhere to the law, then it loses respect and fails to fulfil its contractual obligation to the people as a government.'[73] Sir Robert Thompson made those remarks in elaboration of his second principle of counter-insurgency operations. The principle, *per se*, is: 'The government must function in accordance with the law.'[74] That principle is equally correct in responding to the threat of terrorism. Sir Robert's first principle is also germane, and refers to a government's political aim: 'to establish and maintain a free, independent and united country which is politically and economically stable and viable'.[75] Despite the unhappy history of Britain's relations with many of its overseas possessions following the Second World War, those two principles were the embodiment of British policy throughout the period. It was through the use of such guidance that insurgencies in Malaya and Kenya were overcome. Circumstances which transcended the intent of those policies were responsible for the outcome of events in Palestine, Cyprus, and Aden.

The British Government has adhered to a policy of the rule of law in its efforts to combat terrorism in the United Kingdom. Sir George Baker emphasizes the fact in his review of the Northern Ireland (Emergency Provisions) Act (EPA): 'The Government have ... always sought to act within the law.'[76] A reading of the proceedings of the British House of Commons from 1969 provides numerous references to policy based upon rule of law. All major legislation associated with response to terrorism has been passed after debate in the House, not by arbitrary decree. Notwithstanding, frequent criticism has been put forward alleging the draconian nature of some of the emergency legislation framed to counter the terrorist threat. Both the EPA and the Prevention of Terrorism (Temporary Provisions) Act (PTA) have been the subjects of complaints about infringements of civil rights. The British Government has answered charges, in part, by investigative reviews of the legislation and by official inquiries on a number of occasions. The purpose of the examinations has been to ascertain the correctness, effectiveness, and continuing need for the legislative measures, as well as to seek the means to lessen their impact upon, or their abridgement of, the fundamental liberties of British citizens.

Speaking at a conference on terrorism, Mr. Merlyn Rees explained that:

Any legislation of this kind clearly necessitates some loss of liberty and human freedom. The powers which have evolved nonetheless represent a determination by British Governments that such a legislation will depart as little as possible from internationally agreed principles, and from the traditions of British justice. The aim is to ensure that the security forces have every assistance in their task of bringing terrorists before the courts and that the integrity of the legal system is maintained.[77]

In a report to Parliament in 1977, the Standing Advisory Committee on Human Rights made the following comments:

There is no doubt that the application of some of the emergency measures would, in normal times, constitute serious violations of basic human rights ... it is relevant to recall that in response to those who suggested that the emergency provisions ... should be abolished on the grounds that they constitute a basic violation of human rights, the Gardiner Committee said:

We are unable to accept this argument. While the liberty of the subject is a human right to be preserved under all possible conditions, it is not and cannot be, an absolute right, because one man may use his liberty to take away the liberty of another and must be restrained from doing so. Where freedoms conflict, the state has a duty to protect those in need of protection.[78]

With specific reference to the Ulster situation, William Whitelaw, speaking in debate in the House of Commons, said that 'The Government made it clear in a White Paper on 28 and 29 March 1973 that it is fully committed to restoration of rule of law in Northern Ireland...'.[79]

Terrorists frequently have two aims which they hope to achieve by means of their actions: (1) to cause a government to over-react and impose unpopular sanctions; and (2) to undermine the public's confidence in a government. Recognition of those aims is frequently mentioned in the records of the proceedings of the British House of Commons, as well as in a number of reports submitted to the British Government concerning its anti-terrorist legislation. Mr Rees pointedly alluded to such terrorist intentions in the aforementioned conference address:

in a democratic society the terrorist's aim is to discredit the Government.... He tries to do this ... by trying to bring about the steady erosion of civil liberties to a point where the Government and society's commitment to democratic values is fatally weakened.[80]

The fact that the British Government and leading members of the public are aware of such dangers is an indication of concern that the terrorist does not succeed.

The British Government has also been a leading advocate of international co-operation in the combating of terrorism. Britain is a signatory of the major international conventions and resolutions against terrorism, as well as a party to the Bonn, Venice, Ottawa, Tokyo, and Toronto agreements. In fact, it was the perseverance of the British Prime Minister, Mrs Thatcher, during the London and Tokyo Conferences which resulted in statements condemning terrorism and encouraging multinational efforts to defeat the threat.

Wilkinson has pointed to a pair of significant realities in his assessment of the British position in relation to terrorism. They are as follows: (1) 'it should be obvious that Britain has the strongest national interest in formulating an effective policy to counter domestic and international terrorism';[81] and (2) 'Britain has been able to develop special strengths and resources to deal with the challenges of modern terrorism.'[82] The two statements reflect the British perception of the threat; it is a perception which began (albeit somewhat unwittingly) in colonial problems overseas, and later became much more distinct and uniform as a consequence of events closer to home. It is a perception which also mirrors the character, tradition, experience, and determination of the British nation.

Viewed in retrospect, Canadian, British, and American policy development in response to terrorism can be seen to have evolved in an individual manner. Perception of the threat has been a significant motivating principle in all cases, however, and has influenced the pace, nature, and extent of development and implementation of policy and policy measures. In conjunction, the principle of the rule of law has been, and remains, a constant in the formulation of counter-terrorism policy.

## Fundamental policy

The fundamental counter-terrorism policies of Canada, the United States, and the United Kingdom contain several parallels. Each nation observes the rule of law as a foundational principle of response, treating terrorism as a criminal offence under the law. The three governments also firmly agree on the principle of international co-operation to combat terrorism, and each state is associated with policy of that nature. Each nation, however, has responded to terrorism in accordance with its individual perception of the threat. Thus, certain dissimilarities exist in their respective policy positions and measures of response.

The Canadian attitude, especially through the decade following the October Crisis, has not reflected a perception of terrorism as constituting a major or immediate danger to the nation or to its interests overseas. Understandably, other matters (e.g. the state of the economy, unemployment, and the Constitution debate) have brought more pressure to bear on legislators and on public opinion than a phenomenon which lacked prominent domestic visibility from 1970 until the early 1980s. While sympathetic to the problems of terrorist threats and activities elsewhere in the world, Canadians have not felt endangered by such developments. It has been a narrow perception which failed seriously to take into account the numerous and growing ethnic communities within the nation and their potential as sources of terrorist activism.

Nonetheless, the effects of the FLQ experience, combined with the spectre of atrocities at Munich and Lod, encouraged early and continuing Canadian participation in attempts to achieve solutions in international fora. Throughout those proceedings, Canada has been a leading advocate of the principle that terrorism is a criminal offence and that policies of response should approach the threat in that manner. L.C. Green has carefully pointed to the fact that Canadian policy-makers have consistently endeavoured to divorce political justification from legal obligations.[83] Canada's position was made clear in the 1972 statement of the Canadian ambassador at the United Nations: 'We do not wait for solutions to complex underlying causes of violence and crime in our societies before adopting laws and penal systems to combat individual acts of violence and crime.'[84]

In keeping with that viewpoint, responsibility for response to terrorism in Canada remains primarily a concern of the intelligence and law-enforcement agencies. Military aid to the civil power is a measure available to the government in extraordinary circumstances, as was the case in 1970, but Canadian policy does not include the use of the Canadian Forces (CF) as an instrument of retaliation. Similarly, the decision to allocate responsibility for SERT to the RCMP removed the CF from any possible role mirroring that of Britain's SAS. Hostage-taking and kidnapping were central features of the October Crisis, the outcome of which has raised questions about Canadian policy in such matters. The events of 1970, however, should be treated in isolation, as with the British Government's release of Leila Khaled during the same period. Inexperience, concern for the safety of Mr Cross, and the co-operation of the British Government were influential factors bearing on the incident. Subsequent actions of the Canadian Government in its support of international conventions aimed at inhibiting hostage-taking and kidnapping, in company with changes to Canadian criminal law in that regard, are more valid demonstrations of the Canadian position.

Canadian policy in the situation of a hostage-taking or kidnapping is that of no concessions, with some flexibility attached. Much like the British attitude, but unlike that of the USA, Canada includes a willingness to negotiate. The Canadian policy does not incorporate the possibility of yielding to demands, but it does not preclude the granting of minor concessions which would be limited to the immediate time and place of the incident. Minor concessions would be allowed in the interest of reducing risk to hostages, to facilitate surveillance procedures or to permit a dialogue to be conducted with the hostage's captors. The policy illustrates the Canadian view of terrorism as a criminal act, especially as it is applicable equally to terrorist incidents as to those of a purely crime-oriented nature.

Considered to be hawkish on the subject of response to terrorism, Secretary of State George Shultz emphasized the basis of American policy during a speech on 25 October 1984. At a time when many critics were calling for a less reserved posture, Shultz made it plain that 'We will certainly not alter the democratic values that we so cherish in order to fight terrorism.... I can assure you that in this Administration our actions will be governed by the rule of law....'[85] American policy has displayed some changes in response to terrorism during the years from 1968. Notwithstanding controversy over use of military resources in 1985 and 1986, the policy has been rooted in the principle of rule of law. Domestically, the American Armed Forces remain constrained from employment in the counter-terrorist role by legislation, and responsibility for the task rests with the nation's law-enforcement bodies. American endorsement of a wide range of international conventions opposing terrorist acts, as well as the US Government's recourse to the International Court of Justice in the face of Iranian intransigence in 1980, underline Mr Shultz's claim.

The no-concessions policy of the US Government was a decision which emanated from the Nixon administration and is a policy which has not altered since that time. Despite arguments that the policy has been side-stepped on occasion, government announcements and publicity have not wavered from the conviction 'that to give in to terrorists' demands places even more Americans at risk'.[86] When describing that policy in 1979, Ambassador Anthony Quainton, former head of the State Department's Office for Combatting Terrorism, alluded to two other principles:

(1) All terrorist acts are deemed to be criminal.
(2) Host governments are expected to exercise their responsibilities under international law when Americans are abducted abroad.

Quainton's remarks can also be seen to substantiate the principle of rule of law and the American policy of seeking international co-operation to combat terrorism. The experience of the embassy seizure in Tehran, plus later events in Lebanon, probably influenced the US Government to place less faith in the second of Mr Quainton's stated principles of American policy. Certainly the context did not appear in the expression of the American position as outlined by the 1986 *Public Report of the Vice President's Task Force on Combatting Terrorism*.[87] Two years prior to that Report, however, President Reagan had introduced a major modification to US counter-terrorism policy when in April 1984, he signed National Security Decision Directive (NSDD) 138, authorizing pre-emptive strikes and reprisal raids against terrorists abroad. By that means, the nature of American policy changed from reactive to having the potential of being pro-active.

It was concern 'about the increasing loss of American lives, as well as repeated terrorist threats ...' which induced President Reagan to order 'a Cabinet-level Task Force on Combatting Terrorism' in 1985.[88] The Report of the Task Force included a comprehensive statement of American policy in response to terrorism:

> The U.S. position on terrorism is unequivocal: firm opposition to terrorism in all its forms and wherever it takes place. Several National Security Decision Directives as well as statements by the President and senior officials confirm this policy:
>
> The U.S. Government is opposed to domestic and international terrorism and is prepared to act in concert with other nations or unilaterally when necessary to prevent or respond to terrorist acts.
>
> The U.S. Government considers the practice of terrorism by any person or group a potential threat to its national security and will resist the use of terrorism by all legal means available.
>
> States that practice terrorism or actively support it will not do so without consequence. If there is evidence that a state is mounting or intends to conduct an act of terrorism against this country, the United States will take measures to protect its citizens, property and interests.
>
> The U.S. Government will make no concessions to terrorists. It will not pay ransoms, release prisoners, change its policies or agree to other acts that might encourage additional terrorism. At the same time, the United States will use every available resource to gain the safe return of American citizens who are held hostage by terrorists.
>
> The United States will act in a strong manner against terrorists without surrendering basic freedoms or endangering democratic principles, and encourages other governments to take similar stands.[89]

American policy has evolved very much in relation to the changing perception of the threat on the part of the nation's government and citizens. The Task Force discovered 'that Americans view terrorism as one of the most serious problems facing [the US] government, ranking it along side such issues as the budget deficit and strategic arms control'.[90] The attitude was a considerable change from preoccupation with the Watergate scandal and concerns about human rights which absorbed American interest in the 1970s. It also reflected the impact of the increased terrorist activities against US citizens and interests abroad in the seven years between Ambassador Quainton's observations and the Vice President's investigation.

The rule of law has been a corner-stone of British democracy at least from the time of the Civil War. It is not surprising, therefore, that it should feature as a major policy in the United Kingdom's response to terrorism. From the principle of rule of law has evolved the concept of the Queen's Peace, a condition of law, order, stability, tolerance, and personal freedoms. Responsibility for the maintenance of that status is the duty of the police, with the assistance of the public and the support of the judiciary. A major concern of the British Government is that actions taken to cope with the threat of terrorism adhere as closely as possible to the rule of law. 'The reality of terrorist activity ... is the commission of criminal acts of extreme violence.'[91] Lord Shackleton expressed that judgement in his 1978 report to the Secretary of State for the Home Department on completion of the official review of the operation of PTA's 1974/1976. Terrorism is viewed as a criminal offence in the United Kingdom, and is prosecuted as such. Only in discrete circumstances of extradition, discussed later, does British policy allow consideration of a political dimension.

When describing the initial sequence of events of the 1980 siege at the Iranian embassy in London, Sir David McNee wrote of demands made by the hostage-takers: 'I said that I needed to know what line the Cabinet would take in response to the terrorists' demands.... The Home Secretary ... gave me the answer that I wanted to hear: the Cabinet were unanimous that none of the terrorists' demands should be met.'[92] Similar to that of Canada, British policy holds to a no-concessions position coupled with limited negotiation in situations of hostage-taking and kidnapping.

The no-concessions policy was essentially followed in the case of the FLQ's kidnapping of Mr James Cross, the British trade commissioner who was held hostage in Montreal in 1970. Arguably, concessions were made on that occasion, but they were the responsibility of the Canadian Government and were relatively narrow in their application. Cross's kidnappers, although subject to an offence under the Canadian Criminal Code, were not involved with the murder of Pierre Laporte. In order to ensure Mr Cross's safety, the kidnappers were given immunity on the basis that they depart Canada and not return. 'When it was rumoured in mid-1974 that some or all of them ... were hinting that they might return to Canada, the authorities reminded them that, were they to do so, criminal proceedings ... would be instituted.'[93]

Similarly, when the Tupamaros seized Ambassador Sir Geoffrey Jackson in Uruguay in 1971, and held him captive for nine months, the British Government refused to give in to the terrorists. Only in the release of Leila Khaled, who was involved in the 1970 attempt to hijack an El Al airliner which had taken off from London, could Great Britain be accused of some ambivalence in its no concessions policy. Again, however, the circumstances of that situation tend to mitigate criticism. Hijacking of the sort in which Khaled was a participant was in its infancy; inexperience on the part of the British Government, combined with a serious threat against the lives of the passengers and crews of three other airliners held captive at Dawson Field in Jordan by Khaled's compatriots (the PFLP), as well as threats against other British residents in the Middle East, had a major influence on the government's decision.

On the basis of the British Army's lengthy contemporary involvement with security duties in Northern Ireland, it might be suspected that the military holds a paramount role in responsibility for counter-terrorism in the United Kingdom. Such is not the case; it is British policy that law and order in the United Kingdom is the responsibility of the police. The military is a resource available to assist the police in times of emergency under the terms of Military Aid to the Civil Power, similar to circumstances which prevail in Canada. The Ulster situation is an example of such aid, as was the brief use of the SAS at the Iranian embassy in 1980. Hence, response to terrorism in the United Kingdom is first a matter for the police, who will call for other assistance only when necessary.

British perception of the threat of terrorism, like that of Canada and the United States, was developed through the pressure of events. While Britain had the unpleasant benefit of considerable early experience overseas, for the most part that reality was blurred by its label of counter-insurgency warfare. The contemporary violence in Northern Ireland, and its transfer to the British mainland, however, created an awareness that began in 1969 and which has been evident since that time. The close proximity of Europe and the Middle East, whose rich modern history of terrorism has spilled into the United Kingdom, has been another factor of influence. Britain has been unable to ignore the threat or to view it from a distance, resulting in experience and expertise which 'have provided an invaluable continuity [especially] at governmental level'.[94]

Fundamental policies represent the roots of government response to terrorism, the platforms from which policy measures evolve. Just as the fundamental policies of Canada, the United States, and the United Kingdom exhibit similarities and differences, so do the policy measures adopted by the three nations. Perception of the threat is responsible for the variances to some degree, but other factors also intrude. The constitutional basis of government, the governmental infrastructure, history, national values and the many other constituents of the *Envelope* make their presence felt. The influence of such matters must be appreciated when considering the measures which have sprung from the fundamental policies that form the basis of the liberal-democratic response to terrorism.

### Direct (active) measures

The system of Federal Government in Canada places certain qualifications on the development and introduction of counter-terrorism measures. Examples of provisos, and their implications, are discussed in this chapter and those which follow. It is sufficient for the moment to recognize that Canadian Governments at all levels accept the need to maintain constitutional principles throughout any crisis situation; that is, barring a major catastrophe, one level of government will not arbitrarily impose its will or sanctions on a subordinate body. During the October Crisis, for instance, the Quebec Government requested assistance from the Federal Government of Canada in the form of Military Aid to the Civil Power.

Because of its responsibility for national security, the Federal government plays a leading role in the planning and development of counter-terrorism policy and policy measures. The mandate for that task rests primarily with the Department of the Solicitor General of Canada, principally with the Police and Security Branch (PSB) of the Department. Notwithstanding, for reasons of jurisdictional legalities associated with the Canadian Constitution, the Federal government must consult and co-ordinate with the provincial governments. Thus, the initiation and implementation of measures in response to the threat of terrorism are often complex matters. The problems are magnified when international diplomatic conventions and considerations must also be taken into account.

The prompt and 'successful' resolution of the FLQ crisis was one of the factors which contributed to a lessening of Canadian concern about terrorism. The affair, however, also had the opposite effect of promoting measures which strengthened Canada's fundamental resource structure for combating terrorism. One measure, which arguably belongs under the heading of 'indirect', was the increased emphasis given to the Francophone position in the fabric of the national character. The subsequent vigorous attention given to the bilingual and bicultural nature of Canada helped to reduce frictions which had been a feature of the FLQ platform. In that sense, the activity represents a clear example of a prophylactic measure (i.e. long-term prevention effort) of response to the threat of terrorism.

A second positive measure resulting from the FLQ experience was a review of 'Crisis Handling Capability within the Canadian Federal Structure'.[95] This took the form of a study conducted under the leadership of Lieutenant-General M.R. Dare, for whom the study report was later named. The Dare Group's findings called for:

a comprehensive system within the federal structure which would confirm and formalize the primary responsibilities of departments in crisis handling matters and which would provide the Cabinet with an enhanced capacity for crisis management.[96]

While not all of the study's findings were accepted, and portions remain classified, in 1973 the government did act on the aforementioned recommendation by establishing the 'lead Minister' concept for crisis management, which still prevails.

The system in its basic form is not unique to Canada; both the United States and the United Kingdom have adopted a similar procedure. Essentially it is explained as follows:

The 'lead Minister' or 'lead Department' concept is simply the appointment of a particular Cabinet Minister to automatically assume the responsibility for coordinating government response at the federal level, in an emergency or crisis situation.... The Solicitor General of Canada has been designated the 'lead Minister' for coordinating federal government response to internal security emergencies such as terrorist activities within Canada. The Secretary of State for External Affairs is the 'lead Minister' responsible for coordinating federal government response to emergencies affecting Canada outside Canada. An example, of course, would be a terrorist attack on a Canadian Mission abroad.[97]

The description goes on to explain that each government department has a fundamental responsibility for planning, preparing, and operating in relation to emergencies. Similarly, under certain circumstances a department may hold resources or provide services during one type of emergency, while being a lead department under different conditions. The functioning of this system is given more detailed scrutiny in the next chapter.

Another important measure stemming from the after-effects of the October Crisis was the formation, in 1971, of the Security Planning and Research Group (SPARG) in the Department of the Solicitor General. Originally devised as a means to 'assist the Solicitor General in assessing the significance of security intelligence reports from the

R.C.M.P.',[98] the Group underwent a series of vicissitudes to emerge in the 1980s as the PSB. The PSB also receives closer attention in the following chapter; its responsibilities, however, include 'analyzing and proposing measures in response to':

— threats to the internal security of Canada from organizations, groups and individuals either in Canada or elsewhere;
— policy formulation for the protection of personnel, property and equipment in the federal government;
— the role of the federal government in law enforcement in Canada; and
— contingency planning for Ministry crisis handling in emergency situations.[99]

It is a mandate which, as mentioned earlier, places the focus of counter-terrorism planning on the Department of the Solicitor General.

While the Dare Group and other government departments examined operational problems and the need for possible organizational changes, questions were raised in public about the activities of the security forces at the time of the October Crisis. The performance of some members of the RCMP, in particular, was subject to serious criticisms and allegations of misconduct. The persistence of the queries, some prompted by the separatist-oriented PQ Party in Quebec, eventually resulted in two official inquiries in that province.[100] In conjunction, in July 1977, the Federal government appointed a Commission 'to inquire into and report upon certain activities of the Royal Canadian Mounted Police'.[101] The work of the Commission, named after its Chairman, Mr Justice D.C. McDonald, was instrumental in bringing about a major restructuring of the Canadian government's intelligence organization.

Prior to June 1984, security and intelligence matters relating to threats to the security of Canada were the responsibility of the RCMP Security Service, a branch of Canada's fabled and respected Mounties. Historically, it was a responsibility which could be traced to the days of the Yukon gold rush at the turn of the twentieth century. Other Federal departments, such as Defence, also maintained intelligence cells of a sort to serve their own specific needs, but none possessed the broad mandate accorded to the RCMP. The RCMP's mandate was originally threatened in 1966, by the MacKenzie Royal Commission on Security. The then Prime Minister, Lester B. Pearson, instituted proceedings in the wake of public controversy over the handling of security matters which had been highlighted by Cold War developments. The Report of the MacKenzie Commission, delivered in October 1968, urged the 'establishment of a new civilian non-police agency to perform the functions of a security service in Canada'.[102] Such a dramatic change was not to be, however, and Mr Pearson's successor, Prime Minister

Trudeau, only went so far as to provide for a decision to 'civilianize' the position of the head of the Security Branch of the RCMP. But the Pearson government made other moves in 1966 which had a bearing on the RCMP. As part of the Government Organization Act, the Solicitor General's Department was formed to take over responsibility for penitentiaries, parole, and the RCMP from the Department of Justice. Henceforth, the Solicitor General of Canada was the Federal Minister responsible for the RCMP, including the Security Service.

The publicity surrounding the events which led to the McDonald Commission, the findings of that Commission, and details revealed by the Quebec-government investigations, encouraged support for a change to the federal intelligence and security infrastructure. The outcome was very much in keeping with the MacKenzie recommendations: to divorce the Security Service from its parent body and to make it a non-police agency. Mr Robert Kaplan, the Solicitor General of Canada, initiated such an action in 1983 by means of legislation in Parliament. Under the legislation, the Canadian Security Intelligence Service (CSIS) was to be formed as a separate branch of the Solicitor General's Department, and the Security Service of the RCMP would cease to exist. Despite considerable resistance from many quarters, the legislation received Royal Assent on 28 June 1984, and the CSIS was established.

The Provincial governments strenuously opposed the legislation in its initial form, fearing *inter alia* some of the investigative powers which were to be given to the new agency. The objections were eventually overcome, especially in view of oversight constraints built into the mandate. Similarly, members of CSIS were not given 'police' powers under the legislation; the role of CSIS is the collection, analysis, retention, and dissemination of information and intelligence relating to threats to the security of Canada as defined in the CSIS Act. Investigation of criminal offences uncovered by CSIS remained a function of appropriate law-enforcement bodies. The significance of the role of CSIS is perhaps lost on those who are accustomed to the reality of a discrete national intelligence organization within government. The move was an exceptional departure for Canada, especially in light of the traditional respect accorded to the RCMP. But, as the McDonald Report made clear, 'the rule of law must be observed in all security operations'.[103] During its deliberations, however, the Commission found the view 'expressed within the R.C.M.P., that when the interests of national security are in conflict with the freedom of the individual, the balance to be struck is not for a court of law but for the executive'.[104]

Separation of the law-enforcement and the security-intelligence functions at the federal level was one step toward ensuring that the rule of law would be maintained. The move provided for greater control and supervision of intelligence operations, while allowing the law-enforcement bodies to continue the investigation and prosecution of offences without government interference. CSIS operations require specific judicial involvement in the issue of warrants to undertake certain investigations, and are subject to oversight by an Inspector General and an appointed Review Committee. In a more practical vein, the formation of separate entities holds the potential for independent professional development and advancement, as well as for a more objective assessment of security matters.

The federal structure of the Canadian governmental system, the principle of the rule of law, and the fact that terrorism is treated as a criminal offence under the Criminal Code in Canada place the law-enforcement agencies in the front line of defence against the threat of terrorism. The passage of the CSIS Act, however, brought about a fundamental change to law-enforcement jurisdictions with regard to terrorist offences. Part IV of the Act, known as the Security Offences Act, assigns primary responsibility to the RCMP for peace-officer duties involving a threat to the security of Canada or an Internationally Protected Person (IPP).[105] That is, while the initial response to a terrorist incident in Canada would be the responsibility of the police force on the spot, the RCMP have the authority to assume responsibility for the resolution of the incident and for the investigation in the aftermath. The Security Offences Act also permits the federal Attorney General to issue a fiat permitting the Department of Justice to assume responsibility for prosecution of an offence relating to the security of Canada or an IPP. Threats to the security of Canada are defined in Section 2 of the CSIS Act and include terrorism, which is defined as:

> activities within or relating to Canada directed toward or in support of the threat or use of acts of serious violence against persons or property for the purpose of achieving a political objective within Canada or a foreign state.[106]

The jurisdictional implications of the Security Offences Act in terms of policy and operational concerns are examined in the next two chapters.

Generally speaking, the absence of a prominent threat of terrorism in the years after 1970–1 has tended to ease police concerns in Canada. Special anti-terrorist units have not been the norm, although more emphasis has been placed on their development since the beginning of the 1980s decade. Special Weapons and Tactics Teams (SWATs) designed for crime-oriented situations have been in place in metropolitan areas for many years, but they do not compare in role or capabilities with a counter-terrorist force such as the West German GSG-9. Similarly, the RCMP has developed Emergency Response Teams (ERTs) of a SWAT nature; they, too, have not been principally intended as an anti-terrorist measure, although more properly directed towards that role than the standard police SWAT. Until 1986, Canada was almost alone among NATO countries, and many other nations in the world, in lacking a standing force specially trained and equipped for terrorism response. The decision to launch SERT changed that condition, providing Canada with a substantial resource in the event of a terrorist hostage-taking or barricade situation. SERT was included as part of a package of measures announced by the Federal government in an effort to improve counter-terrorism defences following terrorist incidents in Canada during 1985.

The 1985 attack on the Turkish embassy in Ottawa drew attention to inadequacies associated with the use of commercial security guards for such duties. As a result of that perceived weakness, the government directed the RCMP to undertake the guarding and patrolling of the perimeters of diplomatic missions across Canada. Implementation of that order necessitated an increase in RCMP personnel strength and the introduction of a special RCMP training programme for the constables assigned. In conjunction, as a consequence of the Air India disaster of June 1985, 'unspecified steps to improve security [were taken] at all airports in Canada'.[107] The government also proposed to meet with the nation's media leaders to 'reconcile the demands of a free press with the protection of public safety in times of crisis'.[108]

While the police have a front-line responsibility for response to terrorism in Canada, should their resources be overstressed in an emergency the Canadian military is available to provide assistance. The CF, especially the Army, have a long history of providing military aid to the civil power. During the early years of the nation, the call for such aid was frequently abused by municipalities that disliked the idea of funding a regular police force. The years between the two world wars brought a distinct change to the policy, and in recent times the military has been more usually summoned to assist at time of national disasters, e.g. floods and forest fires. With the exception of the October Crisis, a strike by the Montreal City Policy in 1969, and several incidents of riots at penitentiaries, the military has not had a high profile in the law enforcement or control of civil-unrest functions since the end of the Second World War. The internal security role is a major task of the CF, however, but it is not accorded a high priority in terms of training or equipment, especially in regard to the threat of terrorism. The fact that responsibility for SERT was given to the RCMP illustrates the military's lack of interest in the problem of terrorism.

Despite the general Canadian indifference to the dangers of terrorism, the Federal government *has* demonstrated an awareness of the threat. Mitchell Sharp's 1972 address to the United Nations General Assembly was commendable in its recognition of the need for international co-operation, particularly in the realms of law enforcement and the strengthening of sanctions. Canada has also been a leader in bilateral agreements, such as the 1971 extradition treaty with the USA and the 1972 anti-hijacking arrangement with Cuba. The US–Canada treaty is particularly notable for the provision of Article 4:

> a kidnapping, murder or other assault against the life or physical integrity of a person to whom a Contracting Party has the duty according to international law to give special protection, or any attempt to commit such an offense with respect to any such person, shall not be regarded as of a political character.[109]

Earlier mention has been given to Canada's participation in major international conventions against terrorist acts, as well as the nation's support for the Summit Seven declarations.

From the standpoint of physical security measures, Canada has provided an overwhelming array on special occasions, e.g. the 1976 Olympic Games, the 1981 Economic Summit, the 1984 visit of the Pope. Referring to US preparations for the 1984 Olympic Games, a planner stated that 'There is no way the Los Angeles security forces can provide the kind of comprehensive protection that Canadian army did ... in Montreal. There was a soldier ... every 25 yards at the Olympic Village for three weeks.'[110] Unfortunately, such impressive and laudable efforts also contained the drawback of creating a dangerous sense of well-being. Naturally, terrorists would hesitate to attack under those circumstances, plus Canadian security planners had ample time to prepare. Under normal everyday conditions terrorists face a much less formidable defence.

Considerable publicity was devoted to Solicitor General Perrin Beatty's March 1986 announcement of SERT, and accompanying anti-terrorist measures. Mr Beatty's statement was described as a 'strongly-worded address [which] makes it clear that Canada will not deal lightly with terrorism'.[111] His comments were also deemed to reflect a get-tough policy on the part of the Canadian Government. Publicity of that nature represents a direct and active counter-terrorism measure by providing a forceable statement of the government's position, determination, and intentions. It delivers a clear warning to terrorists, while offering reassurance to the public.

Admirable though Canadian counter-terrorism activities have been over the years, they were also hesitant in their development and gradual in their implementation. Terrorism continues to be given rather grudging recognition as a threat to Canadian security at home and overseas, especially by certain government departments which should display a greater interest (e.g. the Department of Defence). One example of that attitude is associated with the improvement of legislation for situations of national emergencies. Despite the considerable criticism of The War

Measures Act as being a draconian instrument for peace-time application, it was not replaced until 1988 when the Emergencies Act[112] was passed by Parliament.

The US and Canadian governmental systems share a number of common features, predominant among them the fact that they have a federal basis. Under the Constitutions of each nation, the respective central authority holds sway over certain matters such as defence, foreign policy, the treasury, and similar areas of national concern. Unlike Canada, however, the Federal government of the United States does not have the sole right to legislate criminal law. It is a factor which contributes to jurisdictional problems in law-enforcement matters and complicates the development of counter-terrorism measures. State and local governments in the USA, not unlike the federal–provincial arrangement in Canada, have primary responsibility for protecting lives and property, maintaining public order, and enforcing the laws. In most cases, therefore, the Federal government should be seen to defer to state or local authority in a criminal matter. But in some situations, such as a terrorist incident, it could well be advantageous for a federal agency to be directly involved for reasons of experience, resources, or diplomatic considerations. Unless the circumstances meet the criteria making the incident a federal offence, however, central-government involvement is precluded except on a requested basis.

Many acts of terrorism *are* crimes under both federal and state laws, permitting concurrent jurisdiction. But exceptions do exist, as in the situation of a hostage-taking; to be a federal offence the victim must be a federal or foreign official, or be transported across a state line. A number of such jurisdictional loopholes have been closed by the passage of the Comprehensive Crime Control Act of 1984, although effectiveness is by no means complete. Similar federal legislation has also attempted to bring terrorist-related crimes under the federal umbrella, such as making criminal acts involving aircraft the purview of the Federal Aviation Administration (FAA). Actions of that sort, however, have necessitated the establishment of inter-departmental Memoranda of Understanding (MOUs) to overcome resultant contention between federal agencies.

While federal–state jurisdictional disputes are one area in which friction occurs, interagency competition is another. For instance, the planning and conduct of security arrangements for the 1984 Los Angeles Olympic Games raised a storm of controversy for months prior to the event. The FBI and the Los Angeles Police Department, as well as local bodies, hotly debated authoritative responsibility until a solution was agreed. Admittedly, the standards of many US police departments are sufficiently high that federal agencies do not always attempt to intervene. The Hanafi Muslim affair in Washington, DC was resolved through major strategic and tactical decisions of the District of Columbia Police. Notwithstanding, interagency and interdepartmental rivalry is particularly the norm in US law-enforcement and security circles, and a similar friction exists within and between the Armed Forces. One of Robert Taylor's principal criticisms was 'a lack of effective agency communication and coordination at the operational level'.[113] The latter is a consequence of the immense size of the bureaucracy and the fact that responsibilities tend to overlap or lack clear definition, and it also extends down to state and local levels. As Taylor illustrates, 'an estimated 26 federal agencies, 14 state agencies and six local agencies may have direct or indirect involvement in responding to any terrorist incident in the United States'.[114] This condition leads to jealousies, protective behaviour, reluctance to share information and 'turf' problems which are not conducive to a smooth and harmonious development or implementation of policy.

The 'separation of powers' principle which characterizes the US federal system of government contributes to problems of central oversight. A division of loyalty exists between the President, nominally responsible for the bureaucracy, and the Congress. The President may provide direction to the departments and agencies, but Congress controls the funding. This creates a situation where the bureaucracy, in effect, serves two masters and is frequently pulled in two directions. In conjunction, the President may issue directives or express his wishes on a matter, but if he cannot convince Congress to legislate the finances required, the matter will make little progress.

In an effort to resolve the inherent organizational complexities in response to terrorism, the US Government has made use of a version of the 'lead Ministry' concept. The measure is largely identical to that which applies both in Canada and the United Kingdom; that is, one government department has authority for the management of a terrorist incident under given conditions. In the United States, the responsibility is shared, in the main, between the Department of Justice and the Department of State. The Department of State has been given overall authority for co-ordinating policy measures in response to terrorism, as well as responsibility for operational control of international incidents. The Department of Justice (through the FBI) has operational authority over domestic incidents, and works closely with state and local agencies where there is a concurrent jurisdiction. Similarly, the FBI and State Department work together when an incident has both domestic and international ramifications.

The 'lead agency' arrangement, as it is known, was one other positive measure resulting from the Nixon administration's Cabinet Committee to Combat Terrorism. On paper, the process appears reasonably satisfactory, but it does contain many unseen stumbling-blocks. Blurred jurisdictions and 'intricacies of real world agency distrust and parochialism'[115] remain as negative influences, as well as the proverbial bureaucratic red tape. In his book describing the US counter-terrorism unit, *Delta Force*, Colonel Charles Beckwith mentions one occasion when a request to visit the American embassy in Tehran prior to the Iranian takeover was refused for minor budgetary reasons. Beckwith goes on to explain that, had he and State Department security personnel been given the opportunity to inspect the embassy, many of the later events may have had a much different result.[116]

A direct and active measure of response to terrorism is represented by the US intelligence community. The community is large, complex, and highly sophisticated in terms of resources; it was American communications intelligence interception capability which identified Libyan involvement in the 1986 Berlin discotheque bombing. Much of the US intelligence infrastructure and functions are classified, but the basic responsibilities are readily apparent. The FBI is the lead agency for the gathering of domestic intelligence at the federal level, whereas overseas requirements are the domain of the CIA. The CIA is precluded by its Charter from operations within US territory, but the problem of blurred lines of jurisdiction led to questionable Agency intrusion into domestic issues in the 1970s, eventually prompting congressional inquiries in the wake of the Watergate disclosures.

The subsequent debate over alleged abuses by the intelligence community in the United States was said by many observers to have had a consequence in operational constraints which practically emasculated the community's effectiveness.

> By 1980, as a result of widespread concern about protection of citizens' civil liberties, about conforming US behaviour abroad to standards of decency and 'fair play' and about reigning in an 'imperial presidency', restrictive rules and formal executive and congressional oversight practices had been instituted....[117]

Attorney General Levi's Guidelines of 1976 were considered to have had a paralysing effect, to the point where in 1978 FBI Director William H. Webster claimed that the FBI was 'practically out of the domestic security field'.[118]

The Reagan administration took steps to ameliorate the adverse conditions, to revitalize the intelligence community, and to restore public faith in it. A new Attorney General, William French Smith, provided a wider scope of operational latitude for the FBI by the publication of less restrictive guidelines in 1983. The Comprehensive Crime Control Act of 1984 expanded previous legislation in relation to electronic surveillance, making the wire-tap statute less inhibiting. Congressional attitudes changed to the point where the President was authorized to implement covert actions overseas with the need only to notify two congressional oversight committees, or in 'extra-ordinary circumstances' (sic) he is only required to do so 'in a timely fashion'.[119]

Terrorist events in the Middle East and Europe during the 1980s undoubtedly had a marked influence on congressional opinion. Approval was given in 1983 'to provide training in the United States for foreign law enforcement officials in combatting terrorism'.[120] Under the Comprehensive Crime Control Act, authority was delegated to the Attorney General and the Secretary of State to pay rewards of up to $500,000 for information about domestic or international terrorist activity. 'The new act also makes it a Federal offense to use an inter-state or foreign commerce facility to commit a murder-for-hire.'[121] Aimed at would-be assassins, the legislation is another positive measure, although limited in its proscription of such acts on the basis of the commission being for money or economic advantage.

In keeping with its changed perspective, Congress authorized the expenditure of $365 million 'for making the USA's 262 diplomatic posts around the world impervious to terrorist attack'.[122] While overly optimistic in use of the term 'impervious', the report correctly identified a greatly enhanced physical security programme introduced by the State Department in 1985. Estimates placed the total bill to bring embassies and consulates up to adequate modern standards at over $3 billion. One of the recommendations of a high-level State Department advisory panel was the establishment of a 100-foot security zone outside diplomatic buildings overseas. Implementation would necessitate the moving of many facilities to less crowded and less centrally located areas.

Efforts to improve physical security measures have increased dramatically in the wake of terrorist attacks in Beirut, Athens, and major European cities. Children of NATO personnel in Brussels have been given classroom instruction to help to protect them from terrorist threats. The US Secretary of State made an appeal to the American business community in February 1985 to

> join in a worldwide effort to frustrate terrorists by improving security at business facilities abroad.... [The Secretary] announced the creation of an organization called Overseas Security Advisory Council with members drawn from the State Department, U.S. law enforcement agencies and American businesses operating abroad to permit regular exchanges of ideas and information between public and private security programs.[123]

Resented by sections of the US public and by some government officials for reasons of a forbidding atmosphere and appearance, embassies and installations in foreign countries have increasingly begun to resemble small fortresses. Unwelcome or not, the moves have been necessary in an effort to forestall hostage-takings, embassy seizures, and attacks by suicide bombers. A variety of protective devices have been installed, including crash-barriers, metal gates, bullet-proof enclosures, explosive-resistant glass, and electronic screening. The entrance to the American embassy in London has been fronted with a row of immense concrete 'flowerpots' whose purpose (decorative though it may be) is to prevent a vehicle from crashing through the lobby. Visitors to the embassy must immediately step through an electronic screening device upon entering the front door. (Similar protective measures are to be found around and within government buildings in Washington, DC.)

The role of the US Armed Forces in the combating of terrorism has not been as prominent as the casual observer would tend to believe. Akin to the attitude of the Canadian Forces, during the 1970s American military authorities paid little attention to the threat of terrorism, preferring to focus on problems associated with a possible battlefield confrontation with Soviet bloc forces. President Carter did provide an important impetus in 1977 when he ordered the formation of the special Army counter-terrorist team, Delta Force. The story of the development of that team provides a fascinating insight to inter- and intraservice rivalry and bickering.

President Reagan's 1980s policy, involving the use of military force for pre-emptive and retaliatory strikes against terrorists, demanded a much more active interest on the part of the US military. Concern was also raised as a result of the increased number of terrorist attacks against US military personnel and installations overseas, as well as by a critical assessment of protective measures on the part of US Marines who formed an element of the Multinational Force in Beirut, and who suffered appalling casualties in a 1983 terrorist suicide bombing in that city. Nevertheless, although representing a direct measure for response to terrorism in certain situations overseas, the military is constrained by legislation from general use in a domestic role. The Posse Comitatus Act of 1878 expressly forbids the employment of US military forces for law-enforcement duties in the USA, unless in accordance with specific limitations of the Constitution or with the consent of Congress. The President may direct that federal troops or the militia be used in emergencies, just as State Governors may call out their National Guard units in times of extreme civil disobedience or rebellion. But such actions are not an accepted practice in the United States, and local law enforcement agencies must be hard-pressed before consideration will be given to providing military resources for assistance.

The American Delta Force might be reasonably described as a military 'Super SWAT', whose intended task is to resolve foreign terrorist incidents involving the seizure of US hostages or installations.

Because of what was considered the potential for a serious international terrorist attack during the 1984 Olympic Games, presidential authority was obtained to place the unit on a reserve status to assist local law-enforcement bodies within the USA. The FBI, however, formed its own special response team for the Games, and subsequently the decision was taken to keep the unit as a full-time counter-terrorism resource. Law-enforcement SWATs are a standard anti-crime measure in the USA, but, like many of their counterparts in Canada, they are not adequate for the professional counter-terrorism role.

On the domestic scene, the appearance of a number of extremist groups has created concerns for federal and local law-enforcement agencies, especially during the 1980s. Many of the organizations have masqueraded under the guise of 'survivalists' or 'patriots' seeking to prepare for a possible national emergency. Some have adopted the role of 'vigilantes' or quasi-religious sects, who allege a need to protect their rights and heritage from the influence or other militants or issue groups. Groups such as The Order, or Posse Comitatus, have demonstrated the use of terrorist tactics as part of their operations. Efforts to control these groups through investigations and surveillance on the part of the law-enforcement community also illustrate positive measures to counter the threat of terrorism. Domestic terrorism, however, has not been a major problem for the United States, despite the activities of the FALN, the Weathermen, the Symbionese Liberation Army, and other militant groups. The largest number of terrorist attacks against US citizens and interests have occurred overseas, and markedly in the 1980s. Thus, many of the counter-terrorism measures instituted by the US authorities in the 1970s were of a cosmetic nature, even the Office for Combatting Terrorism in the State Department was looked upon as a graveyard by diplomatic personnel during the 1970s decade.

Similar to Canadian endeavours, nonetheless, the American Government did seek an early encouragement and development of international measures to combat terrorism. In 1972, the US Secretary of State attempted to achieve United Nations agreement on a resolution condemning terrorism, but was unsuccessful due to definitional controversy. The US did reach a formal arrangement with Cuba on airline hijacking at the beginning of the 1970s, complemented by the introduction of airline security measures that have become accepted world-wide. The US has also been a firm supporter of international conventions and resolutions opposing acts of terrorism. The 1979 seizure of the US embassy in Tehran, and the 444 days of captivity endured by the American hostages, graphically returned US attention to the reality of the terrorist threat. President Reagan's campaign speeches promised a response to terrorism, as well as placing more focus on the problem. But, it was not until the bombings of US embassies in Beirut, and the tragedy which befell the US Marines in that city, that a real urgency was given to improving physical measures of protection. The most dramatic measure of response, however, was the use of American military force in 1986 to counter terrorist actions in the Mediterranean and Europe.

Yet, in spite of much publicized and forceful moves against terrorists and terrorism, the US has also displayed ambivalence. The reluctance to modify the nation's extradition treaty with the United Kingdom, a measure having serious consequences for Irish terrorists, has demonstrated that equivocation (albeit also a reflection of the influence of the Irish–American lobby). Concern over the definition of terrorism has been a contributing factor, but the complex structure of the bureaucracy, the broad representational nature of Congress, and the President's position in relation to that body and the bureaucracy, have also played a major role.

The unitary system of government in the United Kingdom, by comparison, is a distinct advantage in coping with the threat of terrorism. Problems associated with federalism as exist in Canada and the United States do not arise; the British Parliament is the supreme ruling body. Parliament makes the laws for the nation, and local councils have a very limited scope in terms of the regulations which they may frame and proclaim. The development and implementation of policy measures are not routine or simplistic, nevertheless. As described in the next chapter, the role of Her Majesty's Loyal Opposition in Parliament has a very real influence on policy evolution and stability. For the most part, however, there has been bipartisan agreement on counter-terrorism policy in the United Kingdom. It has been a situation allowing for steady progress toward improved resources and, in particular, a reduction of violence in Northern Ireland.

At the upper echelons of government, responsibility for response to terrorism may be said to lie with two principal departments: the Home Office, and the Foreign and Commonwealth Office. Since the introduction of Direct Rule for Ulster in 1972, a third department has also been included: the Northern Ireland Office. Inter- and intradepartmental frictions are not as evident as they appear in similar North American governmental bodies. Possibly that fortuitous ambience is a consequence of much clearer distinctions of responsibility in the United Kingdom's bureaucracy. Certainly jurisdictional conflicts are not as readily apparent as they are in Canada and the USA.

Very similar to the system which obtains in Canada in regard to a terrorist or other emergency situation, the British Government follows a 'lead Minister' procedure: that is, the Minister and department for which the incident has immediate concern adopt responsibility for the handling of the incident. For instance, in the case of the occupation of the Iranian embassy in London in 1980, the Home Secretary and the Home Office had the task of overseeing the resolution of the incident. A similar condition prevailed during the 1984 St James's Square problem at the Libyan 'People's Bureau'. Because of the international nature of those two events, the Home Secretary acted with the advice and support of the Foreign Secretary and the Foreign and Commonwealth Office, although not always in complete agreement.

Friction is not entirely missing from the British scene, however. Both the law-enforcement agencies and the intelligence services have been known to experience disagreements between each other and amongst themselves. The military, on the occasions when it has been involved (e.g. Northern Ireland), has also been a source of controversy. When the policy of restoring police primacy in Northern Ireland came into effect in 1977, the military was not fully co-operative and nearly two years were to pass before general acceptance was established. The overall situation is best understood by a brief examination of the relationships of the various agencies.

In its most basic form, the British intelligence community is comprised of the Security Service (MI-5) and the Secret Intelligence Service (MI-6). The former is technically a branch of the Home Office, and is responsible for counter-intelligence functions within the United Kingdom. MI-6 is a Foreign Office responsibility, and deals with intelligence gathering abroad. Working in conjunction with these two agencies is the police Special Branch; it is the officers of Special Branch who actually conduct arrests arising from the investigations of the Security Service. Akin to members of CSIS, personnel of MI-5 and MI-6 are not police officers.

Much confusion surrounds the organization and the role of the Special Branch. Originally formed in 1883

> as a response to Irish terrorist movements ... until 1961 [it] existed only as part of the [London] Metropolitan Police. Since 1961 regional Special Branch Squads have been established. In the regional forces, the Special Branch officers are responsible to their Chief Constable for their activities. In the Metropolitan Police, the Special Branch ... are responsible to the Commissioner....[124]

One of the primary duties of the officers of the Branch is the investigation of subversive or terrorist organizations. Special Branch, therefore, like the British police as an entity, is not a monolithic organization or national force. Within the United Kingdom there are fifty-two separate police forces, not counting extraneous bodies such as the Ministry of Defence Police or the Transport Police: forty-three police forces in England and Wales, eight in Scotland, and one in Northern Ireland. Each police force is an independent body headed by a Chief Constable. Contrary to some popular opinions, the United Kingdom does not have a national police force.

It is reasonable to suggest that occasions do arise when controversies exist between different agencies and within departments. A recent newspaper article claimed that petty rivalry and a lack of co-operative spirit had developed between the Metropolitan Special Branch and Scotland Yard's Anti-terrorist Branch, C13.[125] (Scotland Yard is the title given to the Headquarters of the London Metropolitan Police – it is not a separate organization.) Such rivalries were even more pronounced in Northern Ireland for much of the 1970s decade when police and military forces shared the front line in the battle against terrorist activities of both the Republicans and the Loyalists. In the matter of jurisdiction, an incident is the responsibility of the law-enforcement body whose duty it is to maintain law and order where the event occurs. Sussex police, for instance, were responsible for security in Brighton during the 1984 Conservative Party Conference when PIRA succeeded in planting a bomb in the Grand Hotel, and the Sussex police were also responsible for the investigations resulting from the incident. Expertise from other forces can be called upon if considered necessary, or if the Home Office should suggest that such a move would be advisable in extraordinary cases. (The cinema portrayals of 'call for Scotland Yard detectives' is based on the fact that originally only Scotland Yard had a department devoted to specialist crime investigations.) But such actions are not the norm, and would be looked upon with disfavour, if not open hostility, by the police force concerned.

Because of the historical tradition of unarmed police forces in Great Britain, SWATs, as have developed in North America, are not a standard arrangement. The Metropolitan Police do have a Special Patrol Group, and a Royalty and Diplomatic Protection Group, whose members may carry arms in the performance of their duties, and also a team of specialist marksmen, D11. But resistance has been strong against the arming of police in Great Britain. Regular (selected) police officers are trained in the use of weapons, nevertheless, and such officers are tasked on occasions when it is considered that small arms will be needed. Several unfortunate incidents in recent years, however, have stimulated increased public demands that weapons should not be issued to police. In the event of a terrorist incident where weapons are involved, the police make every effort to contain the problem using their own resources. Regular officers, with weapons, form an immediate perimeter, and special squads, such as D11, may then be called upon. It is British policy in a serious terrorist incident to request military assistance should it become necessary to carry out an assault upon the terrorists. The assault force, under such circumstances, would most likely be a team from the SAS.

The British Army has a long and varied history of fulfilling the role of Aid to the Civil Power in the United Kingdom and overseas. From at least the turn of the century, however, that role has continually lessened in Great Britain. When giving evidence in 1908 to the Select Committee on Employment of Military in Cases of Disturbance, Lord Haldane, Secretary of State for War, said: 'In the War Office we are very averse to allowing the military to be employed.'[126] That attitude and policy have prevailed, although circumstances in Northern Ireland have not allowed it to be absolute throughout the United Kingdom. Thus, while the Army has always been viewed as having a back-up role to assist the police in the event of serious civil disturbance, the role has been principally envisaged as an overseas task. To some degree, that is the reason why the Army had considerably to modify its training and methods of operation to meet the challenges of the Northern Ireland conflict. The SAS, on the contrary, have been a special-operations unit from the outset of their formation, making it logical and relatively easy for them to acquire the particular specialist skills demanded of a counter-terrorist force. Police and military personnel at all levels in the United Kingdom agree that tasks involving maximum force and the 'ultimate sanction' are best delegated as responsibilities of the British Army or Marines.

In Great Britain, and to a growing extent in Northern Ireland, the police have responsibility for protective measures for major events such as international sports contests or visits of foreign dignitaries. The Army, nonetheless, has a supporting role which is evident in the occasional appearance of armoured vehicles and personnel at London's principal air terminals at times of a high level of terrorist threat. The presence of the military on those occasions is for the purpose of additional manpower and specialist equipment in support of the police; any necessary arrests or interrogations of suspects would remain a duty of the police.

In contrast with its limited counter-terrorism employment in Great Britain, the military has played a leading part in security tasks and in attempts to restore stability in Northern Ireland. Much attention has been focused on the challenges faced by the Army, especially during the first half of the 1970s decade, when the badly shaken RUC was in the process of re-establishing its capabilities, presence, and authority. The Royal Air Force and the Royal Navy have also been significantly involved as well, the Air Force flying transport and surveillance missions, and the Navy providing valuable coastal patrols to interdict the smuggling of arms and terrorist personnel. Despite the change in government policy in 1977, which returned dominant security responsibility to the RUC, the three military services continue to operate as measures of support.

'The Government have said on frequent occasions that there is no purely military solution and that unquestionably a political solution is also involved.'[127] British policy associated with the Northern Ireland conflict has not been confined to security measures, albeit the latter have commanded the greatest publicity.

> I begin by stating as clearly as I can the broad principle of the Government's policy. The principle is to work for the same standards in Northern Ireland as in the rest of the United Kingdom in community relations, in economic and social progress and in the maintenance of law and order.[128]

Prime Minister Heath's remarks to the House of Commons reflect the range of policy measures which have been part of the British Government's response to terrorism in that area of the United Kingdom where the threat has been so openly manifest.

The British Government has maintained a search for a suitable political solution from the beginning of the unrest in 1969, allowing time in the early stages for Ulster to seek its own answers before imposing Direct Rule in March 1972. Subsequently, the Government endeavoured to restore self-government in the Province by means of an elected assembly in 1973. It was a substantial move which progressed to the establishment of a power-sharing executive involving the Unionists, SDLP, and Alliance parties. Late in the year a conference was held at the Sunningdale Civil Service College (England), attended by members of the Executive and representatives of the British and Irish Governments. The purpose of Sunningdale was to formalize the political framework for the new government; included in the arrangement was a proposal for a Council of Ireland, composed of a Council of Ministers and a Consultative Assembly from both parts of Ireland. The Sunningdale Agreement, although never formally signed, was intended to spur co-operative functions in security and the development of resources. The project did not succeed; it collapsed in the face of Unionist intransigence and the Ulster Workers' Strike, both opposed to power-sharing and the concept of the Council of Ireland. The Executive was forced to resign in May of the following year, the Assembly was prorogued and Direct Rule continued.

A Constitutional Convention was announced almost immediately in an attempt to break the deadlock. The Convention was elected in 1975, but also failed within a year's time. In 1981, the new Secretary of State for Northern Ireland, James Prior, investigated the possibility of an assembly on the US model, with a separation of administrative and legislative responsibility. Early the next year he 'settled on the idea of "rolling devolution," a system where an Assembly would start off with only a consultative and scrutiny role'.[129] Little movement was achieved towards the aim of shared power between the majority and minority groups in Ulster, and the Assembly was finally prorogued in 1986 following vigorous opposition to the Anglo-Irish Agreement.

Financial support from the British Government has also been extremely liberal, rising steadily from 1969, as a measure to improve the economy and reduce sectarian frictions based on deprivation. The amount was £1.3 billion in 1982–3, 'with another 140 million pounds of British army costs on top'.[130] The DeLorean automobile manufacturing fiasco, which cost the British Government over £80 million, was another example of an effort to counter terrorist recruiting by providing jobs for the unemployed. Such moves are perhaps more accurately seen as indirect measures, but their intent has been directly linked with reducing the potential for terrorist violence in the province by improving the standard of living among Protestants and Catholics alike.

The British Government has demonstrated leadership in the development of legislative measures in response to terrorism. Foremost are the previously mentioned EPA and the PTA, both of which were passed 'to deal with problems arising out of terrorism in Northern Ireland'.[131] A degree of foresight was present in regard to the PTA: although not introduced until 1974, the bill was prepared in draft one year earlier, and was actually passed into law in one day's sitting of Parliament in the aftermath of several horrific PIRA/INLA attacks in England. Despite the Act's purpose as a measure to combat terrorism emanating from Northern Ireland, the PTA has also been used to detain and investigate suspected international terrorists. Out of respect for fear of 'the addictive effect of anti-terrorist measures'.[132] limitations were placed on the life of anti-terrorist statutes. Initially six months was the maximum time span before review; later that was extended to the period of one year for the PTA, which must be re-introduced as a new bill at the end of five years (one significant consequence of the Jellicoe Review).

In keeping with the direct and active policy of rule of law, the government has been prompt in implementing official inquiries into controversial incidents, as well as in conducting frequent reviews of special legislation. The Widgery Tribunal, which inquired into the events of 'Bloody Sunday' (30 January 1972) was initiated on the day following, and formally approved by Parliament on 1 February 1972.[133] Similarly, the EPA and the PTA have undergone several reviews by eminent jurists and senior public figures of wide knowledge and experience, often with the support of public and private hearings. Police interrogation procedures in Northern Ireland were the subject of a searching and detailed committee of inquiry, headed by Judge H.G. Bennett, in 1978,[134] and which subsequently resulted in improvements not yet standard in many large North American law-enforcement bodies.

The problem of terrorism associated with the Irish dimension has been a principal focus of British security measures. The 'Bikini Alert' system which warns of bomb threats, for instance, is one outcome; well-known to the public through publicity, the various colours (e.g. black, amber, red) indicate the levels of danger. But the threat of international terrorism has not been ignored, and the United Kingdom has supported efforts to combat terrorism through the medium of international agreements and conventions. The nation was an early ratifier of the European Convention on the Suppression of Terrorism, as well as pressing for co-operation in law enforcement through arrangements such as the Trevi system.

The United Kingdom, as with the two North American states, has responded to terrorism in accordance with perception of the threat. The domestic reality, in terms of Ulster, has been much more substantial, painful, and of longer duration than has been the terrorist experience of Canada or the USA. International terrorist pressures have not been as obvious as those known by the United States, but Great Britain has been the scene of spectacular incidents and has faced a more immediate danger as a consequence of its proximity to Europe and the Middle East and London's position as a centre of international affairs. The British Government, as a result, has had to develop a broader range of measures against the threat of terrorism than has previously been deemed necessary in Canada or the USA.

## Indirect (passive) measures

By virtue of their nature, such measures are more difficult to identify and the issues can be contentious. Immigration procedures, as an example, are receiving more attention as a means of controlling the movements of suspected terrorists; but, on balance, they remain passive in their nature.

> The Immigration and Nationality Act of June 27, 1952, as amended, is very specific concerning who may enter [the USA] and who may subsequently be deported.... Specific modification of the Act, therefore, to include terrorism is not deemed necessary.[135]

The relatively few terrorist incidents in the United States involving foreigners would appear to lend credence to that opinion. The US has a very substantial immigration-enforcement program, which includes the US Customs Service and the Border Patrol. Two long, undefended borders with neighbouring nations make control of illegal immigrants a difficult process, nonetheless. In recent years it has also become a hazardous task in the southern United States where narcotics and illegal alien smugglers use weapons to protect their activities. Co-operation with Canadian authorities is of a very high level, and a number of significant detentions have been made over the years.

Under the Immigration Act, 1976, the screening of immigrants to Canada reflects changes in the international environment over the years from the Second World War. 'Concerns with treason and wartime activities against Her Majesty's allies have shifted to acts of violence and terrorism.'[136] Quoting further from the Report of the McDonald Commission, the Immigration Act 'attempts to strike a balance between administrative efficiency and respect for civil liberties. It accords the government increased power to deal with terrorists, subversives, criminals and those seeking to circumvent the laws; ....'[137] While not identifying terrorism specifically, the Act does make a sweep in that direction. Canada has a well-deserved reputation for a humanitarian approach to the problem of refugees and has been an attractive haven for many decades. This situation poses many problems in the development and administration of immigration policy, forcing it to become increasingly attuned to 'more positive emphasis on the reasons and means for admittance'.[138] It is noteworthy that security concerns at the time of the 1976 Olympics, which gave rise to a Temporary Immigration Security Act, have been permanently implemented. Visitors can be turned back at a port of entry or deported after a hearing by a departmental adjudicator.

British procedures are rather more oriented to controls associated with the EPA and the PTA, and provide immigration officials with wide powers for detention and questioning of persons wishing to enter the country. Movement to and from Northern Ireland and Great Britain is controlled by landing cards and the screening of individuals, a process often conducted by Special Branch officers. Persons may also be precluded from entering any part of the United Kingdom by means of an Exclusion Order if it is considered they are implicated 'in the commission, preparation or instigation of acts of terrorism'.[139]

The ability of Irish terrorists to find sanctuary in the United States has drawn more attention to extradition agreements between the two nations.

British law and practice includes a variety of extradition arrangements. There is ... no extensive network of bilateral extradition treaties. With respect to some countries – for example, the United States – a bilateral agreement is required. As to the Commonwealth countries, however, the United Kingdom is 'able to operate satisfactory extradition arrangements ... on the basis of substantially uniform legislation unsupported by any kind of formal agreement'.[140]

Notwithstanding, the Hague and Montreal Conventions, as well as the United Nations Convention concerning internationally protected persons, all confer formal extradition rights. Continuing problems with extradition, however, prompted promises of 'radical changes to the law on extradition' in the United Kingdom in 1986.[141]

British difficulties with extradition in the United States have also been a major problem in relations with Eire, where safeguards against 'political offenders' have made the Irish nation a sanctuary for PIRA/INLA terrorists. Some successes have been achieved in recent years in obtaining the return of offenders from Eire who were charged for terrorist acts in the United Kingdom. Unfortunately, they have been marred on several occasions by faulty administrative work on the part of British law-enforcement agencies. But,

> Also noteworthy is British legislation, which confers on the courts in Northern Ireland jurisdiction over certain offenses committed in the Irish Republic and which also gives courts in Great Britain as well as in Northern Ireland jurisdiction in certain circumstances where a British citizen causes an explosion in the Republic or when such a citizen conspires to cause an explosion in the Republic. The Republic of Ireland's criminal law contains parallel provisions for jurisdiction over such offenses committed in Northern Ireland,[142] and mainland Britain.

Acts of terrorism are treated as criminal offences under the laws of Canada, the United States, and the United Kingdom. Terrorists are arrested, tried, sentenced, and incarcerated in the same manner as other criminals. Judicial procedures differ in Northern Ireland, however, where the Diplock Courts system is used for the trial of persons accused of terrorist crimes. A controversial arrangement (discussed in detail in Chapter Four), the system consists of non-jury trials presided over by one judge, with certain specific qualifications on evidence and witnesses. Essentially, the procedure is an effort to overcome problems of unfair trials resulting from threats against jury members and witnesses. (The name derives from an official report submitted by Lord Diplock in December 1972.) It has also been British policy to house terrorist prisoners in separate accommodation in Northern Ireland.

Control of weapons varies in the three nations, and is a particularly contentious matter in the United States. Canada and the United Kingdom have relatively strict regulations on the sale and ownership of personal weapons, with British legislation containing the most stringent prohibitions. But, despite the expressed concerns of many law-enforcement agencies and public pressure groups in the USA, Congress further eased controls on automatic weapons in 1985. The easy availability of weapons in the United States makes the nation an attractive source for terrorist groups, such as PIRA, to seek arms supplies. International co-operation between law-enforcement agencies, nevertheless, has begun to make that activity less practicable; the seizure of a large shipment of weapons in 1984, in the Marita Ann Incident,[143] resulted from the joint efforts of Irish, British, and American authorities, and was a significant blow to PIRA.

Neil C. Livingstone, in his book *The War against Terrorism*, states,

> the application of force against terrorists, without any corresponding effort to understand their grievance or to implement specific reforms to rectify what may be legitimate problems, may produce some immediate results but usually does not constitute a viable strategy and may, in fact only postpone the ultimate threat.[144]

Canada's efforts to improve the Francophone position across that nation illustrate the positive aspect of Livingstone's context. Similarly, American moves in respect of its Black and Hispanic communities have had an ameliorative effect, but urban overcrowding and economic disparities still give rise to dissent. Unfortunately, some incidents of extreme violence in Britain (e.g. Brixton and Tottenham), which could easily be viewed as an escalation towards urban guerrilla and terrorist tactics, have created demands for serious reappraisals of policing methods, as well as consideration of inner-city problems. It is a situation which could provoke an increase of unrest and civil disobedience in the future.

> For several years, academic circles have discussed the origins and tactics of terrorism.... In recent years, scholars and the United States Government have begun to share information on terrorism ... the cooperation between academia and governments is not without friction.... Still, the overriding view is that academic involvement is crucial to an understanding of terrorism.[145]

American academics have been particularly active in research devoted to the phenomenon of terrorism, producing an impressive array of authorities on the subject. The US Government has not been reluctant to make use of the expertise: the Defence Nuclear Agency, for example, has sponsored a number of symposia associated with anti-terrorist security problems, and the Department of Energy has utilized facilities such as the Rand Corporation and Sandia Laboratories as a means to gain a better understanding of the terrorist threat. The American authorities have also not been hesitant in expanding their search overseas, and have consulted and co-operated with a number of leading scholars in other western countries.

Academic interest in terrorism has not been overly marked in Canada, although the Centre for Conflict Studies at the University of New Brunswick has conducted a number of research projects in that vein. The Operational Research and Analysis Establishment (ORAE) of the Department of National Defence has, as well, displayed a marginal concern. The Federal government has access to the Special Threat Assessment Group, 'a team of scientific and technical experts who advise on how to respond to the threat or use of nuclear, biological or chemical weapons'.[146]

Extremes of ideology have not been a major problem in Canada, the United States, or the United Kingdom. Militant radicalism in the form of terrorist groups of the Right and Left of the political spectrum has made an appearance in the USA, but has rapidly come to the attention of the FBI. While worrying in its potential, the reality has not had a significant disruptive influence. Similarly, the marshalling of public opinion in Canada has provided strong resistance against the growth of neo-Nazi groups or the establishment of organizations such as the Ku Klux Klan. The traditionally tolerant British attitude and low-key approach has done much to defuse extremists in the United Kingdom, where violence has been most evident between supporters of the far Left and the far Right (e.g. Lewisham).

The openness of liberal-democratic societies is a factor in making them vulnerable to terrorist assault. In recent years, the passage of the Freedom of Information Act in the United States, and the Access to Information Act in Canada, have been criticized on such grounds. Undoubtedly the two acts do contribute to difficulties on the part of the law-enforcement and intelligence services, especially in terms of information sharing within the international community. The legislation has also resulted in the destruction of valuable intelligence records, created expensive administrative arrangements and caused ridiculous use of security classifications. Nonetheless, it has added to the nations' strengths by allowing citizens to observe the workings of their respective governments at close range, be reasonably certain that covert wrongdoings will ultimately be exposed and that the democratic system of government will not be subverted or undermined.

The British governmental system tends to take an opposite approach, preferring to cloak its workings in secrecy. Access to information, other than that which the government itself chooses to make public, is difficult to obtain. Even if information is gained, it is often subject to the terms of the Official Secrets Act, rendering it useless for publication purposes. The British attitude reflects faith in the rectitude of its public servants, but arguments surrounding such incidents as the sinking of the *Belgrano* and the Ponting disclosures, *inter alia*, have suggested a desire by the public for a more liberal approach to information sources.

The role of the media has been mentioned earlier as having a significant place in terrorist strategy. Terrorists obviously 'want a lot of people watching' for the purposes of spreading the terrorists' message and to increase the impact of the terrorists' deeds. Television has been a great boon to terrorist activity in that regard, as have modern communications methods which allow rapid dissemination of news on a global basis. Competition among journalists and the eagerness to achieve a scoop have placed the terrorist in a favourable position. In May 1986, NBC News made an agreement with Mohammed Abbas 'to keep secret [his] whereabouts in exchange for an interview'.[147]

The NBC incident is only one of many occasions when the media has been the subject of debate over the propriety of its coverage of terrorist events. 'During the TWA hijacking, for example, American television conferred tacit legitimacy on the skyjackers by interviewing them on nationwide broadcasts.'[148] From a different standpoint, television coverage of the Iranian embassy incident in London risked the SAS operations by showing the rescue team moving into position.

> The media are important to terrorists because they not only relay information, but, like good drama critics, interpret it as well. The slant they give – by deciding which events to report and which to ignore, by intentionally or unintentionally expressing approval or disapproval – can create a climate of public support, apathy, or anger.[149]

The media, therefore, can have a very direct influence on terrorist activity; because of the principle of a free press in liberal democracies, however, the media cannot be employed as a direct measure of response to terrorism.

Nonetheless, proper use of the media, including a co-operative and understanding relationship, can provide government with an indirect measure of response. Solicitor General Beatty's announcement of stiffer Canadian measures against terrorism mentioned the government's intention to meet with media leaders as a step in such a direction. During the 1970s, the British military and the RUC realized the need for close liaison with the Press to the extent that they established elaborate media-relations cells. The NBC–Abbas affair served to underline the complex problems which continue to arise in respect to American journalists and their concern about First Amendment rights as enshrined in the US Constitution. Despite efforts to improve the position of the media *vis-à-vis* reporting of acts of terrorism, the situation in Canada, the United States, and the United Kingdom, however, remains delicately balanced and requires much greater mutual understanding and a closer exchange of views with government and government agencies.

Policy and policy measures are important aspects of governmental response to terrorism. They represent the foundations and perspectives of government activity, as well as reflecting the influence of history, culture, tradition, values, experience, and the many other factors of the *Envelope*. But they are not self-generating, and result from decision-making and management mechanisms which are also deserving of examination. Those features of government response to terrorism in Canada, the United States, and the United Kingdom are the subjects of the next chapter.

Chapter three

# Decision-making and crisis-management machinery

## Introduction

The challenge of the FLQ, and the October Crisis in particular, evoked a singular response on the part of the Canadian Government. Given the time and the circumstances, that response should not be viewed as surprising or extraordinary. Modern terrorism was in its infancy, and the government had only the lessons of marginal historical experience of civil violence for guidance. Indeed, in 1970, Canada lacked the benefit of later British enlightenment in Northern Ireland, and American problems with civil-rights agitation in the 1960s offered little instruction in how to cope with terrorists. The Canadian Government responded in accordance with precedent, in the manner it best knew, and with the resources available to it.

Judy Torrance has produced an interesting and valuable study that provides a background to Canada's introduction to terrorism, and aids with an understanding of government reaction in 1970.[1] It also helps to signpost Canadian counter-terrorism policy and policy measures developed in the years that followed. Torrance reached her verdicts on the basis of analyses of five major incidents in Canadian history, – Red River Rising of 1869–70; Northwest Rebellion of 1885; Quebec City Riots of 1918; Winnipeg General Strike of 1919; Regina Riot of 1935 – but she purposely excluded the October Crisis because the necessary primary sources were not open at the time of her research. Nonetheless, she did suggest that the handling of the affair was similar to previous policy, and represented a typical Canadian Government attitude and approach. Torrance effectively postulates that at the national level, Canadian Governments have historically been highly attentive to violence, responding promptly and with visible concern. In conjunction, governments have treated incidents of violence as a grave threat to internal security and the integrity of the nation. But, in such cases, the militants were generally classified as misguided criminals, rather than persons acting out of political conviction. 'Thus in 1885 the minister of justice (sic), Alexander Campbell, urged that Riel go to the scaffold as a criminal, not a political, offender.'[2]

The FLQ threat loomed much larger in perception than in reality, with the influence of history and contemporary events in Cuba, Algeria, and Viet Nam contributing to the impression. In view of those circumstances, it is not surprising that the Canadian Government should have acted as it did when confronted by the FLQ attacks. The Federal government had played a prompt and prominent role in the major disturbances cited by Torrance, and certainly had every reason to take a leading part in responding to events in 1970. The terrorist activities of the FLQ blurred the legitimate expressions of political dissent urging independence for Quebec, making the two appear almost synonymous in the minds of the authorities, as well as in the opinions of many citizens. Firm, rapid, determined action was deemed the solution to 'criminal actions' (i.e. FLQ incidents) that had to be stamped out before they had an opportunity to spread. What was later to be criticized as the government's use of legislative extremes, coupled with the unnecessary deployment of overwhelming security resources, can be appreciated in the light of precedent and values associated with the rule of law. Similarly, the nature of response by the security forces was in keeping with the training, experience, and resources of that era. Noteworthy was the fact that in the overall context the methods of response adhered to the rule of law, to the use of minimum force, and remained under the control of government at all levels throughout the perceived crisis.

From the standpoint of terrorism, the FLQ threat can be said to have created a far-reaching influence on Canadian policy and policy measures of response. It was in the immediate aftermath of events in 1970 that the government initiated a comprehensive examination of its decision-making and crisis-management infrastructure for use in time of emergency. Much of the framework and realignment were established in the first half of the 1970s, and remain in current use. Even the McDonald Commission, which prompted changes to security arrangements in the 1980s, was principally a result of accusations of misconduct on the part of the RCMP during the FLQ period. Canadians have not ignored terrorist threats and activities elsewhere in the world; the broad overlap of American television into Canada alone would make such a circumstance an impossibility. Concern for the security of foreign participants and spectators at the 1976 Olympic Games, as well as for the heads of state at the 1981 economic summit, also kept awareness alive. But the Cross–Laporte affair, and the FLQ, dominated Canadian thinking in relation to terrorism through the decade of the 1970s and into the 1980s. It has taken several tragic acts of international terrorism involving Canada and Canadians in the 1980s to engender a much wider perspective.

The lyrics of a commercial message popular in the 1970s described 'hot-dogs, baseball, Chevrolets, and apple pie' as distinctly American. Missing from the list was violence. S.E. Finer and Ernest Evans both cite violence as characteristically part of the American tradition, although not for the same reasons.³ Finer associates violence with motivations in US society, whereas Evans explains that the prevalence of violence in the USA has caused Americans to lack an appreciation of terrorism as a political phenomenon. Finer and Evans are correct in their allusions to a nation historically steeped in the habit and experience of violence. Originally a British colony carved out of struggles with native Indians and encroaching French traders, the USA was founded on the outcome of a revolutionary war. Wracked by the trauma of fearsome civil conflict less than a century later, the developing state expanded its continental borders westward through a lengthy series of sanguinary battles with indigenous tribesmen. Growth, maturity, and limited imperialism brought war with Britain in 1812, with Mexico in the 1840s, with Spain at the turn of the century, participation in the major global strife of the early and mid-twentieth century, leadership of the UN intervention in Korea at the beginning of the 1950s, and prominence in the Viet Nam war during the 1960s and 1970s.

An independent spirit and the freedom to bear arms have been two endowments of the nation's genesis. But 'frontier justice' also translated into brutal confrontations in reaction to growing labour unrest accompanying attempts to unionize industry during expansion in the decades following the Civil War. The same conditions prevailed in the rise of gangsterism in the Roaring Twenties era of prohibition, and in the 'Bonnie and Clyde' exploits of criminals throughout the Depression years. Large conurbations with ghetto-like sectors populated by underprivileged minorities fostered the spread of violent criminal behaviour, abetted by the emergence of Mafia families, and more recently by the illegal narcotics trade. While terrorism of a criminal variety featured in American violence, the activity in most cases was more correctly that of terrorizing individuals, or segments of the population, on a limited basis. Homesteaders were forced off lands claimed by cattle barons, unions were broken by unscrupulous commercial security agencies, and protection rackets operated under the supervision of local gangland bosses. The Ku Klux Klan, generally depicted as an archetypal terrorist group, had an erratic regional influence marginally political in nature. Violence attached to acts of crime has been the principal reality in the USA, promoting an American fixation with the concept of terrorism as a criminal activity, or as a humanitarian problem.

'Bomb Blast at the Capitol'.⁴ Headline news reports of terrorist incidents began to awaken US citizens to the phenomenon within American borders during the 1970s and 1980s. Excluding the FALN bombings, however, many of the domestic incidents appeared as irrational, criminally inspired events and usually were not spectacular or sustained. Rumours of Libyan hit-teams and Iranian suicide squads eventually did have an impact on public opinion, creating a near siege mentality in Washington which has continued to linger. Memories of the 1972 Munich disaster so haunted US authorities preparing for the 1984 Los Angeles Olympics that anti-terrorist security precautions became a subject of national news coverage. The most potent signals of danger, nonetheless, have come as a consequence of international terrorist actions of extraordinary dimensions such as the Iranian Crisis, the Beirut suicide attacks, and the TWA hostage-taking. Also, although not aimed directly at the United States, the Munich massacre and the 1976 Entebbe and 1977 Mogadishu aircraft hijacking incidents served as warnings. Those events were incapable of dismissal, of treatment as ordinary guerrilla warfare, or classification as purely psychotic criminal outrages. Gradually the threat and reality of terrorism as a political device has been brought home to the American public. In turn, that realization has generated an overhaul of US response mechanisms.

Before examining those mechanisms, reference must again be made to the largely unacknowledged pre-1968 American experience with terrorism. Critics fault US response policies over the past two decades, while apologists offer the defence of American historical tradition combined with a low level of domestic threat. Both err in not taking account of US civilian and military experience with terrorism abroad prior to that date. Many US commercial and government operations, personnel, and facilities were subject to, or witnessed, terrorist violence in foreign countries before the late 1960s. Some American authorities are now using the example of Jeffersonian response to the maritime terrorism of the Barbary pirates to recommend US military intervention on occasions of extreme terrorist provocation, but the fact remains that there was an early contemporary failure to recognize that terrorism could become a threat to American national security. Experience and evidence gained overseas were not correlated and communicated as warnings, which might have emphasized the developing trend.

The evolution of American response to terrorism in terms of policies, infrastructure, and capabilities has suffered as a result of the inability to capitalize on early experience with terrorist behaviour. Domestically, a rationale has existed for viewing the phenomenon as criminal violence posing little threat to US political stability. Internationally, however, examples were manifold and should have provided guidance for the future. Unfortunately, military preoccupation with evidence of terrorism as a guerrilla warfare technique, the impression of the USA as a comfortably invulnerable giant, and the complexities of American bureaucracy and politics have all combined to overshadow suggestions that terrorism could represent a potential threat to US global influence and interests.

Turning to British experience, tourists visiting London flock to the Bloody Tower to view relics and sites associated with England's violent early history. During their tour of the massive stone fortress they gaze at awesome displays of feudal armour and weapons, as well as the spot where queens and courtly gentlemen were beheaded. Impressively clad Beefeaters (Yeomen of the Guard) regale the visitors with colourful and gory tales of famous (or infamous) events spanning 600 years from William the Conqueror to Oliver Cromwell. Similar historic loci dot not only London, but are situated throughout the British Isles, and provide tangible evidence of violence coupled with the evolution to mature nationhood. The British Isles have traditionally been the land of raiding Norsemen, of knights in armour, gallant longbowmen, stubborn Welsh nobles, Border 'reevers', and fiercely independent Scots clansmen, all famed in song and legend for their prowess in battle. The history of the United Kingdom presents a thrilling pageant of conflict, intrigue, and deeds of valour.

Less likely to incite the curiosity of sightseers are records which mark the nation's transition from turmoil to stability. The Bill of Rights in England, the Act of Settlement, the Reform Acts of 1832 and 1867, and legislation proclaiming adoption of the secret ballot in 1872 which was followed by other significant electoral reforms in 1883 and 1884, were all major steps in *The Conquest of Violence*.[5] Not without reason may it be said that 'for centuries the British were themselves amongst the most turbulent of peoples ... who have settled down to be one of the most tranquil'.[6] While violence has not been a stranger to the development of the United Kingdom, 'For upwards of one thousand years the whole nation has been involved more or less closely in the arrangements for maintaining the peace.'[7] Critchley's statement underlines the principle of self-policing which originated in Saxon times, and which survived through the parish constable, the militia, and the magistracy. Britain's modern police force did not emerge until Sir Robert Peel successfully introduced the Metropolitan Police Act in 1829. 'The law of the land still requires every citizen to respond to the call of a magistrate or constable to aid in suppressing disorder.'[8] Such shared responsibility and commitment has made possible the reality of a dignified, respected, unarmed police force in Great Britain.

Other factors bear upon the *Envelope* to influence the British characteristic of self-discipline, and have encouraged the flowering of liberal, humanitarian attitudes. Britain's island status, lack of internal natural boundaries, homogenization of culture, and the passage of time have contributed to the growth of stability and the current actuality of nearly 200 years of absence of major internal strife. During the centuries when both Canada and the United States were in their adolescence, Great Britain was well advanced into the Industrial Revolution, prosperity, Empire, and mature statehood. Edward Hyams, an early observer of the contemporary phenomenon of terrorism, remarked on the stability of the British establishment in the late nineteenth century. Hyams described the activities of anarchists in Great Britain, who 'seemed to regard England as a sort of apolitical enclave isolated from the vast field of their operations'.[9] It was 'a product ... of the British policy of letting men say and write whatever they pleased, however fiery, provided they did not actually try to put any of their theories into practice, at least in Britain....'[10]

Not everyone obeyed the tacit rules, however. Archetypal anarchist Johann Most was sentenced to eighteen months in prison for publishing an overly enthusiastic article applauding the assassination of Czar Nicholas II in 1881. Shortly thereafter, Fenian adventurers brought their nationalist aspirations to the British mainland in the form of bomb plots, and labour unrest turned ugly at the beginning of the twentieth century. Nevertheless, Great Britain was spared the revolutionary barricades and open warfare which troubled Europe for much of the 1800s. Foreign wars and colonial disputes did have their impact, and perhaps, to some extent tempered frustrations at home. It would have been difficult to originate, let alone sustain, extremist anti-government behaviour in the face of patriotic support for troops fighting in far flung corners of the Empire. But, despite such Kiplingesque influences and social reform in the years 1900-9, public order became an increasing concern through 1910-14. Disruption and the threat of serious violence resulting from workers' protests, suffragettes, and the promises of Home Rule for Ireland were only averted by the catastrophe of the First World War.

The war exhausted the nation to the point where men, equipment, and resolve were not available for a prolonged struggle against the Irish insurgents in 1919. By 1922 the battle was over, the Irish Free State and the Province of Ulster were established, allowing the British Government to turn its back on problems across the Irish Sea for the better part of sixty years. With the exception of the General Strike of 1926, the years leading to the Second World War were not times of particular violence within the United Kingdom. The aftermath of the Second World War brought peace to the British mainland, but engendered violent reactions in many colonial possessions overseas. The concept of Empire collapsed in waves of nationalist fervour, often abetted by left-wing doctrines, and was replaced by the Commonwealth and United Nations ideals of self-determination and international co-operation. The war-weary nation did not possess the resources to cope adequately in all circumstances, although it made an effort to prepare former colonies for self-government. In any case, even if it had wanted to halt the developments, it was not feasible to resist the overwhelming pressure of the emerging international consensus on decolonization and the universal right to self-determination.

The insurgencies which arose overseas, however, provided many lessons in the law-enforcement and military spheres of operation. General Sir Frank Kitson and Sir Robert Thompson have previously been mentioned as authorities in counter-insurgency who acquired their expertise in Kenya, Malaya, and Cyprus. Dr Richard Clutterbuck is a former British Major-General who became a specialist writer on political violence as a result of his active duty overseas. British military doctrine came to reflect a considerable experience with, and grasp of, the problems of insurgency and guerrilla warfare. Widely and correctly respected as being eminently authoritative, the doctrine did contain one dangerous weakness: it was not designed for use at home. Nearly twenty-five years passed from the end of the Second World War until major outbreaks of violence again disturbed the British Isles. Indeed, in 1968, while serious civil disorder was evident in France, Germany, Japan, and the USA, peaceful protest remained the norm in twentieth-century mainland Britain. It was not until the civil-rights marches inflamed conditions in Northern Ireland that physical conflict appeared on the streets of the United Kingdom. It is from that time that the British Government and people have had to learn to cope with politically motivated violence and the contemporary phenomenon of terrorism in their own homeland.

It cannot be said that the use of terrorism came as a complete surprise or shock to the British Government. The Stern Gang assassinated Lord Moyne in Cairo in 1944 to focus world attention on the plight of the Jews under the British mandate in Palestine. Malaya, Kenya, Cyprus, and Aden provided ample evidence of the use of terrorism to foster political aims. What was initially perplexing was the scope of that use, first in Northern Ireland and later on the British mainland. Undoubtedly of greater consternation was the inability of the RUC to contain the early effects of the violence, or for the later military presence to end the problem quickly. Compounding the difficulties has been the fact that terrorism in the United Kingdom has not been confined to circumstances associated with Ulster. International terrorism has also played a significant role, particularly in certain major urban centres of England, e.g. London, Liverpool, and Manchester. Unlike conditions in Canada and the USA, acts of international terrorism have occurred with greater frequency, and the presence of the threat of such attacks is more substantial. Various reasons involving the ease of travel, proximity to Europe and the Middle East, as well as London's large cosmopolitan population make it unlikely that the threat will subside in the foreseeable future.

British police forces have not shared the same advantage as the military in terms of experience with terrorism. They have not the benefit of that considerable service in trouble spots around the world. Nonetheless, the traditional role and discipline of the British policeman have been effective in maintaining an air of calm and normalcy, even in the face of horrific bombing incidents such as took place at Harrods in 1983. In what might be described as a characteristic approach, the British Government has resisted the temptation to be stampeded into policy decisions in response to terrorism. On the other hand, the government has not moved ponderously or ineffectively. Troops have been deployed when needed, special police units have been formed as circumstances warranted, weapons have been issued to police when required (and in the face of growing public concern), legislation has been passed with speed when conditions demanded, and inquiries have been implemented when questionable actions occurred.

The British Government and British authorities have not demonstrated a perfect reaction to the threat of terrorism, and the same can be said of their counterparts in Canada and the United States. Circumstances have differed for each of the three nations, however, and mitigating factors associated with the *Envelope of Influences* must be taken into consideration. To appreciate better how each nation has approached the threat of terrorism, how policy has unfolded, and how policy measures have developed, it is instructive to examine aspects of the decision-making and crisis-management machinery related to the response to terrorism.

## Decision-making machinery

A brief review of the broad structure of the Canadian governmental system and constitutional framework is helpful before embarking on a closer look at specific institutions and measures. Recalling Canada's status as a federal state, the central governing body (Parliament) shares power with institutions which appear almost its mirror-image in each of the ten provinces. While a somewhat similar situation obtains in the USA, there is a major difference between Canada and the United States in regard to the constitutionally granted distribution of power. In Canada, those matters not specifically allocated to the provinces are considered to be the purview of the Federal Parliament: that is, the Federal government has inherent jurisdiction over legislation and administration not originally and specifically granted to the provinces by the Constitution of Canada. Power, therefore, flows down to the provinces, and through them to counties and municipalities, as opposed to the two-way flow in the USA, where State governments do have considerably more freedom of initiative even though the Federal government has become increasingly powerful and pervasive in the past 100 years.

Canada, like the United Kingdom, combines the executive and legislative functions of central government in a national bicameral parliament. Similarly, Cabinet government is the nature and form of the executive body. In contrast with the United States, the Cabinet is a powerful institution which may actually be termed 'the Government' of the nation. Headed by the Prime Minister, who is the leader of the political party having a majority in the elected House of Commons of the legislature, the Cabinet is comprised of members of the majority party who hold seats in the House. Both the British and the Canadian House of Commons have a maximum elected term of five years. Selected by the Prime Minister, Cabinet members are appointed to head government departments, and are known as Government Ministers. (In some cases, a minister may not head a department, and is known as a Minister Without Portfolio.) On rare occasions, the Cabinet in Canada may include a member from the Senate, an appointed body. It is standard practice for the British Cabinet to include members of the House of Lords.

Simple in concept, Cabinet government does not readily lend itself to explanation. It is essential, however, that the workings be differentiated from those of the executive and Cabinet of the US Government, which are separate from the legislative branch. 'The outstanding duty of the cabinet is to furnish initiative and leadership; to provide the country and Parliament with a national policy and to devise means for coping with present emergencies and future needs.'[11] That activity is achieved by the Cabinet taking collective responsibility for major policy decisions. Partially because of that requirement, the inner workings of the Cabinet are veiled in secrecy, and Cabinet documents are generally not open to public scrutiny. Ministers, however, are individually responsible for the efficient functioning of their departments, and, as members of the legislature, may be called to account for their administration by means of legislative debate. A wise minister works closely with the permanent bureaucracy of the department; department policy, eventually presented to the Cabinet for decision, is usually the result of collaborative effort between a minister and his departmental subordinates. In Canada, the immediate subordinate is the Deputy Minister (DM); in the United Kingdom, it is the Permanent Under-Secretary of State.

The Cabinet is also a co-ordinating body, so that when two or more departments are involved in a particular matter, a resolution of conflicting opinion may be attained within that forum. Control of the Cabinet is very much vested in the Prime Minister, and in cases of that individual having a strong personality, there have been substantial allusions to 'prime-ministerial government'. The 'basic legislative power of the cabinet is the general control which it is able to exercise over the [elected legislature] at all times ... [the] Prime Minister assisted by the cabinet, leads and directs [it] in virtually everything it attempts to do'.[12] By far the majority of all government business is initiated by the Cabinet, which controls the legislative timetable, as well as the nation's financial budget.

Subordinate legislation is another prerogative of the Cabinet, and is known as an Order-in-Council. Authority for the passage of such legislation is the result of delegation by Acts of Parliament. Orders-in-Council may have wide-ranging application, and are discussed later in relation to The War Measures Act of Canada. A further power of the Canadian Cabinet is the right to disallow and render void any Act of a provincial legislature, provided such action takes place within one year after receipt of such Act by the Federal government. The Cabinet also performs executive functions of a broad nature, such as the appointment of ambassadors, judges, and members of the Senate, (the Upper House in Canada) as well as the ratification of international agreements and treaties. Notwithstanding, 'the cabinet is more a political than an administrative institution ... and as such its concerns are to plan the strategy of the ruling party in Parliament, and to keep the public image of the Government as favourable as possible'.[13]

Closely tied to the executive and legislature in the shaping of policy is the bureaucracy, or administrative branch of the government. Within Canada, as in the United Kingdom, the bureaucracy is made up of professional civil servants who are independent of political control – that is, they are permanent employees who are hired on a merit principle through an independent government agency. It is understood, however, that the civil service works for the government in power, i.e. the permanent heads of departments take their orders from the ministers who are appointed by the Prime Minister to have control of the various departments. Civil servants in Canada and the United Kingdom have a tradition of not dealing directly with Parliament, and rarely give interviews with the Press, although they do meet with members of the public as the situation permits. In general terms, what has been said about the federal structure of government in Canada obtains at the provincial level, with the exception that the system is unicameral. Despite the rather specific distribution of power in Canada, there is ample room for jurisdictional dispute, and provincial authorities traditionally guard against intrusions by the federal body. Canada, like the United States, does have a final arbiter in the form of a Supreme Court which may rule on the constitutional propriety of legislation and the jurisdictional scope of government.

The federal system of government in Canada, in keeping with the nation's Constitution, places the matter of security under the aegis of the national Parliament in Ottawa. That responsibility derives from Parliament's power to make laws for the peace, order, and good government in Canada, and Parliament's exclusive jurisdiction over national defence, criminal law, and criminal procedure. The provinces, on the other hand, have the significant responsibility for the administration of justice. Expressed in very simple terms, the Federal government makes the criminal laws and, with certain exceptions (e.g. The Customs Act), the provinces enforce them. While that is an accurate statement, areas exist where federal and provincial responsibilities tend to overlap. Response to terrorist incidents is one such area where controversy could arise, especially in regard to on-scene jurisdiction of police forces. The issues involved in this matter are described later in this chapter in the discussion of crisis-management machinery.

Ultimately it is the Prime Minister, in consultation with the Cabinet, who holds responsibility for matters affecting the security of Canada. Major decisions, therefore, emanate from that level. Because of the scope of government business facing the Prime Minister and Cabinet, however, it has been found necessary to establish specific Cabinet committees as a means to deal efficiently with the range of judgements and decisions which must be included. The purpose of the Cabinet committees is the review of matters within their purview, and the provision of information and advice to the Cabinet. In some cases, that function works in the opposite direction, and flows back to the departments associated with the committees. The burgeoning growth of government business, and the demands for increased efficiency, have encouraged the use of the committee system which first accelerated and proliferated during the Second World War. One such example is the Cabinet Committee on Security and Intelligence (CCSI), which oversees matters relating to the internal security of Canada. It is chaired by the Prime Minister, and includes those Ministers having a direct concern (within the scope of their departmental responsibilities) with threats to the nation's stability. The Committee, and certain bodies subordinate to it, function within the Privy Council Office (PCO); in layman's terms, the PCO may reasonably be called the Prime Minister's Department (*not* the Prime Minister's Office (PMO), which is a separate administrative agency).

A level below Cabinet there exist interdepartmental committees comprised of senior civil servants, frequently of deputy-minister status. The interdepartmental committees report to a Cabinet committee, or to the Cabinet itself in some cases. Below Cabinet level, for instance, is the Interdepartmental Committee on Security and Intelligence (ICSI). Prior to 1972, the ICSI existed as two separate components, one concerned with internal security matters and the other primarily devoted to intelligence of an external nature. 'The reason for merging these ... was recognition of the close relationship between external intelligence and domestic security, especially in an era of international terrorism....'[14] The change reflected a divorce from past practice which harked back to the years of the Second World War. The role of intelligence in that earlier period had been viewed as relating to matters of national defence, involving saboteurs and subversives of the standard cloak-and-dagger concept. The purpose of the new organization is to review proposals and recommendations being made to CCSI and, among other responsibilities, provide general oversight of federal counter-terrorism arrangements. It is through the ICSI, and its subordinate elements, that Canadian security policy is developed and monitored. Membership of the ICSI is shown in Figure 4.

*Figure 4* Interdepartmental Committee on Security and Intelligence (ICSI)

(DM Level)

Clerk of the Privy Council/Secretary of the Cabinet – Chairman
Intelligence and Security Co-ordinator of the Privy Council Office – Vice-Chairman
    Department of External Affairs
    Department of National Defence
    Department of Justice
    Department of Solicitor General
    Treasury Board
    RCMP
    CSIS
    Department of Transport
    Employment and Immigration
    Communications Security Establishment (Associate Member)
    Assistant Secretary to the Cabinet (Security and Intelligence), Secretary.

Reporting to the ICSI are two sub-committees which were also created during the reorganization in 1972. Those committees are: (1) the Intelligence Advisory Committee (IAC); and (2) the Security Advisory Committee (SAC). Composition of the two committees is shown in Figure 5. The IAC 'pools and reviews intelligence and threat analyses from a range of sources within the government and ensures that intelligence and information are disseminated to appropriate authorities'.[15] While the IAC prepares weekly assessments and other reports, it does not have a large permanent staff and makes use of 'working groups' comprised of members of appropriate government departments and agencies (e.g. CSIS, External Affairs, and Defence) to prepare its reports. It is of importance to note that Canada does not possess an external intelligence-gathering agency of the nature of the United Kingdom's MI-6, or the American CIA. In other words, the

Canadian Government does not engage in covert intelligence collection or operations in a formal sense. Intelligence is gained through a number of government sources, as explained later, but not through an organizational structure as is the situation in the other two nations.

The SAC, as its title implies, is concerned with issues relating to security activities of the government. The Committee reviews inter-departmental co-ordination and management and provides advice to ICSI on security policy and programmes, including counter-terrorism. A network of sub-committees and working groups operates under the supervision of the SAC to provide specialized knowledge and advice in such matters as computer security and the protection of nuclear materials. A major sub-component of the SAC is the Counter-Terrorism Sub-Committee.

*Figure 5* Intelligence Advisory Committee (IAC) and
Security Advisory Committee (SAC)

Intelligence and Security Co-ordinator of the Privy Council Office – Chairman
Department of External Affairs
Department of National Defence – Vice-Chairman
CSIS
Communications Security Establishment
Privy Council Office
Department of the Solicitor General
Employment and Immigration
RCMP
Senior representatives of other departments and agencies, on the invitation of the Committee.

Security Advisory Committee (SAC)
Deputy Solicitor General – Chairman
Privy Council Office
Treasury Board Secretariat
Department of Justice
Department of External Affairs
Department of National Defence
Department of Transport
Employment and Immigration
CSIS
RCMP
Communications Security Establishment

Before moving to the Department of the Solicitor General of Canada, which holds overall responsibility for counter-terrorism policy development, it will be useful to review briefly the roles of other government departments as they apply to counter-terrorism. In keeping with the rule of law as an underpinning of Canadian policy, the Department of Justice is a consultant on the legality of proposed measures, providing legal opinion on legislation as well as operational matters. The Department of National Defence (DND) has an obvious involvement directly associated with the physical protection of

Canadian sovereignty rights, and the responsibility to respond to a request for Aid to the Civil Power. The Department also maintains a standard military intelligence capability similar to that of other nations. The security of DND bases in Canada and overseas is shared with local police forces, but the Department does have its own Military Police (MP) component which includes responsibility for counter-terrorism functions.

The Department of External Affairs shares a close relationship with the Solicitor General's Department in matters of security. External Affairs has the task of ensuring the physical protection of Canadian missions and staff overseas; in that regard, some missions are provided with a small internal security body of Canadian Forces police (MPs). Members of CSIS are included in foreign posts for the purpose of vetting applicants seeking immigration to Canada. Guidelines for the screening of such persons, and any reason for a refusal to issue permission for entry to Canada, must be agreed between the two Departments. The Department of External Affairs is directly concerned with the conduct of foreign diplomats in Canada, especially in relation to unacceptable activities involving intelligence-gathering or subversion. Under such circumstances, it may well be the Department's task to declare those representatives as *persona non grata*, and demand their removal. The Department, as well, maintains a foreign geographic information section, and a Bureau of Economic Intelligence to assist with the development of Canadian trade and commerce at home and abroad. Within the Department there is a Coordinator for Emergency Preparedness who holds responsibility for preparing plans to cope with terrorist attacks on Canadian missions or citizens overseas. The task also involves co-ordination with the Solicitor General's Department to assist in the event of a terrorist threat to a foreign mission in Canada, as in the case of the seizure of the Turkish embassy in Ottawa in 1985. In conjunction, the Department of External Affairs works closely with the RCMP to ensure the protection of foreign diplomatic personnel and premises in Canada.

Three other departments having a place in response to the threat of terrorism are Supply and Services, Revenue Canada (Customs and Excise) and the Canadian Employment and Immigration Commission (CEIC). Supply and Services has responsibility for ensuring the adequacy of industrial-security measures, especially the protection of classified or sensitive information held by Canadian companies working on behalf of the Canadian, or other, governments. The task would be particularly applicable in regard to defence-related industries, or those producing goods and materials under a defence contract with other NATO nations. Employment and Immigration shares responsibility with CSIS in the review of the background of applicants for entry to

Canada. Revenue Canada has responsibility for operation of the Primary Inspection Line (PIL) at all official points of entry into Canada. The Customs officers endeavour to ensure that persons attempting to enter Canada are not known or suspected terrorists. Similarly, Customs officials must guard against the smuggling of contraband (weapons or explosives) into Canada or prevent the transit of such prohibited items through the nation.

Two other departments also have significant responsibilities within the federal counter-terrorism infrastructure. The Privy Council Office (PCO) 'supports the Prime Minister in the exercise of his general responsibility for national security and may review and comment on the operational effectiveness of the government's departments, agencies and systems in the aftermath of a specific terrorist incident'.[16] The Department of Transport is responsible for planning and directing policies and procedures concerning the security of the Canadian transportation system (land, air, marine). The Department maintains liaison with international organizations such as the International Civil Aviation Organization (ICAO), the International Air Transportation Association (IATA), and the International Maritime Organization (IMO). Airport security is a major responsibility of the Department; all international airports in Canada have an RCMP detachment which provides immediate security of a policing nature under an agreement with the Department. The Minister of Transport shares a lead Minister role with the Solicitor General and the Secretary of State for External Affairs. In the event of an aircraft hijacking, the minister has lead responsibility for response to the incident while the aircraft is in flight.

The development and oversight of Canadian counter-terrorism policy, nevertheless, is primarily vested in the Department of the Solicitor General of Canada. The Department was established under the Government Organization Act of 1966, which transferred powers, duties, and functions from the Minister of Justice and Attorney General of Canada in respect of:

(a) reformatories, prisons, and penitentiaries;
(b) parole and remissions; and
(c) the RCMP.

Since June 1984, the Department has also been assigned responsibility for the newly created Canadian Security Intelligence Service (CSIS), formerly the Security Service of the RCMP.

Located within the Solicitor General's Department is the Police and Security Branch (PSB); see Figure 6. The PSB grew out of the Security Planning and Research Group (SPARG), an advisory group formed after the October Crisis for the purpose of assisting the Solicitor General in the assessment of intelligence reports from the RCMP. SPARG was a badly misunderstood organization, considered by many members of the public and Parliament to represent the initial framework of a civilian security service. But the McDonald Report confirmed that SPARG had no operational duties of any sort and was not a parallel civilian Security Service. From December 1972, despite contention over its purpose and role, the original small Group expanded to a Branch with certain responsibilities for crime prevention and law-enforcement matters. The current mandate of the PSB is the 'analyses [of] policy initiatives, operational policy issues and operational submissions in the areas of law enforcement and national security to provide appropriate advice to the Minister and the Deputy Solicitor General.'[17] It is also the responsibility of the Branch to initiate, develop, and administer government and Ministry policy for law enforcement and national security matters, and to manage the Solicitor General's direct responsibility for the national-security programme including contingency planning and co-ordination of the Federal government's counter-terrorism programme. The PSB, headed by an Assistant Deputy Solicitor General, consists of three major components; counter-terrorism matters are the concern of the Security Planning and Coordination Directorate. It should be noted that the SAC Secretariat also comes under the purview of that organization. Thus, it might be said that much of Canadian counter-terrorism policy originates with the Security Planning and Coordination Directorate of the Solicitor General's Department.

*Figure 6* Police and Security Branch (PSB)

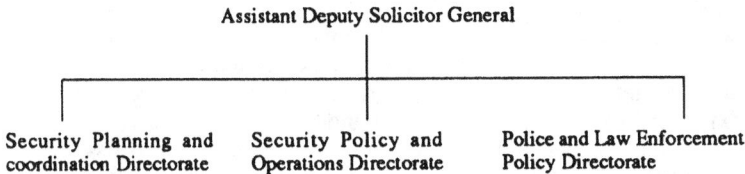

Assistant Deputy Solicitor General

| Security Planning and coordination Directorate | Security Policy and Operations Directorate | Police and Law Enforcement Policy Directorate |
|---|---|---|

At the provincial level, it is the function of each province's Attorney-General (or Minister of Justice) to oversee the operations of the provincial/municipal law-enforcement agencies, as well as the administration of justice. Operations of federal agencies within the provincial sphere are arranged and co-ordinated by that means. Within each province there are Police Acts and police commissions which establish regulations and advise upon the standards and operations of provincial and municipal law-enforcement bodies. A detailed explanation of policing arrangements, organization, and relationships in Canada is provided in the next chapter.

'In the USA [sic] the governmental system starts at the bottom and works to the top and the top merely caps an already existing edifice'.[18] Similar by virtue of a federal character, government in Canada does not share that definition in the sense that authority tends to flow downwards in Canada to the provinces, and through them, to the counties and municipalities. The closest approximation in the United Kingdom is the system of municipalities, who derive their limited span of responsibility from Parliament, and exist at the pleasure of Parliament. Conspicuous differences of this sort necessitate a brief examination of the features of the US governmental system which impact upon counter-terrorism policy development, decision-making, and crisis-management.

Foremost is the Constitution of the United States, which is a written document whose provisions determine the structure of the government, assign authority, and enshrine human rights. Guarantees of personal freedoms are contained in the Bill of Rights, and cannot be abridged by the Federal or State governments. Attempts to introduce legislation or to tighten laws directed toward constraining terrorism have continually encountered opposition based upon fears of endangering the civil rights of American citizens. Controversy was acrimonious in the debate over relaxing the Levi Guidelines imposed on FBI operations in the post-Watergate period. Eight years passed before President Reagan's Attorney General, William French Smith, managed a loosening of restrictions on the domestic intelligence-gathering community. The American Constitution established the principle of 'separation of powers' in the US Government, a system of checks and balances between the executive (President), the legislature (Congress), and the judiciary (Supreme Court). Each holds certain reserved powers so that neither the executive nor the legislature can act to much effect without the concurrence of the other, and, in turn, their action might possibly be declared unconstitutional by the judiciary. As Finer explained, 'the existence of a set of political checks and balances ... imports friction and delays into the decision-making and policy-executing processes of the government. The USA is particularly rich in such devices'.[19]

The Cabinet system of government does not obtain to the same degree in the United States as it does in Canada and the United Kingdom; that is, the actions and decisions of government are not focused in one powerful directing body. A presidential Cabinet does exist and has a significant role, but it is essentially an advisory grouping composed of the heads (Secretaries) of major government departments, and who are non-elected appointees of the President. The President may, or may not, make much use of his Cabinet because it is a non-statutory adjunct, lacking the political or administrative power of its Canadian and British counterparts. Similarly, a government or administration will not be forced to resign as the consequence of an embarrassing error of management or mistaken policy decision on the part of the executive body, as would occur in Canada or Britain. Leading the executive branch of the US Government is the President of the United States. The incumbent is constitutionally head of the Civil Service, commands the Armed Forces, appoints and receives ambassadors, signs treaties, and proposes legislation to the Congress. Powerful and prestigious as the office may be, the President's capability to 'get things done', in his way and in a hurry, is much more constrained than is that of a Prime Minister in Canada or the United Kingdom. Graham Allison's descriptions of President Kennedy's problems in resolving certain situations during the Cuban Missile Crisis provide excellent illustrations of the frustrations and hurdles which must be overcome.

The Congress, a bicameral legislature, is yet another brake upon 'hasty, rash and ill considered legislation'.[20] The House of Representatives and the Senate have roughly equal powers, but their membership and tenure are dissimilar. The House of Representatives (Congressmen) is elected every two years, and representation is based upon population distribution within the States. One-third of the Senate (Senators) is elected every two years, with representation fixed at two Senators per State. Congressmen, facing an election challenge every two years, must be extremely sensitive to the immediate currents of opinion within the districts which they serve. Senators, on the other hand, have a certain advantage of experience over a longer period, and tend to be regarded with rather more importance. The latter factor can be disadvantageous when a Senator, representing a sparsely populated constituency, rises to the chairmanship of an influential Senate committee simply by means of seniority (number of terms in office). One other factor associated with the electoral process is the manner by which candidates seek and obtain their election. Selection is not made by political party organizations, as in Canada and the United Kingdom, rather the aspiring candidate simply runs in a primary election, and is chosen by the local electorate. Because political parties exercise little control in this procedure (with certain exceptions, e.g. where a powerful political 'machine' has traditional influence), members of Congress tend to support their chosen party on many issues while, at the same time, continuing to regard themselves as independent representatives of their districts or States. Thus, they often vote as they believe best suits the interests of their constituents. It is because of this degree of independence that a President may be able to move Congress to support his legislative proposals, even when Congress is not controlled by the President's political party. The opposite situation can also arise of course.

A significant difference between the legislatures of the United States, the United Kingdom, and Canada is the fact that Congress is a law-initiating body. Bills may be introduced in either chamber, although both must concur before a measure is passed into law. The President may propose legislation, but only Congress may legislate. Congress may refuse to pass measures that the President puts before it, or it may amend the measures (sometimes beyond recognition), or it may pass measures which the President dislikes, forcing them through by overriding the presidential veto by means of a two-thirds majority in both Houses. In that manner, Congress has the power to control finances, granting the amounts it wishes, or attaching riders to bills appropriating money. Similarly, presidential appointments, and treaties negotiated by the President, must be approved by a two-thirds majority vote of the Senate. The delay in achieving a new extradition treaty between the United States and the United Kingdom, finally authorized in 1986, was a consequence of the need to convince the Senate; the Irish–American lobby put much pressure on the Senate in an effort to block the ratification.

The President is not helpless in the face of congressional powers. S.E. Finer described the weapons which lie at the President's disposal, perhaps one of the strongest being the President's position as the perceived focal point of American Government.[21] President Lyndon Johnson was possibly the most adept in the modern use of a President's major resource: the ability to bargain and to parley. Notwithstanding, the President of the United States does not have the scope to function with the the almost arbitrary disdain of a Canadian or British Prime Minister and Cabinet. Nor has an American President the possibility of an unlimited tenure in office; not for him the fifteen years of government leadership enjoyed by Pierre Trudeau. In fact, a President enjoying a second term finds that his influence begins to wane as time passes his mid-term mark.

Passage of bills in the US legislature is a much more complex and less direct system than that which obtains in Canada and the United Kingdom. It is much more straightforward and controlled by the executive in the Canadian and British Governments, and is a matter of some consequence in relation to the budget process. Descriptions of the procedure are available in several texts noted in the bibliography of this research. Sufficient for the moment is to note that bills originated in either US legislative chamber must reach, and survive, committee, and frequently sub-committee, hearings in a gradual progression toward legal status. Differences of opinion must be settled in conference committees, and compromise versions returned to each House for final approval. The President may then veto a bill, which must be returned to Congress in an attempt to secure the necessary two-thirds majorities for passage. It can be seen that it is not a simple matter to obtain the needed consensus to enact legislation, or to obtain funding to implement measures in response to terrorism.

As with Canada and the United Kingdom, the American bureaucracy is allied to the legislature and the executive in the shaping of policy. The bureaucracy in the USA, however, is not dominated by the executive to the extent known in the Canadian and British Governments. Senior appointments in the US bureaucracy are made on a political basis:

> The American practice of staffing their top ranks with politicians, the friends of the administration in power, rather than with career-bureaucrats (the permanent secretaries, etc., of the British [and Canadian] system) has permitted the departments to crumble into their primary units, and bureaux. Unlike the departments themselves, these are headed by career officials and are cohesive units, although few, if any, of these bureau chiefs care a fig for the bureau next to them.[22]

Finer's comments provide an insight into some of the problems related to policy development within the US government. His remarks also serve to indicate the reality of 'turf' and jurisdictional frictions raised by policy critics such as Motley, Livingstone, *et al.* A further complication, again pointed to by Finer, concerns control and influence over the bureaucracy:

> ... each of the main secretaryships – the main departments of state, whose members sit in the Presidential Cabinet, like the Department of State and the Treasury – is subjected to a two-way stretch. In theory it owes its allegiance only to its head – the president. In practice, if it wants to see its budget through, if it wishes to retain its powers and its private way of doing things, it had best be friends with the congressional committees which exercise the power, not only of scrutinizing proposed legislation and of withholding funds, but of generally supervising groups of executive agencies. The department, or a bureau in a department, faces two ways.[23]

Department and bureau heads, therefore, must not only seek the President's support for programmes and measures, but must also secure the approval of Congress. Lacking one or the other makes it an extremely difficult proposition to initiate action. Agreement of the two major bodies (i.e. the executive and the legislature) does not guarantee unopposed implementation. Pressure groups may decide that a constitutional principle has been violated or threatened, and may turn to the Supreme Court for a decision.

As stated previously, government in the USA begins at grass-roots level in villages, townships, counties, and municipalities, and works its way up to State level. At that juncture, each State possesses a governor, legislature (bicameral in all but one), and a supreme court. The State and federal bodies are mirror images in most respects and they are legally co-equals; that is,

> neither may legally invade the jurisdiction of the other, nor override nor veto the operations of the other in the conducting of its own peculiar set of duties; the operations of each governing authority (i.e. the national and the state authorities) are usually executed by their own sets of officers, neither of whom may invade or veto the work of the other set in the execution of their due powers.[24]

Power not specifically allocated to the Federal government is assumed to belong to the States. While the Supreme Court has extensively widened the powers and influence of the federal sector in recent years, the States still maintain broad local control. The enactment of criminal law, for instance, is not the sole prerogative of the central governing body. Jurisdiction becomes a major issue under such conditions, as in the cases of the assassination of an anti-Khomeini supporter in Maryland, and the attempted murder of a Libyan student in Colorado. The multiplicity of governing authorities, and legal disputation, has bedevilled the expeditious development and implementation of Federal government policy.

Despite the 'separation of powers' principle and the checks and balances operative between the three branches of US Government, the President stands at the pinnacle of the nation. Particularly in times of tension and stress, it is the President who must shoulder the overall responsibility, making the crucial judgements and decisions involving domestic and international issues. Congress and the Supreme Court may criticize, amend, or support in the aftermath, but at the time of crisis the Office of the President must assume immediate control. It is one reason why the President is accompanied everywhere by an aide who carries the electronic means to release the nation's awesome nuclear arsenal.

'The President needs help.' (The reader may also require assistance with an understanding of the profusion of names and titles associated with the bureaucracies in Canada, the USA, and the United Kingdom. For that reason, a brief comment is provided at note 96.)[25] Staff members of the White House Office, the Bureau of the Budget, and the Cabinet form part of the response to that observation. One other senior forum is available to the incumbent for assistance in analysing, integrating, and facilitating foreign, defence, and intelligence policy decisions. That agency is the National Security Council (NSC), created by an Act of Congress in 1947 in recognition of the relationship between diplomatic, military, and political affairs which grew out of the Second World War experience.

The National Security Council is unique among U.S. governmental agencies. Aside from the President's Cabinet, it is the highest level, executive branch advisory and coordinating body on national security affairs. Unlike the Cabinet, it is based on statutory authority.[26]

Because the US counter-terrorism infrastructure functions under the aegis of the NSC, the Council is of some consequence in the development and direction of policy and policy measures.

The original membership of the NSC included only the department heads of State, Defence, Army, Navy, and Air Force, with the CIA acting in an advisory capacity. The President could, as required, name other executive department heads to sit on the Council. From the time of its inception, the NSC has undergone changes and various degrees of influence. Under President Truman, the Council was of subordinate use, whereas Eisenhower made it a principal instrument in both the formulation and implementation of national-security policy. Suffering varying fortunes in the Kennedy–Johnson–Nixon–Ford–Carter years, the NSC under President Reagan again adopted a position more in keeping with the Eisenhower era. The posture of the NSC in the 1980s returned to that of a decision-facilitating instrument, with the NSC staff co-ordinating policy formulation among the agencies represented, and ensuring that decisions taken by the President have effective implementation.

The goal is to provide the President with the means to make the most vital decisions as related to national security, including defense programs, budget, force structures, and resource allocations – in brief, to create and implement national strategy.[27]

The Lod and Munich massacres demonstrated to the world that terrorists were capable of more than kidnapping and hijacking; even individual assassinations paled in the glare of publicity attached to the two atrocities. Recognizing a need for co-ordinated federal action to counter the menace, President Nixon directed the formation of the Cabinet Committee to Combat Terrorism in September 1972, as another resource for presidential assistance. Chaired by the Secretary of State, the Committee was comprised of the Secretaries of the Treasury, Defence, Transportation, the Attorney General, the Ambassador to the United Nations, the Directors of the CIA and the FBI, and the Assistant to the President for Domestic Affairs. The early perception of terrorism as principally a foreign, or international threat was reflected in the allocation of the chairmanship. It is an influence which continues through current arrangements in terrorism response.

The Cabinet Committee met only once, and was abolished in 1977 during the Carter administration. The solitary meeting was not quite as unremarkable as it may appear, however, as several important and lasting decisions were achieved at the gathering. A Working Group, consisting of designated senior representatives of the Cabinet Committee, was established. The Working Group provided the impetus for an ongoing recognition of the threat of terrorism, and for a modicum of co-ordinated response by various agencies. One failed effort of the Cabinet Committee meeting was the President's direction that the UN ambassador, in conjunction with the Secretary of State, should attempt to secure a draft convention opposing terrorist activity. While the proposal foundered in the General Assembly on the inability to obtain a consensus in regard to a definition of terrorism, the publicity generated was of considerable value. The singular meeting of the Cabinet Committee also resulted in the establishment of certain fundamental guidelines for response to terrorism which have essentially remained unaltered. The guidelines, arguably followed by every US administration since 1972, were as follows: (1) a no-concessions policy in reply to terrorist demands; (2) host governments have a responsibility for anti-terrorist protective measures; and (3) terrorist acts should be dealt with as criminal matters. The approach of the Committee was a preventive mandate, laying emphasis upon the sharing of intelligence information on an international basis.

For those persons who have worked in a government bureaucracy, William R. Farrell's description of 'How the Organizations Responded' makes understandable, if not surprising, reading.[28] 'Immediately after President Nixon's mandate in 1972 there was a high-level interest, but this soon trailed off as matters became more routine.'[29] A corresponding magazine article is even more illuminating, and is deserving of lengthy quotation:

> It is axiomatic in government that a committee's importance diminishes with the passage of time, no matter what its business. At first, assistant secretaries and under-secretaries attended the meetings [of the Working Group]. After a while, however, no one above the rank of colonel was showing up. Moreover, some two dozen departments and agencies were represented ... The meetings were usually 75 or 100 people strong. Not only were there too many people in one room to get anything done but the various representatives wouldn't talk with one another. The issues were too sensitive. A lot of information was classified, and no one was sure who could (or should) know what. The FBI, for example, steadfastly insisted that it had the terrorist problem solved.[30]

Between the years 1972 and 1978, the chairmanship of the Working Group, a State Department responsibility, changed seven times. A review of the qualifications of those who held the chairman's post reveals little background experience which would have supported appointment for the purpose of counter-terrorism policy development. In the summer of 1976 the State Department established the Office for Combatting Terrorism to assist the chairman, and to provide an operational focus for managing international terrorist incidents. But service in that cell was known as a 'dead-end assignment, graveyard, and a no-win situation'.[31] Terrorism response was obviously not a high priority or high-profile task throughout the period. The attitude prevailed despite the Hearst incident, the death of Ambassador Davies in Cyprus, the seizure of the French embassy at the Hague by members of the JRA (during which the nearby US embassy served as a command centre), an attempt to fire a RPG-7 rocket launcher at an El Al flight at Orly airport, the Fraunces Tavern bombing by the FALN in New York, the kidnapping of Peter Lorenz in West Berlin, and the seizure of the US consulate in Kuala Lumpur by the JRA, amongst a host of other prominent terrorist attacks, many of which directly involved Americans.

The Carter administration received much criticism for errors and blunders surrounding its counter-terrorism policy. Human-rights concerns, which formed the core of the Carter approach, have been particularly subject to condemnation. Nonetheless, as Livingstone grudgingly admits, a favourable revamping of the institutional machinery for response to terrorism was initiated during the Carter era. The changes came about as a result of an extensive review of US Government policy and capabilities with regard to responding to the problem of terrorism. The review, ordered by the NSC, prompted the issue of Presidential Review Memorandum 30 (PRM-30) which recommended a number of changes to the US counter-terrorism programme. A tri-level organizational structure was introduced (see Figure 7), in conjunction with four basic programme components: Prevention; Deterrence; Reaction; and, Prediction. Two other steps were taken slightly later: the position of the head of the Office to Combat Terrorism in the State Department was elevated to the rank of ambassador, and Anthony C.E. Quainton was appointed as incumbent. Quainton held the responsibility for an unprecedented three years, an achievement sufficient to generate the phrase 'pre-and-post Quainton' to signify the gradually increased influence of the Office.[32]

The Carter Memorandum (PRM-30) abolished the Nixon Cabinet Committee, replacing it with a Special Coordination Committee (SCC) of the NSC. The SCC functioned under the chairmanship of the Assistant to the President for National Security Affairs, with membership duplicating that of the NSC. The SCC was expected to provide support for the President should he have wished to participate in the management of response to a specific terrorist incident. The SCC, therefore, was both a policy directing body and an advisory body for operational situations. It was constrained in its role, however, by the mandate: 'Only in the event of a major incident, requiring the highest level of decision-making, will the SCC become involved.'[33]

*Figure 7* US trilevel counter-terrorism structure

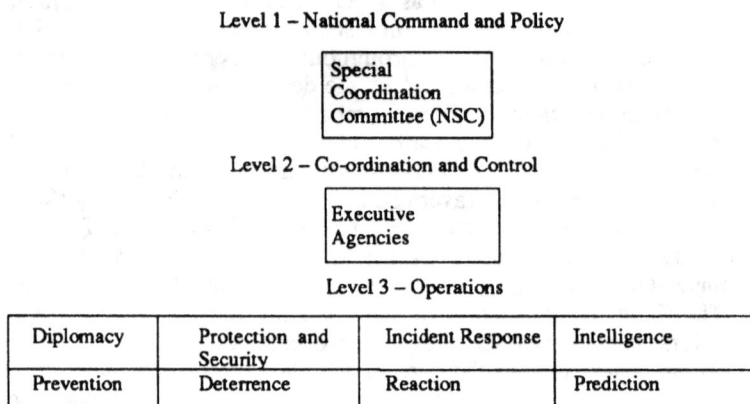

Level 1 – National Command and Policy

| Special Coordination Committee (NSC) |
| --- |

Level 2 – Co-ordination and Control

| Executive Agencies |
| --- |

Level 3 – Operations

| Diplomacy | Protection and Security | Incident Response | Intelligence |
| --- | --- | --- | --- |
| Prevention | Deterrence | Reaction | Prediction |

*Figure 8* US anti-terrorism programme organization

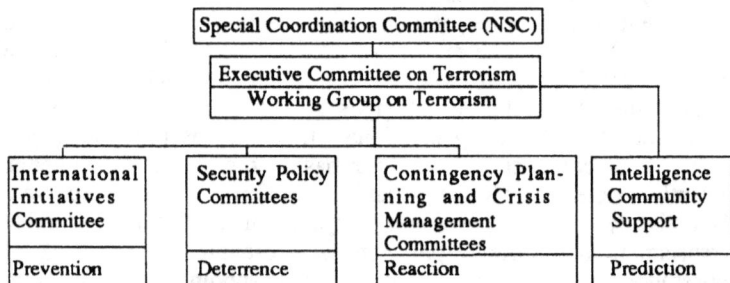

| Special Coordination Committee (NSC) |
| --- |
| Executive Committee on Terrorism |
| Working Group on Terrorism |

| International Initiatives Committee | Security Policy Committees | Contingency Planning and Crisis Management Committees | Intelligence Community Support |
| --- | --- | --- | --- |
| Prevention | Deterrence | Reaction | Prediction |

Directly subordinate to the SCC was the interagency Executive Committee on Terrorism (ECT), with its own Working Group on Terrorism (WGT). The chairman and deputy-chairman for each body were the State and the Justice Department representatives, respectively. The ECT was charged with matters of government-wide policy formulation and operational co-ordination. It was, as well, 'especially concerned with response to major terrorism incidents and related issues, including periodic testing and evaluation of response capabilities. The ECT was responsible also for long range anti-terrorism [sic] program planning and analysis.'[34] National Security Advisor Zbigniew Brzezinski clarified the role of the ECT and its Working Group in 1977, stating in a memo that its 'primary concern' would be 'policy, coordination and information exchange'.[35] The two groups were not to have responsibility for the management of a terrorist incident. The latter task fell under the operation of the 'lead agency' system, essentially similar to the 'lead Minister' concept used by the Canadian and British Governments. The NSC/SCC, as well, would only take control if the responsible agency was unable, or failed, to resolve the incident.

The ECT had a relatively small membership, consisting of representatives from the departments of State, Defence, Treasury, Transportation, Energy, the CIA, and the NSC staff. In contrast, the Working Group was much larger, and eventually included 'some twenty-nine agencies with an interest in the four basic anti-terrorist program components'.[36] Some controversy arose over the effectiveness of the WGT based on its size, the comments reflecting similar criticism of the Nixon Committee's Working Group. The WGT has been described as a 'valuable forum', but also castigated because the chairman often 'found it easier to work with members on a one-to-one basis rather than as part of a fully constituted committee'.[37] An attempt was made to lessen the traditional interagency jurisdictional infighting, while developing better working relationships, through the establishment of WGT sub-committees. Four major sub-committees were formed which conformed to the four components of the anti-terrorism programme (see Figure 8), and which permitted a degree of specialization as well as a division between foreign and domestic responsibilities. The Carter administration continued with the original Nixon approach of viewing terrorism as primarily a non-domestic threat, but took that perspective a step further by assigning to the State Department the oversight for co-ordination of US response to both domestic and international terrorism. The arrangement still prevails, although the operative function conforms to the lead agency concept.

Ambassador Quainton left office in 1981, to be replaced by Robert M. Sayre, and the programme underwent yet another reorganization. Secretary of State Alexander Haig quickly proclaimed that 'clear signals were broadcast to the world that terrorism would be an extremely sensitive topic'.[38] The ECT (in what was fundamentally a change of title) became the Interdepartmental Group on Terrorism, known in bureaucratic shorthand as the IG/T, and the WGT was disbanded. In a move to enhance the influence of the Office for Combatting Terrorism, and to combine resources, the Office was placed in a direct reporting position to the Department of State's Under-Secretary for Management. The State Department's Office of Security was in a similar position, so that by such an arrangement 'planning and policy as reflected in the counterterrorism [sic] office, and the resources for response to threats represented in the security office ... [were] ... both under a single jurisdiction'.[39] Ambassador Sayre held his post for two years, then was replaced by Ambassador Robert B. Oakley. Ambassador Oakley said of yet another organizational change: 'Over the past five years we have tried several configurations and have now settled down to a reasonably effective structure.'[40] Chairmanship of the IG/T remained the task of Oakley's renamed Office for Counter-Terrorism and Emergency Planning. Oakley's Office for Counter-Terrorism and Emergency Planning also acquired a new acronym: M/CTP. The M/CTP retained the traditional task of co-ordination of US agencies in the combating of terrorism, plus provision of technical support, as opposed to involvement with counter-terrorist operations.

Returning briefly to the IG/T, its role of developing policy recommendations for consideration by the President and the NSC continued as before. The responsibility included issues which ranged across

> improvements in U.S. domestic legislation, bilateral treaties, and multilateral conventions, through collection, analysis, and exchange of intelligence, to programs for assistance to or exchange with other governments in various fields of anti-terrorist activity, better physical security and warning systems for our missions abroad, and the consideration of more active measures to deter or preempt terrorist action.[41]

The IG/T was supported in that work by two adjunct groups: a Technical Support Working Group (TSWG), with the objective of exchanging information and co-ordinating research and development on technical measures; and, an Exercise Committee to co-ordinate national-level multi-agency counter-terrorism exercises. Both the IG/T and the M/CTP developed certain goals to guide and govern their deliberations: attainment of effective co-ordinated action; integration of passive and active measures; the full utilization of intelligence efforts; and increased international co-operation. Activity in the latter area, international co-operation, has extended to bilateral talks with senior officials in foreign countries with the aim of improving intelligence sharing, provision of better physical protection of US facilities overseas, and the closing of legal loopholes in extradition procedures. Other diplomatic exchanges have extended to NATO meetings, summit talks, and through EEC conferences.

The M/CTP was given additional responsibilities over the period from 1982, specifically in regard to emergency-action planning, conduct of exercises, and anti-terrorist assistance programmes. To carry out the new duties, the M/CTP was organized into three basic divisions: (1) Counter-terrorism Policy; (2) Anti-terrorism Assistance; and (3) Emergency Planning and Exercises. The Counter-terrorism Policy cell was designated to have an analytical base in terms of geographic areas, terrorist groups, and functional matters, for the purpose of interfacing with other bureaux and agencies at the working level. The underlying concept was to 'pull together for senior decision-makers and the IG/T the kind of information they must have in formulating policy and resolving a crisis'.[42] The Anti-terrorism Assistance cell was organized as a technical group with the task of assisting and conducting professional exchanges with civilian anti-terrorism authorities around the world. Under the Anti-terrorism Assistance Program, authorized by Congress in 1983, training has been made available for members of friendly foreign governments, and includes basic functions such as airport security as well as more sophisticated aspects of government policy. The role of the Emergency Planning and Exercise group has been primarily that of preparing US personnel to meet terrorist threats overseas and to develop emergency action plans at US facilities. It has been a requirement that engendered a close working relationship with the US Department of Defense.

Comfortable though he may have been with the revised infrastructure, others did not share Ambassador Oakley's opinion. The *Report of the Secretary of State's Advisory Panel on Overseas Security*, (known as The Inman Report from the name of its chairman, Admiral Bobby R. Inman, USN (Ret.)) published in June 1985, recommended a number of changes.[43] Among the suggestions put forward were the dismantling of the Office of Counter Terrorism and Emergency Planning, and the subsuming of its responsibilities elsewhere in the State Department. A major proposal, in conjunction with that suggestion, was the formation of a new Bureau of Diplomatic Security. The concept was based on two perceived needs:

(a) To improve physical security measures, both for US facilities overseas and for protection of foreign diplomatic missions in the USA.
(b) To pursue counter-terrorism efforts by means of international diplomacy.[44]

The Inman Advisory Panel believed that the aims could best be accomplished by enlarging the responsibilities of the Office of Security, requiring the creation of a new bureau which would remain the purview of the Under Secretary for Management. At the same time, it was recommended that the diplomatic activities of Ambassador Oakley's Office should be transferred to the Under Secretary for Political Affairs.

The Inman Report provided an indication of the continuing controversy over counter-terrorism policy and policy measures within the US Government. Notwithstanding, many of the report's proposals were accepted; several of those agreed for adoption are examined in the next chapter. Prominent restructuring was announced in November 1985, as follows:

— formation of a new Bureau of Diplomatic Security;
— reorganization of the Bureau of Administration and Security, to become the Bureau of Administration; and
— establishment of the Office of Ambassador-at-Large for Counter-Terrorism (S/CT).

The responsibilities of the M/CTP were transferred to the newly created Bureau of Diplomatic Security, Chairmanship of the IG/T remained with the S/CT. An outline of the Bureau's structure is shown at Figure 9.

The outcome of the Inman Report has resulted in an enlarged physical-security organization within the US Department of State. Protective measures in response to the threat of terrorism have received increased emphasis, and operational matters have been placed under one head. But, while the terrorism cell has been enlarged, it is the smallest of three bodies vying for the attention of the bureau head who holds the same status (i.e. assistant secretary), as did Oakley when in charge of the Office of Counter-Terrorism. An advantage could obtain, however, from the closer positioning of the counter-terrorism resources of the former M/CTP with those of the operationally oriented security personnel. The overall consequence, of course, has been yet another division in matters of response: the S/CT pursuing diplomatic avenues (which the Inman Report considered 'may not produce substantive results, but an aggressive, determined effort must be undertaken ...'),[45] and the new bureau seeking to improve protective security.

Farrell had an interesting observation on the earlier juxtapositioning of the M/CTP and the Office of Security:

> The melding of the Office to Combat Terrorism with those dealing with security will be interesting. The former is composed of foreign service officers where the latter is not. Both offices have different career patterns and world views.[46]

Intra-agency friction and opposition is a well-known source of difficulty at government level, to say nothing of inter-agency and interdepartmental conflicts. Farrell's comments remain very appropriate under the new organizational structure.

The decision-making machinery associated with US response to terrorism has been dynamic, in the sense that it has undergone frequent modifications. The focus is at a high level, including the President and the approximately ten departments and agencies comprising the IG/T, as well as the influence of the NSC. That level of decision-making was clearly illustrated in the proceedings associated with the US military

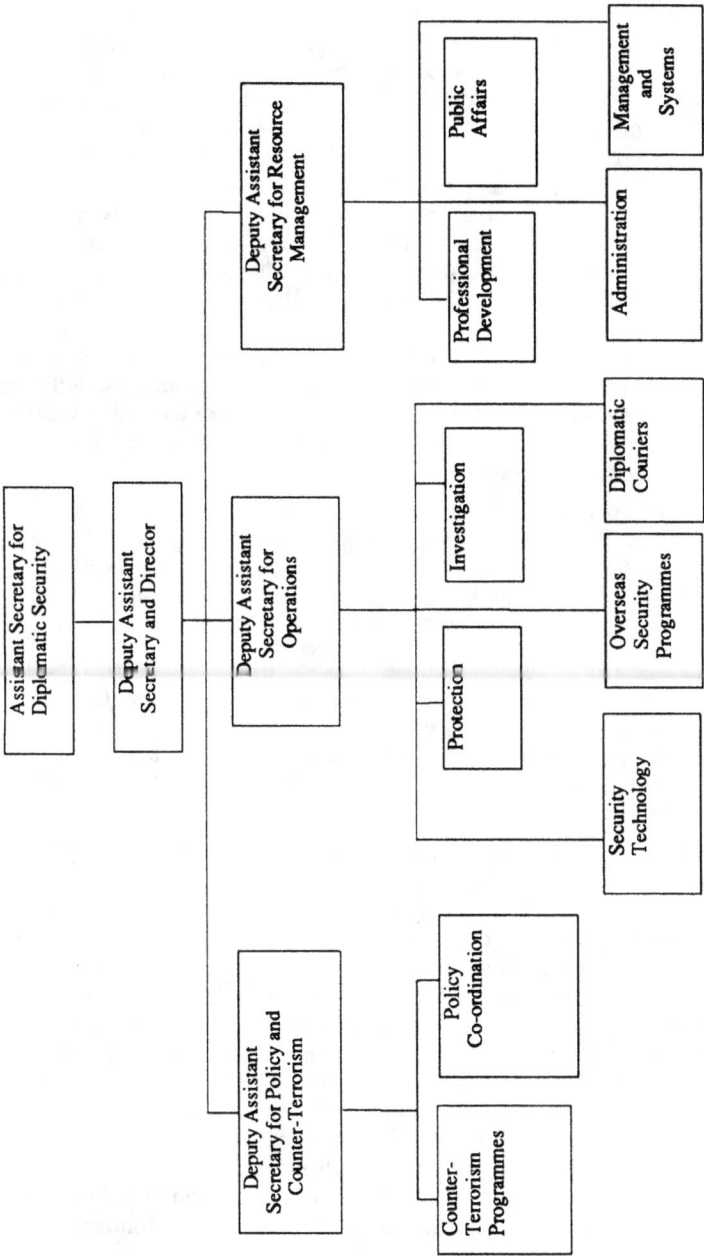

*Figure 9* US State Department Bureau of Diplomatic Security

retaliation raid on Libya in 1986, and the earlier incident with an Egyptian commercial airliner in 1985. Under certain circumstances it could 'involve as many as 30 or more Federal agencies ... in one situation or another'.[47] The heads of the principal departments of the US Government (e.g. Justice, Treasury, Defense) play a major role in the decision-making process through the IG/T and NSC. Similarly, the elaborate American intelligence community has a significant place as a contributor. The participation of the various departments and the intelligence resources are better illustrated as part of the crisis-management mechanisms, and in the next chapter on Resources and Capabilities. Prior to that, however, the British system of decision-making is examined next.

'American commentators and students often think there is something incongruous about the existence of monarchical institutions within a democratic system of government. In fact, many ... of the world's stable democratic systems are monarchical in form ....'[48] The United Kingdom is a constitutional monarchy whereby

> law the government ... is vested in a composite body styled the Crown-in-Parliament. This consists of the Sovereign, nominally the supreme executive, in whose name ministers carry out duties with which they have been charged – either by custom and precedent (the 'prerogative powers') or by statute; of the House of Lords; and of the House of Commons.[49]

The circumstances of a constitutional monarchy, the Crown, and the Royal Prerogative frequently give rise to some confusion. Anthony H. Birch clarifies these matters to a reasonable degree in his publication *The British System of Government*, a portion of which is quoted as follows:

> The roles of the British monarch may be categorized as symbolic, social and political. The first two need not concern us ... The political role ... has changed dramatically since the beginning of the nineteenth century, though without any legislative measure or other overt action to which a date can be given. To explain how this change took place it will be helpful to distinguish the nature of the Royal Prerogative from the personal discretion enjoyed by the reigning monarch. The Royal Prerogative is a term which denotes the authority which rests with the Crown, as distinct from that which rests with Parliament or the courts. Thus, it is within the Royal Prerogative to enter into diplomatic relations with other states and to conclude treaties with them; to command the armed forces, to declare war and to make peace; to appoint judges, to initiate criminal prosecutions, and to pardon offenders; to

summon, prorogue and to dissolve Parliament; to appoint ministers, including the Prime Minister; to confer honours; to create peers, and to appoint bishops of the Church of England. All these acts, and others, are acts performed in the name of the Crown, and the way in which they are performed cannot be questioned or controlled by the courts. Most of them are equally free from parliamentary control ....

The extent of the Royal Prerogative has not diminished appreciably during the last 200 years. What has happened is that, whereas 200 years ago the reigning monarch performed many or most of these acts at his own discretion, today the monarch performs the acts on the advice of ministers or other persons. The acts are performed in the name of the Crown, but except in a few special cases the decision is no longer taken by the monarch. The conduct of foreign affairs is in the hands of the Prime Minister and the Cabinet, as are decisions about defence policy; judges are appointed by the monarch on the advice of the Prime Minister or the Lord Chancellor; ministers are appointed on the advice of the Prime Minister, and on his advice alone; honours are conferred and other appointments are made on the advice of a variety of persons.[50]

Birch goes on to compare the monarch's role today with that of a sports referee, wherein the referee is in charge of the match. But, the referee 'exercises ... control within strict rules which he did not make and cannot influence'.[51] To maintain his 'career' as a referee there are three indiscretions which must be avoided: (1) interference, except when a rule has been violated; (2) partiality; and (3) involvement in disputes between players. The British monarchy has mastered these rules admirably and appears unlikely to have its career disturbed.

A second, sometimes confusing, feature of British Government is the unitary nature of the state. Within the United Kingdom, 'No territorial assembly inside its frontiers enjoys a coequal legal status to that of the Parliament of Westminster.'[52] Despite the existence of the territorial areas of England, Wales, Scotland, and Northern Ireland, government emanates from Parliament. As discussed later, until 1972 Northern Ireland did have a semi-autonomous parliament at Stormont, but that right was rescinded by Westminster following the outbreak of the troubles in 1969. Thus, unlike the federal structures of Canada and the USA, the United Kingdom does not contain major governing subunits within its regional entities of England, Wales, Scotland, and Northern Ireland. The closest approximation in the United Kingdom may be the system of local authorities. It must be noted, however, that specific ministries (e.g. the Scottish Office, Welsh Office, and Northern Ireland

Office) within the government structure have a primary responsibility for the administration of many policy areas for these three regions. Illogically, there are no equivalent regional departmental offices for areas of England such as the South-West, the Midlands, the North-West, or the North-East.

Scotland joined with England and Wales in a voluntary political union in 1707. Some Scottish institutions remained intact, nonetheless, such as 'a distinctive legal system, a distinctive (and rather advanced) educational system, and the Presbyterian Church of Scotland'.[53] A separate ministry, the Scottish Office, exists within the British Government to administer the internal affairs of Scotland. Legislation, if it pertains only to Scotland, is scrutinized by the Scottish Grand Committee before being enacted by Parliament. Controversy over matters resembling provincial or States 'rights' as occurs in North America is the subject of Cabinet discussion and decision in the United Kingdom, not intergovernmental or judicial debate. Northern Ireland, which enjoyed a degree of internal autonomy through its own parliament at Stormont from 1921 until 1972, is now governed directly by the British Parliament at Westminster. Akin to the Scottish situation, a separate ministry, the Northern Ireland Office, has been formed in the British Government. Similarly, legislation affecting Northern Ireland is drawn up, debated, and passed by Parliament with Cabinet sanction.

Jurisdictional problems, therefore, do not arise in the United Kingdom to the extent that they create difficulties in the two North American nations. That is not to say that such conflicts do not occur; jurisdictional parameters are very much a reality, for instance, both within and between law-enforcement agencies, and such frictions are examined in the next chapter. It is sufficient for the moment to state that the centralized nature of British Government significantly precludes many of the obstacles facing legislators and administrators in Canada and the USA. Before looking more closely at the structure of government, mention must be made of the British Constitution. Many authorities refer to it as being unwritten; S.F. Finer preferred what is, perhaps, a more accurate distinction: 'uncodified'.[54] 'To find the constitutional position on any one point, any (or all) of five different sources must be consulted.' Finer cited: (1) statutes; (2) judicial pronouncements; (3) principles of Common Law; (4) the *lex et consuetudo parliamenti* (body of law relating to status and operation of Parliament and its members); and (5) 'the conventions of the Constitution'.[55] As Finer pointed out, all of the foregoing with the exception of the conventions are 'in one way or another, written down'. The British Constitution, therefore, is more correctly described as not being codified in the manner of the Constitutions of Canada and the USA, although to a large degree it is in a written form.

Reference has been made earlier that Canada, like the United Kingdom, combines the executive and legislative functions of central government in a national bicameral parliament. Parliament, in the United Kingdom, is comprised of the House of Commons and the House of Lords; Parliament

> is regarded as the highest court in the land ... Parliament is supreme. The courts of law recognize a statute, passed in due form by Parliament, as being binding upon them, and they must therefore apply it. Neither they nor any other authority in the U.K. is competent to set statutes aside or override them. This holds true irrespective of the content of the laws – even of laws that act retrospectively.[56]

In technical terms, 'in the British system of government supreme power lies with Parliament, which has direct and exclusive control over legislation and indirect control over the actions of the executive and the central administration'.[57] However, in practice, the House of Commons is the centre of power, and that power is exercised in the main by the senior level of the executive – the Cabinet. Generally speaking, when reference is made to 'the Government' in the United Kingdom, the comment alludes to the innermost governing body, or Cabinet. The system of Cabinet government has been described earlier, in relation to Canada. Essentially the two systems closely resemble each other because Canada inherited its governmental structure from the parent nation, Great Britain. The major difference lies in the fact that Canada, like the United States, is a federal entity. It becomes obvious that in many respects the operation of government in the United Kingdom is less difficult and less convoluted than that of its counterparts in Canada and the USA. Certainly it is more direct in effect and application, and in many respects it is more standardized.

The infrastructure of government in the United Kingdom is based, as in Canada and the USA, upon departments and ministries which form the bureaucracy. Government ministers are the heads of the principal departments, and the majority of such ministers have a place in the Cabinet. Career civil servants, as also explained earlier, provide the permanent staff of the bureaucracy; the ministers are elected Members of Parliament, or Members of the House of Lords, who have been appointed by the Prime Minister to head a department. The government departments having a primary concern with current manifestations of political violence and terrorism are: (1) the Home Office; (2) the Foreign and Commonwealth Office (FCO); (3) the Ministry of Defence (MoD); (4) the Northern Ireland Office (NIO); and (5) the Cabinet Office, which serves Ministers collectively. While the functions of each of these departments are generally recognized, a few comments will assist to focus their roles and responsibilities in the task of combating the terrorist threat.

The Home Office could be said to incorporate some of the responsibilities of the Justice Departments in North America, as well as that of the Solicitor General's Department in Canada. Law enforcement, public order, and the administration of the penal system in England and Wales fall within the Home Office purview. The Home Office also has the task of monitoring the law in the courts, the sentencing policies, and the application of the Criminal Code. Because the majority of terrorist attacks in Great Britain have taken place in England, the Home Office enjoys the dubious distinction of being the most experienced mainland department in matters of counter-terrorism. Understandably much of the onus for counter-terrorism planning and operations in Great Britain essentially rests with the Home Office. It must be noted, however, that the Scottish Office has certain parallel functions for Scotland, making co-ordination and co-operation between the two departments a necessity. In a similar vein, the NIO has responsibility for such activity in Ulster, and works closely with the Home and Scottish Offices. This nature of reciprocity is especially important in relation to illegal activities of Republican and Loyalist militants in Northern Ireland which spill across to mainland Britain, and vice versa.

Overseas involvements are the purview of the FCO. Again, because of international terrorist incidents which occur in Great Britain, and because of foreign terrorist links with the Irish dimension, the FCO collaborates with each of the aforementioned departments. The FCO, of course, maintains significant diplomatic relationships with other nations in regard to counter-terrorism matters. The British ambassador in the United States had a large role in efforts to secure improved extradition arrangements between the two nations. Similarly, the British ambassador in Dublin plays a continuing part in exchanges between the United Kingdom and Eire aimed at reducing the terrorist threat.

The MoD's place in counter-terrorism response has become more prominent over the past two decades primarily because of the demand for aid to the civil power tasks in Northern Ireland. (The military's responsibilities are discussed at greater length under 'Crisis-management machinery,' and in the next chapter.) 'In the war against the bombers, Northern Ireland terrorists are not the only enemy. London has become [one of the many arenas] for Arab and other foreign groups waging bombing campaigns against a variety of international targets.'[58] Coping with bomb threats has been only one of the military's jobs, however, which have also included security duties at major airline terminals during times of extreme terrorist threat.

The Cabinet Office, headed by the Cabinet Secretary, has the traditional responsibility 'to service the Cabinet and its committees'.[59] It has been a task 'concerned more with the smooth movement of paper [rather] than with the evaluation of policy'.[60] To avoid any possibility of confusion, it should be noted that the Prime Minister's Office is a separate entity within the Cabinet Office in much the same manner as obtains in Canada in regard to the PMO. The Cabinet Office in the United Kingdom also has oversight of the intelligence and security services, and the resources allocated to them, but the precise status of that relationship is unclear.

The official origination of counter-terrorism policy in the United Kingdom rests with the British Government – the Cabinet. The Prime Minister, in conjunction with appropriate ministers, arrives at the decisions relating to the security of the nation. Advice is given on matters concerning defence, foreign affairs, law enforcement, and those items peculiar to Scotland and Northern Ireland by ministers of those particular departments. The Prime Minister, and the individual ministers holding the appropriate portfolios, are ultimately answerable to Parliament for policy development and implementation. Judgements, however, are also based upon information and recommendations obtained through the use of the Cabinet-committee system.

Several Cabinet committees have an influence upon the development of counter-terrorism and security policy and the actions taken to oppose or to disrupt terrorist intrusions. A differentiation in the nature of the committees must be understood from the outset: on the one hand are the permanent (standing) political committees made up of politicians, and on the other hand are parallel official (shadow) committees made up of civil servants. A third category, *ad hoc* committees, are occasionally formed in the same manner to serve a specific purpose. The committees of interest in the subject of counter-terrorism are subsumed under three principal Cabinet Office functional parameters: (1) overseas and defence; (2) home, legislation, and information; and (3) intelligence and security.[61] A variety of committees have a place under those major headings, but only certain of them are concerned with problems related to terrorism, as displayed in Figure 10.

The Prime Minister chairs the committee for Foreign Affairs, Defence, and Northern Ireland, which has its parallel in the permanent-secretaries group under direction of the Cabinet Secretary. The latter person is, of course, the senior civil servant in the government infra-structure. The Home Secretary is both a principal decision-maker and a crisis manager. This situation stems, in part, from his or her position as chairman of the Civil Contingencies Unit (CCU). The CCU represents 'permanent machinery authorized by the Cabinet for dealing with civil emergencies',[62] dating from an internal review in 1972. While the purpose of the CCU is primarily to plan for and initially to manage civil emergencies such as might arise from an industrial dispute, it has responsibility 'to keep COBRA [Cabinet Office Briefing Room] ... in running order'.[63] COBRA is discussed in more detail under 'Crisis-management machinery' as it denotes the Home Secretary's other role. The workings of the CCU are one means by which Cabinet decisions are reached in the event that the police request military assistance in Great Britain. A feature of the CCU is its composition, 'a mixture of ministers and officials'.[64]

Intelligence and security matters are the subjects of the attention of four individual committees. The Prime Minister chairs the Ministerial steering committee on Intelligence and Security (MIS) which has responsibility for supervision of MI-5, MI-6, and GCHQ (Government Communications Headquarters), and which fixes budget priorities for the intelligence community, as well. A permanent-secretaries steering group, chaired by the Cabinet Secretary, prepares briefing materials for the Prime Minister. The Joint Intelligence Committee (JIC), whose history dates back to 1927, collates intelligence from all sources and prepares assessments for ministers, circulating its material weekly in what is known as the Red Book. Until 1983 the JIC was chaired by an official from the FCO (and earlier by the MoD), but in an effort to avoid problems which led to the Falklands conflict the position was given to an appointee of the Prime Minister in an effort to give the JIC 'a more critical and independent role in intelligence assessment'.[65]

*Figure 10*  Cabinet Office Organization

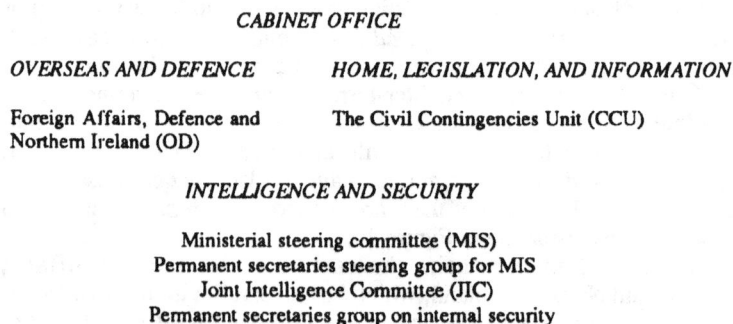

**CABINET OFFICE**

*OVERSEAS AND DEFENCE*          *HOME, LEGISLATION, AND INFORMATION*

Foreign Affairs, Defence and          The Civil Contingencies Unit (CCU)
Northern Ireland (OD)

*INTELLIGENCE AND SECURITY*

Ministerial steering committee (MIS)
Permanent secretaries steering group for MIS
Joint Intelligence Committee (JIC)
Permanent secretaries group on internal security

The Cabinet Secretary chairs a parallel permanent secretaries group on internal security. These various committees provide input upon which decisions are made concerning, *inter alia*, government response to the threats and realities of terrorism. The permanent secretaries groups fulfill an important role by establishing common ground between departments and permitting unanimity in the briefing of ministers. Because intelligence forms a major resource in the combating of terrorism, it is obvious that the intelligence committees, and the community as a whole, have a significant part to play. To improve upon the overall assessment capability of intelligence within the Cabinet Office, a post of Intelligence Co-ordinator was established in 1968.

A Joint Intelligence Organization (JIO) was created to prepare assessments for consideration by the JIC and circulation to ministers and officials. According to the Franks Report of 1983:

'(The JIO) draws for its assessments on all relevant information: the diplomatic reports and telegrams, the views of Government departments and publicly available information, as well as secret intelligence reports. It also has a coordinating role in respect of the work of the security and intelligence services.'[66]

Unlike the US attitude, which is shared to a considerable extent by Canada, the British Government maintains a very secretive and tight-lipped approach toward the operation of its intelligence resources. 'The policy of all post-war governments has been conditioned by two highly questionable pre-war constitutional principles: that intelligence is undiscussable in public, and that parliament surrenders all its powers in intelligence to the executive.'[67] While some slight lessening of that policy has been necessitated as a consequence of controversy over labour relations at GCHQ, the essential features remain intact. Research data are, therefore, extremely difficult to obtain under such circumstances and, if gained, are all too frequently subject to classification.

Decision-making and the place of responsibility in response to the threat of terrorism appear reasonably clear-cut from the standpoint of the British governmental system. Fundamentally it is a centralized and compartmentalized arrangement with relatively little overt evidence of jurisdictional overlapping. Beneath the surface, however, problems do exist which can give rise to incidents such as the bomb attack in Brighton in October 1984. These difficulties, and the relationships which give rise to frictions and faults, are examined in later portions of this chapter, as well as in Chapter Four.

## Crisis-management machinery

Prior to the time of the Dare Committee's findings, contingency planning for a national emergency in Canada was primarily associated with a perceived need to prepare for conditions of nuclear warfare. The Emergency Measures Organization (EMO) had been established in the 1950s, during the tenure of Prime Minister John Diefenbaker, with a central focus of developing resources to assist the Canadian population in the event of global nuclear conflict. But, 'the responsibility for coordinating assigned to the ... (Canada EMO) ... was only partial and lacked authority'.[68] Thus, government departments tended to develop *ad hoc* arrangements to cope under the threat of possible national disasters, nuclear or otherwise.

Circumstances at the turn of the 1970s decade demanded a changed perspective. Not only did the FLQ crisis sound an alarm, but a serious oil spill which created dangers of environmental pollution on Canada's east coast also warned of inadequacies in organizational response. The Dare Report brought the shortcomings to the attention of the government in 1972, and many of the recommendations were adopted. EMO continued to function (now known as Emergency Preparedness Canada), with cells in each province working with the provincial governments, and with a mandate aligned to planning for a broad range of national civil emergencies such as floods, forest fires, and similar calamities. A significant measure implemented as an outcome of the Dare Report, however, was the 'lead Minister' concept for crisis management.

Under the concept, government departments were assigned responsibility for specific response to national emergencies – that is, departments were required to prepare co-ordinated plans, develop resources, and ready themselves to play a role which might be either supportive or leading. The Solicitor General of Canada, for instance, was tasked to co-ordinate federal response to internal civil emergencies of a security nature. It is a responsibility which includes widespread civil disobedience, such as riots and other major disturbances, as well as the threat of terrorist activities. Similarly, the Secretary of State for External Affairs became responsible for co-ordinating federal measures in response to emergencies affecting Canadian citizens and diplomatic missions overseas. Each of the two departments, therefore, has a leading role in those assigned tasks: in the one case involving internal security problems, and the other involving external threats. From a supportive standpoint, the Department of External Affairs, for example, would assist the Solicitor General's Department in the event of terrorist activities which posed a danger to a foreign diplomatic mission in Canada.

The fact that the Solicitor General is responsible for internal security (as well as for the RCMP and CSIS) largely contributed to a decision by ICSI in 1984 that the Department be confirmed as the focal point for co-ordination and planning of the Federal government's counter-terrorism activities. As mentioned earlier, the responsibility *per se* lies with the Security Planning and Coordination Directorate (SPAC) of PSB. Within that mandate is the task of co-ordinating the crisis management of terrorist incidents occurring within Canada, for which purpose the PSB maintains a co-ordination centre, or operations room, staffed by members of SPAC. When activated the co-ordination centre is augmented by representatives of other departments and agencies (e.g. CSIS, RCMP) as required. The centre has direct open and secure communications links with other major operations centres such as those maintained by External Affairs (for overseas requirements), Department of National Defence, Department of Transport,. Emergency Preparedness Canada, the RCMP, and CSIS. The following examples illustrate the subject areas and tasks which would concern the SPAC operations room staff during an emergency:

— alerting and consulting other departments and agencies;
— establishing communications with appropriate provincial and municipal authorities;
— collecting, collating, analysing, and disseminating information relevant to the situation;
— providing situation briefings;
— coordinating release of information to the media; and
— recommending suitable courses of action for consideration by the minister.

To assist with readiness and co-ordination, SPAC developed the Interdepartmental Terrorist Alert System (ITAS) as a means of providing a measured activation of the crisis-management network in response to apprehended terrorist threats. Based on three Alert Conditions, the system automatically triggers pre arranged, appropriate responses across the security infrastructure at the federal level.

The problems of co-ordination are complex and are compounded by jurisdictional overlap. While jurisdictional concerns at departmental level can appear reasonably straightforward (e.g. a hijacked aircraft in flight is the responsibility of the Minister of Transport), the division of responsibility in relation to the enactment, and the administration and enforcement, of the criminal law in Canada creates difficulties. Policing, except for limited areas of specific federal responsibility, is considered primarily a provincial matter. In 1983, however, the Supreme Court of Canada held that the Federal government has inherent jurisdiction to enforce all federal laws, including the Criminal Code. Under that ruling, provincial authority can be displaced by federal legislation and, in a limited manner, that was accomplished in 1984 with the passage of the CSIS Act.

Part IV of the CSIS Act (known as the Security Offences Act) permits the Attorney General of Canada to issue a fiat to take over the prosecution of criminal offences involving threats to the security of Canada or directed against Internationally Protected Persons. Under the CSIS Act, terrorism is a threat to the security of Canada. Similarly, Part IV specifies that the RCMP have primary responsibility to perform 'peace officer' duties in respect to such offences.[69] In other words, the RCMP have primary responsibility for response to terrorist threats or incidents; that is, while a local police force in many situations would be first on the scene, the RCMP arguably have the right to intervene and to resolve the incident and to conduct the subsequent investigation.

In circumstances where a small, less sophisticated police force was involved, the assumption of responsibility by the RCMP might be welcomed. A different attitude might well prevail, however, in a large metropolitan area (e.g. Montreal or Toronto) where the police justifiably consider themselves adequate to cope. The ramifications of the new conditions are currently undergoing careful study, discussion, and negotiation within the law-enforcement community.

Opposed to the normal concept of power flowing downwards in Canada, the reverse is more accurate when dealing with the practicalities of enforcement of legislation and regulations. The development of policy, therefore, must be coloured by the need to permit a latitude and flexibility that caters for the ability of the lowest echelons to work with freedom and initiative. Such efforts require considerable prior and ongoing consultation and agreement, and often the successful outcome of ventures is a result of the co-operative attitude and personalities of individuals, rather than a strict adherence to the rules.

In the United States, the Reagan administration confirmed the Department of State's role in the co-ordination of the US response to terrorism. The Department of State won the interagency battle to head the federal counter-terrorism programme with the argument that most terrorist incidents had been directed against US interests or diplomats abroad. The responsibility, however, does not impinge on the shared tasking of the lead-agency concept. Fundamentally, jurisdiction for domestic and international incidents is divided between the Department of State and the Department of Justice, with the FBI (an agency of Justice) responsible for domestic situations. One other agency also has a prominent role: the Federal Aviation Administration (FAA) of the Department of Transportation. The FAA has jurisdiction in terrorist incidents involving aircraft.

Akin to the lead-Minister concept in Canada, the lead-agency system is simply a recognition of specific expertise and functional authority. In the event of a domestic or an international incident, the FBI or the Department of State assumes respective leadership in the management and resolution of the matter. Both agencies assist each other as required by the circumstances, and may call upon other departments for advice or resources. The Department of State and the FBI both maintain sophisticated operations centres of the nature previously described when discussing the PSB. The centres have a 24-hour watch-keeping arrangement, and are linked to each other, to other government facilities, and to subordinate elements by a comprehensive and secure communications network. Information and reports are also received from the large American intelligence community which includes the CIA, the National Security Agency (NSA), the Defense Intelligence Agency (DIA), and the intelligence resources of the US Armed Forces.

Presidential direction is an important factor in the progress of a crisis situation, and an operations centre is located within the White House. Presidential direction can become a problem, however, if it tends to draw the President directly into the crisis-management process. During the early Carter years, a worrisome precedent was set when the President allowed himself to be involved with negotiations in a domestic hostage-taking. In the later and more spectacular Hanafi Muslim seizure of hostages and buildings in Washington, the President was dissuaded by his advisors from direct participation. Since that occasion, efforts have been made to keep the executive office out of the immediate progress of a terrorist incident. The IG/T and the NSC provide the means of keeping the President informed, advised on policy and recommended measures, and of transmitting the President's decisions to the scene of an incident through appropriate channels, i.e. the lead agency. Carter was severely criticized for permitting himself to become a virtual prisoner of the Iranian crisis, and for interference in the rescue attempt. President Reagan, on the other hand, refused to allow himself to be seen as behaving in that manner during the 1985 TWA hijacking.

Jurisdictional difficulties are something of a paradox within the United States. The problems begin with the multiplicity of agencies that could be involved in a terrorist incident, compounded by the application of federal or state law. In most criminal situations the local authorities have initial responsibility for responding to, resolving, and investigating the matter. Unless a federal law has been violated the federal authorities, such as the FBI, are precluded from involvement; 'murder, standing alone, is a local offense'.[70] Thus, in the incident of the assassination of an anti-Khomeini supporter (cited earlier in this chapter), the FBI was only able to enter the investigation because 'of the unique Federal status of the District of Columbia'[71] which includes Bethesda, Maryland, where the murder took place.

Despite the FBI's role as the lead agency for response to domestic terrorist threats, incidents could occur in which the FBI would be unable to participate other than from a monitoring and advisory standpoint. Federal laws, however, have increasingly broadened the scope of responsibility of federal law-enforcement agencies in recent years. The Comprehensive Crime Control Act of 1984, for instance, has accomplished the following:

Current Federal law ... *is* generally effective in dealing with terrorist acts. Certainly, if the target is a U.S. official or a United States installation, Federal law provides effective statutory coverage to permit both Federal investigative jurisdiction and Federal prosecutive jurisdiction. Similarly, Federal law provides effective coverage for terrorist actions against foreign officials and foreign property located in the United States. Further, Federal laws regulating the use of firearms; the possession, sale, and use of explosives; and the possession of nuclear material provide sufficient linkage for Federal input.[72]

The federal authorities have few difficulties to surmount with jurisdiction in regard to international terrorist activities in the United States. The provisions of the Attorney General's Foreign Counter Intelligence Guidelines, the Foreign Intelligence Surveillance Act, and the Omnibus Diplomatic Security and Anti-terrorism Act (1986) provide the FBI with the necessary investigative authority. Domestic terrorist threats are approached as criminal investigations, often a means of circumventing legal obstacles. Joint Terrorism Task Forces, composed of FBI and State and local law-enforcement officers, are another means whereby the FBI has been able to implement its lead agency responsibilities. Such task forces were successful in obtaining arrests and convictions of FALN terrorists in the Chicago area, and in the terrorist-linked Brink's robbery in Nanuet, New York. A series of terrorist incidents carried out by the United Freedom Front (UFF) over a period of two years ended by the combined efforts of 'representatives from three State police forces, several FBI Field Divisions, and a number of local law-enforcement entities'.[73]

The situation, nonetheless, is not entirely straightforward. The FAA, for example, has responsibility for the direction of any law-enforcement action aboard an aircraft in flight within the US territorial jurisdiction. As with the Canadian ruling, 'in flight' is determined as the moment the aircraft doors are closed for embarkation until such time as they are opened again for disembarkation. The FAA, therefore, has jurisdiction throughout that period. But, since incidents involving aircraft are a federal offence, the FBI would be able to act once the aircraft was deemed to have landed. If the passengers included a foreign diplomat, however, the FBI would have to consult with the State Department before taking action. Under the terms of an MOU (Memorandum of Understanding), even the Department of Defense would have to defer to the FAA in the case of a hijacking of a military aircraft. If the incident occurred in the USA, the FAA would request the FBI to engage in the necessary law-enforcement and investigative response. Military involvement in counter-terrorism response is inhibited in the United States by the Posse Comitatus Act, which precludes the use of Army or

Air Force personnel from the execution or enforcement of law except as authorized by the Constitution or by Congress.

The Department of the Treasury has a significant role to play in counter-terrorism which has little association with financial matters. Under the Assistant Secretary for Enforcement and Operations are the US Secret Service, the US Customs Service, and the Bureau of Alcohol, Tobacco, and Firearms (BATF). The Secret Service is tasked with responsibility for the security of the President of the United States, and for all very senior visiting dignitaries. Members of the Secret Service accompany the President wherever he travels, domestically or internationally, and must vet all security arrangements related to his safety. The Customs Service works closely with the FBI and the BATF in efforts to restrict illegal shipments of weapons and equipment from the USA to terrorist organizations overseas. The BATF is also directly responsible for the control of certain proscribed armaments in the United States (e.g. fully automatic weapons), a task of increasing importance in relation to the growing number of 'survivalist' groups within the nation.

The safeguarding of nuclear materials and nuclear facilities is the responsibility of the Department of Energy (DOE). The DOE employs specialist contract agencies, under DOE policy and supervision, to conduct security operations at its facilities. Once again, however, should a criminal violation occur, the FBI would be called upon to manage the incident and conduct the investigation. A special Nuclear Emergency Search Team (NEST) also operates under the aegis of the DOE. The purpose of NEST is to assist civilian and government agencies in dealing with the hazards of nuclear materials, and for locating and neutralizing explosive nuclear devices. NEST has purposely maintained a low profile for fear of creating alarm among the civilian population, or for drawing attention to the potential of nuclear terrorism.

> So far, NEST has assisted with 20 cases in which the danger of a nuclear device being set off seemed real. All proved to be hoaxes but one. That involved a former employe [sic] of a Wilmington, N.C., nuclear plant who obtained spent fuel and demanded $100,000. He was caught.[74]

One offshoot of the trilevel response organization established in the Carter era was the Federal Emergency Management Agency (FEMA). FEMA came into existence in June 1978, when the federal emergency preparedness and disaster response programmes were merged into one body. 'Two emergency functions not previously assigned to any specific agency were also placed under the purview of FEMA – coordination of emergency warning, and federal response to the consequences of terrorist incidents.'[75] FEMA is an interesting example of a reasonably valid concept which was not properly developed before implementation. Similar to the original Canadian EMO in its purpose, FEMA (as with EMO) was not given sufficient authority to carry out its duties. It was pointed out 'in testimony before the Senate ... that regardless of FEMA's responsibility ... executive branch responsibilities for prevention and control of terrorist incidents are not altered'.[76] Thus, FEMA might produce plans and issue directions, but the receiving departments and agencies do not necessarily have to comply with them.

The lead-Minister concept is well-entrenched in the British Government more so on the basis of tradition than as a discrete response to terrorist violence. Historically, the Prime Minister has been a focal point in times of crisis or during the proceedings of a critical incident. The situation still obtains, but with the advent of television, the principal minister responsible for coping with a particular problem has increasingly been publicly in the forefront. During the Libyan People's Bureau affair at St James's Square in 1984, it was the Home Secretary who most frequently appeared in the media as the spokesman on government policy. Despite the international implication, resolution of the impasse was pre-eminently the task of the Home Office in so far as the public domain was concerned. Obviously, the Prime Minister and the CCU were very much involved, and the Foreign Secretary had a major role to play in negotiations and as an advisor. Nonetheless, the 'on the ground' development of the matter was a Home Office responsibility.

The point to be noted is that the Home Office held that responsibility because of its oversight of law and order and supervisory position in regard to the police in England and Wales. It was doubly germane on the basis that the 'Commissioner of the Metropolitan Police [of London] is directly responsible to the Home Secretary',[77] the Metropolitan Police being the only police force with such a relationship in the United Kingdom. On the other hand, had the incident occurred in Scotland or Ulster, the ministers of those Offices would have held primary jurisdiction. Even in regard to London, however, it is not government practice to interfere openly in police operations unless requested to do so. Chief Constables jealously defend their independence, and the influence of local police authorities is generally limited 'to provision of adequate staff, accommodation and equipment....'[78] Thus, when an incident occurs, it is the police on the spot who take charge and who conduct the operations. The local Chief Constable is responsible for the outcome, although in the case of an international terrorist incident, there would be consultation with the appropriate ministry, e.g. the Home Office.

Military assistance, historically, was summoned through the local magistrate. Currently, the 'civil power' that may [seek the assistance of] the armed forces appears no longer to be the local magistracy, but the Home Secretary [in England and Wales], acting on a request from a chief officer of police. It is then for the Secretary of Defence to respond to the call. In such a situation, conventions of individual and collective responsibility must merge.[79]

(Technically, of course, only the Defence Council can issue authorization because Ministers cannot give orders to the military.) In very extraordinary circumstances the military would be expected to act on its own initiative in the normal responsible role of citizens, but a situation where police would not be first involved is difficult to imagine.

During the siege of the Iranian embassy in 1980, the conduct of operations remained with the senior police officers of the Metropolitan Police assigned to that duty. The then-Commissioner, Sir David McNee, retained overall supervision and regularly visited the police 'command post' established at the site.

> My instinct was to take charge of the tactical operations and this was a feeling difficult to quell. But it had to be done in order to retain objectivity in making a continuous assessment of the operations and the participants – including police commanders. Further ... there was still a force to be run.[80]

Ultimately, when the terrorists began killing hostages, the decision was made to permit an assault by the SAS. That decision was based upon consultation by the Commissioner with the Home Secretary and supported by Cabinet ministers. '[The Home Secretary] authorized the commitment of the SAS, saying that the precise timing of the assault was to be a matter for the police forward control outside the Embassy in consultation with the military commander.'[81] Immediately following the conclusion of the SAS operation, control of the situation reverted to the police.

Special operations rooms within government departments as exist in Canada and the USA are not the norm in Great Britain. Indeed, during the evacuation of British nationals from Aden in early 1986, television coverage showed very *ad hoc* arrangements in the FCO. Such facilities as operations centres on a formal basis *are* found in police and military establishments throughout the nation. The closest approximation at central-government level in Great Britain, excluding the MoD, would be the Cabinet Office Briefing Room, or COBRA. Quoting Sir David McNee, 'Backing up the work of the police control was ... [COBRA], staffed by civil servants and others.'[82] The purpose of COBRA, aside from keeping the Cabinet informed, is to facilitate and to expedite the smooth functioning of events such as the police operations during the

Iranian embassy siege. One of its tasks on that occasion, as an example, was to attempt to arrange the services of Arab ambassadors as negotiators. COBRA was established during the mid-1970s by the then Home Secretary, Mr Merlyn Rees. COBRA is located in the Cabinet Office, 'just around the corner from 10 Downing Street'.[83] In the 1980 situation, 'it was composed of 15 staff members augmented by about 20 specialist advisors on standby'.[84] A junior minister represented the FCO, the 'number two' was present for the MoD, 'the security and intelligence services had their own men on the committee',[85] and the British ambassador to Iran was also summoned home to provide advice on the political context. To use Mr Rees's description, 'There is only one god in there ... and that is the bloke in charge – the Home Secretary.'[86]

Within the United Kingdom, responsibility for counter-terrorism in the operative sense is the concern of the security and law-enforcement agencies, with the support of the military where applicable. Much weight rests on the shoulders of the intelligence community, particularly MI-5, MI-6, Special Branch, and the military elements. The Security Service, MI-5, whose jurisdiction lies within the United Kingdom, is the responsibility of the Home Secretary. The Secret Intelligence Service, MI-6, which functions overseas, is the responsibility of the Foreign Secretary, although retaining direct access to the Prime Minister. Both MI-5 and MI-6, however, are monitored by the MIS, and reports from the two agencies are submitted to the JIC.

Because of its focus in regard to terrorist activities, necessitated by virtue of the number of incidents in the London area, the Metropolitan Police have taken the lead in the development of specialized law-enforcement and counter-terrorist units. One such group is the Special Branch, plain-clothes officers whose task is the gathering of intelligence. Contrary to some popular belief, the Special Branch is not a national body. Organized in 1883 as a response to the Irish terrorist movements of that period, it existed until 1961 only as part of the Metropolitan Police. Since that time regional groups have been formed and each is responsible to their own Chief Constable. While the Branch does not have any special powers beyond those of ordinary policemen, it does work closely with MI-5, especially as the latter does not possess powers of arrest. Both the Special Branch and MI-5 activities have tended to raise the concerns of civil-liberties groups on occasion. It is perhaps unfortunate that the 'unnecessary amount of official reticence about giving information'[87] has been a continuing policy in the United Kingdom, thereby creating fears where fears may not have a reason to exist.

'The British police began seriously to evaluate the threat from terrorism in 1968 — the so-called "year of the barricades".'[88] In reality the evaluation was more a part of 'a wider and extremely thorough examination of the whole force, and the Metropolitan Police in particular'.[89] The action, however, undoubtedly paved the way for changes in organizational structure and methods of operation that would be needed to combat the terrorist threat as it developed in succeeding years. In 1971 the Bomb Squad was organized at Scotland Yard as a counter to the Angry Brigade. Five years later the unit gave birth to the Anti-Terrorist Squad, C13, which now bears the brunt of response to terrorism in the Metropolitan area. Providing support for the C13 group, or as needed, is D11 which is the expert firearms section of the Yard and is better known as the Blue Berets. D11 is responsible for the use of firearms, plus the training of Metropolitan Police officers in the use of weapons, and is backed by a sophisticated array of modern training devices. A second support element, C7, is the Technical Support Branch; C7 develops the comprehensive surveillance, monitoring, and communications specialties such as were employed during the St James's Square confrontation.

Pre-dating the aforementioned evaluation, the Metropolitan Police formed the Special Patrol Group (SPG) in 1965, 'to assist divisional police units ... where and whenever needed'.[90] Originally conceived as a highly mobile support unit to deal with serious disturbances and crime, it has since become a valuable resource for perimeter control during terrorist incidents. Akin to the SPG, the Royalty and Diplomatic Protection Group (RDPG) provides permanent surveillance of embassies and private residences with mobile and static patrols, as well as conducting close protection for members of the Royal Family. Members of this security group are frequently armed; Trevor Lock, the RDPG police officer who figured so prominently as a hostage in the Iranian embassy siege, managed to conceal his weapon on his person throughout the incident. Although he could not prevent the takeover of the embassy, Constable Lock played a valuable role of calm courage and leadership which greatly assisted in the ultimate hostage rescue.

Following London's lead, other urban centres have established similar groups on an as-required basis. For instance, the Birmingham Police formed a bomb squad in response to the PIRA bombing campaign in the 1973–4 era. British police, nonetheless, are reluctant formally to organize special groups for fear of being accused of developing the 'Third Force' concept so prevalent on the Continent. Sir Robert Mark, noted former Commissioner of the Metropolitan Police, stressed 'that policing in a free society depends on a real measure of public approval and consent'.[91] It is the generally held opinion in British police circles that support of that nature 'has never been obtained by military or paramilitary means'.[92]

The Northern Ireland police force presents a fundamentally different picture of a divided society, although it is making great efforts at establishing British-style impartiality. From 1969, when British military forces were first committed, until 1977, when the policy of police primacy was restored, responsibility for security was vested in the local military commander. The RUC did maintain control over normal police functions; but during the approximately eight years of military ascendancy, the police had to defer to Army decisions in security operations. Those circumstances, to all intents and purposes, are now reversed. It was the matter of control of security by Westminster which brought about the final collapse of the Stormont Government and initiated Direct Rule from London. Northern Ireland politicians could not abide the concept of security policy being dictated by the British Government, despite the fact that British troops were being deployed in Ulster for internal security purposes. On the other hand, the British Government could not delegate its command of British military forces to a subordinate governing body. Even after the imposition of Direct Rule the military commander, in a sense, served two masters: the Northern Ireland Office and the MoD. It was not an entirely comfortable or perfect solution, but it was expedient and it worked.

The change from military to police control, or 'Ulsterization', which took place in 1977 was not accomplished easily and met with some resistance from the Army. It was not until the Warren Point incident in August, 1979, that a 'decisive move settled once and for all the disagreement over "police primacy".'[93] On that date, eighteen soldiers of the British Army were killed in a bombing incident by the PIRA. The Prime Minister flew to Ulster to discuss security policy with the Army and the police. During a series of briefings it became apparent that the police and the military were not in accord over security policy and on return to London the Prime Minister appointed Sir Maurice Oldfield as overall security co-ordinator. With the continued withdrawal of troops from the province, coupled to the increasing confidence and effectiveness of the RUC, security policy has become a matter for the NIO. Development of that policy is accomplished in conjunction with a Security Committee which includes the Chief Constable of the RUC, a military representative, and civilian appointees. Considerable weight is given to the opinion of the Chief Constable, and the implementation of policy is his responsibility.

Various measures which have been applied to the Northern Ireland problem (e.g. detention, judicial inquiries, Diplock Courts) are discussed in Chapters Four and Five. Two major pieces of legislation, however, which are a direct outcome of the prevalence of terrorism in the United Kingdom must be mentioned. They are: (1) The Prevention of Terrorism (Temporary Provisions) Act 1984, hereinafter PTA 1984; and (2) The Northern Ireland (Emergency Provisions) Act 1978, hereinafter the EPA 1978. The former was originally passed in 1974 in response to a wave of PIRA bombings in England, and the Birmingham pub explosions in particular. The EPA was created to provide emergency powers to cope with circumstances in Northern Ireland following the suspension of Stormont and the imposition of Direct Rule. Initially authorized in 1973, the EPA was followed by similar, modified versions in 1975 and 1978.

PTA 1974 was passed very quickly, in the space of twenty-four hours, although 'the Bill was the product of more than a year of Home Office contingency planning'.[94] The first Act was replaced two years later with some modifications to the strengthening of police powers and the protection of civil liberties. Two reviews have subsequently followed, one by Lord Shackleton in 1978 and a further investigation by Lord Jellicoe in 1983, which led to changes and ultimately to the passage of a new Act in 1984. The life of the PTA 1984 is now limited to five years and is subject to annual renewal by Parliament. The EPA was initially renewable annually, but that term has been reduced to confirmation every six months. Both the PTA 1984 (more especially, its predecessors) and the EPA 1978 have made inroads into the cherished traditions of civil liberties in the United Kingdom. Between them they allow for, *inter alia*, exclusion of certain persons from parts of the United Kingdom, wider powers of search, and modifications to the legal procedures and conduct of trials in Northern Ireland. One obvious result is the requirement to complete landing cards when travelling between Ulster and the British mainland and to be in possession of adequate identification – a minor demand, but nonetheless another example of how terrorism has intruded upon public freedoms.

The PTA and the EPA have been subject to much criticism, and also to extensive and intelligent scrutiny by experienced and learned authorities on an official basis. As Earl Jellicoe made plain:

> I was invited in March 1982 to review the operation of the Prevention of Terrorism (Temporary Provisions) Act 1976. I took some time to consider my reply ... partly because of my proposed terms of reference ... required the acceptance of 'the continuing need for legislation against terrorism.' I satisfied myself ... that some form of special legislation was indeed required to deal with the continuing threat posed by terrorism throughout the United Kingdom ... I have since become convinced ... that if special legislation effectively reduces terrorism, as I believe it does, it should be continued as long as a substantial terrorist threat remains.[95]

The decision-making and crisis-management machinery of Canada, the United States, and the United Kingdom are functions of the respective governments, and reflect those governmental systems. Advantages and disadvantages can be seen in the workings of the individual machinery, and in the relationships which exist between the various bodies which have responsibility for response to the threat of terrorism. Before commenting directly on those matters (see Chapter Five) it is beneficial to examine the resources and capabilities that are part of the response in the three nations.

Chapter four

# Resources and capabilities

## Introduction

Government policies in response to terrorism extend beyond courses of action, or intended courses of action, to include the resources and capabilities available to government in the pursuit of its policies. Thus, the means (or 'tools', e.g. police, legislation, equipment) and methods (use of the tools) must also be identified, together with an assessment of their utility and effectiveness. For instance, it would be quite possible for a government to establish a large security force, and to provide that force with the most modern equipment available. But, if the force lacks adequate training, experience, and leadership, it could prove worthless, or even dangerous under certain circumstances. In conjunction, if government authorities do not possess the knowledge, experience, or suitable sources of competent advice, the force could be committed to a task beyond its capabilities or under conditions which would only serve to exacerbate a serious situation. The attempted rescue of Egyptian hostages aboard a Cyprus Airways plane at Nicosia airport in 1978 is a case in point.

The *Envelope* also exerts pressures which bear upon the resources and capabilities available to government, especially in response to terrorism. Geography and history may affect perception of the threat, while ideas, institutions, precedents, and constitutional principles may influence the development of legislation and various other tools, as well as the manner in which they are employed. The use of the SAS in the maximum-force role of law enforcement in Great Britain, for example, is a natural outcome of the nation's tradition of an unarmed police force. Conversely, in the United States the military is precluded by law from such an involvement in the domestic environment, and historically the task has belonged to American police forces.

The Prevention of Terrorism (Temporary Provisions) Act 1984 (hereinafter PTA 1984) permits the British Government to exclude certain persons from specific parts, or all, of the United Kingdom. Under the terms of the US Constitution, and given the influence of American civil-rights lobbies, it is difficult to conceive of similar legislation ever being enacted in the United States. The Constitution of Canada would also make such action difficult for the Canadian Government, although various factors of the *Envelope* (e.g. history, system of government, use of British precedent) would tend to make the task easier than in the USA. The foregoing are some of the circumstances which must be borne in mind when examining the resources and capabilities associated with implementation of government policies in response to the threat of terrorism.

## Background

When questioned about Canada's counter-terrorism policy, some persons have replied with the rhetorical statement: 'What policy?' Answers of that nature have generally come from individuals with a genuine lack of knowledge, stemming from Canada's relatively limited modern experience of terrorism. Occasionally the response originated with persons involved with national security who had been frustrated in the past by the apparent reluctance of Canadian authorities to introduce more positive measures to cope with the threat. Statements by the Solicitor General in 1986, however, coupled with actions announced at the time, have helped to ameliorate the perception. Canada does have a fundamental policy in regard to terrorism, and one which is clearly and continuously exhibited by the national ethos: to uphold the ideals of freedom and democracy and the dignity of the individual. From that elementary foundation the twin principles of the rule of law (incorporating use of minimum force), and the perception of the threat, have provided guidance for policy development. Acts of terrorism are treated as criminal offences in Canada, with demands by terrorists opposed by a modified no-concessions response. In addition, the Canadian Government has been an early and consistent supporter of international co-operation as a means to combat terrorist activity.

The speech by the Canadian Solicitor General on 10 March 1986 proclaimed a much greater awareness on the part of the government: 'Terrorism is no longer something that just happens somewhere else.'[1] In subsequent paragraphs of the speech, the Solicitor General identified two major threats to Canada: 'We can be the immediate target of terrorists attempting to intimidate our government ... We can become the innocent victims of foreign battles being staged on our territory.'[2] Perhaps of greater consequence was recognition of the fact that' 'Countries that fail to take adequate measures to defend their citizens invite terrorists to victimize them.'[3] The Solicitor General then outlined a series of counter-terrorism measures to be undertaken by the Canadian

Government, and which are discussed later in this chapter. Regrettably (although in all fairness not within his purview), he failed to mention the threat to Canadian interests overseas or measures of response which might be entertained to cope with that nature of danger. As he said, 'Canadians are, by and large, a peaceful people ...; Canadians have yet to fully appreciate that [Terrorism] knows no boundaries.'[4]

'I can't explain the mentality of terrorism'.[5] Assistant Secretary of State Richard Murphy made that remark when viewing the devastation following the September 1984 car-bomb attack on the US embassy's new annex in East Beirut. Expressed sixteen years after the acknowledged beginning of modern terrorist assaults against American interests at home and abroad, Mr Murphy's comment is perhaps difficult to fathom. Yet the phenomenon of terrorism is so foreign to the US democratic ethos, constitutional principles, and concept of an open society, that it does become possible to comprehend his perplexity. Terrorism is considered to be a criminal activity under US law and legislation, and policies of response are framed from that approach. US counter-terrorism policy is essentially a reflection of the American ideal and way of life. The rule of law underpins the US approach, with an expectation that people and nations will obey the rules. The astonishing behaviour of the Khomeini regime in the seizure of the American embassy in Tehran almost paralyzed the Carter administration by the blatant flaunting of international diplomatic conventions and legal precedents.

The foundation of American counter-terrorism policy has been translated into a set of guiding principles. One of the earliest fundamentals has been the no-concessions rule, which includes a refusal to negotiate even to save lives. The United States has long maintained that it is the responsibility of host states to provide protection against terrorists, and the USA is prepared to act in concert with other nations to prevent or respond to terrorist acts. Although a strong advocate of international co-operation in opposition to terrorism, the United States has recognized the role of rogue states that practise terrorism or actively support it, and the nation has demonstrated its willingness to take measures to protect its citizens, property, and interests, unilaterally if necessary. A number of complex factors intrude upon the simplicity of those basic guidelines. The place of the United States as a leading global power makes the nation's citizens, facilities, and interests attractive targets for terrorist attacks, especially overseas. The desire to retain the openness of its society, and its representation abroad, injects conflict into efforts to develop protective measures to counter terrorist activities. Also, American support for what are seen as right-leaning, but often despotic, 'friendly' governments or insurgencies tends to cause confusion. The result is a compounding of definitional controversy and bewilderment amongst legislators, decision-makers, and members of the public. Friendly governments and civil-rights agitators alike find it easy to be critical of American behaviour, with the influence of civil-rights lobbies prompting other governments to be chary about the sharing of intelligence with US agencies.

Controversy over the threat of terrorism and the policies and policy measures of response has been a feature of the American reaction to terrorism. As an example, three articles published between July and September 1982 took widely differing views of the problem. One stated that 'Experts believe they are winning the battle against terrorism';[6] a second warned that the 'U.S. is not immune to terrorism, and had better get its act together'.[7] The third declared that airport security was a '$310 million paranoia subsidy'[8] that should be dropped in favour of letting the Federal Aviation Administration (FAA) crisis centre simply manage all aircraft incidents by negotiation as they occur. (The problem of terrorist bomb threats, as in the Air India incident of 1985, was not considered.) Similar controversy has been evident at the highest levels of the American government, within the legislature, and amongst the security agencies. A bitter feud erupted between the FBI and the Los Angeles police over responsibility for control of anti-terrorist protection for the 1984 Olympic Games. Conflicting statements by senior officials have also contributed to misunderstandings; in 1984 the Director of the FBI was quoted on two separate occasions, as follows:

(1) We have seen an increased propensity on the part of terrorist groups to plan and carry out terrorist acts in the United States.[9]
(2) There is not really a rising tide of terrorism, but rather a rising tide of concern for terrorism in America.[10]

In a lighter but equally significant vein, an investigation by the General Accounting Office (GAO) into difficulties associated with State Department protective measures overseas reported that an ambassador demoralized his security guards by having them walk his poodle.

The American media has been another source of difficulties in the development of the US response to terrorism. Much criticized for its behaviour during the 1985 TWA hijacking in Beirut, the media has sought a good story wherever it could be found. Frequently an eagerness to attract public attention, or to achieve a scoop, has overridden solid investigative journalism or sound factual reporting. The NBC News interview with Mohammed Abbas was assailed by the US State Department as encouraging 'the terrorist activities we're all seeking to deter',[11] and 'Terrorism thrives on [that] kind of publicity.'[12] It is not surprising, therefore, to discern a lack of clarity in American perceptions of terrorism. Criticisms of erratic and incohesive postures in US policy have a valid basis. A spokesman for the Department of Energy's Office of Safeguards and Security remarked that in the absence of an overt terrorist incident there is not much that could be done other than basic planning. When ranged alongside such attitudes of complacency, the demands for more centralized control, direction, and emphasis in American response to the threat of terrorism take on greater meaning.

In Great Britain, a precis distributed in 1984 to military students at the Staff College, Camberley, stated that 'most recent British experience [with political violence] has been in former colonial territories'.[13] Included on the same page was a comment from a 1973 *Times* article by Claire Palley (now Professor of Law at the University of Kent): 'Twentieth century colonial insurgency in India, Malaya, Kenya and Aden was, without much regard to legality, subjugated by methods which would not have been countenanced in the United Kingdom.'[14] The accuracy of Professor Palley's remarks will not be taken to task. Coupled with the preceding statement, however, they serve to underline two realities: (1) until events of the past two decades, most of modern British experience with terrorism had been overseas; and (2) adept as it was in coping with foreign insurgencies, the British military had not been prepared to cope with political violence in the United Kingdom. Nonetheless, as Sir David McNee observed, 'The Metropolitan Police experience of terrorism goes back to 1829, but particularly to March 1883 when ... the Irish Fenian dynamiters ... were then putting down bombs in London.'[15] Terrorism is not a distinctly new phenomenon in the annals of British history; it is, however, largely a novel development within Great Britain and particularly on the scale that has been witnessed over the past fifteen years. London, especially, has been a primary target area and has been the scene of more bombings, shootings, and persons injured as a result of terrorist activity than the whole of the rest of Britain.

The British response to terrorism, as a consequence, has been coloured to a considerable degree by perception of the threat. During the post-Second World War years through to 1969 the threat was principally confined to events in overseas territories. Professor Palley's suggestion notwithstanding, a respectable body of evidence exists to the effect that methods generally employed by the British were not extreme under the circumstances, and that policy conformed to the rule of law. As described in Chapter Two, Sir Robert Thompson emphasized the correct approach to procedures adopted in Malaya, and he strongly advocated such an attitude in the combating of insurgency and terrorism elsewhere in the world. The modern threshold of British perception of the threat of terrorism was raised by the outbreak of major violence in Northern Ireland in 1969. It was heightened further when PIRA attacks began to occur on mainland Great Britain, as in the explosion at the Parachute

Regiment headquarters in Aldershot in February 1972. A very appreciable reaction did not set in, however, until PIRA increased the ferocity of its intermittent bombing campaign in England in the latter half of 1974. Since that time, despite numerous and sometimes prolonged lulls in the PIRA/INLA bombing campaigns, the perception of the threat in major urban centres and at government facilities has not waned markedly. Threat perception in England has also remained at a higher level partially because of the incidence of international terrorist activity which became apparent at the beginning of the 1970s. Centred on the Metropolitan area of London, it has spread to Manchester, Birmingham, Liverpool, and even to the seaside resort town of Brighton. Attacks against British diplomats overseas also served to increase awareness, as in the cases of the abductions of Mr Cross in Canada in 1970 and Sir Geoffrey Jackson in Uruguay the following year. More recently, the assassinations of Mr Norris in Bombay in 1984, and of Mr Whitty in Athens in the same year, shocked the government and public alike.

Disregarding the Northern Ireland situation, domestic terrorism has been a factor in Great Britain as well, albeit in a relatively sporadic and minor fashion. One of the better-known examples was the anarchistic Angry Brigade who were accused of a series of explosions at the homes of Cabinet ministers, leading industrialists, and at state buildings between August 1970 and the end of 1971. The Angry Brigade was virtually destroyed as a functioning entity by a series of arrests in 1971, although responsibility for incidents is occasionally still claimed in its name, e.g. a bomb at the London offices of American Express in August 1983. Separatist movements in Scotland and Wales have intermittently made their presence felt by means of bombing and incendiary attacks. The Scottish National Liberation Army (SNLA) took responsibility for a series of letter-bombs in 1982 and 1983, including one sent to the Lord Provost of Glasgow on the day of the visit of the Prince of Wales. Several Welsh groups purport to exist, such as the Welsh Army of Workers, the Sons of Glendower, the Movement for the Defence of Wales, and the Keeper of Wales. These organizations have been accused of arson attacks on English-owned holiday cottages in Wales. Like the SNLA, they are small extremist groups motivated by hatred of the English and by local economic grievances. Extremists of both the Left and Right of the political spectrum have participated in violent street demonstrations, one of the more notable being the Red Lion Square incident of June 1974. The far Right is represented predominantly by the National Front, a fascist group which appears to have been significantly infiltrated by fugitive members of a similar organization in Italy. On the Left are the Socialist Workers' Party (SWP) and the International Marxist Group (IMG), and some of the membership have allegedly been active in street clashes.

Racial tension has increasingly been cited as the cause of recent incendiary attacks and harassment, particularly of Asians, in large urban areas of England. Compounding the situation has been the obvious willingness of 'Trotskyites, Socialist extremists, revolutionary Communists, anarchists, and black militants'[16] to use such frictions for political advantage. At a public protest meeting held in Tottenham in October 1985, several hard-left speakers openly called for more riots, and threatened that 'there will be a revolution'.[17] Such actions serve only to promote recruiting by opposing extremist groups and create a vicious circle of violence. Not to be ignored has been the growing militancy of issue groups, particularly those associated with the animal-rights movement. Activities of the Animal Liberation Front and the Hunt Retribution Squad have exceeded normal lobbying procedures to the point where they have moved into the realm of terrorism.

> There can be little doubt ... about the fear engendered by claims of poisoned candy and other consumer goods, by abusive and threatening telephone calls, by the posting of letter bombs, the destruction of property, or even slogans painted on walls. By definition valid not only in Great Britain, such actions are deemed to be acts of political terrorism ...[18]

Throughout, in Northern Ireland or on the British mainland, British Government policy has reflected the principle of the rule of law in response to terrorism. Acts of terrorism have been classed as criminal offences, with the responsibility for prevention, investigation, and the apprehension of offenders primarily a police concern. Only in Northern Ireland have the military been called upon for a prolonged front-line role, and that task has been dramatically reduced during the past eight years. Within the United Kingdom, of course, specific Army units continue their assignment as the ultimate sanction for the resolution of extraordinary terrorist incidents, i.e. the SAS and the Royal Marine Commandos. A pivotal link in the government's security policy has been the concept of no concessions when faced with terrorist demands. Such an approach was clearly illustrated in the 1975 Balcombe Street incident, and again five years later during the Iranian embassy seizure. The only major exception in the area of international threats occurred in 1970 when Leila Khaled was released in response to the PFLP Dawson Field adventure in Jordan. The circumstances surrounding that occasion, combined with a lack of governmental experience, undoubtedly had much to do with the decision. In general, however, the policy has been adhered to, and is one which even the 1980-1 PIRA/INLA hunger strike could not topple.

The British Government has achieved notable success in its response to the threats and actions of both domestic and international terrorist groups within the United Kingdom. Impressive headway has been made against the activities of PIRA/INLA in Northern Ireland, as well as on the British mainland. The accomplishments have been the result of the use of a range of resources and capabilities which continue to be developed in the face of changes in terrorists' methods, tactics, and targets.

## Resources and capabilities

### Policy

Government counter-terrorism policy is, *per se*, a resource. It indicates, at the very least, recognition of a threat and the government's position in relation to the threat. Policy provides guidance in the development of policy measures, to include plans, organizational arrangements, equipment acquisitions, training, domestic and international agreements and co-operation, introduction of regulations, passage of legislation, and publicity. Policy can represent a major and extremely valuable resource in response to terrorism.

But policy can have negative aspects, as well. The wrong policy, for instance, or poorly directed policy, or inconsistent policy, or policy inadequately expressed or publicized can be as dangerous as the absence of policy. Questions arise in relation to a government's counter-terrorism policy: (1) is the threat assessment accurate and complete? (2) is the selected policy correct (e.g. too weak, too draconian, too narrow or two broad in scope, constitutionally permissible, or illegal)? (3) are the policy measures suitable, and capable of implementation (are the tools ready and available)? (4) have the policy and policy measures been given sufficient public notification? and (5) how can the foregoing queries be judged to the best advantage? The benefit of policy lies in the achievement of positive answers to those questions, not always an easy task when combating terrorism. As an example, if government introduces legislation designed to suppress terrorist activity, does that legislation make unacceptable inroads upon civil liberties or threaten the liberal-democratic structure of the nation? Similarly, if terrorism thrives on 'the propaganda of the deed' how does government respond with its own public-awareness campaign, and how does it cope with media demands for freedom in the coverage of terrorist incidents?

Canadian counter-terrorism policy was first evolved as a response to the FLQ crisis. Prime Minister Pierre Trudeau, on Friday 16 October 1970, made a national radio and television broadcast to announce the proclamation of The War Measures Act as a consequence of serious FLQ provocations. Mr Trudeau's speech made reference to a number of significant considerations: to the terrorists' motivation in their attempts to destroy the very basis of freedom, to the fragility of a democratic society if democracy is not prepared to defend itself, to the government's recognition of its grave responsibilities in interfering with civil liberties, to the dangers of being entrapped in alleged authoritarianism, and to the need 'to maintain the rule of law without which freedom is impossible'.[19]

Those considerations established a framework of Canadian counter-terrorism policy which continues to provide guidance to government authorities. Mr Trudeau's speech, however, was also important for several other reasons, amongst them the fact that it illustrated the government's early recognition of the fundamental aims and threats inherent in terrorist activities. Despite later claims that the Trudeau Government acted with an unnecessary display of strength, the government did appreciate that 'It is a well-known technique of revolutionary groups ... to goad the authorities into inflexible attitudes'.[20] Important, as well, was a warning to Canadians of their complacency in assuming that terrorism 'could not happen (in Canada)',[21] and the foundational basis of the no-concessions policy: '... it is the responsibility of the government to deny the demands ...'[22]

Mr Trudeau's remarks in regard to the no-concessions principle warrant some detailed expression:

> It is a responsibility that the Government will discharge according to law. To bow to the pressures ... would not only be an abdication of responsibility, it would lead to an increase of terrorist activities ... The Government's decision to prevent this from happening is not taken just to defend an important principle, it is taken to protect the lives of Canadians ... Freedom and personal security are safeguarded by laws; those laws must be respected in order to be effective.[23]

No concessions, with minor exceptions, has remained a policy of the Canadian Government in response to terrorist demands. During the October Crisis, nonetheless, a notable bargain was concluded with some of the terrorists in regard to the release of Mr Cross. The circumstances of that incident, which were not entirely dissimilar to those faced by the British Government in the Leila Khaled affair, involved a decision to avoid the risk of injury or worse to Mr Cross.

The policy of the Canadian Government was also enunciated at the United Nations on several occasions in the 1970s, but, on balance, counter-terrorism has not had a high public profile in the nation. Admittedly, the October Crisis initiated new policies to improve the decision-making and crisis-management infrastructure, and events such as the 1976 Olympics kept awareness alive on an intermittent basis, as has Canadian participation in the Summit Seven conferences. In 1981, the McDonald Report generated an interval of renewed interest which was carried forward by the government's decision to form the Canadian Security Intelligence Service (CSIS). The CSIS debate, however, centred more pointedly on the operative scope of that organization rather than on a potential terrorist threat to Canada or Canadians. It has not been until well into the 1980s decade that terrorism received greater public notice in Canada, and publicly acknowledged government attention. Two events in 1985 (i.e. the Turkish embassy siege in Ottawa, and the combined Air India/Canadian Pacific Airlines bombings) stirred considerable reaction in the nation. The Turkish embassy incident shattered the normal bipartisan attitude in Parliament, with Opposition parties accusing the government of inadequate security arrangements. The result was a number of well-publicized exchanges in the news media between members of the Government and the Opposition which placed a focus on Canadian counter-terrorism policy measures.

Arguably the most comprehensive and direct public statement since 1970 regarding Canadian counter-terrorism policy was made by the Solicitor General in March 1986. His speech echoed Mr Trudeau's warning to Canadians about the threat of terrorism, and outlined salient features of Canadian policy and measures of response:

— Canada is resolved to protect both its own citizens and foreign diplomatic personnel resident in Canada;
— the lead-minister concept remains operative for crisis management, with the Solicitor General's Department responsible for the counter-terrorism programme and response to terrorist incidents in Canada; the Department of External Affairs holds responsibility for terrorist incidents affecting Canadian interests abroad;
— Canada has forcefully pressed for concerted international action to combat terrorism, and regularly consults with NATO and the Summit Seven, as well as continuing to work in the United Nations;
— no concessions remains government policy; the government will not make deals, pay ransoms, release prisoners, or make other concessions that would encourage terrorists;
— Canada recognizes the vital role of reliable intelligence in preventing terrorist acts; CSIS monitors terrorist organizations, and exchanges information with other nations;
— the RCMP shares criminal intelligence with CSIS, and other government departments and counterparts in other countries; the RCMP also continues its role of investigating offences that constitute a threat to Canadian security;

— the RCMP, in conjunction with other police forces, provide security for diplomatic missions and prominent persons; the RCMP also has Emergency Response Teams in centres across Canada ready to respond to terrorist situations;

— military and police bomb disposal squads are available, and the RCMP's Bomb Data Centre provides analysis of bomb incidents and keeps abreast of the latest techniques;

— the Special Threat Assessment Group provides scientific and technical advice in matters of nuclear, biological or chemical threats;

— the Police and Security Branch (PSB) co-ordinates the federal government's counter-terrorism programme, and works closely with appropriate federal agencies (e.g. RCMP, CSIS, Privy Council Office, Departments of External Affairs, Transport, Employment and Immigration, National Defence, and Health and Welfare); the PSB also consults with the provinces to delineate the authorities and mechanisms to deal with terrorist acts;

— the RCMP will increase its strength and responsibilities to improve security for foreign missions and their personnel;

— improved security arrangements will be introduced at all airports in Canada, pending a Cabinet review;

— the RCMP will create a permanent Special Emergency Response Team (SERT) for hostage taking incidents; and

— the Solicitor General will meet with media leaders to seek their views and advice on how to best protect the public while respecting journalists' democratic right to information.[24]

Further evidence of greater concern about the threat of terrorism, and a strengthening of government policy, was demonstrated in the aftermath of a recent trial of three men charged in the 1982 attempted assassination of a Turkish diplomat in Ottawa. Two of the accused, who pleaded guilty to conspiracy to commit murder, received sentences of six years in prison and two years less a day, respectively. The Crown Prosecutor for the Province of Ontario lodged an appeal on the basis that the judge erred by 'imposing a sentence "which fails to reflect the primary need to deter politically motivated acts of violence committed by organized terrorist groups..."'.[25]

Counter-terrorism policy in Canada received an early impetus as a consequence of the FLQ and the October Crisis of 1970. Ensuing developments were somewhat erratic, with increased emphasis occurring when threat perception demanded. From the beginning of the 1980s, however, more attention has been devoted to the problem and significant domestic measures have been introduced. Nonetheless, despite the Canadian perception of a favourable national image abroad, Canada clearly cannot depend upon that factor to protect the nation's citizens and interests from the threat of terrorist attacks overseas.

Until the early 1980s, American counter-terrorism policy founded in the rule of law had been essentially of a reactive and protective character. Policy development originated in a perception of the threat, a threat not seen as being of significance within the continental USA. Indeed, because the majority of contemporary American experience of terrorism had occurred abroad, little publicity was given to policy guidelines for response to domestic attacks. Terrorism equates with criminal activity in the United States, and law-enforcement authorities have approached domestic incidents with that attitude. For instance, the hijacking of an airliner by Croatian activists in 1976 involved negotiations and the granting of some concessions, quite out of keeping with the standard American no-concessions policy.

'US policy on terrorism has evolved through years of experience in combatting terrorism and is an outgrowth of responses by various Administrations'.[26] Formal policy action began with the Nixon Cabinet-level committee to combat terrorism, but moved slowly through the 1970s decade. President Carter initiated a more responsive programme which established the lead-agency concept for managing terrorist incidents. It was the Iranian embassy crisis, however, and the spate of terrorist attacks against American personnel and facilities overseas in the 1980s, which introduced major changes to American counter-terrorism policy, as well as providing a much greater emphasis on policy development. The American counter-terrorism programme has been subject to much comment over the years from 1972. Critics have faulted government for inadequate policies, lack of organization and direction, and a failure to develop suitable policy measures of response. Flawed though the endeavours may have been, they have provided a framework and a means of assessing success or failure: President Reagan, for example, was able to make certain judgements for his reactive posture during the 1985 TWA hijacking on the basis of President Carter's experiences throughout the 1979–80 embassy seizure in Tehran. Similarly, the abortive attempt to rescue the hostages in Iran provided lessons and guidance for necessary preparations in any like situation, as well as a means of determining the circumstances under which such an action might be feasible.

The Reagan administration came to power riding a wave of public reaction to the Iranian hostage crisis and promising strong measures to oppose the threat of terrorism. Aside from the rhetoric, coupled with some mainly cosmetic changes in organizational structure, few major developments were immediately obvious. American counter-terrorism policy, however, began a shift towards a more aggressive, Israeli-style approach following the 1983 truck-bombing of the US Marine base in Beirut. 'From that moment on, a military counter strike in response to terrorism was inevitable in the hearts and minds of the Reagan leadership'.[27] But not all of the Reagan leadership favoured such an idea. Secretary of Defense Caspar Weinberger voiced his misgivings repeatedly over the subsequent two years. Weinberger's reluctance, in part, stemmed from his awareness that the American military structure was designed to defend the nation in a global nuclear war, and was unsuited for battling terrorists or conducting small, swift actions. The difficulties encountered in the Grenada invasion and the casualties sustained underscored his reservations. He emphasized his position in a review of the Long Commission Report, when he agreed with a recommendation that alternative means be found to achieve United States' objectives in Lebanon.

Secretary of State George Shultz, on the other hand, became increasingly outspoken in support of pre-emptive actions against known terrorist groups. Shultz had originally been an advocate of the two-track diplomacy which placed the United States in the role of a mediator between Arabs and Israelis in the Middle East. It was Shultz who, in the wake of the 1982 Israeli invasion of Lebanon, 'devised a policy that saw American troops providing stability to permit the withdrawal of the Israeli forces and the restoration of a Lebanon with a Lebanese Christian and Moslem government'.[28] The terrorist attacks on US facilities and personnel in Beirut during 1983, beginning with the car bomb which destroyed much of the US embassy (killing 86 and wounding 100) and reaching a peak in the Marines' disaster, brought about a distinct change in his attitude. Shultz succeeded in convincing the President to sign a policy directive in April 1984 authorizing the principle of pre-emptive strikes against terrorists abroad. On the day following the signing, Shultz made the first of several speeches which signalled his altered stance, emphasizing the need 'to take "preventive or pre-emptive action" against state-sponsored terrorism'. In June, the Secretary of State called for 'a tough line on Middle East terrorism ... [and] ... pre-emptive actions against terrorist groups before they strike'.[29] Later that year, while providing assurances of adherence to the principle of the rule of law, he said that the United States (and others) 'must be willing to use military force [against terrorists, even though] ... there is potential for ... the loss of life of some innocent people'.[30] Included in this context was the suggestion that the 'rest of us would do well to follow Israel's example'.[31]

The debate between Shultz and Weinberger continued, gradually developing into a significant bureaucratic struggle. The controversy spread beyond immediate government circles to include the influence of think-tanks and lobbyists (especially of a hawkish right-wing nature).[32]

The Jonathan Institute, and Robert Kupperman of the Georgetown Institute of Strategic Studies, were among those advocating military reprisals and strikes against terrorists. Other authorities, such as Admiral Stansfield Turner,[33] shared beliefs that such actions were, *inter alia*, not in keeping with American ideals, constitutional principles, and moral tenets. Civil libertarians feared the development of assassination squads or a renewal of CIA 'Phoenix' operations of the Viet Nam era. The Reagan administration, however, claimed that it did not 'contemplate any assassination conspiracies ... preemptive action [being] based on a specific planned event ... and could only be made after complete information about a terrorist plan [was] gathered'.[34] While the arguments raged, the United States 'shied away from the Israeli tactic of launching an immediate, indiscriminate attack'[35] partially because of concern over public reaction. But the government became increasingly vocal about proposed active and military measures of response. As each new terrorist incident occurred, official US statements promised retaliation; correspondingly, each unfulfilled threat eroded American credibility and confused the American public. The open disagreement between Shultz and Weinberger, the repeated claims of US readiness to strike militarily, and the clamour of right-wing opinion combined to leave the government with fewer and fewer options. In 1985,

> Robert McFarlane, then the President's national-security advisor, told the National Strategy Information Centre that the U.S. 'must be free to consider an armed strike against terrorists or those who support them .... We need not insist on absolute evidence ... Nor should we need to prove beyond all reasonable doubt the tie between terrorists' actions and their supporters'.[36]

In his search for an answer to the problem of terrorism, Secretary of State Shultz 'introduced what would become a key factor in forming the Reagan administration's policy: "state-sponsored terrorism"'.[37] Although the US Government had long known of financial support given to the PLO by moderate Arab states, as well as suspecting Soviet involvement with terrorist groups, it could not act forcibly against those sources. Evidence existed of Syrian and Iranian complicity in attacks against US personnel and installations abroad, but both of those nations did not provide sufficient open provocation to warrant American military action. Nor did they present suitable or attractive targets. Almost conveniently, Colonel Gaddafi, with his blatant public statements in support of terrorist activity, brought Libya into prominence as the archetypal rogue state and leading practitioner of state-sponsored terrorism. Libya, a relatively safe and easy target, became the villain in 'an orchestrated confrontation with America's President'.[38] Nevertheless, the first clear demonstration of US willingness to pursue an Israeli-style policy direction came in October 1985, following the hijacking of the liner *Achille Lauro*. American military aircraft intercepted an Egyptian commercial airliner carrying the Palestinian hijackers from Cairo to Tunis, forcing the plane to land at the Italian NATO base at Sigonella where the Palestinians were taken into Italian custody. Subsequently, US military forces were used again in April 1986, and on that occasion the target *was* Libya. American military aircraft based in Britain, and on aircraft carriers in the Mediterranean, conducted a bombing raid on installations in Libya which were alleged to facilitate terrorist activities. The raid was proclaimed as a punitive and retaliatory action for Libyan involvement in the December 1985 terrorist attacks at the Rome and Vienna airports, and particularly in response to the bombing of a West Berlin disco in April of 1986 in which an American serviceman was killed.

Generally applauded in America, the two military actions by the United States received considerable censure in many foreign nations. While some disapproval centred on the question of legality in terms of international law, a greater fear was voiced about the precedent established for similar behaviour by other states. Despite the expressed concerns, President Reagan stated that he would not hesitate to repeat the blow against terrorism, and that the United States reserved the right to act unilaterally. His rhetoric and public posturing notwithstanding, the negative reaction did prompt the White House to consider the creation of a special new State Department 'public diplomacy' office for the purpose of seeking to make foreign public opinion more sympathetic to US anti-terrorist activities.[39]

Prior to the above-mentioned events of 1985–6, frustration over the inability to implement a programme of perceived substantial response to terrorist attacks, and recognition of the need for public support for retaliatory measures, led to President Reagan's request in July 1985 that Vice President Bush form a Cabinet-level Task Force on Combatting Terrorism. The result was the *Public Report Of the Vice President's Task Force On Combatting Terrorism* issued in February 1986, representing the first truly collective public statement of American counter-terrorism policy. To achieve the objective, the Vice President reported that:

> Our Task Force was briefed by more than 25 government agencies, visited 14 operations centers to observe our capability first-hand, met with over 100 statesmen, military officers, scholars and law enforcement officials, and traveled to embassies and military commands throughout the world where discussions with both U.S. and foreign officials were conducted.
>
> I personally met with many members of Congress, airline chief

executive officers, media executives, and former Cabinet officials and diplomats.[40]

The scope of the Report was very broad, ranging from discussion of the growing threat of terrorism, through US policy and response, to the role of Congress, the viewpoint of the American people, and the relationship of the media. Significantly, the Report acknowledged both the dramatic increase in international terrorist incidents and domestic vulnerability. It also underscored the US readiness to act in concert with other nations or unilaterally in response to terrorism, as well as providing a warning to states involved in the sponsorship of terrorism.

The Report was optimistic in tone, concluding that the US policy and programme to combat terrorism was tough and resolute. In reference to the opinion of the American people, while alluding to continued respect for national values, it indicated qualified agreement on military actions. 'There is growing evidence the American people support timely, well-conceived, well-executed operations, such as the capture of the *Achille Lauro* hijackers.'[41] Nonetheless, the Report acknowledged that a 'U.S. military show of force may intimidate the terrorists and their sponsors', [but]:

> There are, however, some distinct disadvantages: a show of force could be considered gunboat diplomacy, which might be perceived as a challenge rather than a credible threat; it may require a sizable deployment of support activities; it may provide our enemies with a subject for anti-American propaganda campaigns worldwide; and most important, an active military response may prove necessary to resolve the situation if a show of force fails.[42]

Several pages of recommendations were contained in the latter half of the Task Force Report, some of which (e.g. extradition agreements, payment of rewards) have been acted upon. The recommendations included suggestions to improve airport and maritime security, and a review of the vulnerability of State and Defense Department facilities and the level of overseas personnel needs, as well as:

— a National Programming Document to list agencies responsible for response to terrorism and their resources;
— a policy criteria for deciding when, if, and how to use force to pre-empt, react and retaliate;
— a full-time National Security Council (NSC) position, with support staff, to co-ordinate the national programme;
— a consolidated intelligence centre on terrorism;
— the death penalty should be established for the murder of hostages by terrorists;

— a public education programme should be introduced to inform American citizens about the counter-terrorism programme and the aims of the US Government;
— the US Government should provide the media with timely information during terrorist crises, and the media, in turn should ensure high professional and ethical standards in reporting. Regular meetings should occur between the media and government officials regarding the coverage of terrorism.

Like the Report, the recommendations were broad in their coverage, and both general and specific in nature. They have value in their identification of matters requiring revision or improvement; but they also allow for latitude of action – especially in association with pre-emptive and retaliatory actions in response to terrorism. Taken overall, the Report was a milestone in progress toward a coordinated US counter-terrorism programme based on stated policy guidelines. The system of government in the United States, however, does not lend itself to an easy application of many of the recommendations. The 'separation of powers' principle, plus the existence of inter- and intradepartmental and agency conflicts, rivalries, and protectionism, as well as political factors and the powerful influence of various lobbies, will affect the outcome of the Report and the implementation of suggested policy measures.

American counter-terrorism policy has come a long way from the early 1970s, when no concessions, host-country responsibility, and criminality of terrorist actions were the fundamental underpinnings. It has moved through the inclusion of the recognized need for international co-operation, a growth in organizational resources, increased physical protective measures, to retaliation and preemptive actions against terrorists at home and abroad. (Arguably, the 1985 FBI investigation of, and subsequent raid on, the Arkansas compound of the extremist group known as 'The Covenant, the Sword, and the Arm of the Lord' was pre-emptive.) Two aspects of policy, however, have been particularly contentious: no concessions, and retaliation and pre-emption. Unlike the Canadian and British Governments, the American authorities have made tra her greater efforts to emphasize the no-concessions rule publicly in dealing with terrorist demands. On the surface, the firm policy has resulted in casualties on occasion, e.g. Khartoum, 1973. The Vice President's Report reaffirmed that position: 'The U.S. Government will make no concessions to terrorists.'[43] On the other hand, the Americans do take a pragmatic approach and have demonstrated a willingness to negotiate through third-party intermediaries, as was done during the Iranian crisis of 1980. 'The [financial] settlement obtained the release of the hostages.'[44]

Some critics have assailed the Carter administration for its actions in negotiating with the Khomeini regime, stating that the United States paid a ransom and performed in a manner which made America appear weak and which led to an increase in terrorist activity. In fundamental terms the US did not pay a ransom, and the declared American policy of not doing so, or releasing prisoners, or changing policies, or agreeing to other acts which might encourage terrorism remains essentially intact. It has been said that terrorists are waging a war against America; flexibility is a principle of warfare, and in the battle against terrorism every legitimate resource should be brought into play. Negotiation, even if only through intermediaries, is one such resource that should not be ignored. But, as the Irangate affair clearly demonstrated, there are limits to the methods and instruments to be used in such bargaining.

The retaliatory-cum-pre-emptive raid against Libya in April 1986 raised considerable protest on the eastern side of the Atlantic Ocean. While 77 per cent of the American population applauded the raid, 59 per cent of Britons condemned it.[45] France refused permission for US aircraft to use French airspace to fly to and from Libya to conduct the attack. The issue was not so much concern about international law, although in January of the same year the British Prime Minister had opposed such strikes for that very reason. Major worries centred on the establishment of an example that some less-responsible nations might follow in the future, as well as stirring queries about the effectiveness of such a policy in Lebanon in 1982 where 'after all the bombardments, the terrorists were more active and more desperate than ever ...'[46] The raid did spur many European nations to place constraints on the activities of Libyan diplomats within their borders, even to the extent of expulsion of some Libyan representatives for alleged complicity in terrorist activities. The raid did not initiate the feared and predicted immediate large-scale response from terrorist organizations, although several incidents were related to the event: two Britons and an American held hostage in Lebanon were executed by an Arab extremist group; a US Foreign Service officer was shot in Khartoum; and a US Marine barracks at the embassy in Tunis was firebombed. The threat of terrorist response, however, did have the effect of reducing the influx of tourists from North America to Britain by 40 per cent in July 1986, causing appreciable alarm in the tourist industry.

From a practical standpoint the April 1986 demonstration of the United States' determination actively to pursue its policy of retaliation and pre-emptive action did little to eliminate terrorists. Evidence points to civilian casualties in Libya, rather than terrorist leaders, plotters, or activists.[47] But the action did raise the threshold of violence associated with response to terrorism, and placed the United States in the equivocal position of possibly having to resort to similar action in the future just to maintain the nation's credibility. Laudable though the intent may have been, as well as momentarily satisfying, it did not illustrate a policy which redounds to the credit of a world power with other sophisticated resources available to it, nor did it reflect positively on the diplomatic and foreign policy strength and prowess of the United States.

Moving to the British situation, the first chapter of Sir George Baker's review of the Northern Ireland (Emergency Provisions) Act (EPA) 1978 is devoted to General Considerations. A section of that chapter states the broad security policy of the British Government:

— to end terrorist crime from whatever source, through the effective and impartial application of the law... This means that terrorists ... are already criminals and will be treated as such regardless of their motives. They will not, for example, be prisoners of war...

— to create conditions in which the RUC no longer require the support of the Army in enforcing the law.[48]

Sir George's comments are flavoured by his necessary regard for the Northern Ireland situation, but they also reflect the government's policy in response to terrorism in the general application. A similar review of the PTA 1976 by Earl Jellicoe is equally revealing. In his Background chapter, Jellicoe has pointed out that the 'most notable trend in this area [the terrorist scene] in Great Britain has been the increasing threat posed by international terrorism'.[49] To combat that trend Jellicoe recommended that the arrest powers available under the Act be extended 'to be used against terrorists not suspected of any connection with Northern Ireland'.[50] His recommendation was subsequently embodied in the new PTA 1984.

As described earlier, British policy in response to terrorism is based upon the rule of law and incorporates police primacy, the criminal nature of terrorism, no concessions in the face of threats, and continued efforts to secure international co-operation. The intent of that policy has been the eventual defeat of terrorist activity in the United Kingdom, coupled with a return to a state of normalcy, and that 'democracy will prevail'[51] throughout the process. In that regard, Jellicoe echoes the sentiment of Parliament by writing:

[special legislation] should remain in force only while it continues to be effective, only if its aims cannot be achieved by the use of the general law, if it does not make unacceptable inroads on civil liberties, and if effective safeguards are provided to minimise the possibility of abuse.[52]

In what was later to produce serious and embarrassing repercussions for the British Government, however, a decision was made in 1972 which departed from the strictly criminal-justice approach to terrorist violence. It was a concession which applied only to Northern Ireland and came about principally as the result of a prolonged hunger strike by prisoners in Belfast prison. (It was also claimed that it was a means to facilitate negotiations between the British Government and the IRA.) At that time the then Secretary of State, Mr Whitelaw, accorded 'special status' to members of paramilitary organizations sentenced to more than nine-months imprisonment for offences related to civil disturbances. Under the terms of the special category, or 'political status', such prisoners were housed in separate compounds (primarily because of a lack of cell accommodation), 'they were not required to work, could wear their own clothes, and were allowed extra visits and food parcels'.[53] Boyle, Hadden, and Hillyard describe the conditions in some detail in their volume *Ten Years on in Northern Ireland*.[54] Essentially the prisoners lived in compounds accommodating up to ninety persons, with each compound being allocated to a particular paramilitary group. Each compound had its own 'commanding officer' and warders only entered twice a day for a head count, or on special occasions 'when search operations were carried out to prevent the accumulation of weapons and other prohibited articles ...'[55]

'This system clearly afforded a great deal of autonomy to paramilitary groups within the prison system and was in effect a recognition by the authorities of a form of political status for terrorist offenders.'[56] The Gardner Report of 1975 was strongly critical of the system, condemning it on several counts which included the likelihood that special-category prisoners would become more committed to terrorism, that they would expect an eventual amnesty, and that they would not consider themselves to be convicted prisoners. It was the report's recommendation that the earliest practicable opportunity should be taken to bring special-category status to an end. The recommendation was accepted and special-category status ceased in 1976, in conjunction with the phasing out of the much-disputed policy of internment which had been instituted in 1971. Under the conditions of the rescinding of the special status,

> no one convicted of a scheduled [i.e., terrorist] offence committed after February 1976 would be granted special category status, but ... the existing privileges of those who had already been granted special category status would not be affected, [and] those who were subsequently convicted of offences committed before March 1976 would also be permitted to claim special category status.[57]

All new admissions were stopped in 1980.

Unhappily for the government, the matter did not rest with its decision to cease the arrangement in 1976. Despite an inducement which entitled co-operative prisoners to a remission of half of their sentence, 'there was never any doubt that IRA members would continue to demand political status'.[58] Within a year the protests began; the first stage was known as 'going on the blanket' by which offenders refused to wear prison clothing and wrapped themselves in their bedclothes. Later they initiated the 'dirty protest' by refusing to wash or use the toilets and of smearing their cells with excreta. The dirty protest continued through March, 1981, 'when it was dropped so as to focus attention on Bobby Sands's hunger strike'.[59] Sands's action was taken in an attempt to coerce the authorities into a return of the special category, and it included five major demands: (1) the right to wear own clothing; (2) no prison work; (3) freedom of association; (4) extra recreational facilities and more visits and letters; and (5) restoration of remission lost on protests. 'Basically it was a battle of wills between the prisoners and the British Government.'[60] In the course of the protest ten PIRA/INLA prisoners who took part in the hunger strike died from the effects of their fasting. Fundamentally the government did not give in, despite considerable international publicity and pressure, although once the strike was over a decision was taken that prisoners could wear their own clothing and 50 per cent of lost remission times was restored.

> For the IRA it is vital to assert the legitimacy of their campaign and to emphasize that they are fighting what amounts to a war against Britain as a foreign occupying power in Northern Ireland ... For the authorities it is equally important to insist that those found guilty of ... offences are just like ordinary criminals and cannot therefore be entitled to any special treatment in prison.[61]

Boyle *et al.* cannot be accused of favouring the British position in the context of *Ten Years On* ..., but they could not, by their own admission, offer a legal basis to support the concept of special treatment for terrorist offenders or for prisoner-of-war status.

Lord Gardner, the Committee Chairman, was particularly emphatic about the criminal aspect of terrorism, stating that 'terrorists who break the law ... are not heroes but criminals; not the pioneers of political change but its direct enemies.'[62] He continued,

> The Rule of Law is presently under attack in many places throughout the world. Sometimes this takes the form of blatant terrorism; sometimes more sophisticated methods are employed. But when the attack, whatever its nature succeeds, ordered democratic government is in jeopardy. The Rule of Law must therefore be maintained ...[63]

The term 'criminalization' (which Sir George Baker considers to be a 'horrible word') has been applied to policy in Northern Ireland following the end of internment and special-category status and in conjunction with the renewal of police primacy in 1977. The description is less than accurate, and certainly could not be associated in a similar sense with Great Britain where terrorism has not been construed as other than a criminal offence. Criminalization derives its marginal legitimacy from the semblance of political status related to the special category, as well as the predominant role played by the military in the years from 1970 to 1976. Nonetheless, the rule of law continued to be upheld throughout that period, and security policy was directed towards an eventual return to normal police supremacy in law-and-order duties.

A second area of contention in regard to terrorism-response policy in Northern Ireland involves judicial procedures, particularly the system of Diplock courts. Fundamentally it is a system whereby an accused faces trial before a single judge and without the presence of a jury. Only 'scheduled offences' are tried in such a manner; that is, offences which are likely to have been committed by terrorist offenders. Within the United Kingdom the procedure is unique to the Province of Ulster. The Diplock courts were established in 1973, following the report of a Commission, headed by Lord Diplock, which was required to consider 'arrangements for the administration of justice in Northern Ireland ... to deal more effectively with terrorist organizations by bringing to book ... individuals involved in terrorist activities ...' [64] The Commission found that the 'main obstacle to dealing effectively with terrorist crime in the regular courts of justice is intimidation ...'[65] The intimidation extended not only to witnesses, but to members of juries and attempts to influence judges as well.

Intimidation was not the only problem, however; bias on the part of juries was also a factor, as was the practice of attempting to pack the juries with Protestants. Procedures were needed which would overcome these obstacles and which would facilitate the presentation of evidence. The result was a system of non-jury trials of scheduled offences in which much of the evidence is based upon written statements, and the onus of proof as to the possession of firearms and explosives lies with the defendant. In cases where a defendant refuses to recognize the legitimacy of the court, it amounts to a plea of guilty, although the prosecution must produce convincing evidence of guilt. 'It is fair to conclude ... that the Diplock court system has continued to operate without discrimination and from the point of view of the authorities it has worked smoothly and efficiently.'[66] The system has not, however, won overwhelming public approval, and criticism has been raised by jurists on various aspects. Recommendations have been made that a three-judge arrangement would be more suitable to preclude 'case-hardening', as well as to offer a wider point of view. The latter might induce a better acceptance on the part of the public, especially in trials involving members of the security forces.

Two other aspects bear upon the judicial policy operative in Northern Ireland; they are the matters of interrogation of suspects, and the use of 'supergrasses.' Interrogation is a particularly sensitive subject because many cases in the Diplock courts are decided by the testimony or confessions of the accused.

> The efficient operation of the Diplock court system ... is largely dependent on confessions which have been obtained during prolonged interrogation. A very large number of convictions are based entirely on such confessions, and a high proportion of contested cases revolve around their admissibility and reliability.[67]

Interrogation procedures in Northern Ireland were first the topic of investigation following the introduction of internment in 1971, discussed later. Extraordinary methods, such as hooding and sleep deprivation, were halted by the British Government in the wake of an inquiry headed by Lord Parker.[68] Matters came to a head again in early 1978 as a consequence of the publication of a report of an Amnesty International mission which visited Northern Ireland between 28 November and 6 December 1977. The substance of the report prompted the government to institute a Committee of Inquiry under the chairmanship of His Honour Judge H.G. Bennett, Q.C.[69]

The Bennett Committee did find evidence 'in which injuries, whatever their precise cause, were not self-inflicted and were sustained in police custody'.[70] In fairness, however, Bennett also stated that 'There is a co-ordinated and extensive campaign to discredit the RUC ... No other police force in the United Kingdom is called upon to deal with so much violent crime in such uncompromising circumstances as the RUC.'[71] Boyle *et al.*, commenting on the increase in complaints during 1976–7, allude to 'the pressure put on police by the Northern Ireland Secretary, Roy Mason, to obtain convictions and the failure of ministers and senior officers in the RUC to make it clear that malpractice during interrogation would not be tolerated'.[72] A number of recommendations were made by the Bennett Committee, among which were a need for increased vigilance by supervisory personnel, closed-circuit television in interview rooms, more frequent inspection by medical officers, and the unconditional right to access to a solicitor after forty-eight hours of detention. The majority of the Bennett recommendations were implemented, and since 1980 the level of complaint has dropped sharply. (During a research visit to Northern Ireland in 1985 permission was granted to witness the interrogation of suspects via the closed-circuit system, without the knowledge of the interviewing officers, and the supervisory method did appear to function as Bennett had intended.)

The EPA 1978 confers on the police the power to detain and interview a suspect for a period of up to seventy-two hours. The RUC may also detain a suspect under the PTA 1984, and thereby make application to hold the suspect for a total of seven days. The Diplock Commission made it very clear that

> If human lives are to be saved and destruction of property prevented ... it is inescapable that the security authorities must have the power to question suspected members of terrorist organizations ... The whole technique of skilled interrogation is to build up an atmosphere in which the initial desire to remain silent is replaced by an urge to confide in the questioner.[73]

The detention, interview, and arrest powers conferred, function in combination with the Diplock court system in which evidence is accepted unless it can be shown that it was obtained by torture or inhuman or degrading treatment. It is imperative, therefore, that police interrogation methods be seen to conform as closely as possible to those currently in use in Great Britain, as well as to the recommendations of the Bennett Committee.

Supergrass is a term which derives its meaning from the reference to 'a snake in the grass', an expression used by members of the British underworld when describing an informer. It is simply a system in which an accomplice agrees to give evidence which will lead to the arrest and trial of terrorist offenders. The concept is not new; it has been so known for three centuries in English law. The difference in Northern Ireland has been the fact that individuals have implicated large numbers of offenders; that is, one supergrass has implicated more than twenty offenders on occasion. A complicating factor in the conduct of such trials is that when such evidence is given in a jury proceeding, the judge warns the jury about the competency of the witness; under the Diplock system, the judge must warn himself. Sir George Baker has commented at length on the supergrass procedure in Northern Ireland. While he did not disagree with the concept, he did voice reservations about 'the wisdom of having so many defendants, so many charges, such delay in starting, and such long trials'.[74] Undoubtedly the system has not been an unqualified success, and several trials have ended in acquittals because the supergrass recanted his testimony at the last moment, or the judge decided that the testimony was unsatisfactory.

Discussion of British policy as a resource in response to terrorism would not be complete without mention of the use of internment during the early years of the current Northern Ireland troubles. Internment is not unique to circumstances in Ulster in the first half of the 1970s decade; it has been employed as security policy in both Northern Ireland and in Eire on previous occasions. In fact, it enjoyed a large measure of success at times when both the North and the South entered into its use conjunctively. The failure of internment in the 1970s was partially a consequence of adverse publicity, partially a result of mishandling, partially the fault of poor intelligence, and partially because the Republic chose openly to oppose implementation at that time.

The contemporary account of internment is long and involved; implementation of internment was not a quick and easy decision reached by the British Government. Agreement of the latter was a necessity because control of security in Ulster had been a Westminster responsibility from the time that troops were formally introduced into the disturbances in 1969. Until March 1972, however, Northern Ireland had its own parliament and government within the UK, and it was that body which favoured the policy of internment and which pressed at length to obtain the concurrence of the British Cabinet. Writing ten years after the event, Edgar O'Ballance said that the 'British Government's reaction to the IRA terrorism that developed in 1971 was uncomprehending, hesitant, and piecemeal'.[75] Viewed in retrospect, undoubtedly the comment is not without some justification. But the developments in Northern Ireland had come as a considerable surprise to the British Government, which had not paid much heed to events in the province since 1922. Intimate knowledge of the affairs of Ulster was not readily at hand in Whitehall and, as O'Ballance observed, 'The GOC [General-Officer-Commanding] [at the time] ... was conditioned by colonial methods of dealing with insurrections, which were hardly suitable for a Northern Ireland setting.'[76]

Originally welcomed as saviours by all concerned (excepting the IRA), the Army rather quickly became the butt of criticism. Catholics claimed that the Army favoured the Protestants, and the latter argued that the Army was not hard enough on the Catholics. Controversy was especially heated over the policy which allowed no-go areas in large Catholic enclaves in Belfast and Londonderry, a policy which London was reluctant to attempt to change for fear of causing casualties amongst the civilian population. What

> began as a fairly straightforward peace-keeping operation gradually developed into a series of confrontations between the Army and the civilian population in the main Catholic areas in Belfast and elsewhere, and then into sporadic guerrilla warfare between the IRA and the Army.[77]

Internment had demonstrated evidence of success in past use, although under conditions which did not approximate the circumstances of 1971. Nonetheless, vociferous and influential (in Ulster) political figures such as Ian Paisley and William Craig denounced the Army's efforts, and many called loudly for the detention of terrorist sympathizers. Two Prime Ministers of Ulster resigned in the space of two years as a consequence of the troubles and the third, Brian Faulkner, was considered to offer the best hope for a solution. Faulkner espoused the idea of internment as a remedy to the chaos, and in mid-1971 he managed to negotiate agreement with the British Cabinet.

The policy was charged with controversy from the outset. Poor intelligence, in part a result of a lack of co-operation between the military and the police, led to the arrest of significant numbers of non-involved persons. Initially the announced aim of the action was to smash the IRA, and Catholic communities were the targets of the security sweeps. But many of the PIRA ringleaders escaped arrest because they were unknown or intelligence was faulty; some of the IRA appear to have had some foreknowledge of the plan and were in hiding or managed to cross into the Republic. The operation itself was carried out in a heavy-handed manner and was subject to much adverse publicity based upon alleged incidents of maltreatment by members of the military and the police. The complaints gave rise to the Compton Inquiry 'into allegations against the security forces of physical brutality in Northern Ireland arising out of the events on 9 August 1971'.[78] The Compton Report did not uncover evidence of brutality as alleged in many cases, and which had received considerable negative attention from the media. The Report did, however, highlight the use of methods of interrogation of a sort not acceptable in the United Kingdom. The Committee judged that the 'interrogation in depth' of a 'small number of persons ... who were believed to possess information of a kind which it was operationally necessary to obtain as rapidly as possible'[79] did constitute ill-treatment but not brutality.

The findings and the surrounding publicity over the incident eventually prompted the initiation of another inquiry, this time headed by Lord Parker. The purpose of the inquiry was to establish if 'the procedures currently authorized for the interrogation of persons suspected of terrorism ... require amendment'.[80] Two of the three members who participated replied in the negative; the dissenting opinion of the third, Lord Gardner, was sufficiently impressive to cause the Heath Government to ban any further use of the methods. Reaction to internment was disastrous. As previously mentioned, the main target of the policy was the Catholic population, although Faulkner threatened to employ internment 'against any individual or organization which might pose a threat in the future.'[81] The Catholics, however, saw the move as simply another attack upon the minority community and not as the announced attempt to strangle the IRA. Serious rioting ensued, as well as increased violence by the terrorists whose recruiting efforts benefited from the policy.

'After internment had been introduced ... the new Provo policy was to intensify its bombing campaign ... and also to step up the antipersonnel campaign, especially against British soldiers and the UDR.'[82] 1971 became the worst year to date in terms of violence; following the introduction of internment to the end of 1971, '146 people were killed, including forty-seven members of the security forces, and ninety-nine civilians, and there were 729 explosions and 1,437 shooting incidents'.[83] On the surface, internment cannot be seen to have achieved very much of positive value. It served to increase the alienation of the Catholic population, assisted the PIRA with recruiting and support, caused some IRA units to join the Provos, and gave a fillip to violent actions. Claims have been made that it precluded a threatened Protestant backlash against no-go areas and the Catholic population in general, and that in the first two days 'over eight officers of the Officials and the Provisionals had been arrested...'.[84] Perhaps more noteworthy was the fact that the increased level of violence over the ensuing eight months ultimately led to the decision by the British Government to take control of all security and law-enforcement matters in Northern Ireland. The latter action brought about the resignation of Faulkner's Government at Stormont, the suspension of that governing body, and the initiation of Direct Rule from Westminster.

British policy from the beginning of the disturbances in 1969, and particularly through the continuing period of Direct Rule, has been an endeavour to find a means to return domestic jurisdiction to Northern Ireland. Various attempts have been made to develop a solution, one which must include a form of participation on the part of the minority Catholic community. A promising effort occurred in 1973 when an elected Assembly and a power-sharing Executive were established. The arrangement included the concept of a Council of Ireland which was intended to generate a co-operative relationship between the Province of Ulster and the Republic. The entire proposal collapsed, however, when Loyalist opposition to power-sharing and the Council proved too strong. A Worker's Strike in May 1974 paralysed the province, forcing the Executive to resign, and the project was abandoned. Various other moves were attempted over following years with little success, although another Assembly was elected in 1982 based on the formula of 'rolling devolution'. The plan was to begin with a consultative and scrutiny role for the Assembly which would progress towards devolved power. Progress was to be based on agreement of all parties represented, with a weighted majority requirement to guard against Unionist domination. Following the election of the Assembly only the Unionist and centralist Alliance parties took their seats; the Social Democratic and Labour

Party (SDLP) and Provisional Sinn Fein refused to do so. The Assembly became principally a forum in which the Unionist parties could voice their opinions concerning the British Government's administration of Ulster. Eventually even the Alliance Party withdrew from the Assembly, which was prorogued in June 1986.

In November 1985, following lengthy negotiation between the Governments of the United Kingdom and Eire, the two nations signed the Anglo-Irish Agreement at Hillsborough in England. 'The result is certainly the most innovative and courageous effort made to evolve a stable and peaceful political framework for the bitterly divided Province since the Sunningdale power-sharing experiment of 1974.'[85] Under the terms of the Agreement an Intergovernmental Conference was established, with a secretariat based in Belfast, by which the Dublin Government was accorded a consultative role in the government of Ulster. Significantly, 'the Republic's government for the first time [accepted] that there shall be no change in the constitutional status of the Unionist majority without their consent'.[86] The underlying philosophy of the Agreement is based on recognition that the IRA's terrorist campaign, 'which threatens democracy on both sides of the border',[87] feeds on the alienation and despair of the Catholic minority who 'feel that their identity and fundamental rights are not recognized or protected in a Province so long dominated by an intolerant and aggressive Protestant sectarianism'.[88] Politically, the Agreement aims at enhancing support for the SDLP, as well as mitigating some of the criticism originating in the USA. The Agreement was generally well received by the Catholic population of Northern Ireland; it received positive press reaction in mainland Britain, was welcomed by the Labour Party, enthusiastically endorsed by the US Government and Congress, and overwhelmingly supported by the European Parliament. The Unionist parties in Ulster, on the other hand, bitterly opposed the accord.

The Unionist arguments are principally centred on three main objections: (1) that the Agreement was forced upon them without their consent; (2) that they are being handed over to a foreign government and 'sold out' by Great Britain; and (3) they have become second-class British citizens because of the consultative role of the Irish Government. The Unionists resented the fact that they were not consulted on the terms of the Agreement, and felt that a referendum should have been conducted in Northern Ireland before the document was signed. To demonstrate their opposition the fifteen Unionist Members of Parliament at Westminster resigned their seats and forced an election as a means of obtaining their referendum. The result was not completely as they had hoped; only fourteen were returned to office. Subsequently, Unionist supporters indulged in public disturbances, demonstrations, and a one-day strike to call attention to their claims and their dissatisfaction with the Agreement. Threats of rent and rates (taxes) strikes have also been put forward, but the British Government has remained firm in its resolve not to be intimidated. The Agreement has encountered some unfortunate moments, as in the case of ill-considered public statements by officials of both the British and Irish Governments. Similarly, incidents involving the extradition of terrorist offenders in which documentation errors resulted in adverse publicity have created strains.

The expressed objections of the Unionists have no basis in fact, especially as it is the right of the government at Westminster 'to make treaties and agreements with any other government ... provided it can carry the support of Parliament ...'[89] Indeed, since it is the responsibility of the British public as a whole to provide for the security and well-being of Northern Ireland, a referendum would have to include the entire British population, and the outcome would most likely be in favour of the Agreement. Contrary to claims of being sold out, the Unionists are actually in a better position by virtue of Dublin's recognition of their rights, and 'the Agreement is perfectly explicit that full executive control ... rests ... with the *British* government'.[90] In terms of being second-class British citizens, the reality is that the Unionists will have to become accustomed to being British citizens instead of a privileged ruling class. The PIRA has realized the importance and the danger (to itself) of the Anglo-Irish Agreement. They have increased their bombings and their mortar attacks against police stations, as well as assassinations of police and military personnel. Of particular concern have been their attempts to intimidate construction firms and workers involved in the building and repair of security facilities throughout the province. A major improvement in cross-border security arrangements and the successful disruption of terrorist operations would have a significant positive influence on the public and political support for the Anglo-Irish Agreement in the United Kingdom and the Republic. But the biggest problem remains 'those who fuel and fan the fires of sectarian bigotry, hatred and suspicion'.[91]

Sir George Baker included a memorable quotation in his review of the EPA 1978:

'Amid the clash of arms the laws are silent' so Cicero exclaimed over 2,000 years ago ... Now, too, peace, order and society itself are under fierce and constant attack and that is why we must remember Lord Atkins's famous dictum: 'In this country, amid the clash of arms the laws are not silent. They may be changed, but they speak the same language in war as in peace.'

This war is being waged by organizations which style themselves armies and observe military procedures, but it has not invaded, and will not be allowed to invade, the courts. The rule of law has prevailed and will continue to prevail there.[92]

British policy has continually adhered to the principle of the rule of law. Terrorists have been treated as criminals; when apprehended for attacks in the United Kingdom, they have been tried in British courts and sentenced to incarceration in British jails. Policy primacy has been maintained in Great Britain and has been restored in Northern Ireland. Perhaps slow and shaky in the early stages of response to modern terrorism, British policy has developed steadily and has gained strength through the benefit of experience.

### Experience

Not always the best teacher, experience can be a valuable resource if studied carefully. It has been said that rules are for the obedience of fools, and the guidance of wise men. So it is with experience; it can prove dangerous if slavishly followed, but very useful if employed judiciously. Canada, the United States, and the United Kingdom have had differing experiences of terrorism and each nation has been guided, albeit not always wisely and well, by those experiences.

Canadian experience came early, in the form of the domestic terrorism of the FLQ. It was a traumatic event for the nation which had the positive value of alerting government to weaknesses in emergency-response infrastructure. The expeditious manner in which the FLQ threat was suppressed also had the negative effect of convincing many Canadians that terrorism was not a serious concern for Canada. Consequently, aside from special preparations for potentially high-threat attractions (e.g. the 1976 Olympic Games in Montreal), counter-terrorism measures did not receive particular attention by the public or government authorities through the latter half of the 1970s. The impact of terrorist attacks elsewhere in the world did not pass unnoticed by Canada; thus, the careful arrangements in Montreal as a result of the Munich massacre in 1972, and similar stringent precautions during the Summit Seven conference near Ottawa in 1981. In conjunction, the McDonald Report of 1981 stirred renewed interest in Canadian organizational structure for terrorism response. But Canada and Canadians largely escaped experience of terrorist activity, domestically or abroad, until April 1982, when a member of the Turkish embassy staff was seriously wounded in an assassination attempt in Ottawa. The attack was an incident of international terrorism carried out by the Armenian Secret Army for the Liberation of Armenia (ASALA).

Four months later the Justice Commandos of the Armenian Genocide (JCAG) struck in Ottawa, murdering the Turkish military attaché as he sat in his automobile at a traffic-light. During the same year a domestic terrorist group, known as Direct Action, claimed responsibility for two bombing incidents. One involved (Canadian) $6 million damage to a power substation on west-coast Vancouver Island, and the other injured ten people and caused considerable structural damage to a missile component manufacturing factory in east-central Canada. Nonetheless, except for a pointed warning to Canadians about the dangers of doing business in South Africa issued in 1983 by the African National Congress (ANC), Canada continued to enjoy a somewhat privileged status *vis-à-vis* encounters with terrorism. It was not until 1985 that several dramatic and tragic events again demonstrated to Canadians that they, and their nation, were not immune to terrorist attack. In March three Armenian terrorists stormed the Turkish embassy in Ottawa, killed a security guard, and held the ambassador's family and staff members hostage for four hours before surrendering to police. Two incidents followed in July: a bomb allegedly placed aboard an Air India jet by Sikh extremists in Canada destroyed the aircraft over the Atlantic Ocean with a loss of 329 lives; and on the previous day a related explosion occurred while baggage-handlers were unloading a Canadian Pacific Airlines jumbo jet at Tokyo airport, killing two people, and was also traced to Sikh militants in Canada. Six months later two Canadian citizens were killed during the Egyptian rescue of hostages aboard an aircraft in Malta.

Compared with the United States and the United Kingdom, however, Canada's experience of terrorism has not been as frequent in terms of incidents, or in numbers of casualties suffered, domestically or internationally. For a decade after the FLQ affair Canadians felt secure from any danger at home as well as abroad. Canadian citizens, government facilities, officials, and interests overseas have been relatively free of terrorist threats. It is not surprising, therefore, to note a rather low level of concern about terrorism amongst Canadians in all walks of life for better than ten years following the October Crisis. As mentioned earlier, while the FLQ threat shook Canadian complacency, the impressive suppression of the movement had a dangerous side-effect of inducing a degree of over-confidence. When questioned in 1981 about preparations for countering any possible recurrence of an FLQ-type experience, some Canadian Forces officers replied that: 'We'll just dust off the plans we used before.'[93] Admittedly, certain senior officials did not hold the same opinion; but the overwhelming defeat of the FLQ, combined with Canada's apparent splendid isolation, had an inhibiting effect on the perceived need to develop significant anti-terrorism measures. Fortunately, the distressing events of the 1980s have not gone unheeded, and the Canadian Government has taken positive steps to improve its capability to meet the threat of terrorism.

Nonetheless, the FLQ experience should have provided a guide; not so much as an example of success, but as a warning of terrorism's disruptive potential. Similarly, the experience of other nations in regard to international terrorist attacks should make Canada more aware of its vulnerability, especially in association with its overseas missions and interests.

Americans have not had the dubious benefit of experiencing the domestic violence of groups such as the FLQ or PIRA. The Puerto Rican FALN bombing attacks have probably come closest to approximating terrorism of that nature. 'A handful of terrorist organizations account for most bombings and other terrorist actions in the United States.'[94] Bombings, in fact, have been the most prominent form of incident because 'the simplicity ... is most attractive to the small, relatively unsophisticated terrorist groups currently operating in the United States'.[95] With a few notable exceptions (e.g. FALN, Weathermen, Symbionese Liberation Army), the United States has escaped the terrorist outrages that have plagued Europe, the Middle East, and Latin America. For the most part, terrorist incidents have been judged as criminal acts and treated with a standard law-enforcement approach. It is one reason why to an extent, the American public has been able to ignore the problem of terrorism. Domestic terrorism has simply not been a major concern within the USA, especially when compared with the high levels of violent crime, e.g. thirteen terrorist incidents in 1984, and seven in 1985.[96] A British newspaper editorial commented, for example, that 'though American cities are afflicted by rates of criminal violence that have no counterpart in Europe, political violence is almost unknown'.[97]

It is somewhat paradoxical that the United States has had a marginal experience of domestic terrorism. During the civil-rights disturbances and campus unrest of the 1960s and early 1970s a profusion of underground publications offered a wealth of ideas pertaining to civil disobedience and outright revolution. Strategies, tactics, instructions on the manufacture of lethal weapons and explosive devices became readily available for general readership. A number of publishers, many associated with the growing survivalist culture, still offer a wide range of similar material for sale. Jay Mallin's book, *Terror and Urban Guerrillas*,[98] provided a warning about the possibilities of terrorist activity in the USA. One particular chapter, 'Terror in the United States', cites militant writings *circa* 1969 which predict 'direct action [that] will take two forms, terrorism and sabotage'.[99] The suggestions for disruptive action which follow are realistic and fully within the capabilities of determined activists. 'If practiced by a great number of individuals, in a great number of places, they could effectively ... drive the authorities wild.'[100] That the disgruntled minorities in the United

States have not elected to adopt such methods is a tribute to the American democratic system and its adaptability.

The openness of American society, its dependence on technology, and two long undefended borders contribute to an assessment of the United States as 'a soft terrorist target'.[101] Yet because 'the world is full of American targets',[102] international terrorism has rarely made an appearance within the nation.

American embassies, American bases, American businesses and American overseas residents provide terrorists with all the victims, and opportunities for sensation that they require. The profession of the American diplomat, for example, has become an appallingly high-risk way of life, more have been killed abroad since the Second World War than American generals or admirals, despite the Korean and Vietnam [sic] wars.[103]

It has been American experience with major terrorist atrocities abroad that has produced the greatest impact upon US response policy. Regrettably, experience overseas in the years between 1945 and 1970 was ignored, and it has taken the serious incidents of the 1970s and 1980s to draw attention to the problem.

Yet even that was slow in coming, and was coupled with failures to appreciate the magnitude of the threat. The initial lack of protection for the US embassy in Beirut in 1983 is difficult to comprehend in the light of experience of earlier attacks on US diplomatic facilities in Viet Nam, Iran, Pakistan, Cyprus, and a number of other locations. It is also difficult to understand the inadequate security arrangements at the US Marine compound in Beirut six months later. Rather than being 'frustrated by a sense of helplessness',[104] Americans should be looking to experience for the necessary positive lessons. Granted, several obviously tempting targets in the United States in 1984 (Los Angeles Olympics, New Orleans World's Fair, Republican and Democratic Party Conventions in Dallas and San Francisco, respectively) did foster improvements in domestic security measures. American perception of terrorism has been hampered somewhat in perspective by preoccupation with the influence of communism and the role of Soviet Russia. Claire Sterling's book[105] created something of a sensation, largely as a result of its allegation of Soviet complicity in the organization and support of terrorism on a global basis. Many US authorities and politicians have been unable to accept the concept of terrorism as a threat to US security unless in association with a communist motivation. In a parallel vein, elements of the American population continue to provide assistance to front organizations acting on behalf of Irish terrorists in the belief that they are promoting the cause of freedom.

Included in its findings, the Vice President's Report on terrorism makes reference to the viewpoint of the American people, a viewpoint based on experience up to November 1985. According to the report, 78 per cent of all Americans believed terrorism to be one of the most serious problems facing their nation. The attitudes expressed anger, frustration, fear, and vulnerability, as well as a concern for the perception of the United States as a world leader. Most Americans thought that a cohesive policy on terrorism did not exist, but that such a policy should be developed which reflected national values, e.g. respect for individual life, law, and the sovereignty of nations. While military response was considered controversial, although welcomed by many Americans, there was evidence of growing support for well-executed, swift, and forceful actions against terrorists. Experience has not been a resource which Americans have employed to the nation's best advantage in response to, or in the appreciation of, the threat of terrorism. A tendency toward re-learning old lessons the hard way, or of neglecting previous experience, has been evident. Americans are not noted for patience in dealing with problems; valuable though the trait may be under certain circumstances, it becomes a liability when it does not allow time for consideration of the past.

Earlier reference has been made to the wealth of British experience in contending with insurgency and terrorism in overseas colonies. The main benefactor was the Army, although service abroad did not prepare it for related duties in its own homeland. Also, as Kitson has observed, 'one ... requirement [was] to maintain a force in Europe which would appear ... as a convincing contribution to a credible deterrent'.[106] Training, organization, and equipment for that role and risk meant expertise in conventional warfare, not proficiency in dealing with riotous mobs and terrorists. The venue, too, was northern Europe, not Northern Ireland. A lack of experience was not the reason for not sending police from Great Britain to assist the RUC. The suggestion was put forward in the weeks before the civil disturbances went beyond the control of the RUC in August 1969, and was repeated a year later. As former Prime Minister James Callaghan explained:

> ... until the Police Act of 1970 there was no legal provision by which this could be done, and the British police objected in principle to serving when the Special Powers Act was in force ... and it was the last I ever heard of the plan.[107]

British experience with terrorism in Northern Ireland grew rapidly in the early 1970s. For mainland Britain, however, it was a time of vicarious learning gained from almost daily scenes of the violence portrayed on television screens, by radio broadcasts, and through the printed media. The need for mainland response was not immediate; it was not until 1973, when PIRA exported its threat to Great Britain as a matter of policy, that major efforts were required to curb terrorist inroads. By that time the law-enforcement and security agencies had almost five years of Ulster's experience to draw upon for guidance. Incidents of international terrorism in Great Britain were rare during the 1970s, and events on the Continent had little tangible impact across the English Channel. Nonetheless, isolated attacks in 1972 and 1973, such as the PLO letter-bomb campaign against Jewish targets and the seizure of the Indian High Commission by Pakistani militants, served warnings of the need for special security measures. Britons, however, have not been the object of terrorist threats domestically (excluding the Irish dimension), and infrequently overseas in recent years. In view of the magnitude of the Northern Ireland problem, the absence of international terrorist attention has been fortunate.

But the situation may not continue undisturbed, as events in 1986 have indicated. British permission for the US Government to use military aircraft based in England for the raid against Libya incurred the wrath of Arab extremist groups. Two Britons were murdered in Lebanon as a direct consequence, and a British military base on Cyprus was subjected to a rocket, mortar, and small-arms attack four months later, although the motivation and links of the group which carried out the raid remain unclear. The years of coping with terrorism in Northern Ireland have prepared the British Government and people to meet the threat reasonably well. A possible danger lies with overseas diplomatic posts and commercial enterprises, or citizens working abroad, in locations previously considered safe. It is in those places that the earlier British colonial experience should prove of value.

## Infrastructure

The very nature of liberal democracy makes it vulnerable to, and attractive as, a target of terrorism. Those circumstances are enhanced by the openness of government and society in Canada, the United States, and the United Kingdom, as well as by the technological dependency of the three nations. In response to terrorism, however, the system of Cabinet government in Canada and the United Kingdom confers some advantages over the 'separation of powers' in the United States. The dominating position of the Cabinet permits a central national focus of direction and control, and allows for a reasonably speedy passage of legislation in times of emergencies. The latter is particularly true when coupled with the provision for issuance of Orders-in-Council. Such conditions, of course, are dependent upon the government having a majority position in Parliament or, in the case of a coalition, being able to secure a consensus.

The Canadian Government, as with those of the United States and the

United Kingdom, possesses overriding powers which it can exert in times of a national emergency. Normally, the federal body monitors the progress of a serious situation and awaits a provincial request for assistance, as in providing Military Aid to the Civil Power. But in some circumstances it may act arbitrarily; during the October Crisis, for example, the Federal government deployed troops in Ottawa to protect diplomatic premises and vital points without a request from the Government of the Province of Ontario. The Dare Report stated, in part, that in Canada 'Responsibility for managing the great majority of emergencies lies with the municipal [and] provincial ... governments ... [and] ... harmonious and efficient federal-provincial co-operation is an important condition for crisis-handling....'[108] That observation, and supporting evidence, helped to bring about the lead-minister system of crisis-management within the Canadian Government. Both the Dare Report and the McDonald Report also called for a more centralized arrangement of control at the level of the Privy Council and the Cabinet for use in times of emergency, and for the monitoring and direction of national-security matters. The McDonald recommendations are discussed in following paragraphs.

The report was critical of the functioning of the Cabinet Committee on Security and Intelligence, or rather the infrequency of its functioning because of inadequacies in the operation of its supporting Interdepartmental Committee (ICSI) and sub-committees. Suggestions were made for modifications to the responsibilities and workings of those subordinate bodies to allow the Cabinet Committee to meet on a regular basis to establish the government's intelligence priorities. Fundamentally the Report observed that:

> Weaknesses in the internal security system can have drastic consequences for the well-being of the nation. The secret, intrusive nature of security work makes it dangerous to permit any Minister to become overly dominant in this field. The consideration of intelligence needs to be a balanced process free from domination by any single government department. It is doubtful that any other area of government activity has as much potential for damaging civil liberties. For all of these reasons we think it essential that the Prime Minister continue to be chairman of the Cabinet Committee on Security and Intelligence ...[109]

The report also recommended that the Privy Council's Security and Intelligence Secretariat should play a co-ordinating, not an operational role, in government activities involving security and intelligence matters.

'Virtually everyone who discussed the interdepartmental committee system with us ... said that though the basic structure ... is sound it is not working as well as it should.'[110] The report identified problems involving the ICSI and the two sub-committees of that body: the Security Advisory Committee (SAC), and the Intelligence Advisory Committee (IAC). A major concern was the fact that the ICSI was not providing the initiative and leadership necessary to enable the SAC, in particular, to work effectively.

> We recommend that in the future the *initiative* in policy issues such as personnel security, physical security and emergency planning not be delegated to a junior committee. Leadership in determining which security policy issues need resolution, in assigning policy problems to the [SAC], and in monitoring the impact of security procedures, must be exercised by Ministers and Deputy Ministers. The Cabinet and [ICSI] should establish clear mandates with firm completion dates for working groups at the [SAC] level.[111]

In keeping with that comment, it was recommended that the Solicitor General be designated as lead Minister for most security policy matters, and that the Assistant Deputy Solicitor General in charge of the Police and Security Branch (PSB) of that Department continue to chair the SAC.

Turning to the IAC, the McDonald Committee was troubled by the fact that 'the [SAC] collates and prepares assessments of current security intelligence, the [IAC] does the same for foreign intelligence'.[112] In its report, the McDonald Committee urged that those responsibilities held by SAC be transferred to the IAC.

> As we have pointed out many times in this Report, many of the threats to Canada's internal security have international dimensions. The collation and distribution of reports about such threats should not be split up into foreign and domestic compartments.[113]

It was further suggested that membership of the IAC be expanded to represent the community of intelligence producers and its major customers. Such a broadening of the IAC should include the head of the new Security Service (Canadian Security Intelligence Service (CSIS)), as well as representatives of the Departments of Finance, Industry, Trade and Commerce, and Energy, Mines and Resources, and the Treasury Board. In conjunction, a change to the IAC's chairmanship was recommended to preclude one government department having more influence than another on the intelligence assessment process.

> [The] central co-ordinating work must not be dominated or be perceived to be dominated by one or two departments of

government. It is essential that the perspectives of the various collecting departments be reflected in the intelligence products the government receives. We think ... this process will be enhanced if the [IAC] is chaired by the Assistant Secretary of the Cabinet (Security and Intelligence) rather than by the Deputy Under Secretary for External Affairs (Security and Intelligence).[114]

A very significant conclusion of the McDonald Report was associated with 'a deficiency in the machinery available to do strategic long-term assessments within government of intelligence from various sources ...'.[115] To rectify that lack of capability, the report recommended that the IAC continue to provide current intelligence, but that a Bureau of Intelligence Assessments be established for the purpose of 'longer term, strategic estimates assessing the likelihood that certain situations will exist or that certain events will occur'.[116] Located in the Privy Council Office, the Bureau would not be an intelligence-collecting agency; rather its

functions would be confined to using the intelligence collected by other departments and agencies of the Canadian government and that obtained from other sources, and combining this with the best available public sources of information to produce long-term assessments of threats to Canada's security and vital interests.[117]

While some of the proposals of the McDonald Report were not implemented (e.g. the Bureau of Assessments), a number of changes have been effected. The IAC now prepares intelligence assessments and reports on both foreign and domestic matters, the latter no longer a purview of the SAC. Further, the Coordinator (Security and Intelligence) of the Privy Council Office (PCO) is the chairman of the IAC. On the other hand, in an attempt to give the SAC more sectoral perspective, the Deputy Solicitor General presides as the chairman. Security matters, including the threat of terrorism, have received increased attention by the Canadian Government in the 1980s, as was illustrated by the Solicitor General's public statements in March, 1986. The most widely publicized and controversial outcome of the McDonald Commission, however, was the establishment of the civilian security agency: the Canadian Security Intelligence Service (CSIS). In keeping with the McDonald recommendations, the CSIS was placed under the aegis of the Solicitor General's department. The CSIS was created by divorcing the RCMP's Security Service from that law-enforcement body, allowing the RCMP to continue its primary role of policing and enforcement. Although many of the RCMP members of the former Security Service moved across to the new organization, they ceased to function as police officers. The CSIS role is to collect and analyse information and intelligence on activities that are reasonably suspected of constituting threats to the security of Canada, and to report its findings to the government. Much like MI-5 in the United Kingdom, it is not an enforcement or prosecuting agency with powers of arrest or criminal investigation. Needless to say, the creation of CSIS was resented by many within the RCMP who regard it as a negative reflection on the history and performance of the Force.

Before examining the British and American infrastructures, one aspect of the Dare Report bears mention. The Dare Committee argued the need for a central-government situation centre, with a supporting secretariat and a Cabinet briefing room for use during emergencies. The Senate Committee Report of 1987 also recommended the establishment of 'a central, crisis management centre for the federal government'.[118] Attractive though the concept may appear in theory, the proposal overlooks the fact that many government departments must maintain individual operations centres for the conduct of their day-to-day affairs. The Departments of National Defence, External Affairs, and Transport are examples of this need. The Solicitor General's Department must also maintain its operations centre for other purposes than the possible requirement to co-ordinate response to a terrorist threat or incident in Canada. The fundamental requirement is for a more closely co-ordinated and structured linkage, or plan, joining the various centres as a means to provide a centrally directed response managed by the Solicitor General.

A Cabinet briefing room, however, could prove advantageous by allowing ready access to the Prime Minister and senior decision-makers, and to facilitate the process of crisis management in critical situations. A danger lies in the possibility of senior officials becoming too involved in the progress of an incident, nonetheless, as occurred on at least one occasion with President Carter. An alternative would be the installation of sophisticated, secure communications links between the major operations centres and a central location adjacent to the Privy Council Office. Such an improved communications system is one matter which does require attention within the Canadian crisis-management organization and is currently under review.

In the United States, the

way in which the organs of government are arranged in relation to one another — what we might call the functional structure of the federal government and each of the individual governments within the fifty states that comprise the USA – is both incoherent and self-stultifying ... It requires the coalition of a large number of different interests before a measure of government can be put through.[119]

The federal system of government in the USA, emphasizing the separation of powers, does not facilitate a smooth, rapid response or development of policy. The President may proclaim his administration's policy intents, but translating the ideas into practical reality is rather more complex. The situation is not eased by the existence of a large and cumbersome bureaucracy containing many rivalries and frictions. An example was the contention between the Departments of State and Justice over responsibility for counter-terrorism prior to President Carter's decision to issue PRM-30. Justice feared that State would give too much attention to international concerns, whereas State viewed Justice's actions as an attempt to invade its turf and an endeavour to wrest control of the Executive Committee on Terrorism (ECT).

Bureaucratic in-fighting is not confined to the federal level, but occurs between federal and state agencies and down through subordinate levels. Jurisdictional conflicts were obvious in preparations for control of security at the Los Angeles Olympic Games; in an extraordinary drama prior to the Games, disagreement over a jurisdictional issue involved a local police officer snatching a telephone from an FBI agent conducting a hostage negotiation because the police officer believed the incident was not a federal matter. Serious debate has taken place in Congress over the organization of the command structure of US military resources assigned to counter-terrorism functions. Some Congressmen and Senators have suggested the creation of a National Special Operations Agency responsible directly to the President and the Defense Secretary which would bypass the military Joint Chiefs of Staff in the control of such forces. A frequently cited criticism in the United States is that 'no single department, agency or office has total responsibility for combatting terrorism nor the authority and means to do so'.[120] Robert W. Taylor has suggested that the US Government's anti-terrorism programme 'should include the establishment of a separate and distinct agency to address holistically the international and domestic phenomenon of terrorism'.[121] Conversely, the result of the Inman Report has produced a further division of responsibility and tasking within the State Department. Notwithstanding, the National Security Council (NSC) and the Interdepartmental Group on Terrorism (IG/T) head the list in providing advice to the President, and in the co-ordination of 'the development and implementation of programs to combat terrorist attacks or threats'.[122]

The NSC is the senior advisory body to the President, assisting him in the decision-making process. On the other hand, the 'IG/T provides a single point to which the various departments and agencies can address questions and make proposals.'[123] The role of the IG/T has been given different expression in various documents; one of the more precise is:

The [IG/T] is intended to coordinate policies of the U.S. Government concerning terrorism, whether domestic or international in character, and to assure that the various operational programs to deal with terrorist attempts, including intelligence and incident management are effective ... [it is] primarily a policy-shaping group ...[124]

While co-ordination of policy is regularly cited as a principal function of the group, Ambassador Oakley qualified the task: '[the IG/T makes] recommendations on policy and programs.... The conclusions and recommendations of the IG/T then go to the NSC and the various agencies involved'.[125] Even more specifically, he stated at a symposium in 1985 that: 'The function of the IG/T ... is to develop policy recommendations for consideration by the [NSC] and the President.'[126]

Farrell considered the IG/T to be the closest approximation to a 'terrorism czar' in the US structure, and which he suggested was the answer to coping with the problems of terrorism, although he also believed it was a position impossible to achieve. Motley, too, recommended a similar arrangement whereby a small permanent NSC staff should be established to provide a focal point for directing the US anti-terrorism programme. In a parallel vein, the Vice President's Report urged a 'full-time NSC position with support staff ... to strengthen coordination of our national program'. The functions of the position would be:

— participation in all interagency groups;
— maintenance of the national programming document;
— assistance with co-ordination of research and development;
— facilitation of development of response options;
— oversight of implementation of the Vice President's Task Force recommendations.[127]

As previously mentioned, the lead-agency system is the means by which the US Government plans for and manages terrorist incidents. The principal agencies are: the Department of State for matters outside the United States; the Department of Justice (FBI) for those within the United States; and the Federal Aviation Administration (FAA) of the Department of Transportation for hijacked aircraft incidents. Other government bodies with a major interest are the Departments of Defense and the Treasury, and the Central Intelligence Agency (CIA).

Lead Agencies assume coordination responsibilities in addition to their statutory functions. The Lead Agency cannot exercise exclusive jurisdiction, but has the lead because of primary operational and functional responsibilities in the area concerned.... Between incidents, [it] works with other agencies to develop policy approaches, maintain necessary relationships with other governments and organizations, keep current on intelligence and other developments in the field, and maintain a readiness to respond whenever an incident occurs. During an incident, [it] establishes and maintains a Working Group to coordinate with other agencies and to discharge its own primary responsibilities. Accordingly, State, the FBI, and the FAA maintain operations centers with staff support, secure and non-secure voice communications, and satellite capabilities worldwide.[128]

The functions of the Department of Defense and the FBI are discussed later in this chapter; the roles of the principal Treasury agencies (US Secret Service, BATF, and the US Customs Service) were described in the previous chapter. 'The [CIA] and other elements of the intelligence community contribute vitally important intelligence to the NSC and Lead Agencies before, during and after terrorist incidents.'[129] Within the CIA analytical units prepare current and long-term reports on terrorist organizations, individuals, and trends, and disseminate the reports to all government agencies having counter-terrorism responsibilities. 'The Director of Central Intelligence has overall co-ordinating responsibility within the intelligence community for counter-terrorism.'[130] Other departments and agencies also maintain intelligence resources; the military facilities, for instance, include the ultra-classified National Security Agency and the Defense Intelligence Agency. The State Department has a Bureau of Intelligence and Research which is 'the principal point of contact between the Department and the rest of the Intelligence Community and directs research and analysis on terrorism and intelligence activities'.[131] Within the US counter-terrorism programme it is becoming increasingly accepted that intelligence is clearly one of the keys to an effective counter-terrorism strategy.

When examining the British infrastructure, it quickly becomes apparent that the system offers the beneficial resource of centralized control. Policy can be developed and implemented without the need for concern about the reactions of state and provincial governing bodies, as in North America. Granted, the Scottish Office and the Northern Ireland Office (NIO) must be consulted and participate in policy formulation, but decisions are essentially finalized at the Cabinet level. The Cabinet system and the bureaucracy of specialized ministries facilitate the arrangement. In times of crisis it is possible for direction to be given from the Cabinet Office virtually straight to the agencies involved. The terrorist conflict in Ulster has had an influence upon the structuring of organization to achieve a more efficient and effective response formula. A fundamental cog in that machinery is the Civil Contingencies Unit (CCU), founded in 1972 'when an internal review ... led to "a refashioned, streamlined emergencies organization"...'.[132]

Before discussing the CCU and other agencies, a portion of an article from *The Times, circa* 1984, warrants mention:

> This week at least ten and maybe as many as 25 Cabinet Committees will meet either in the Cabinet Office of the Cabinet Room at Number Ten. Unless the Downing Street press secretary is authorized to brief political correspondents, non-attributably, naturally, on what transpired at the meetings, there is little chance of MPs or the public finding out until a White Paper is published, a decision announced or even, in many instances, until January 1, 2025 when the files will be broken open at the Public Record Office under the 30-year rule.
>
> Yet since 1916, when Lloyd George established the Cabinet Secretariat, the Cabinet machine has been the engine room of British central government and the Cabinet committees its working parts. They are where political power and bureaucratic power meet. They are the forum in which options are considered before decisions are set in concrete.
>
> Anyone interested in understanding the real hidden government in Whitehall – as opposed to the visible, semi-artificial version, shaped largely by presentational factors – which dominates life at Westminster, must concentrate on the Cabinet committees. Very rarely is life in the engine-room penetrated by outsiders, whether they be journalists, MPs on a select committee or scholarly researchers. When it is, another time-honoured part of the Whitehall apparatus creaks into action – the leak inquiry machine.
>
> Only one other nation in the western world practices private government on this scale: the Republic of Ireland. A study conducted last year by Dr. Brian Hogwood and Mr. Tom Mackie of Strathclyde University discovered that all the OECD nations which operate a parliamentary system were prepared to give them their Cabinet committee lists, with the exception of Whitehall and Dublin.[133]

One further paragraph offers some explanation for this practice:

> The second person a new premier sees on entering Downing Street ... is the Cabinet Secretary ... He delineates certain urgent matters crying out for decision and suggests the kind of groups the prime minister's newly-appointed senior ministers might like to form for

the purpose. Before a new incumbent knows where he or she is, there before his or her eyes is a 68-year-old system for running Britain.[134]

Without attempting to appear facetious, it would seem that the television programme so popular in Britain, known as 'Yes, Minister', provides an accurate reflection. The Thatcher Government, however, has been rather more economical in the formation of committees compared to some of its predecessors. Attlee had 466 in his six-and-a-quarter years; Callaghan formed 190 in his three years. Over a five-year period, Mrs Thatcher had only established some 130–140, of which (in 1984) only four were officially acknowledged.[135]

The CCU, as mentioned previously, has the status of a standing Cabinet committee. The smooth functioning of COBRA, the 'Cabinet Office's "doomsday" operations centre',[136] is the responsibility of the secretary of the CCU; the arrangement is abetted by their co-location in the Cabinet Office. Excepting the MoD and law-enforcement facilities in London, COBRA is the government's emergency-operations centre. During labour troubles in 1978–9, a system of Regional Emergencies Committees (RECs) was established based upon regional economic planning boards. While these RECs are not properly related to the resolution of a terrorist incident, they could be a basis for organizational assistance in the event of a major terrorist attack, e.g. one in which a threat of use of nuclear, biological, or chemical materials was involved. The CCU has a central role in planning the response to major industrial disputes and to managing them to avoid the use of emergency powers. If the latter must be employed, it is the CCU's task to judge when to invoke them; for instance, the CCU provides the machinery for facilitating a decision to use the military when a request is made for Aid to the Civil Power. The CCU also has a planning and crisis-management role in response to terrorist incidents.

Within the United Kingdom, responsibility for counter-terrorism is principally the concern of the security and law-enforcement agencies with the support of the military where applicable. Both the military and the law-enforcement agencies are described later in this chapter, as well as the police Special Branch. From the intelligence standpoint, national security, aside from defence and law enforcement, is primarily the task of the Security Service, popularly known as MI-5. 'The Security Service is not established by statute nor is it recognized by common law.... The cardinal principle of operations is that the Service is to be used solely for the purpose of the defence of the realm.'[137] Established just prior to the First World War, MI-5 'has continued to grow into what is now a major department of State ...'.[138] The Service functions much like the new CSIS in Canada, and would be comparable to the FBI in the United

States if that agency were relieved of the powers of arrest and prosecution. The Security Service is an intelligence-gathering body which shares a close and co-operative relationship with the Special Branch of the police forces in the United Kingdom. Lacking any special powers, MI-5 officers cannot effect a formal arrest, and if a search warrant is required it is issued to a police constable. The Service is nominally the responsibility of the Home Secretary, but its operations are monitored by the Prime Minister's Cabinet steering committee on intelligence (MIS). Reports from MI-5 are collated and analysed by the Joint Intelligence Committee (JIC) in conjunction with similar data received from other sources.

Working in tandem with, but independent of, MI-5 is the Secret Intelligence Service which is concerned primarily with overseas matters, and is better known as MI-6. 'MI-5 and MI-6 have always been jealous of each other ...',[139] an indication that jurisdictional frictions do exist in the British security system. While the 'ancestry of Britain's foreign intelligence service goes back at least as far as Robert Cecil, Chancellor to Elizabeth I at the time of the Spanish Armada',[140] MI-6 evolved from a passport control system originated during the First World War. MI-6 is a function of the Foreign and Commonwealth Office (FCO), although it is also monitored by the Prime Minister's intelligence committee and its reports are submitted to the JIC.

> There is a well established convention that ministers 'do not concern themselves with the detailed information which may be obtained (by MI-5 and MI-6) in particular cases, but are furnished with such information only as may be necessary for the determination of any issue on which guidance is sought'.[141]

### Law enforcement agencies

These resources form a principal domestic response to terrorism in Canada, the United States, and the United Kingdom. It is a reality which originates in the concept of the rule of law, and the fact that terrorist activities are treated as criminal offences under the laws of the three nations. It is the law-enforcement agencies, who, making use of organic and associated intelligence facilities, and supported by the military and the courts, implement the government's counter-terrorism legislation through the application of the law. The Criminal Code of Canada uniformly governs the description of criminal offences in Canada. The making of criminal law is a Federal-government responsibility, but the administration of that law is a provincial matter. Certain exceptions do exist (e.g. control of many narcotic substances, tax fraud and evasion), and remain the purview of federal agencies such as the RCMP, and

Canada Customs and Excise. Provincial and municipal authorities have a degree of latitude in the framing of regulations under the law (e.g. nature of traffic violations), and in the application of penalties. Similarly, especially at the municipal level, variations are apparent in the standards of law enforcement.

Canadian police forces are based on the British colonial model; that is, they are armed and, particularly in the case of the RCMP, have a somewhat paramilitary complexion. Canadian police, however, are not organized on the lines of a Third Force, and are not employed as such even though they do undertake riot-control training. In Canada police forces are of a national, provincial, and municipal character, with a growing trend to the amalgamation of the latter into metropolitan or county groupings in areas of large conurbations. Only two provinces, Ontario and Quebec, maintain their own provincial forces for policing duties outside municipal jurisdictions and for purely provincial matters. The RCMP is the federal law-enforcement body, with a mandate for national security in relation to criminal activities. That responsibility includes sabotage, subversion, and actions of foreign nationals which might be detrimental to the welfare of the nation. The RCMP also contracts with many of the provinces and municipalities to provide standard policing services as an economical measure. Under those circumstances, the RCMP members involved do not perform federal tasks, reporting instead to the Attorney General of the respective province. Thus, while Canada does have a federal body of police, it is not a national force of the type found in many totalitarian countries. Within Canada there are other law-enforcement and regulatory elements such as railway and port police, military police, and forestry and fish-and-game authorities. Private security firms have become a growth industry, providing industrial security patrols, guards, and armoured vehicles for the transportation of valuables. Depending upon the circumstances and the nature of duties, such personnel may be armed and have the status of a 'peace officer'. All major police forces have a criminal intelligence and investigation branch, and the RCMP maintains a central computer resource for criminal intelligence data which includes information about terrorist groups and activities.

Law-enforcement jurisdiction in Canada essentially begins at the lowest level working upwards if the gravity of the situation so demands. Responsibility for the security of Federal government property, personnel, information, and 'VIPs' (including foreign diplomats, resident or visiting) is vested in 'P' Directorate of the RCMP. The role of the Directorate is the provision of protective services, as opposed to concern with investigation. Because the provinces and municipalities have jurisdiction in law enforcement, frictions have occurred between federal agencies and provincial/municipal authorities on occasions of visits of foreign dignitaries and VIPs. It is one area which, as the Dare Report stated, requires 'harmonious and efficient federal–provincial cooperation...'.[142] The situation has been compounded by the provisions of the Security Offences Act (Part IV, CSIS Act) which gives the RCMP 'primary responsibility to perform the duties that are assigned to peace officers in relation to any offence referred to in section 57 [of the Act] or the apprehension of the commission of such an offence'.[143] (Section 57 refers to offences constituting a threat to the security of Canada within the meaning of the CSIS Act, or if the victim is an internationally protected person within the meaning of the Criminal Code.) Under the Security Offences Act, for instance, the RCMP have authority to assume authority for the resolution of a terrorist incident and for the conduct of the subsequent investigation.

The circumstances become more understandable when related to the employment of the RCMP's new Special Emergency Response Team (SERT), whose formation was announced by the Solicitor General in March 1986. The RCMP have maintained Emergency Response Teams (ERTs) for many years in detachment locations across Canada; they represent the RCMP's version of Special Weapons and Tactics Teams (SWATs) so popular in standard police forces. But, as with most SWATs, the ERTs only train regularly on an average of one day per month, and their orientation is primarily towards contending with violent criminal situations as opposed to terrorist operations. (An exception is the Ottawa area, where full-time ERTs exist because of the large diplomatic and government community.) Despite the enthusiasm and high standards obtained by the 'Blue Soldiers' (a title given to some SWATs), however, they do not approximate the virtuosity and surgical precision found in full-time, discretely equipped, tasked and organized groups such as the SAS and the GSG-9. In an attempt to obviate that shortcoming, the Canadian Government has adopted the SERT concept and allocated responsibility to the RCMP. SERT is comprised of two twenty-four-man teams of specially selected members of the RCMP that are on a constant stand-by status. (Consideration is being given to increasing the size of the SERT to at least seventy-five members.) The teams rotate on a monthly basis, with one team on call and the other 'taking training to hone its skills'. The Canadian Forces support the SERT by provision of transport aircraft to move the team wherever it is needed. The purpose of SERT, 'to resolve incidents beyond the capability of normal protective arrangements',[144] is particularly to cope with terrorist activities involving hostage and barricade situations. In conjunction with SERT, the RCMP has significantly increased its personnel resources in order to replace commercial security firms in the task of providing security for foreign diplomatic missions and personnel in Canada. These changes were given impetus as a consequence of the terrorist assault on the Turkish embassy in Ottawa in March 1986.

While the CSIS is not a law-enforcement body, certain aspects of its mandate warrant discussion at this point. CSIS provides support to the RCMP and other law-enforcement agencies (domestically and internationally) through the provision of information and intelligence relating to 'threats to the security of Canada', specifically:

— espionage or sabotage that is against Canada or is detrimental to the interests of Canada or activities directed toward or in support of such espionage or sabotage;
— foreign influenced activities within or relating to Canada that are detrimental to the interests of Canada and are clandestine or deceptive or involve a threat to any person;
— activities within or relating to Canada directed toward or in support of the threat or use of acts of serious violence against persons or property for the purpose of achieving a political objective within Canada or a foreign state;
— activities directed toward undermining by covert unlawful acts, or directed toward or intended ultimately to lead to the destruction or overthrow by violence of, the constitutionally established system of government in Canada.[145]

CSIS personnel do have the 'same protection under the law as peace officers have in performing their duties and functions',[146] but they are not police officers, and their conduct is subject to a ministerial report should they act unlawfully.

The functions of the CSIS and the activities of its members are monitored by an Inspector General appointed by the Federal government. The Director of the CSIS must submit an operational report to the Solicitor General at least annually, with a copy for the Inspector General. In addition, a Security Intelligence Review Committee was established to oversee the operations of the CSIS, and to receive and investigate any complaints made against the Service. Members of the Review Committee (consisting of a chairman and not less than two or not more than four members) are appointed on a stringent basis to hold office for not more than five years. Selection of the Committee is made from members of the 'Queen's Privy Council of Canada' (primarily former Cabinet ministers, but also distinguished Canadians) who:

are not members of the Senate or the House of Commons, after consultation by the Prime Minister of Canada with the Leader of the Opposition in the House of Commons and the leader in the House of Commons of each party having at least twelve members in that House.[147]

One section of the Act which established CSIS was severely

criticized by many of the provincial governments. Under Section 57 (Part IV, Security Offences Act), the Attorney General of Canada 'may conduct proceedings in respect of an offence under any law of Canada' where:

— the alleged offence arises out of conduct constituting a threat to the security of Canada within the meaning of the [CSIS] Act
— the victim of the alleged offence is an internationally protected person within the meaning of section 2 of the Criminal Code[148]

The section provides authority for the Attorney General to issue a fiat establishing the 'exclusive authority of the Attorney General with respect to the conduct of any proceedings in respect of [the] offence'.[149] The proviso, in effect, allows the federal Attorney General to override a provincial counterpart in the administration of the law. The contention which arose over that stipulation illustrated how jealously the provincial government authorities guard their jurisdictional 'rights'.

Jurisdictional conflicts are understandable in the United States, where '16,000 individual law enforcement agencies nationwide', or '650,000 law enforcement officers' are figures quoted to indicate the size of the policing community.[150] Village, town, city, county, state, and federal law-enforcement bodies exist, as well as regulatory agencies such as the Border Patrol, Customs, Immigration, Forestry, Energy, Internal Revenue, and many others. In most cases, members of this large community are authorized to carry firearms and do so. The United States, as with Canada and the United Kingdom, does not have a national police force, although the FBI is often portrayed as such because of its role as a federal law-enforcement agency. But the FBI may only investigate crimes and enforce laws covered by federal legislation. As mentioned in the previous chapter, even the crime of murder is not necessarily a federal offence. For that reason, authoritative observers such as Neil C. Livingstone have urged that Congress enact legislation which would place acts of terrorism within federal jurisdiction.[151] The Comprehensive Crime Control Act of 1984, discussed later, and the Omnibus Diplomatic Security and Anti-Terrorism Act of 1986, have done much to remedy the situation.

The FBI is the lead agency for response to terrorist incidents (excluding those aboard aircraft, which is an FAA role) which occur within the United States, its territories, and overseas possessions. The FBI also investigate terrorist attacks upon American citizens and facilities abroad, such as the 1984 suicide bombing of the US embassy in Beirut.

While among Federal, State, and local laws, statutes probably exist to cover virtually any type of terrorist act, the combination of greater resources and wider experience generally leaves effective law enforcement to the Federal Government. A terrorist calling his act a political assassination, capitalist expropriation, or political prison rescue does not change the act from murder, bank robbery, or escape. Yet often even a large metropolitan city does not have the resources to deal effectively with the investigation of a terrorist act, especially if the investigative trail leads out of the country.[152]

Because of its sizeable resources, coupled with its nation-wide representation and overseas relationships, the FBI is able to undertake a broad variety of counter-terrorism tasks which include liaison within local law-enforcement agencies, organization of joint task forces, operation of a national/international training academy (the FBI Academy, Quantico, Virginia), maintenance of intelligence on terrorists and their movements/activities, collection, and dissemination of technical information on explosives and bombings, and computer-assisted research and analysis.

The initial tactical response to a terrorist incident is made by the FBI Special Agent in Charge (SAC) at the scene. Realistically, depending on the location and the circumstances, some time might elapse before an FBI agent reached the scene of a terrorist incident, although the Agency has fifty-nine offices across the nation and each office has counter-terrorist contingency plans. The excellent communications facilities in the USA permit direct access to the FBI Emergency Operations Center in Washington in times of crisis.

> Telephone hotlines connect the center with the White House Situation Room, the Department of Justice Emergency Programs Center, the Department of State Operations Center, the National Military Command Center, and other federal agencies that may be involved in the situation.[153]

Agents trained in behavioural science and crisis management are available to assist local police or the on-site SAC with the resolution of an incident.

The FBI also maintains SWATs at each of its field offices, as well as the national Hostage Rescue Team permanently headquartered in Washington, DC. The national team was organized in preparation for the 1984 Los Angeles Olympic Games, and was retained as a consequence over concern about the rising threat of terrorism. Based in Washington so that it can be close to the major federal buildings and foreign embassies, it will 'respond to highly complex hostage situations, and will provide the President and the Attorney General [with] a viable law enforcement alternative to the use of military forces for resolution of a domestic incident'.[154] Former FBI Director William E. Webster's enthusiasm is not shared by Robert W. Taylor, who claimed that the FBI 'has failed to realize that many terrorist groups are militarily trained, well-financed, and heavily armed'.[155] It was Taylor's contention that the SWAT member 'who has been trained to combat a relatively unintelligent person with a "Saturday night special" may indeed be surprised when he faces upwards of 15 to 20 commandos armed with automatic weapons, rocket launchers, and high explosives'.[156]

Before examining current and proposed diplomatic security arrangements, a brief clarification of law-enforcement relationships in the United States is appropriate. Policing begins at the lowest level in the USA; any legally constituted community may provide its own security body. In many states the office of county sheriff is an elective position, and that individual may have authority for policing a number of towns within his jurisdiction, as well as being able to hire and dismiss the officers of his force arbitrarily. The roles of State Police and State Highway Patrol forces are often confusing because frequently their primary mandate is associated with the enforcement of traffic regulation, not major felony prevention and investigation. Taken overall, the situation leads to marked variations in the standard of policing across the nation, although most states and large counties have established police academies as a means of improving the standards of their law-enforcement bodies.

'The organization of the United States Government to protect foreign missions and resident diplomats is shared between the Department of State, the Secret Service, and local police agencies.'[157] Currently, it is a somewhat confusing melange in which the Secret Service provides protective services for the President and for every visiting Chief of State or Head of Government. The rise of terrorism in the mid-1970s brought increased protective requests from other important, but lesser, dignitaries, but which were not within the purview of the Secret Service. The problem was partially remedied by the formation of a uniformed Secret Service guard division for protection of diplomatic missions in the Washington, DC area only. Visiting dignitaries not protected by the Secret Service are the responsibility of the Bureau of Diplomatic Security of the Department of State. The Inman Report recommended that the task of protecting all visiting foreign officials and resident diplomats/missions should be transferred to the Department of State. To undertake that responsibility, the Department would have to increase its resources significantly and conduct training programmes to achieve the necessary 'level of professionalism'. Similarly, the Inman Panel was not satisfied with the use of commercial security firms to provide protection for diplomatic missions in the United States, and recognized the difficulties in having to rely on local police forces who face constraints in terms of manpower and budgetary limitations. The Panel recommended that the Secret Service expand its protective services or, should such not prove agreeable, that the Department of State 'form its own office of trained personnel within the Diplomatic Security service to provide these services'.[158]

> The Panel is disturbed by the diffusion of protective responsibility within our government that is perhaps best exemplified by the inexplicable current practice in which the Secret Service protects a visiting Head of State or Government while the Department of State's Security protects that individual's family and/or the accompanying foreign minister. Often both protective details take place simultaneously.[159]

The quote illustrates an interesting example of jurisdictional overlap which frequently occurs within the US law-enforcement community.

In looking at the British system it must be clearly understood that the United Kingdom does not have a national police force. In fact, 'there are now forty-three police forces in England and Wales including the Metropolitan and the City of London Police'.[160] Scotland has eight police forces, and Northern Ireland has one, the RUC. The title Scotland Yard (now 'New Scotland Yard') refers to the Headquarters of the Metropolitan Police, and is located on Victoria Street in London. The City of London, which consists in the main of the financial district in the heart of the metropolis, has its own separate police force. 'The Commissioner of the Metropolitan Police is directly responsible to the Home Secretary, and like the other forces, half his costs are borne by the local rates [taxes].'[161] Outside the metropolitan area of London the police forces are referred to as 'the Constabulary', and are headed by Chief Constables who are virtually independent in terms of policy and practice. To a large degree, it is because at least 50 per cent of constabulary expenses are allocated by the central government on the basis of annual reports of the Inspectors of Constabulary, who report to the Home Secretary (Scottish Secretary and Northern Ireland Secretary, as appropriate), that accusations have been made of a 'national police' in the United Kingdom.

To clarify matters somewhat, Scotland has eight regional districts in which are located major cities such as Edinburgh, Glasgow, and Aberdeen. The latter, for instance, is situated in the Grampian region; the police headquarters for the region has been established in the City of Aberdeen. The policing body is known as the Grampian Police, headed by a Chief Constable, and is responsible for all policing duties within cities, towns, and villages of the Grampian region. Grampian also has a special additional jurisdiction; it is tasked with the law-enforcement responsibility for the offshore North Sea petroleum and gas fields. The

Chief Constable, while generally independent in so far as the operations of his force are concerned, responds to the local civil police authority and to the Scottish Secretary through the Scottish Inspector of Police.

Partially because of its larger experience of mainland terrorist threats and attacks, the Metropolitan Police of London has taken the lead in developing specialized law-enforcement units. One such group is the Special Branch, plain-clothes officers whose task is the gathering of intelligence. Their duties are defined as: 'the investigation of subversion or terrorist organizations; concern with offences against the security of the state (e.g. espionage and treason; and offences against the Official Secrets Act and the Public Order Act)'.[162] As explained in Chapter Three, the Special Branch originated as a response to Irish terrorist attacks in the early 1880s, and it was not until eighty years later that separate regional groups were formed. Although independent and reporting to their own Chief Constables, the regional units are linked to Scotland Yard via a communications service and the facilities of the Yard are available for assistance. Chapter Three also provides a description of other special units of 'the Met' (Metropolitan Police of London): the Special Patrol Group (SPG); the Royalty and Diplomatic Protection Group (RDPG); the Anti-terrorist Squad (C13); the Blue Berets (D11); and the Technical Support Branch (C7). Recently a new unit, T8, was established to provide advice to 'specialist police units vulnerable to bombing and sniper fire from terrorist groups on how to protect their vehicles and buildings'.[163]

In Great Britain the tasks of preventing and protecting against terrorist acts are the responsibility 'of the ordinary police, the police of government departments and other statutory bodies, and the Army, the latter operating under police control'.[164] Since 1974 local forces have begun to take over the policing of airports from the British Airports Authority Police, and training exercises have been held with the military to practise the co-operative methods necessary if a situation demanded support from the armed forces, especially the use of armoured vehicles. Under such conditions it would be standard procedure for Army units to establish a perimeter 'screen' and access control, while a body of SAS personnel worked with the police at the actual scene of the incident. The Ministry of Defence and the Atomic Energy Authority (AEA) are among other government bodies having their own police force. The AEA police have been somewhat controversial because of their 'powers of a constable to pursue, arrest, or place in custody a person or persons anywhere when necessary on reasonable grounds...'.[165] Even more a source of criticism is the authority for AEA police to carry arms, although 'as Special Constables [they] are individually accountable in law for their actions'.[166]

Regrettably, in a society where policemen have traditionally been unarmed and have not had to resort to the use of special riot-control equipment in the past, circumstances are showing signs of change. Not only terrorism, but armed raids (hold-ups) have become more frequent with the result that police in Great Britain have had to make a wider use of firearms. Violent labour confrontations and racial unrest, often politically motivated, have necessitated the resort to improved riot protective gear such as fire-resistant shields, sophisticated helmets, tear-gas, the baton-gun, and armoured Land Rover vehicles; even the use of water-cannon has been reconsidered. The Third Force concept, while resisted and not likely to develop to the extent that it exists in Europe, has become marginally visible in major urban centres of England.

Before moving from Great Britain to examine the special situation of Northern Ireland, reference must be made to jurisdiction. In the normal course of events, jurisdiction is not the problem which it can often prove to be in North America. Hot pursuit, as an example, where police pursue suspects from one Constabulary area into another is a standard practice in Britain. But friction does occur, however, both between and within constabularies. The Metropolitan Police is often regarded with suspicion and a degree of barely concealed jealousy by other police forces, a situation which is not uncommon where large and much-publicized forces are concerned. As mentioned in Chapter Two, reports of controversy have surfaced about the élite position of C13, and it was hinted at one point that the group was to be disbanded and merged with the Special Branch. Perhaps the most obvious indication of the existence of rivalries and the lack of complete co-operation between police forces surrounded the Brighton hotel bombing in October, 1984.

On the one hand, it appears obvious that 'Sussex senior officers never considered terrorism as possibility'.[167] (The Sussex Police had jurisdiction for the Brighton area.) With the Miners' Strike in full swing, the emphasis by the police was on the possibility of coping with a mass demonstration by pickets. A report conducted in the aftermath of the bombing indicated that security control at the conference was inadequate, and that the search procedures used to examine the hotel prior to the conference were 'derisory'.

> The prime minister's suite was the only one where a sniffer dog was used. The home secretary's [sic] suite was not searched at all. No use was made of the available technology ranging from electronic detectors, chemical and battery sensors to radio scans.[168]

Under the circumstances, it would have seemed logical for the Sussex Constabulary to have at least discussed the security arrangements and pre-conference search measures with the specialists at Scotland Yard. (The IRA traditionally carry out spectacular attacks prior to their annual meeting in Dublin in November; also, recent successes of the security forces in capturing IRA arms supplies should have warned of a retaliatory attack.) In conjunction, the Chief Constable of Sussex 'insisted ... that he had no prior warning of a terrorist attack at the conference...'.[169] Yet, two days beforehand 'the entire British armed forces had been put on alert "Bikini Black Alpha", which is specifically designed to counter a terrorist attack'.[170] A senior Scotland Yard official also claimed that police had been on full alert before the incident occurred, and that alerts 'had been telexed by Special Branch to police around the country, including Sussex police, who were in charge of security at Brighton'.[171]

One outcome of the Brighton bombing was the formation of a new government committee, nicknamed 'TIGER' in relation to its title: Terrorist Intelligence Gathering Evaluation and Review.[172] The purpose of the committee was described as a means of channelling 'information from the Special Branch and other security agencies and to co-ordinate counter-measures'.[173] Under the direction of a Home Office Deputy Secretary, the interdepartmental committee's membership includes C13, the Special Branch, MI-5, MI-6, and military representatives, with a role of the monitoring of terrorist intelligence received from all sources. Special Branch, nonetheless, remains 'the focal point for the collection and evaluation of intelligence'.[174] One of the committee's tasks is to gather together during emergency situations, such as when alert notices are issued, e.g. prior to the Brighton bombing.

> But there is one fatal snag with all these ideas. These committees can only give advice. Local police forces retain responsibility for specific counter-measures. There is still no proper national task force for combating terrorism with a unified command and control, communications and intelligence .... In addition to our 43 autonomous police forces, we have the Special Branch, M15, M16, and the anti-terrorist squad, all intimately involved in countering terrorism. There is no proper overall co-ordination for this task.[175]

Discussion of the Northern Ireland law-enforcement resources requires a brief introductory historical review. Following the tragic events of early August 1969, which necessitated military intervention in Ulster for security purposes, an Advisory Committee was appointed to: 'examine the recruitment, organization, structure and composition of the Royal Ulster Constabulary [RUC] and the Ulster Special Constabulary [USC] ...'.[176] The committee was headed by Lord Hunt, and had the task of recommending 'as necessary what changes were required to provide for the efficient enforcement of law and order in Northern Ireland'.[177] The third chapter of the Hunt Report provides a description of the RUC, including its history from 1836 when all the constabulary forces in

Ireland were united as The Royal Irish Constabulary. In the aftermath of the Government of Ireland Act 1920, which established the Province of Ulster, the RUC was formed under the terms of the Constabulary Act (Northern Ireland) 1922. The force was placed under the control of an Inspector-General, who was responsible to the Stormont Minister of Home Affairs. It is significant that the committee which originally recommended formation of the force included the stipulation that the strength of the RUC should be 3,000, 'one-third of which was to be recruited from the Roman Catholic faith'.[178]

From 1922 the RUC was 'one [police] force under a single command for the whole of Northern Ireland'.[179] The force was of the colonial model; that is, members of the RUC were armed. Supporting the RUC from the time of its inception through 1969 was the USC, or B Specials. The USC was essentially a part-time force whose strength was considerably increased during the Second World War when it performed a type of paramilitary 'Home Guard' duty. Three categories of USC service were available: (1) full-time duty (Class A); (2) part-time duty (Class B); and (3) reserve status (Class C). The majority of personnel were enlisted for Class B service, hence the nickname B Specials. A large number of the B-Men, as they became known by the IRA, served in county areas. Consequently, the

> requirement to perform ordinary police duty [was] rarely placed upon him and his training and equipment, including the types of firearms with which he [was] issued, [were] primarily of a military nature and not designed for the ordinary police role.[180]

The Specials were not, therefore, trained to a high standard of police work; more significantly, 'Whilst there [was] no law or official rule that preclude[d] any person, whatever his religion, from joining the U.S.C., the fact remain[ed] that for a variety of reasons no Roman Catholic [was] a member.'[181]

The Hunt Committee made wide-ranging and, for that time, very controversial proposals. A portion of the justification for the recommendations is as follows:

> ... efficient enforcement of law and order depends ... [on considerations] ... that the control and administration of any police force should be vested in such manner as will ensure that it will not only be, but will be seen to be, impartial in every sense and that it should be accountable to the public for its actions. Furthermore, in the eyes of the public it must be seen to be civilian in nature....[182]

Probably the most publicized conclusions of the report were 'that the RUC should cease to have any paramilitary role and should be disarmed, and that the USC should be disbanded'.[183] In conjunction, it was urged that the RUC should 'no longer be directed by a government minister but ... be supervised by a new Policy Authority'.[184] The Hunt Report proposals were rapidly adopted, despite strong Protestant opposition in Northern Ireland which viewed 'the disbandment of the USC as removing the bulwark of their defense against republicanism'.[185] The firearms policy was short-lived, however, as a 'general rise in violence in 1971, including more attacks on the police, led to firearms being reissued'.[186] The USC *was* disbanded, and its place was taken by two new bodies: the RUC Reserve (RUCR), and the Ulster Defence Regiment (UDR). The UDR was established as a part-time paramilitary unit that would come under the direct command of the British Army; the UDR is examined in detail later in this chapter.

The RUC and the RUCR have steadily increased in numbers since the time of reorganization in 1970. Initially suffering from a morale problem because of the impact of the Hunt Report and related events in 1969–70, the RUC/RUCR recovered sufficiently by 1977 once again to accept the law-enforcement primacy role in Northern Ireland. Since that time the force has enjoyed a continuing progress from strength to strength, and is now ranked as an extremely competent professional body of police. The establishment figures in 1969 were 3,044 for the RUC; currently that number is 8,250, almost a threefold increase. The RUCR began in 1970 with 1,500 members, and now exceeds 4,500 personnel serving on a full-time or part-time basis.[187] The RUC functions in the manner of a standard police force, with components devoted to traffic, criminal investigation, communications, and community relations, for example. Special units have been created for the specific purpose of countering the terrorist dimensions, amongst them being the Divisional Mobile Support Units (DMSUs) which operate in the twelve RUC divisional areas. The DMSUs are looked upon as élite groups within the force, and engage in covert surveillance operations and interceptions of terrorists as well as their immediate task of mobile support to police units. Not to be ignored, however, is the important RUC policy of committing more police to foot patrols in urban areas, and the concept of community policing. The latter is an extremely valuable means of regaining the respect of the populace on both sides of the sectarian divide, and includes the popular 'Blue Lamp' discos and countryside excursions for mixed groups of children, i.e. Catholic and Protestant. The force correctly attaches great emphasis to the community-relations programme, with one highly capable department solely devoted to the conduct of improving relations with the public, promoting the positive image of the RUC, and encouraging better understanding between the opposing loyalist–republican groups.

Experience with large-scale public disturbances and terrorism has provided the RUC with a respectable knowledge of the more suitable methods and tactics for coping with those problems. Consensus does not favour the use of water-cannon for contending with rioters or violent demonstrations; rather, the armoured Land Rover equipped with extendable side-screens is the recommended measure for containment and control of crowd movement. Considerable emphasis is placed upon the value of the baton-gun, with its plastic bullet, as the effective and non-lethal (under most circumstances, and if used properly and with due care) method to keep at bay persons throwing missiles or Molotov cocktails. The armoured Cortina automobile used by mobile RUC patrols has been criticized because of inadequate protective characteristics, as well as the linked inability to roll down the armoured windows and lack of interior cooling capability. The seriousness of that weakness was demonstrated in mid-summer of 1986: three RUC members were shot by terrorist gunmen when a police patrol halted and opened their vehicle doors to cool the interior. From a purely technical standpoint, a 'Computer Assisted Policing' system was introduced in 1980. Together with a Criminal Information Retrieval System (CIRS), it provides for the efficient deployment of resources and the central collation of all incident reports and other information. The RUC has also successfully implemented a confidential telephone operation whereby information can be provided by informers using a province-wide toll-free telephone number coupled with an automatic tape-recorder. Training resources for the RUC are of the latest modern and sophisticated variety, including a mock village which permits practical exercises in dealing with a broad range of terrorist situations.

'Despite its [previous] close relationship with the Stormont government, the RUC has *never* been a wholly sectarian body.'[188] Even in the years prior to 1969, approximately 11 per cent of the force was Roman Catholic. Currently that force level and recruitment level are running at about 10 per cent Catholic, but 'the proportion of Catholics in the officer ranks [is] rather higher'.[189] PIRA/INLA, of course, continue to pursue the aim of attempting to discourage Catholics from enlisting in the RUC or the RUCR. PIRA/INLA see the rejuvenated RUC as a principal threat to their goal of a united Ireland. One means of trying to dissuade Catholics, as well as Protestants, from serving in the RUC is the terrorist policy of concentrating their attacks upon the security forces of Northern Ireland.

### Armed forces

Much publicity was given to the unification and integration of the Canadian Forces (CF) at the beginning of the 1970s. Despite considerable reorganization, however, the CF remains little different from the tri-service military defence forces of other NATO nations. A recent decision by the Canadian Government restored much of the former individual service appearance through the re-introduction of the distinctively separate uniforms of the naval, army, and air-force branches. Generally based upon the British system in terms of structure and discipline, the CF have adopted certain features of US practice in the years since the Second World War. Most weapons and equipment in the CF are obtained abroad because Canada does not maintain a large defence industry geared to the development and manufacture of military requirements.

'The Canadian Forces are the military element of the Canadian government and are part of [the Department of National Defence]'.[190] The CF is comprised of both Regular (full-time) and Primary Reserve (part-time) personnel, all of whom serve on a voluntary enlistment. The roles of the CF are:

— surveillance of Canadian territory and coastlines (protection of sovereignty);
— defence of North America in co-operation with U.S. forces;
— fulfillment of NATO commitments as agreed upon;
— performance of international peace keeping roles as assumed by the Canadian government.[191]

The stated roles include duties involved with Aid to the Civil Power, Assistance to Other Federal Departments, and Assistance to Civil Authorities, discussed later.

Compared to the armed forces of the United States and the United Kingdom, the size of the CF is not large. The strength of the full-time CF in the mid-1980s was approximately 84,000, and was not projected to increase by any substantial numbers. Relatively, the Canadian military has a considerable range of commitments which are not clearly indicated by the statement of its roles. Those commitments make heavy demands upon CF manpower and resources, a matter of significant consequence in terms of any requirement to perform internal security duties, e.g. response to widespread civil disobedience or terrorism. During the October Crisis, for instance, troops on leave after returning from UN service on Cyprus were recalled because of a shortage of available personnel to meet the demands of the situation.

The CF would have two potential roles should terrorism or civil unrest stress the resources of the law-enforcement community as occurred in 1970. The first requirement would be to provide security for military installations, and possibly assist with the protection of government buildings, vital points, and VIPs. In that circumstance, the Federal government has the power to deploy troops for such duties if it is considered that provincial authorities lack the capability to provide suitable protection, or are unwilling to do so. The second task would involve duties in Aid of the Civil Power, when assistance is requested by the provincial government. Under the terms of the National Defence Act, the Chief of the Defence Staff (CDS) must respond to the request, his only option being to determine the type and strength of the resources to be deployed. Military forces so provided would act in support of the provincial authorities, taking direction from police officers wherever and whenever possible. The police, however, do not have authority to issue orders to the military; rather, the military acts in accordance with the requirements of the police. Members of the CF deployed on Aid to the Civil Power have the powers of a peace officer which, *inter alia*, confer the right of arrest.

During the 1970 October Crisis, the military and the police established a joint headquarters in Montreal, working together to conduct the security operations as directed by the provincial authorities. To expedite this type of function, the nation is divided into six geographical regions which are the responsibility of various senior military commanders, e.g. Eastern region (Quebec), under Commander Mobile Command. Within each region a small military stand-by force is maintained for purposes of immediate reaction in time of emergency. If needed, other forces would be brought in from other regions to supplement the initial deployment. While in its early history Canada had considerable experience of troops used in Aid of the Civil Power (eighty occasions between 1867 and 1914), the requirement has only arisen twice since 1945. The first instance occurred at the time of a brief strike by the Montreal police in 1969, and the second arose shortly thereafter during the October Crisis of 1970. In the years immediately following, training for the internal-security role was given increased emphasis, but gradually such preparation assumed a much lower priority. Some practice and liaison does continue between the military and police, although primarily at the 'staff' level. Several police forces make use of military facilities for training of their SWATs, but CF personnel practise little beyond 'base-defence' duties. The resources of the CF were extensively employed at the 1976 Olympic Games in Canada, with much of the security provided by armed military personnel. Similarly, the CF was involved with the 1981 Summit Seven conference in the Ottawa area, the 1984 visit of the Pope and the 1987 CHOGM conference in Vancouver, but the major portion of the tasking was associated with provision of helicopters for surveillance and transportation, and meeting communications needs. It should be noted that the Primary Reserve may be called upon for full-time duties in time of emergency, and was employed to some extent in 1970, but its nature and level of training do not lend themselves to use under conditions of serious civil disturbance.

Prior to the Solicitor General's announcement in 1986, speculation existed that the SERT role might be allocated to the CF, and such a possibility was studied by the Department of National Defence (DND). It is understood that both DND and the RCMP were instructed to submit proposal documents to Cabinet for consideration. Because Cabinet matters are classified, the contents of those Cabinet submissions and the Cabinet deliberations were not made public. Notwithstanding, responsibility for SERT was not viewed enthusiastically by some members of the CF who feared a drain (especially financially) upon the already extended resources of the CF. The CF did not entirely escape an involvement with the SERT role, however, and have agreed to provide support for SERT in terms of aircraft and helicopters (and other specialized equipment as necessary) to move the team and to aid with tactical operations.

Not to be confused with Aid to the Civil Power are the tasks of Assistance to Other Federal Departments, and Assistance to Civil Authorities. Assistance to Other Federal Departments involves the use of DND personnel, equipment, or facilities to help another Federal government department. One example is the use of military units in the event of a serious disturbance at a prison or penitentiary; under such conditions DND would assist the Solicitor General's Department in the restoration of order and security. Various examples can be provided in regard to the role of Assistance to Civil Authorities wherein provincial or municipal governments require the help of DND in emergency situations, e.g. floods, forest fires, snowstorms, searches for persons lost in uninhabited areas. In conjunction, DND undertake bomb-disposal tasks where a civilian capability is not readily available.

The impressive military resources of Canada's immediate and powerful southern neighbour, the United States, have not been a deterrent to the threat or reality of terrorist attacks. In fact, the presence of US military bases and facilities around the world, controversy over the nuclear issue, the highly visible character of American personnel and equipment, and the frequent vulnerability of the infrastructure have contributed to making the military an attractive terrorist target. Coupled with those factors has been the reasonable guarantee that such attacks would achieve broad and prominent publicity. Conversely, the inability of the technologically large American forces to come to grips with, or thwart, terrorist activities has been a source of frustration for the United States. The organization and composition of the US military is somewhat more complex than the armed forces of Canada and the United Kingdom. The American forces are comprised of the Army, Navy, Air Force, and Marine Corps; in time of war the US Coast Guard (USCG), 'a service within the Department of Transportation',[192] reverts to its role as a branch of the armed forces. In keeping with the separation-of-powers principle, two major elements of the military exist in the USA: Federal and State forces. The 'Regular' full-time armed forces are a federal responsibility; a part-time multi-service Reserve also comes under federal control. The State forces, or National Guard(s), are also part-time military bodies which resemble the Primary Reserve in Canada or the Territorials in the United Kingdom. Each State has its own National Guard (Army and Air Force) commanded by the State Governor in the similar manner that the President is Commander-in-Chief of all US Armed Forces.

State Governors have control over their National Guard to the extent that the Governors may call out those forces in times of emergency, such as floods or other disasters, or in times of serious civil disorder when law-enforcement agencies cannot cope. State National Guards are fully integrated in the US military, however, and represent the primary reserve combat elements. In time of war or other national emergency, the President may activate the National Guard and place its units under federal control; during the Viet Nam conflict, for instance, a number of National Guard units were mobilized for service overseas. Similarly, when some State Governors threatened to use their National Guard forces to oppose integration procedures in the 1960s, the President placed the units under federal control.

> During the past two decades the repeated need for National Guard assistance to quell incidents of civil unrest in the U.S.A. prompted certain European writers to erroneously describe the Guard as a form of 'Third Force.' This led to unfair comparisons with the Compagnies Republicaines de Securite (CRS) of the French Police Nationale.[193]

Because the Guard is correctly a part-time voluntary military force (all US Armed Forces members now serve on a voluntary enlistment) with a primary mission of training for the wartime defence of the nation, its units did not do well when first committed to civil-disobedience confrontations. Experience with riots in Watts, Chicago, Detroit, and Newark brought about changes in training and equipment. When called upon to assist the Florida law-enforcement community during large-scale disturbances in Miami in May 1980, the Florida Guard was demonstrably better prepared. Employed under such circumstances, however, US military forces (Federal or State) do not have civil powers akin to those shared by their Canadian and British military counterparts when acting in Aid of the Civil Power. American military personnel do not have the powers of a constable or peace officer, and cannot arrest persons or search premises in the similar manner.

The major constraining factor on the use of American military resources in the enforcement of civil law is the Posse Comitatus Act passed in 1878 as the consequence of President Grant's controversial use of US troops during the election of 1876. Originally, only the Army was included under the terms of the Act, but the Air Force was specifically added in 1956. The Navy (as well as the Marines, who are a part of the Department of the Navy) have never been legislated into the Act, although the Secretary of the Navy issued a directive in 1974 'forbidding Navy and Marine Corps personnel from enforcing or executing local, state, or federal law in violation of the Posse Comitatus Act'.[194]

Notwithstanding, Navy sea-going resources have been used to assist in countering the incidence of drug trafficking from Central and South America in recent years. (Army personnel and equipment have also been employed in similar activities in Bolivia, raising concerns of US civil-liberties groups about 'the erosion of US laws and traditions separating the military from law enforcement'.)[195] The USCG has an important role in the anti-narcotic effort, especially with the growing significance of narco-terrorism. The USCG does not fall under the Navy purview in peacetime, and is not subject to the Posse Comitatus restrictions. Maritime terrorism is also a responsibility of the USCG: 'there are 2,000 oil platforms and 12,000 miles of pipeline that could be the target of hostile groups. Additionally, attacks against vessels in port or within U.S. territorial waters are also a definite possibility.'[196] In 1979 the FBI and the USCG signed an MOU (Memorandum of Understanding) to provide mutual support and planning to co-ordinate communications, command, and control policies between the two agencies.

The President may call into federal service the militia (National Guard) of any State, as well as the regular armed forces, to suppress 'unlawful obstructions, combinations or assemblages, or rebellion' against the authority of the United States, or any State in particular.[197] He can do this by virtue of constitutional authority or by terms of certain statutes, but, failing a widespread emergency, the Posse Comitatus Act inhibits his action in response to terrorist activities in the United States. The Posse Comitatus Act does not forbid the loan of equipment and material or the provision of advice, as frequently occurs between the military and the law-enforcement community.

The US Armed Forces are 'a military apparatus, designed to fight a world war and unsuited for small, swift actions'.[198] It is partially through a failure to realize that fact that the American public has become frustrated and confused about the lack of success in coping with the threat of terrorism. In conjunction, the conflict at senior government level over use of force in response to terrorism served to further the bewilderment. Speeches by Secretary of State Shultz advocating 'pre-emptive actions against known terrorist groups'[199] were countered by Secretary of Defense Weinberger's cautions about 'employing our forces almost indiscriminately and as a regular and customary part of our diplomatic efforts...'.[200] The debate increased, with President Reagan stating that the US 'would "go to the source" if foreign governments were found to sponsor terrorist attacks',[201] until US retaliatory military action became inevitable, if only to substantiate what would otherwise have appeared as empty rhetoric. But it is only in recent years that the American military has begun to ready itself to undertake special anti-terrorist operations, or even to appreciate the dangers of terrorism seriously. In the decades since 1945 the US Armed Forces, as with those of Canada and the United Kingdom, have prepared themselves for major global warfare. The NATO role of deterring a possible Soviet invasion of Europe has been a primary focus, necessitating the development of large, highly mobile, mechanized armoured forces. Small, specialized units for the conduct of pin-point, surreptitious raids have received little attention, or were treated with disdain. It was not until 1977, following instructions from President Carter, that the US military again gave serious study to Special Operations Forces (SOF).

The SOF has a background of commando-style Ranger units originated during the Second World War, as well as Special Forces units such as the Green Berets and the Navy's SEAL teams (Sea–Air–Land teams) of the Viet Nam era. Those groups, however, fell into relative disfavour in the wake of the Viet Nam conflict, with only vestiges remaining at the time of Carter's directive. The US Army initiated Delta Force, a small company-size element modelled on SAS lines, at Fort Bragg, North Carolina, in response to the President's orders. Nonetheless, the development progress of the unit was plagued by interservice and intraservice rivalries, lack of a central command structure, and continuing disinterest on the part of senior officers.[202] The Tehran embassy seizure brought the role of the SOF into sharp focus. Delta Force was committed to a rescue operation which 'took more than six months and about $250 million to execute, yet still failed to achieve its objective'.[203] The abortive attempt ended in a spectacular catastrophe which cost the lives of eight US servicemen, and humiliated the much-vaunted American military resources. An investigation in the aftermath by Admiral James L. Holloway revealed problems with poor planning, in adequate command, control, and communications arrangements, unreasonably stringent security, and 'deficiently managed and integrated'[204] intelligence assets, amongst other negative factors contributing to the lack of success.

One of the Reagan administration's mandates was 'to restore America's special operations ... capabilities',[205] when Reagan assumed the presidency in 1981.

Since then, America's very own guerrilla army has undergone an unprecedented peacetime build-up. Its budget has shot up from $441 million (about 300 million) in 1981 to a projected $1,600 million (more than 1,000 million) for 1987. By 1990, active duty SOF personnel will total 21,600, almost double the 1981 figure.[206]

In an attempt to provide co-ordination and control of the growing organization, the Pentagon established a Joint Special Operations Agency in 1984. Each of the military branches contributes to the SOF in terms of personnel and equipment as previously described, e.g. Delta Force, Rangers, Green Berets, SEALs, helicopters, transport, and tactical support aircraft. Despite these intense efforts and an appreciation that 'a new form of warfare has emerged ... [which] ... takes the form of terrorist attacks and guerrilla insurgencies',[207] many problems yet remain.

That there is a problem is evident from government studies of the Iran and Grenada missions, the two most high-profile SOF operations in recent years. The studies concluded that in both cases SOF effectiveness was seriously hindered by appalling deficiencies in forward planning and communications. Worse still were the endemic rivalries that prevailed – and still prevail – between the three arms of the military throughout which SOF units are dispersed. The lack of any permanent unified command structure has meant that each time a crisis requiring SOF deployment arises, the Joint Chiefs of Staff have to set up an ad hoc task-force composed of the separate service units.[208]

To compensate for the continued shortcomings, some Congressmen proposed an amendment to 'the 1987 Defense Authorization Bill to allow a National Special Operations Agency to be set up'.[209] Under the terms of the amendment, all the SOF units would be detached from their parent commands and be aggregated in a new separate service. Further to that controversial suggestion, the Congressmen recommended that the service have direct access to the President and the Secretary of Defense, a move which would effectively bypass the Joint Chiefs of Staff and give 'real control to the civilian leadership'.[210] The concept not only created concern in military circles, but alarmed liberal politicians and others who worry about US involvement in non-supervised covert operations and the possibility of the risk of another Viet Nam situation.

'Military Paying Increased Attention to Terrorism Now'.[211] The Iranian debacle, followed by the Beirut bombings, and attacks upon US Armed Forces personnel and facilities in Europe and elsewhere have markedly altered the US military's perception of the threat of terrorism. Protective measures have been improved at bases and installations domestically and abroad, and service personnel and their families have been given special briefings to alert them to the dangers of terrorist attack and the necessary precautions to be taken. The Air Force introduced a 'Dynamics of Terrorism' course at Hurlburt Field, Florida, designed to teach individuals an awareness of terrorism and how to defend themselves against it. The Army, on the other hand, conducts training at Fort McClellan, Arkansas, 'which teaches military officials how to fight terrorism directed at installations'.[212] From a slow start in 1977, the US military has moved to a position of viewing terrorism as 'low-intensity conflict'.

> The threat to American security from low-intensity conflict was summed up by George Shultz, the US Secretary of State, at a conference on special operations and unconventional warfare.... 'The ironic fact is that these new and elusive challenges (of terrorism and guerrilla insurgencies) have proliferated in part because of our successes in deterring nuclear and conventional war.... Our adversaries know they cannot prevail against us in either type of war. Low-intensity warfare is their answer to our conventional and nuclear strength. They hope the legal and moral complexities of these kinds of challenges will ensnare us in our scruples and exploit our humane inhibitions against applying force to defend our interests.'[213]

The Vice President's Report of 1986, while urging a cautious approach to the use of military force in retaliation against terrorism, leaves little doubt that such use is a viable policy option of the American Government, as was demonstrated by US military aircraft in the Mediterranean area in 1985 and 1986.

As opposed to the complex structure of the United States' Armed Forces, and the integrated nature of the CF, the British military follows a standard, fundamental pattern of organization. In basic form the British Armed Forces are comprised of the Royal Navy (RN), the Army, and the Royal Air Force (RAF); the Royal Marines (RM) are a component of the RN. Unlike their US Marine counterparts, however, the RM function as a commando assault unit, and do not compare in size, equipment, or tasking. The British forces are an all-volunteer establishment, with the Army forming the largest body. As a member of the NATO Alliance, the United Kingdom has a major portion of its military forces stationed in, or committed to, the European Theatre of Operations (ETO). A sizeable part-time reserve, or Territorial Army (TA), supports the regular Army, while similar organizations exist for the RN and the RAF. Only regular personnel are permitted to serve in Northern Ireland; at the height of the troubles 21,000 troops were deployed in Ulster, placing a considerable strain on the MoD to meet its commitments elsewhere, especially in Europe.

Within the British Army, regiments and battalions of long and honoured histories and traditions perform specialized roles, e.g. infantry, artillery, and the armoured corps. One unit with a relatively short, but illustrious, record is the Special Air Service Regiment (SAS) which was formed in North Africa during the Second World War. The SAS operated behind enemy lines, creating havoc by raiding airfields, supply dumps, and headquarters facilities. Nearly disbanded at the conclusion of the hostilities because of its discrete role, the SAS was found to be a valuable resource in the post-1945 counter-insurgency campaigns in Malaya, Indonesia, Aden, and the Arabian peninsula. The SAS earned an enviable reputation for its ability to conduct covert patrol and surveillance tasks requiring extensive periods of stealth and concealment. Introduced into Northern Ireland operations in the 'bandit country' of the border areas in 1976, its presence was not immediately acknowledged, in part because the government feared criticism on the basis of the SAS's traditional ruthless efficiency. (Unfortunately, controversy has dogged the SAS in Ulster; two members of the unit were brought to trial for a shooting incident in 1978 in which a teenage youth was killed in error. Contradictory evidence resulted in an acquittal.) More spectacular, in terms of publicity, have been the SAS's exploits in connection with the Mogadishu hijacking and the Prince's Gate incident. At Mogadishu in 1977, SAS members assisted the élite West German GSG-9 in overcoming PFLP terrorists holding ninety passengers hostage aboard a Lufthansa airliner. Three years later it was the SAS alone who stormed the Iranian embassy in London to release nineteen persons held captive by Iranian dissidents. Although the latter operation brought world-wide acclaim and much publicity, the unit shuns such attention for practical reasons as well as a matter of pride. The incident, nonetheless, reinforced the British principle of assigning the ultimate sanction to the military in the event that a terrorist attack requires such action. As part of the British Special Forces Organization, the Royal Marine Commandos also have a role to play in counter-terrorism operations, but little public mention is made of their tasking. Security of the North Sea petroleum industry's oil and gas platforms and infrastructure is the responsibility of the RM, acting in support of the Grampian Police. In conjunction, incidents of maritime terrorism involving ships at sea or in harbour are the purview of the RM in the event that use of maximum force is the only feasible solution.

'Since the kings of England had nothing to fear from land invasion, they did not have the same incentive as their continental cousins to develop a standing army....'[214] It was not until after Cromwell's time that a permanent army was established in the United Kingdom. Britain's colonial empire was shored up by relatively small numbers of British soldiers supported by large locally raised forces. The Army, nevertheless, did play a significant law-and-order role in Great Britain during the periods which Critchley described as the 'Great' and the 'Lesser' struggles from the beginning of the nineteenth century through to 1919. August of the latter year was 'the last time soldiers were called out,' and the 'Riot Act was read for the last time'.[215] Disregarding the Ulster situation for the moment, the Army continues to have a prominent place in the public-order task in Great Britain. It fulfils that requirement, however, in a low-key manner and on the basis of 'the duty of all citizens ... to come to the aid of the civil authorities'.[216] In conjunction, 'where troops are used their legal authority does not rest upon statutory or prerogative powers of the Crown'.[217] Sir Edwin Bramall underscored the position of the military during a speech delivered in 1980:

> If the Armed Forces were ever needed for public order – ... ie, for dealing with law-breakers, then our legality would come from that famous obligation under common law 'to come to the aid of the Civil Power when so required', and from the Criminal Law Act 1967 (Section 3) which requires, that in so doing, the use of no more force than is reasonable and necessary.[218]

Two other circumstances could require the use of the Army (as well as the RN and the RAF): Aid to the Civil Community; and Aid to Civil Ministries. Legislation does exist in regard to those two demands, principally the Emergency Powers Act of 1964, which would allow the Defence Council 'to authorize the use of the Forces on "urgent work of National importance"'.[219] In a specific sense, such would relate to assistance in the time of a national disaster or, in certain cases, when the maintenance of essential services is required, as in the event of a major labour dispute. Critical to the operation of the military under the latter circumstances would be the question of public acceptability and the technical skills of the military personnel in accomplishing the tasks assigned.

While well-versed in the techniques of counter-insurgency operations overseas, the military has had to train itself in the para-military methods and procedures needed in Northern Ireland. It has been a continuous process, and one for which the military is deserving of much credit. At Hythe-Lydd on the south-east coast of England, for instance, special training facilities prepare troops for their period of service in Ulster. The infrastructure of the establishment is extremely sophisticated, practical, and thorough in its range of application. Complete mock villages, similar to those in Northern Ireland, have been constructed, and video cameras film the training exercises for later review by the participants to assist in correcting errors or for improving standards of operations. As mentioned earlier, a like arrangement has been implemented in Northern Ireland for use by the province's security personnel. The security task in Northern Ireland has not been solely an Army responsibility. The RN and the RAF, as well as the RM, continue to have major roles to play. The RM units serve with Army units on a rotational basis (roulement), as explained later, while the RN provides coastal and offshore patrols to cope with terrorist attempts to smuggle ashore weapons, equipment, and personnel. (Frequently terrorists also seek to escape or to hide-out by taking refuge on fishing vessels operating in local waters.) The RAF participate through the provision of aircraft, helicopters, and staff expertise associated with airborne security functions.

'The use of force by soldiers and policemen in the exercise of their powers in Northern Ireland has proved controversial in a number of contexts ... but particularly so in connection with the use of PVC baton rounds [plastic bullets] and of lethal force.'[220] Nevertheless, the Standing Advisory Committee on Human Rights (SACHR) 'were impressed by the strictness of instructions to the security forces' and commented that 'if obeyed by the security forces no member of the law-abiding public need be concerned for his safety and neither need members of the security forces equally fear breaking the law'.[221] Soldiers in Ulster carry a Yellow Card containing instructions on when they may open fire, breach of which could result in disciplinary action even though no breach of the civil law was involved. Similar rules exist for the use of baton rounds, and the RUC have stringent restrictions contained in their Force Instructions. The basis for the Yellow Card and other directions in the matter of using force originate in the maxim that no more force may be used than is necessary for the task at hand.

Before turning to the subject of the Ulster Defence Regiment (UDR), it must be recognized that British troops were present in Ulster prior to the disturbances of 1969, but not for purposes of internal-security duties. Garrisons of Regular British soldiers have always been stationed in Northern Ireland in the same manner as they have in Great Britain. In fact, certain regiments of the British Army have a traditional association with Ulster; they have their headquarters and Regimental Depots in the province, and recruit from the local populace, e.g. The Royal Irish Rangers. For security reasons, however, these units do not serve in Northern Ireland. The permanent British garrisons in Ulster were reinforced following the outbreak of troubles in 1969, a procedure which ultimately necessitated the presence of nearly 22,000 troops by 1972 as opposed to the 2,000 of four years earlier. Over the succeeding years the level has been successfully reduced to approximately 9,000, although in early 1986 two 500-strong infantry battalions of the stand-by 'Spearhead' force returned on temporary duty because of activist militancy associated with the Northern Ireland Agreement. Currently, the Army garrison is made up of six resident units, with a two-year tour of duty during which they are accompanied by their families, and two 'roulement' units. The roulement units are drawn from garrisons in Great Britain and West Germany, and spend 4 months on security duties principally in Belfast and along the Ulster–Eire border.

The newest regiment in the British Army is the UDR, a paramilitary body established in 1970 when the B-Specials were disbanded in the wake of the Hunt Report. The UDR is a locally recruited unit liable for service only within Northern Ireland. An official information release describes the role of the Regiment thus:

> The [UDR] was tasked [by an Act of Parliament] to support the regular force in Northern Ireland, should circumstances so require, in protecting the border and the State against armed attack and sabotage. It was to fulfil this by undertaking guard duties at key points, by carrying out patrols and by establishing check points and road blocks when required to do so. The Regiment was not to be deployed in crowd control duties, and never has been.[222]

The UDR consists of a Regimental Headquarters at Lisburn (near Belfast), and nine battalions responsible for providing military support to the RUC in Tactical Areas of Responsibility (TAORs) throughout the province. Certain locations, such as West Belfast and the urban area west of the Foyle River in Londonderry, remain exclusive to the operations of the regular Army, however. The present strength of the UDR is approximately 6,500, comprising full-time soldiers, part-time soldiers, permanent cadre, and Greenfinches (female members).[223]

The Regiment is an integral part of the British Army, and is commanded by a brigadier from the Regular Army, with a number of command and staff positions in each battalion filled by British Regular Army personnel, e.g. the battalion commanders. The basic equipment of the UDR is the same as that of regular Army units serving in the internal security role in Northern Ireland. The backbone of the unit is the part-time soldier, and over three-fifths of UDR members serve in that category; they hold civilian jobs by day and usually report for duty on two or three nights per week and on weekends. 'Living within the community [at home] itself, members of the UDR – like RUC regulars and reservists – present relatively "soft" targets, and are particularly vulnerable to terrorist intimidation and attack. Of the 151 UDR soldiers killed up to the end of 1985, 123 were off duty at the time.'[224] Despite serious efforts to encourage Catholic enlistment, PIRA/INLA intimidation and a degree of sectarian distrust has kept the numbers low. The first UDR soldier killed by PIRA in 1986 was a Catholic Non-Commissioned Officer (NCO) who was leading a security patrol; the incident occurred within yards of a local Catholic school. Prospective members of the UDR are carefully screened on application for enlistment in an attempt to preclude Protestant extremists. Unhappily, allegations of favouritism towards, or collaboration with, Protestant groups have been made against the UDR, and a small number of UDR soldiers have been convicted of involvement with sectarian murders. Nonetheless, the UDR strives hard to present and maintain an objective position, and to carry out its 'major and valuable role in the fight against terrorism'.[225]

One other military organization is present in Northern Ireland: a branch of the Territorials. 'There are also about 4,000 Territorial Army soldiers in Northern Ireland but the TA is not involved in the security forces. Its soldiers, many committed to NATO, train for general war in Europe'.[226] Like its counterpart in Great Britain, the TA in Ulster is composed of part-time, locally recruited personnel.

## Legislation

In late 1985 it was announced that the Canadian Federal Government had plans 'to repeal the War Measures Act and replace it with "safety and security" legislation which recognizes varying degrees of civil and military emergencies'.[227] The War Measures Act was originally passed in 1914 at the outbreak of the First World War and, with the exception of a small amendment passed in 1960 which affected Parliamentary debate on proclamation procedures, remained unchanged. The Act was only called into use on three occasions: at the beginnings of each of the two World Wars, and once in peacetime during the October Crisis of 1970.

Under the terms of the Act, the government could proclaim sweeping regulations and orders declaring specific organizations to be unlawful, as well as extending the powers of search, seizure, arrest, and internment. While intended as a measure for wartime security, the Act could be used when a 'real or apprehended' insurrection was believed to exist, as was the situation in 1970. The powers available to the government and the security authorities under the Act were draconian, allowing whatever action was 'necessary or advisable for the security, defence, peace, order and welfare of Canada'.[228]

An expiry limitation restricting duration of proclamation was not included in the Act, which could continue in force until the government decided that the state of emergency had ended. The only restriction was that passed in 1960, whereby the government had to forthwith lay before Parliament the proclamation invoking the Act or, if Parliament were not sitting, within the first fifteen days after Parliament next sat. As stated by an Associate Minister of Defence, the Act was 'appropriate when you have war.... Any emergency less than war does not seem appropriate to require the same powers'.[229]

In June 1987, the Minister responsible for Emergency Preparedness in Canada announced the repeal of the War Measures Act and the introduction of new legislation as a replacement. The new measure, entitled the Emergencies Act, distinguishes between four levels of emergency:

— situations affecting public safety and security caused by an accident or act of nature, such as an earthquake, hurricane or massive chemical spill;
— situations caused by civil disobedience 'of a significant nature' requiring emergency action, such as terrorist acts within Canada;
— international situations requiring Canada to take emergency action, such as an increased level of alert problem by NATO requiring the standby of Canadian troops;
— war itself.[230]

The Emergencies Act was passed into law on 21 July 1988. Under the new legislation the powers of the government are less draconian and would permit more flexibility in meeting the challenges presented, especially the threat of terrorism. The introduction of such legislation was one of the recommendations put forward by the McDonald Report in 1981. The Senate Report of 1987, however, did not observe on the War Measures Act but did recommend against special anti-terrorism legislation. The Senate Committee objected 'to any implicit or explicit recognition of terrorism being different from any other crime for legal purposes'.[231] It was the Committee's opinion that the Criminal code did not require amendment to reflect 'politically motivated crime', although a need was seen to extend the extra-territorial jurisdiction of Canadian courts to bring terrorists more effectively under the jurisdiction of Canadian law and courts.

Terrorism in Canada is a criminal offence. 'If a person commits a terroristic act which is an offence under the Criminal Code, and he is within the jurisdiction of a Canadian court, he may be prosecuted by provincial authorities.'[232] Also, 'the motive of persons charged with a criminal offence has no relevance in the assessment of guilt or innocence'. In exceptional circumstances, however, 'motive can affect the sentence which flows from a conviction'.[233] As mentioned earlier, Part IV of the CSIS Act (Security Offences Act) allows the Attorney General to issue a fiat to conduct proceedings in respect of an offence deemed to be a threat to the security of Canada or where the victim is an internationally protected person within the meaning of the Criminal Code.

Canada is a party to the Tokyo, Hague, and Montreal Conventions, as well as the 1974 UN Convention on the Prevention and Punishment of Crimes against Internationally Protected Persons, Including Diplomatic Agents, and the 1979 UN Convention against the Taking of Hostages. Similarly, Canada is a signatory with over fifty other nations of the 1979 Convention of the Physical Protection of Nuclear Materials which was concluded by the International Atomic Energy Agency. Canada also participated in the Bonn, Vienna, Ottawa, London, and Tokyo declarations opposing terrorism and specific terrorist acts. The Criminal Code of Canada has been amended where necessary to provide for those actions on the part of the Canadian Government. The Access to Information Act, passed in 1982, provides for much wider public availability of government records, documents, and information maintained in Canada. As discussed later in regard to similar legislation in the United States, the provisions of the Act have the potential for creating difficulties for security and intelligence agencies, as well as other government departments. Not only does it pose questions about the nature and extent of information that should be collected or disseminated, it makes other nations wary about the matter of sharing information. Administratively, the Act has necessitated the expense of establishing special government sub-departments to cope with requests for information submitted by the public.

'New U.S. unity in war against terrorists.'[234] Important changes to American legislation in response to the threat of terrorism took place in 1984, and continued in following years. The impetus for many of the changes came from incidents such as the Beirut bombings, the TWA hijacking, the murder of four American Marines in El Salvador, and the *Achille Lauro* affair. So great was the impact of those events, that Senate approval of the long-sought modification to the extradition treaty with the United Kingdom was achieved in 1986. It was a move strongly resisted for years by the powerful Irish–American lobby because of concern over the negative effect the new treaty would have on permitting PIRA/INLA terrorists to seek sanctuary in the United States. 'In 1984, several significant bills were passed that have enabled the United States to expand its jurisdiction over terrorists.'[235] Provisions in those bills have made it a federal offence to commit violence against any passenger on a government or civilian aircraft, and the US Government has been enabled to prosecute any person who destroys a foreign aircraft outside the USA if that person is subsequently found in America. Similar legislation provides authority to prosecute persons who commit acts of violence against the immediate family members of the President, Vice President, Members of Congress, all federal judges, the heads of executive agencies, the Director of the CIA, and federal law-enforcement officials.

The Comprehensive Crime Control Act of 1984 closed many of the loopholes that previously inhibited the investigation and prosecution of terrorists by federal agencies such as the FBI. In a chapter entitled 'Terrorism', the 'federal law covering kidnapping [sic] has specifically been expanded to include a new statute called "Hostage Taking"',[236] and provides for life imprisonment for any person convicted of that act. A Murder-for-Hire inclusion allows the United States to 'prosecute anyone who travels or uses transportation or communications facilities in inter-state or foreign commerce with the intent to murder for compensation'.[237] The Omnibus Diplomatic Security and Antiterrorism Act of 1986 assists in establishing jurisdiction over crimes involving US nationals which take place abroad. Congress also approved a measure granting the Attorney General and the Secretary of State the authority to pay rewards for the 'arrest and conviction of any person who has committed terrorist acts against U.S. citizens or property'.[238] The amounts of the rewards may be as much as $500,000; in the wake of the TWA hijacking the Reagan administration was reported to be willing to pay 'a cash reward of as much as $5 million for the capture of the Shi'ite militants'[239] responsible for the outrage. Concern over the use of sophisticated weapons by terrorists prompted a change to the US International Traffic in Arms Regulations to require a licence for anyone in the United States to train any foreign national in the use, maintenance, repair, or construction of certain prescribed munitions.

One area of continuing concern involves the Freedom of Information Act which, like its Canadian counterpart, allows access to government documents and information. 'It is alleged that terrorist and terrorist organizations, in addition to unfriendly foreign governments, have used the Act to gain sensitive information.'[240] The Vice President's Report recommended that possible abuses of the Act be investigated, and if verified, that the Act be suitably amended.

On the international plane, the United States was an early advocate of co-operation amongst nations in response to the threat of terrorism. As described in previous chapters, the Nixon administration concluded an anti-hijacking pact with Cuba in 1973, preceded in 1972 by an attempt to obtain UN agreement on a Convention opposing acts of terrorism. The United States is a signatory of the three major ICAO Conventions, as well as the two principal UN Conventions relating to the subjects of internationally protected persons and the taking of hostages. Similarly, the American Government has played a significant role in counter-terrorism discussions during the Summit Seven meetings. Also, on 9 December 1985, the United States gave strong support to the UN General Assembly resolution condemning terrorism, and eleven days later successfully initiated a UN Security Council resolution condemning all acts of hostage-taking and urging international efforts to resolve the problem.

In the United Kingdom, two major pieces of legislation exist which have singular importance in response to terrorism. They are: (1) The Prevention of Terrorism (Temporary Provisions) Act 1984 (hereinafter PTA 1984); and (2) The Northern Ireland (Emergency Provisions) Act 1978 (hereinafter EPA 1978). A third measure, the Emergency Powers Act 1920 (EPA 1920), amended in 1964, also confers wide powers to govern in an emergency by means of statutory regulations issued by Order-in-Council. The EPA 1920 does not apply directly to acts of terrorist violence, but it could be used in the event of significant disruption stemming from an extraordinary circumstance, e.g. a nuclear, chemical, or biological threat. Its provisions come into force when a state of emergency has been stated by royal proclamation, which may only remain in force for the period of one month without renewal. Parliament, if not sitting, must be summoned to meet within five days.

> Such powers may be conferred on government departments, the armed forces and the police as may be deemed necessary for the preserving of peace or for securing and regulating the supply and distribution of necessities for maintaining the means of transport, 'and for any other purposes essential to the public safety and the life of the community'.[241]

One piece of legislation must be mentioned as a background to an examination of the PTA 1984 and the EPA 1978; the Civil Authorities (Special Powers) Act 1922, passed by the Northern Ireland Parliament at Stormont. The Act was replaced by the EPA 1973 (subsequently the EPA 1978 after revisions) when Direct Rule was imposed by Westminster in the wake of the security breakdown in Ulster. The Special Powers Act (as it was generally known) was the source of much Catholic resentment in Northern Ireland because of the wide latitude of its provisions; for instance, the Special Powers Act was the means by which internment was authorized. Paradoxically, while the Act conferred extraordinary powers much criticized as being draconian in the extreme, similar legislation has existed across the border in the Republic for decades and continues to be in effect.

The PTA 1984 was originally passed in November 1974 in response to a wave of PIRA bombings in England, particularly the Birmingham pub explosions which left a total of twenty-one dead and 160 injured. The Act was not without precedent, however, as a pre-Second World War IRA campaign had resulted in the passage of the Prevention of Violence (Temporary Provisions) Act 1939 (PTA 1939) which contained many like powers. The PTA 1939 lapsed in 1954, and incidents 'in the 1956–62 IRA campaign were met on the mainland by the ordinary law'.[242] The PTA 1974 was passed very quickly, in the space of one day, but 'the Bill was the product of more than a year of Home Office contingency planning'.[243] It was replaced two years later by the PTA 1976 which made some modifications to the strengthening of police powers and the protection of civil liberties. A review of the PTA 1974 and 1976 was undertaken by Lord Shackleton in 1978, and most 'of the relatively minor changes it suggested were implemented by the Government'.[244] A further review of the PTA 1976 was later conducted by Lord Jellicoe in 1983, with the result that of his recommendations those 'that could be effected administratively were promptly accepted and implemented, some through guidance in circulars. Others are enshrined in the PTA 1984.'[245] Amongst the latter is the provision that the PTA 1984 must be re-introduced as new legislation in five years time, although the British Government is considering a proposal to introduce legislation making the PTA 1984 a permanent Act.

> In 1969 in accordance with accepted constitutional proprieties whereby the Northern Ireland Government asked the Westminster Government for such help, troops were deployed in Ulster as a peace-keeping force to aid the civil power to maintain order in the face of sectarian rioting.[246]

The situation continued to deteriorate until, in 1972, the British Government suspended Stormont and instituted Direct Rule from Westminster. To provide for emergency powers to cope with circumstances in Northern Ireland the EPA 1973 was passed, and was followed by similar, but modified, legislation in 1975 and 1978. The EPA 1973 'was based broadly on Diplock who reported in 1972 ... [EPA] 1975 was an amending Act to provide for Gardiner's recommendations and the [EPA] 1978 is a consolidation Act'.[247] A review of the EPA 1978 was carried out by Sir George Baker in 1984. In response to conflicting opinion about such emergency legislation, he replied, 'is it reasonably foreseeable that repeal or amendment [of each provision of the EPA 1978] may deprive yet another man, woman or child of the right to life or to live free from fear?'[248]

The current versions of PTA 1984 and EPA 1978 contain a number of overlapping powers, a matter which Baker argued should be amended to reduce confusing duplication. It is undoubtedly a complex arrangement, requiring a sound knowledge of both Acts to determine their correct applicability. Law-enforcement officers frequently use the provisions interchangeably, especially as the PTA 1984 (as did its predecessors) offers more latitude in the detention of a suspect, i.e. up to seven days, as opposed to seventy-two hours for the EPA 1978. A section-by-section review of the two legislative instruments is beyond the scope of this volume. An excellent examination in detail has been produced by David Bonner, Lecturer in Law at the University of Leicester.[249] An understanding of the legislation, and the rationale for development and implementation, is also available through a study of the various official reviews and inquiry reports. As Bonner has stated, 'All the inquiries into the legislation represent a substantial contribution to the debate on emergency powers. They are essential reading.'[250] Sir George Baker offered the same advice in his description of preparations for this review of EPA 1978: 'More useful was a ... reading [of] the various relevant reports: Jellicoe and Shackleton, Diplock, Gardiner and Bennett, also Compton (1971) and Parker (1972).'[251]

Important highlights of the two Acts, however, have been extracted and summarized. Beginning with the EPA 1978:

| Clause | Item |
|---|---|
| 2 | Bail in cases of scheduled terrorist offences may be granted only by Supreme Court or trial judge. |
| 7 | A trial on indictment of a scheduled offence shall be conducted without a jury. |
| 8 | A court shall have power to exclude a statement by an accused person if it is satisfied that the statement was obtained by torture or by inhuman or degrading treatment. |
| 9 | Where explosives, firearms, or ammunition are found on premises, or in any vehicle, vessel, or aircraft, the onus will be on the occupier to show that he did not know of its presence or if he did, that he had no control over it. |
| 11 | Empowers any constable to arrest without warrant any person whom he suspects of being a terrorist. A person arrested may be held without charge for up to seventy-two hours. |
| 12 | Power to detain without trial (internment). Repealed in 1980. |
| 14 | A member of HM Forces on duty may arrest without warrant, and detain for not more than four hours, a person who he suspects of committing, having committed, or being about to commit any offence. |
| 15 | Gives power to search premises for munitions or radio transmitters. |
| 17 | Empowers a constable or member of HM Forces to search premises where a person is believed to be unlawfully detained. |
| 18 | Allows any constable or member of HM Forces on duty to stop and question any person for the purpose of ascertaining |

the person's identity and movements, and his knowledge of any terrorist incident.

22 Makes it unlawful to collect without authorization any information likely to be useful to terrorists.

23 Provides that the giving of illegal training in the use of firearms or explosives shall be punishable by up to ten years' imprisonment, or £400 fine, or both.

24 Empowers any commissioned officers of HM Forces or officer of the RUC not below Chief Inspector to order the dispersal of any assembly of three or more persons.

25 Makes it an offence to dress or behave in a public place in such a way as to arouse reasonable apprehension that one is a member of a proscribed organization.

26 Makes it an offence to wear a hood or mask in a public place.

29 Only the Director of Public Prosecutions may authorize a prosecution under the Act.

*Schedule*

2 Lists the proscribed organizations: IRA; Cumann na mBan; Fianna na hEireann; Red Hand Commandos: Saor Eire; Ulster Freedom Fighters (UFF); Ulster Volunteer Force (UVR); Irish National Liberation Army (INLA).

3 Gives police the power to fix the route of a funeral or require those taking part to travel in vehicles. Gives the Secretary of State the power to close pubs or licensed premises for specified periods, or indefinitely, and also to control railways or road traffic.

4 Lists the scheduled offences to which the Act applies. (These include murder, manslaughter, kidnapping, riot, false imprisonment, assault occasioning bodily harm, interference with railways, and offences under a series of legislative Acts.)

'The Schedule also covers extra territorial offences under the Criminal Jurisdiction Act, 1975. This is the legislation which, together with reciprocal legislation in the Republic, permits a terrorist to be tried on whichever side of the border he is arrested.'[252]

In regard to the scheduled offences, Bonner has made it clear that 'no express distinction is made between those crimes executed for a political motive and those executed for some private advantage'.[253] The situation is a consequence of the Diplock Commission, which observed that 'terrorist organizations inevitably attract into their ranks ordinary criminals whose motivation for particular acts may be private gain or personal revenge ... the effect on public safety and on public fear is no different'.[254] Bonner continued: 'The present system in Northern Ireland, like that in the Republic, enables serious crimes, unconnected with the emergency, to be tried without a jury. Thus an armed robbery, wholly unconnected with the paramilitaries, must be tried before a Diplock Court.'[255] Nonetheless, it is within the Attorney General's power to certify that certain offences are not to be treated as 'scheduled' in particular cases, e.g. murder and manslaughter in a purely domestic quarrel. Also the Attorney General may certify that certain offences are only to be treated as scheduled offences in certain circumstances.

The PTA 1984 may be summarized in more general terms:

*Part*          *Context*

   I 'Restricts freedom of association in Great Britain, making it an offence to belong to, collect money or invite support for, or to arrange to speak to a meeting in support of any proscribed organization. The Act [INLA] ... It is [also] an offence to wear in public any item of dress or to display any article demonstrating support for a proscribed organization.'

  II 'Restricts the freedom of movement within the United Kingdom by authorizing the Secretary of State to issue exclusion orders to those suspected of being concerned in the commission or instigation of terrorist acts ... "with respect to affairs in Northern Ireland".' (Under PTA 1984 an exclusion order expires after three years if not revoked earlier.)

 III Makes it an offence 'to solicit, receive or make contributions for the support of acts of terrorism connected with Northern Ireland affairs. It is an offence to withhold information from the police which might be of material assistance in preventing such terrorist acts or in securing the arrest or conviction of any other person for such acts.'

 IV Applies to acts of terrorism connected with Northern Ireland and also to terrorist acts in general (but not to terrorist acts concerned solely with the United Kingdom or parts of Great Britain): 'all persons entering or leaving Great Britain and Northern Ireland may be searched and examined with a view to determining whether they are concerned with such terrorism or are subject to an exclusion order.

'By section 12, a constable may arrest without warrant a person reasonably suspected of being (a) guilty of offences against the Act; (b) concerned in the commission or preparation of acts of terrorism; or (c) subject to an exclusion order. Such a person may be detained in the right of arrest for not more than 48 hours, but the Secretary of State may extend the detention for up to a further 5 days. A detained person need not be brought before a court. Thus the police may arrest on reasonable suspicion of terrorist involvement without there being suspicion of specific offences; the extension of detention for up to 7 days in all enables the police to make further investigations before deciding whether to charge a suspect.'[256]

One of Lord Jellicoe's recommendations which was acted upon involved the life of the PTA 1984, which is now limited to five years and subject to annual renewal by Parliament. An observation on the change claimed that

events such as the Harrods bombing in London in December 1983 mean that there is no immediate prospect of the Act being brought to an end. Since there appears to be little scope for judicial protection against those whom the Act is applied, political vigilance continues to be necessary in respect of these exceptional powers.[257]

Both the PTA 1984 (more particularly its predecessors) and the EPA 1978 have made inroads upon the cherished traditions of civil liberties in the United Kingdom. The two Acts have been subject to extensive criticism, but also to extensive and intelligent scrutiny by experienced and learned authorities acting in an official capacity. Admittedly, bipartisan support was lacking in the 1983 general election when the Labour Party's manifesto opposed a continuance of the PTA 1976. Nevertheless, as Earl Jellicoe remarked,

I was invited in March 1982 to review the operation of the [PTA 1976]. I took some time to consider my reply ... partly because my proposed terms of reference ... required the acceptance of 'the continuing need for legislation against terrorism'.... I satisfied myself ... that some form of special legislation was indeed required to deal with the continuing threat posed by terrorism throughout the United Kingdom.... I have since become convinced ... that if special legislation effectively reduced terrorism, as I believe it does, it should be continued as long as a substantial terrorist threat remains.[258]

The British Government has announced plans to enact legislation making the PTA a permanent Act. But a major change to the legislation may also be necessary in the light of the European Court of Human

Rights decision in 1988 that the Act violated human rights by detaining prisoners for seven days without charge or a court hearing.

British activity, however, has not been confined to domestic legislative efforts. As with Canada and the United States, the United Kingdom is a signatory to the major ICAO and UN Conventions opposing terrorist acts. In conjunction, Britain is a party to the European Convention on the Suppression of Terrorism which came into force in 1978, as well as participating in the 'Trevi arrangements'. As previously mentioned, bilateral agreements between the United Kingdom and the Republic of Ireland 'permit courts in both countries to try offenders on a wide range of serious charges in the courts of the country in which they were apprehended, even if the crimes were committed within the other country's jurisdiction'.[259] Amendments to the Extradition Treaty with the United States, approved by the US Senate in 1986, have significantly reduced the attraction of the USA as a safe haven for persons suspected of terrorist offences. Similar recent extradition arrangements between Britain and Spain, and Britain and Italy, 'contained clauses designed to deal with terrorist activity'.[260] The United Kingdom has demonstrated strong leadership in achieving counter-terrorism accords at the Summit Seven meetings, especially in London (1984) and Tokyo (1986). As a consequence of determined efforts by Prime Minister Thatcher, the London Summit issued a declaration with specific proposals,

> such as closer co-ordination between police and security organizations and other authorities, especially the exchange of information, intelligence and technical knowledge and, as far as possible, cooperation over the expulsion from the participants' countries of known terrorists, including those of diplomatic status involved in terrorism.[261]

In July of the following year, in a speech to the American Bar Association in London, Mrs Thatcher made it plain that the British Government would not accede to terrorists' demands, release prisoners, make statements in support of the terrorists' cause, or allow hijacked aircraft to take off from Britain, and that the law would be applied to terrorists as to all other criminals. Speaking to the Police Management Association three months later, the Home Secretary further emphasized the government's commitment to international co-operation. He listed a series of objectives which incorporated:

— promotion of a common interest in fighting all kinds of terrorism;
— creation of an international climate in which State-sponsored or State-supported terrorism is unacceptable;

— agreement that no substantive concessions be made to terrorists;

— ensurance that diplomatic immunities are not abused by States which condone or support terrorism, and that fitting action be taken against such States;

— ensurance that consistent and effective measures are taken to prevent hijacking or sabotaging of aircraft;

— creation of an international environment in which it is difficult for terrorists to operate, and to impede the movement of terrorists from one country to another by use of immigration methods;

— ensurance that there is full cooperation among security services, police forces, and other organizations.[262]

In the aftermath of the American raid on Libya in 1986, the British Government took a leading position at the emergency meetings of the Foreign Ministers of the European Community states. Agreement was reached on the importance of taking collective action to prevent further acts of Libyan-directed terrorism. The member nations undertook to:

— reduce radically the size of the Libyan People's Bureaux and to review the size of their own missions in Tripoli;

— to take steps to reduce the freedom of movement of Libyan diplomats;

— to review the size of all other official Libyan bodies and to reduce their number to a minimum;

— to apply stricter visa practices and to ensure that any Libyan expelled from a member State would be refused admission to all others;

— to study urgently further ways of preventing Libyan abuse of diplomatic immunity.[263]

Subsequently, the Home Secretary 'ordered the expulsion of 22 Libyans on the grounds that this would be "conducive to the public good in the interests of national security" because of "their active involvement in Libyan student revolutionary activity in the UK"'.[264] Two years earlier the United Kingdom broke off diplomatic relations with Libya during the St James's Square incident in which a female police constable was shot and killed and eleven bystanders were injured. The government also announced restrictions on visa applications from Libyan citizens, and that no new contracts for defence equipment would be permitted. Export cover provided by the Export Credit Guarantee Department was suspended, and in May 1986 'even the limited amount of cover under existing credit lines was withdrawn'.[265]

*Media*

The media play an extremely important and obvious role in relation to terrorist activity. Publicity is the life-blood of terrorism. Conversely, the media can provide a valuable resource for government in response to the threat of terrorism. Such a concept does not imply a need for imposition of censorship, 'managed news', or other attempts at dictatorial regulation by government. Rather, the policy should include co-operation, understanding, dialogue, interchange of information, and a reasonable degree of responsibility by both parties. It is not an easy objective to achieve in liberal democracies which adhere to the principle of a free press and where such liberty is protected by constitutional guarantees.

Canadian media do not have a broad or considerable experience of encounters with terrorism in Canada. The October Crisis was a major event, but few incidents have occurred from that time until the 1980s. Crelinsten observed that during the October Crisis,

> In the first two-and-a-half days, reporting was confused, rife with speculation, and lacked accurate information both on the nature of the terrorist demands and threats, and on the extent and nature of police activity. This was consistent with an official policy of silence on the exact nature of the terrorist demands and on police activity. After the terrorists sent copies of their messages to different newspapers and radio stations, creating competition for scoops, newspaper reporting on the terrorists' demands became more consistent.... Consistency and accuracy of reporting on official activity was low.
>
> After the imposition of the War Measures Act, the pattern changed completely. The papers focused exclusively on government statements and actions, the consistency and accuracy of reporting was high for government statements.[266]

Unlike the United Kingdom, but in keeping with the American situation, the media is not concentrated in Canada and often demonstrates a very parochial attitude. Major urban centres in Canada support their own radio and television stations and newspapers; the national media representation of the United Kingdom is not the norm in Canada. A considerable influence is felt from the United States because the majority of the Canadian population lives within range of American radio and television coverage, and many American newspapers and magazines have a wide audience in Canada, e.g. *Time, Newsweek.*

The problem of 'the intelligent controlled release of information to the news media' during a terrorist incident, and 'persuading the news media to behave responsibly' has been recognized for some years by

Canadian Government authorities.[267] Robin Bourne, in his description of official crisis-management arrangements, described three events in the 1970s where media interference had potentially dangerous implications:

— During an attempted bank robbery, the would-be robber took eleven hostages and demanded a CF aircraft to fly him to Uganda. 'Before arrangements could be made to change the telephone number, an enterprising reporter was interviewing the hostage-taker on the national radio network.' Such interference with on-going negotiations might have seriously endangered the lives of the hostages.

— During another hostage-taking, at a jail in Quebec, a reporter contacted the hostage-taker by telephone and in the process of discussion the reporter informed the hostage-taker of the intentions of the police.

— During a third hostage incident, in western Canada, a man guilty of killing several police officers nearly went beserk when a television network helicopter flew low over the building where the killer was holding three persons hostage.[268]

Similarly, during the March 1985 seizure of the Turkish embassy in Ottawa, a reporter was able to interview the hostage-takers by telephone before the authorities could disconnect the lines and change the number.

Such activities by the media, while arguably understandable in the pursuit of news coverage in association with the high level of modern journalistic competition, do not reflect maturity and responsibility. The Solicitor General of Canada expressed those concerns in announcing the intention of the Canadian Government 'to meet with media leaders to seek their views and advice on how we can best protect the public while respecting journalists' democratic right to information'.[269]

Analysts have often pointed out that the goal of terrorists is to use the media to spread their message. Looked at in this context, terrorism becomes a tragic form of guerrilla theatre in which the media audience, and not the immediate victims, are the ultimate target. Hostages or others killed or wounded in terrorist acts are treated as simply theatrical props in a deadly performance.

Media coverage of terrorist threats or acts in progress can pose two problems. First, the release of even certain types of accurate information may inflame events and cost lives.

Second, coverage can encourage terrorists and prolong incidents.[270]

Circumstances in relation to American news coverage of terrorist incidents are more extreme. Earlier reference has been made to the harsh criticism of NBC News over its agreement in 1986 'to keep secret the whereabouts of a terrorist suspect in exchange for an interview...'.[271] The media, and television broadcasters in particular, were also treated to much criticism in the aftermath of the 1985 TWA hijacking in Beirut. In a sense the media were themselves the victims of the terrorists, who used the press coverage to every possible advantage. An article in the *Sunday Times* referred to media role as 'Terrorvision'.[272] The author of the article, Howard Rosenberg, TV columnist of the *Los Angeles Times*, wrote:

> Disregarding the feelings of the victim's family, ABC has several times shown a graphic photograph of the battered, bloodied body of the US Navy diver beaten and shot in the head aboard the TWA airliner. It was shocking television and even more shocking news judgement.[273]

Rosenberg further commented on the 'dangers of inflammatory coverage', and the sort of reporting that seemed to be 'prodding Reagan toward the kind of hasty military action he has seemed determined to avoid'.[274] In the same manner the television networks continued to remind the President of his 1981 promise to conduct 'swift and effective retribution'.[275] As an example, Martin Kalb cited a number of incidents of anti-American terrorism during the Reagan years and then ended each enumeration with the statement: 'Again, none of the retribution this president has promised'.[276] Related to the TWA incident, it was claimed that media reporting of Delta Force movements compromised any attempt by American SOF units to intervene.

The Vice President's Task Force acknowledged the fact that terrorism 'is a form of propaganda, demanding publicity to be effective'.[277] Further, the Task Force Report observed that if 'violence is spectacular, wide coverage is usually assured'.[278] It was also accepted that two viewpoints exist: (1) that the media believe by putting hostages on television they may actually save lives; and (2) government considers that untimely or inaccurate information released by the media can interfere with the resolution of an incident, 'foreclose options for dealing with it, or unwittingly provide intelligence information to terrorists';[279] thus prolonging an incident or creating danger to the lives of hostages. Several media practices were cited as causing problems for government in the conduct of an incident:

— Saturation television coverage, which can limit or pre-empt the government's options;
— Political dialogue with terrorists or hostages;
— Coverage of obviously staged events;

— Payments to terrorist groups or supporters for interviews or access;
— Coverage of military plans or deployments in response to terrorist incidents.[280]

'The solution of these problems is not government-imposed restraint that conflicts with the First Amendment's protection of freedom of speech and the press.'[281] As with the Canadian attitude, the US government holds the opinion that the media must 'serve as their own watchdog'.[282] Similarly, the government has a responsibility to provide information and to maintain communications with the media during a terrorist incident. The Task Force, while cautioning the media (especially the television networks) on the danger of 'making heroes out of criminals and exploiting the privacy and grief of affected families',[283] recommended that regular meetings take place 'between media and government officials on the coverage of terrorism'[284] to achieve more effective government–media relations.

Within the United Kingdom, the 'whole area of media coverage of Northern Ireland affair is ... controversial and has attracted criticism from differing quarters'.[285] Little argument exists over the fact that the early civil-rights marches and the ensuing disturbances received a major fillip from the glare of world-wide publicity. Much concern has been voiced about the extent to which terrorists have benefited from the opportunity to propagate their views by such means. Certainly there were frequent occasions when the media perspective did not present the actions of the security forces in a favourable light. Initially the government and the security forces did little to rectify their often unbalanced position in relation to media coverage and relationship with media representatives. In fact, for a time, an air of hostility existed between the two elements. The Army, in particular, adhered to the age-old policy that only officers should speak to the Press, and even then the conversation should be circumscribed. Security forces press releases were generally issued too late to be effective, and the context was insufficiently detailed to be of much value to the Press. Gradually, however, the situation improved, particularly when a government policy change was introduced which encouraged authority for the media to speak directly and immediately to soldiers involved in an operation. A better understanding developed, and the public were better able to assess events when they heard them presented in a candid manner by working soldiers instead of from often pompous or harried officers. A very real change for the good occurred when both the military and the police established professional media and public-relations departments within their headquarters staff departments.

The military organized a tri-service public relations office at the headquarters at Lisburn, while the RUC formed a Force Control and Information Centre at its Knock Road headquarters in Belfast. Both operations are impressive in their approach to the need for accurate, timely information on the part of the media and the public. The two operations produce attractive, glossy brochures, magazines, and hand-out material in copious amounts. Commenting in his 1984 Report, the Chief Constable of the RUC stated:

> Tens of thousands of inquiries originating locally, nationally, and internationally were dealt with on a 24-hour, seven-days-a-week basis. Briefings, interviews, and extensive facilities were provided for hundreds of visitors from all over the world and the policy, actions and role of the Force were explained.... The service to weekly newspapers throughout the Province continues to expand alongside the firmly established weekly television programme, daily radio programmes and newspaper features.... Our policy of providing as much information as possible about the Force and its work – about the incidents, often traffic, with which we have to deal – is appreciated by the public....[286]

It is noteworthy that in Northern Ireland, until 1988

> there (were) no legal restrictions on interviews with Sinn Fein members (and) use of material about terrorist or extremist political groups (was) constrained principally by the editorial policies of BBC Northern Ireland, Ulster TV and other media organizations.[287]

On the contrary, in

> the Republic there is quite strict control relating to the treatment of terrorist and paramilitary organizations ... (since 1976) no interviews, or reports of interviews, with PIRA or PSF members, or members of any organization proscribed in Northern Ireland, have been broadcast ....[288]

In October 1988, following an upsurge of terrorist shootings and bombings by Loyalists and Republicans, the British Government issued a ban on broadcast interviews with members of legal and armed militant wings of both groups in Northern Ireland. The ban applies to British television and radio, but not to the British print media or foreign broadcasting organizations. Of interest has been the outcry by civil-rights organizations and negative comment in some newspaper editorials, although reference to the existence of similar regulations in Eire since 1976 has been avoided.

While secrecy is a hallmark of government and security-force operations in the United Kingdom, official censorship does not obtain except in time of war, or in relation to the Official Secrets Act. The D-notice system, however, does operate on a voluntary basis. Under the arrangement 'editors are advised by the D-notice Committee, made up of Whitehall and Press and broadcasting representatives, that publication is against the national interest'.[289] Akin to many matters which tend to restrict publicity on the workings of government in the United Kingdom, the D-notice system is the subject of controversy and criticism. In 1984, for instance, the *New Statesman* was reprimanded for publishing the names of intelligence service personnel. But, as the secretary of the Committee commented, 'nothing could be done about it'.[290] In 1985 controversy erupted over a BBC plan to broadcast a television documentary which featured interviews with leading members of Sinn Fein and the loyalist Democratic Union Party. Following pressure from the Home Secretary, the BBC Board of Governors cancelled the programme. Subsequently, after world-wide publicity, and in the wake of a one-day strike by television and radio personnel, the programme was re-scheduled. Opinion generally agreed that the content did little to promote the views of either extremist and, perhaps, produced a negative reaction. The problem, however,

> illustrates ... the continuing difficulty, especially for responsible journalists and editors in a democracy such as the (United Kingdom), of striking a balance between reporting opinions and events as fully as possible while denying unrepresentative and frequently violent minority groups the 'oxygen' which publicity provides.[291]

An equally difficult situation, as in the Iranian embassy seizure, is the restraining of media coverage which might jeopardize the actions of security forces. British journalists have notably demonstrated rather more constraint and responsibility in such matters than have their counterparts in North America, possibly in part as a result of their depth of experience.

## Comment

At the beginning of this chapter an observation was made that the finest resources are of little value lacking suitable preparation or appropriate use. In conjunction, various factors influence the type and nature of resources that may be adopted, and constrain both their development and application. Despite their similarities as liberal democracies, Canada, the United States, and the United Kingdom cannot employ precisely identical resources to combat terrorism. For various reasons, the capabilities of the resources available to the three nations are also different. Constitutional limitations, systems of government, and structures of bureaucracy are some of the variables which contribute to those realities.

Thus, comparative generalizations must be weighed carefully in an attempt accurately to depict strengths and weaknesses associated with resources and capabilities. Chapter Five, which follows next, is a discussion of those topics and the subject matter of previous chapters, taking into account the aforementioned qualifying reservations. Certain factors can be used for guidance in making an overall assessment, as well as for reflecting specifically on resources and capabilities. Approached from practical and philosophical viewpoints they are: (1) perceptiveness; (2) capacity to adapt to new challenges; (3) practicality; and (4) adherence to legal and moral principles.

In brief, they translate as follows:

1. *Perceptiveness.* How well has each nation learned from its own experiences, and the experience of others? Has each nation been able to differentiate between strategic and tactical goals, and to define clearly short-, medium-, and long-term objectives in response to the threat of terrorism?
2. *Capacity to adapt.* How swiftly and expeditiously has each national government and security system been able accurately to assess a new or developing threat and evolve an appropriate response?
3. *Practicality.* Has each nation utilized its resource and capabilities to the best advantage, and how well has each nation developed new measures?
4. *Legal, democratic, and moral principles.* Have these been upheld and maintained, or sacrificed for short-term gains?

It can be seen that experience constitutes a significant element, but cannot rest on a narrow foundation. Individual national experience must be combined with that of others, but perceptively. The desire to achieve a 'quick-fix' solution must not be allowed to cloud long-term issues or influences. What may appear as the answer to an immediate problem may have far-reaching consequences, especially if legal and moral principles are distorted or abrogated, even temporarily. Similarly, practical solutions must also be viewed in relation to their impact on the future and upon legal and moral principles. A simple cost-effective judgement, particularly if based on a short-term or quick-fix perception, is not a sound assessment in response to the threat of terrorism.

Chapter five

# Concluding commentary

## The threat

Because Canada, the United States, and the United Kingdom are liberal-democratic nations they possess characteristics which make them soft targets for domestic and international terrorism. The openness of their societies, concerns for the observance of civil rights, respect for the rule of law, and protection of freedom of expression (especially in relation to the media) are features which provide terrorist groups with opportunities to evolve and to conduct attacks against those nations at home and abroad. Under totalitarian regimes the brutal repression of opposition and firm control of the populace are maintained by the use of all-powerful secret-police agencies combined with strong, well-equipped, and harsh paramilitary forces, and through the suppression of unfavourable publicity and by direction of the media. Such are the 'strengths' which inhibit the growth of terrorist behaviour, except as practised by the state. The 'weaknesses' which make democratic nations attractive targets for terrorists, on the other hand, are the very properties that must be carefully guarded to ensure they are not subverted in efforts to overcome the threat of terrorism. Democratic nations must be constantly aware of the long-term aims of terrorist groups, and must not be lured into opting for quick-fix solutions which may ultimately create greater problems or undermine legal and moral principles.

Equally at risk are the developing Third World countries which lack the experience and resources to combat the subversive actions of terrorist groups effectively. The overthrow of democratic institutions in those nations, and their replacement by governments whose interests are inimical to those of western democracies, could constitute a serious danger to global stability. Western democracies must endeavour to counter such inroads both by offering material assistance and by setting the moral example of constitutionally correct behaviour when battling terrorist aggression.

In broad terms, terrorism presents a parallel threat to Canada, the United States, and the United Kingdom. Each nation is vulnerable from a technological dependency standpoint, as well as in relation to their exposed systems of government. Although Canada and the United States share the benefit of relative isolation from the centres of terrorist violence in Europe and the Middle East, they have overseas interests which offer lucrative targets. Both North American nations also have a number of large ethnic communities that are potential sources of terrorist problems, either in terms of support infrastructure or as centres of unrest. As well, the 'successes' of some recognized terrorist groups in achieving limited gains have tended to engender a certain admiration among issue groups in all three nations, and could promote an increase in acts of domestic terrorism.

Each nation has wisely chosen to treat terrorism as criminal behaviour, and to approach and oppose such activity under the concept of the rule of law. But terrorism must not be regarded simply as ordinary crime, it must be placed in a perspective which views it as a threat to the very concept of the rule of law, the stability and constitutional well-being of nations, and the principles of democratic government and society. For that reason, it is dangerous to consider terrorism as a form of warfare and to allow that attitude to prevail in determining measures of response. Conditions of war tend to permit extremes of laxity and constraint in the functioning of government which are not appropriate to the peacetime environment. Use of such measures in peacetime can make lasting and unwarranted intrusions upon democratic freedoms and principles, as well as providing the 'risk [of] increasing the very anarchy in which terrorists flourish'.[1]

## General policy

### Policy development

Canadian counter-terrorism policy development originated with activities of the FLQ and the resultant October Crisis of 1970. At that time the Canadian Government demonstrated an active appreciation of the dangers of terrorism and took steps to improve the nation's crisis-management mechanisms, as well as advocating international co-operation against terrorism. But during the remainder of the 1970s, as the domestic threat receded and Canada encountered little experience of international terrorist activity, interest in counter-terrorism measures waned. It was not until several tragic incidents of domestic and international terrorism directly affected Canada in the first half of the next decade that counter-terrorism policy development again received closer scrutiny.

Perceptive and responsive in the early years, Canadian counter-terrorism policy development lost its edge in the period between 1973 and 1983. Over-confidence, a smug sense of Canada's position as a UN peacekeeper, distance from the majority of terrorist incidents (literally and figuratively), and preoccupation with domestic concerns (e.g. the economy, native rights, the Constitution issue) overrode attention to the threat of terrorism. Some improvements to organizational structuring which came about in the wake of the 1981 McDonald Report indicated a reawakening to the dangers of terrorism, and particularly as later expressed by government measures announced in 1986. But the nation will have to beware of the trend illustrated by its behaviour in the 1970s, and not lapse back into the comfortable posture of the 'peaceable kingdom'.

The United States gradually became alert to the menace of terrorism in the early 1970s, in part through a spate of aircraft hijackings and the atrocities at Munich and Lod. Recognized by the Nixon administration, attempts were made to generate a collective UN response, an organizational infrastructure was created at senior government level, and a bilateral anti-hijacking treaty was concluded with Cuba, among other efforts. As with Canada, however, interest in the threat of terrorism flagged until the Iranian hostage crisis in 1979–80, although President Carter initiated moves to rejuvenate the US counter-terrorism programme in 1977. Reaction to perceived American inadequacies in coping with the Iranian crisis markedly assisted the election of Ronald Reagan to the presidency in 1981. The new administration came to power 'with bellicose warnings of what it would do if challenged'[2] by terrorists.

> But the astute handlers of the President soon discerned a different problem: By elevating terrorism to a top public concern, the administration inevitably raised public expectations for action and results, something officials doubted they could deliver.[3]

Consequently, through later 1981, 1982, and early 1983 the Reagan administration 'turned down the volume'[4] on terrorism. It was not a difficult move to make because during 1982 only eleven terrorist attacks involved Americans, and only nine US citizens were killed in the incidents.[5]

The US Government did take action against Libya shortly after President Reagan assumed office in 1981. When Gaddafi dispatched his hit-squads in search of dissidents abroad, the US imposed political and economic sanctions on Libya which included a ban on American imports of Libyan oil and the removal of many American technicians from that nation. But the US was unable to rally foreign support for its efforts, especially in Europe, and the American embargoes appeared to have little negative effect. In fact, when the Americans departed, European oil companies stepped in and benefited from the situation, and during 1984, 'European countries exported $4.3 billion worth of merchandise to Libya'.[6]

Circumstances began to change in mid-1982 with the Israeli invasion of Lebanon, followed later in the year by American military involvement in the evacuation of the PLO and then as part of the multinational force. US Secretary of State Shultz viewed the deployment as a means of obtaining an Israeli withdrawal and the restoration of stability in Lebanon. The concept did not prove workable, however, and began to unravel in early 1983 when a suicide car bomber destroyed a large part of the US embassy in Beirut, causing eighty-six deaths and wounding 100 persons. Six months after that incident another suicide vehicle bomber demolished the US Marine headquarters building at Beirut airport, killing 241 American servicemen.

From the time of that event, terrorism moved on to stage-centre in terms of attention from the US government. The event also marked a watershed in US policy in response to terrorism. Increased emphasis was placed on the governmental counter-terrorism infrastructure, and measures were taken to improve physical security at American facilities at home and abroad. Security became a high priority matter, eventually prompting the Inman Report and recommendations for a multi-billion dollar programme to modernize protective arrangements, especially at overseas installations. The most significant change, nevertheless, was a growth in favourable consideration of a policy of pre-emptive strikes and retaliation against terrorists. In April 1984, President Reagan signed a directive authorizing such action on the part of the United States. The issue was controversial within the upper echelons of the American Government; although increasingly advocated in public statements by Secretary of State Shultz, it was openly opposed by Secretary of Defense Weinberger. Weinberger was concerned that the US Armed Forces were neither prepared for, nor suited to, carrying out the task. Further, two problems were directly related to the policy: (1) specific terrorist targets could not be readily and accurately identified; and (2) the American public did not favour indiscriminate attacks, especially if casualties to innocent civilians were likely to result.

A parallel trend developed, however, in the form of pronounced reference to the role of state-sponsored terrorism. In that regard, Gaddafi and Libya provided convenient and easily recognizable attractions, particularly from the standpoint of retaliation. Notwithstanding, American public opinion remained reluctant about military intervention; therefore, the Reagan administration sought support from European countries for more economic and political sanctions against Libya. Despite incidents such as occurred in St James's Square in London, the level and nature of response to American advocacy was not satisfactory. Commercial benefits continued to hold precedence, and even certain American-owned oil corporations did not cease their operations in Libya. The combination of the lack of European co-operation and the strident warnings of retaliation voiced by the American Government led to the availability of fewer and fewer options, and made the possibility of military response increasingly likely.

In late 1985 the hijacking of the liner *Achille Lauro*, and the murder of an aged and crippled American passenger, triggered the use of US military forces to apprehend the terrorists involved. Carrier-borne aircraft intercepted an Egyptian commercial airliner carrying the terrorists to Tunisia and forced the plane to land in Sicily. Jubilantly welcomed in the United States, the action was criticized abroad as a violation of international law; it also raised concerns about the extent to which the US was prepared to use force in response to terrorism.

On 27 December 1985, terrorist atrocities at the Rome and Vienna airports paved the way for further use of American military force. While evidence pointed to some Syrian involvement, Libya was considered to be the base from which the raids were staged. The US Government ordered a total economic boycott of Libya and instructed all Americans to leave that country. Again, 'Reagan ... was unable for the most part to persuade the ... Europeans to join in. Without their participation, U.S. officials acknowledged, the American sanctions would have little bite'.[7]

In February 1986, the US Navy conducted manoeuvres in the disputed Gulf of Sidra, off the coast of Libya. 'As predicted, Libyan forces fired on American jets',[8] which prompted 'brief American counterattacks against two Libyan naval ships and against land-based radar sites'.[9] The outcome of the incident strengthened the arguments of pro-retaliation factions in the American Government and among right-wing hawkish lobbies: the American forces did not suffer any losses, the Soviet Union did not make any overt moves in aid of Libya, and US public opinion polls suggested an overwhelming approval of the action. Not long afterwards, the report of the Vice President's task force on terrorism was made public and it, too, indicated stronger national support of military response to terrorist attacks.

On 5 April 1986, a bomb exploded in a West Berlin disco frequented by off-duty US servicemen. The blast killed an American soldier and a Turkish woman, and wounded 230 other people; communications interceptions by the US intelligence community led to the conclusion that the attack was conducted under Libyan sponsorship. 'From that point, a counterterrorism official said, the administration was both compelled to respond in some way and finally ready to take military action that would "match the rhetoric with action".'[10]

Less than ten days later, American military aircraft from bases in England and aircraft carriers in the Mediterranean took part in bombing raids against targets in Libya. The United States had implemented the promised policy of military retaliation. The American raid was generally well received by the US public, and was officially endorsed by the British and Canadian Governments. It was also subject to much criticism, particularly in Europe and the Middle East (excluding Israel). European concern was illustrated by efforts to increase sanctions against Libya to preclude further US military strikes, although the moves still did not incorporate radical political and economic constraints. Despite the co-operative atmosphere displayed at the following Tokyo Summit Seven conference, President Reagan warned that if terrorist attacks continued the United States would not hesitate to employ military force again.

The change in policy direction begun in 1983 is the result of a range of motivational factors. Among other things, it represents an attempt to find a quick solution to the problem of terrorism, to demonstrate the power and influence of the United States, to assuage the fears, frustrations and anger of the American people, and to restore credibility to US Government statements. The use of American military forces in the aftermath of the *Achille Lauro* hijacking, and the bombing raid on Libya, undoubtedly did satisfy an urge for revenge, as well as providing substantive evidence that terrorists could not act against the United States with impunity. In the latter sense, the American behaviour was not without some positive results. The shock of the actions did produce a temporary lull in terrorist attacks, and gave a clear warning to nations involved in state sponsored terrorism. The proof that the United States was willing to act alone, and in strength, in retaliation against terrorists served notice to other nations as well. It focused the attention of European nations on the need, *inter alia*, to scrutinize more closely the credentials, background, and activities of diplomatic representatives from those states known to be associated with terrorism.

But the policy direction also contains other less commendable aspects. From an elementary standpoint, the policy of retaliation has not lessened the American public's fear of terrorist attacks, as was shown by the reduction of tourist travel to the European area in 1986. More importantly, however, the policy represents a dangerous escalation of violence and suggests the use of one sort of terror to combat another. It has established a serious precedent, and illustrates a lamentable lack of concern for international legal standards. While the Reagan administration declared that 'Libya had engaged in armed aggression against the United States',[11] and cited Article 51 of the UN Charter to defend the bombing of Libya, military retaliation involving innocent civilians violates legal, democratic, and moral values, and is as reprehensible as the terrorist acts which prompt the action. The policy of retaliation embodies the 'might is right' concept, and poses a threat to established democratic mores and constitutional principles. Its use does not demonstrate a mature view of the threat of terrorism, or recognition of the need for a long-range many-faceted response in keeping with the rule of law.

Counter-terrorism policy development in the United Kingdom has been characterized by a rather more measured response than that of Canada or the United States. Undoubtedly that reality is largely a consequence of Great Britain's longer experience with political violence associated with colonial disturbances following the Second World War, coupled with the unbroken years of conflict in Northern Ireland beginning the latter half of 1969. In conjunction, the proximity of terrorist activity in Europe and the Middle East has had a pronounced influence during the 1980s.

British policy development, however, has not been without errors or faults. An early failure was the lack of perception in judging the situation in Ulster and the inability to forecast the evolution of events accurately. Similarly, the use of internment and subsequent introduction of special status for prisoners did not reflect wise, long-range policy decisions. The British military (like its counterparts in Canada and the United States) was not suitably prepared for domestic counter-terrorism duties, especially when trouble first broke out in Ulster. While the London Metropolitan Police have shown admirable initiative in forming special anti-terrorist units, some weaknesses have persisted in the functioning of co-ordinated nation-wide counter-terrorism activity in Great Britain.

British policy development in response to terrorism emanating from Northern Ireland has been steadily fixed on re-establishing conditions of normalcy in that Province. Although different solutions have been put forward, and some criticism may be levelled at a lack of major Whitehall concern over the years, the policy goal has remained consistent. It is an attitude that has been illustrated by the perseverance in restoring the RUC to effective status as a law-enforcement body, and by returning the RUC to primacy in the maintenance of security in Northern Ireland. Mrs Thatcher's Government has also demonstrated a firm resolve to oppose and defeat terrorism, as illustrated in part by the determination to make the Anglo–Irish Agreement a viable working instrument. Accusations have been levelled at the British Government to the effect that measures introduced during the 1980s to combat terrorism, especially Irish-inspired, 'are a real containment of Britain's civil rights'.[12] But the defeat of terrorist groups such as the PIRA will only be accomplished by strengthening the resources available to government. The oversight mechanisms employed in Britain, and the tradition of rule of law, make it unlikely that lasting inroads on civil rights will occur and that the 'fundamental duty of defending ... citizens' right to life'[13] will remain the paramount concern.

The British Government has played a leading role in attempts to encourage international co-operation against terrorism, particularly at the Summit Seven gatherings. Like Canada and the United States, the United Kingdom is a signatory of major international Conventions and agreements designed to combat acts of terrorism, and the nation is a party to the European Convention on the Suppression of Terrorism. In the wake of the American bombing raid on Libya in 1986, Great Britain made prompt efforts to obtain European co-operation to impose a number of restrictions on Libyan activities with a view to precluding the need for further US military actions. (The restrictions were of a limited nature, especially in regard to economic sanctions. The United Kingdom, as with other European nations (e.g. West Germany, Italy) continued to do business with Libya.) Co-operation within the European Community to oppose terrorism will become even more important as 1992 approaches when travel between the nations will not be subject to immigration controls.

## Fundamental policy

From the outset, the three nations have generally adhered to the combined policy of: (1) no concessions in response to terrorists' demands; (2) encouragement of international co-operation and sanctions; and (3) observance of the rule of law in the combating of terrorism. The United States has tended publicly to accord rather more emphasis on the no-negotiation aspect, although the government has displayed a willingness to conduct discussions through third parties. Unfortunately, the latter process got out of hand under the influence of Oliver North, and the resulting Irangate Affair seriously damaged American credibility.

Until the mid-1980s the philosophy of the use of force was shared by Canada, the United States, and the United Kingdom; that is, each nation endeavoured to employ minimum force through the use of police resources in response to terrorism. The military functioned in a supportive role, to be committed only if the police were exhausted or were unable to cope, or if maximum force could not be avoided.

The National Security Decision Directive 138 signed by President Reagan on 3 April 1984, authorizing pre-emptive and retaliatory strikes by the United States against terrorists overseas, followed by the use of American military forces in 1985 and 1986, placed that nation on a different footing. In a sense, the United States adopted a warfare posture in opposition to terrorism, and demonstrated a readiness to rely upon maximum force as a preferred option for dealing with acts of terrorism. While the Governments of Canada and the United Kingdom supported the American raid on Libya in public statements (and Britain permitted the use of US aircraft based in England), the two governments have not adopted parallel policy commitments. Notwithstanding, it must be remembered that the terrorist threat to the United States is principally offshore and American response is not illogically directed towards the use of its powerful military resources as the means to counter the threat.

## *Direct (active) measures*

Canada, the United States, and the United Kingdom have each elected to view terrorism as criminal acts, in keeping with the rule of law. It is an approach which has eased problems with definition, helped to overcome many difficulties associated with political-status claims, expedited use of criminal-law statutes in dealing with terrorist crimes, and facilitated reliance upon law-enforcement agencies in opposing terrorism. It has also encouraged a somewhat reduced tendency to employ special wide-ranging emergency legislation of a draconian nature, as well as stimulating improvements to extradition procedures.

The three nations have implemented individual versions of the lead-minister or lead-agency concept in structuring government organization to cope with terrorist acts. In theory it is a practical idea with many obvious advantages, and allowing for the focus of responsibilities to be established. In practice, particularly in North America, it encounters difficulties with jurisdictional constraints or overlapping that do not permit smooth functioning. Bureaucratic frictions, self-interest, or 'protectionism' at all levels create obstacles which are frequently overcome only through the dedicated efforts of individuals who manage to reduce tensions and induce a co-operative atmosphere. The system requires a central directing and co-ordinating body with the power to ensure that policy decisions of senior government leadership are carried out. Conversely, such a body must also be in a position to provide recommendations and advice directly to senior government leadership. It is not sufficient to assign spheres of responsibility (e.g. response to domestic or international terrorist threats), without capping the infrastructure with a central organ for the purpose of monitoring progress and providing direction and decision-making. More is said on this matter in later discussion.

The United States has proposed a vigorous, ambitious and costly programme to improve the physical security of government facilities at home and abroad. Such improvements are beneficial and obviously necessary, but care must be taken to ensure that the measures are of practical value and not dysfunctional or merely cosmetic. The United Kingdom introduced somewhat similar protective measures in response to PIRA attacks both in Northern Ireland and in mainland Britain. Britain would be wise to review security at overseas installations, however, especially in view of the support given to efforts to stem Libyan activities. Evidence of Canadian concern for physical security measures at home and abroad has not been overly impressive, and the nation would do well to take advantage of the experience of others. The United States has also initiated programmes designed to inform military and civilian personnel serving abroad of the dangers associated with the threat of terrorism. As well, the American Government enlisted the support of that segment of the business community with overseas commitments to provide better security arrangements. Wide dissemination of such information has value in lessening the availability of targets for terrorists, and helping citizens to comprehend the aims of terrorist groups. Even elementary precautions have the potential of deterring a terrorist attack.

Canada, the United States, and the United Kingdom employ a number of active measures in response to terrorism. Included in the spectrum are use of legislation, law-enforcement agencies and military resources, and organizational structuring. Specific reference is made to those subjects later in this chapter.

*Indirect (passive) measures*

Canada deserves commendation for its recognition of Francophone concerns and the corresponding efforts of the Federal government in achieving improvements to that situation. Canada has also taken steps to acknowledge Native Rights within the nation, and to observe the interests of minority groups in the maintenance of their cultural and ethnic heritages. Canada, nonetheless, must take care not to encourage the development of ethnic ghettos or other structures which might have a divisive rather than a cohesive influence on the nation. Civil-rights agitation in the 1960s and 1970s resulted in the amelioration of conditions for minorities in the United States, particularly the Black population. Similar efforts have been undertaken on behalf of the Hispanic communities. In the United Kingdom there has been growing evidence of friction involving the Black, Indian and Pakastani populace in major urban centres which requires government attention.

Immigration and passport controls, generally a source of some complacency as to their effectiveness, warrant more concern. Passports, in particular, require improvements to make them less amenable to forgery or alteration. Political and refugee-status claims are other areas where a more firm application of standards is required to prevent terrorist activities from achieving even limited gains, both in terms of movement of terrorists and the migrations of populace. Canada has faced severe problems with the illegal entry of immigrants and the government continues to receive criticism in regard to its efforts to impose controls. The United Kingdom is particularly concerned over the removal of movement controls within the European Community scheduled to occur in 1992. Undoubtedly some form of scrutiny or restriction must continue if the free flow of terrorists is to be curtailed.

Access to information on the part of the public is a delicate responsibility that government must balance carefully. Too much availability can lead to difficulties in securing international co-operation, as in the case of relationships between intelligence agencies. It can also hamper the functioning of security agencies or provide terrorists with critical knowledge of possible targets. Too little access can cause infringements of civil rights or cause uncertainties among the public in regard to government intentions or operations. The United States has recognized the demands, but also must ensure that the pendulum does not swing too far in the opposite direction. Canada is just beginning to come to grips with the problem and may encounter increasing difficulties as a consequence of its new Charter of Rights and Freedoms. The United Kingdom has been forced to make some disclosures, but is unlikely to alter its fundamental closed attitude to the operation of government and the bureaucracy.

The United States has been an early proponent of the use of academics and research organizations for assistance in understanding the threat of terrorism. Canada and the United Kingdom have not displayed the same level of interest, but would demonstrate greater perceptiveness were they to do so. Advisedly, however, use of such resources must be broad in scope and caution must be observed that the advocacy of any one source does not become paramount. Undoubtedly in the United States certain right-wing institutions, and lobbies, have influenced the government in its decisions to pursue the policy of pre-emptive strikes and retaliation.

## Decision-making and crisis-management

### Decision-making mechanisms

Top-level government leaders (e.g. Prime Minister and Cabinet; President and National Security Council) are the source of major decisions in response to terrorism. Such may involve policy matters, or the choice of options to pursue during an incident. This set of circumstances should prevail, within reason, because government is responsible to the public under the rule of law. Nonetheless, subordinates must have substantial leeway to make decisions involved with the implementation of government direction. For instance, senior government leadership should not become part of the decision-making process in the actual operational conduct of an anti-terrorist incident, other than to authorize use of maximum force if required. As mentioned previously, however, an organizational structure should exist to facilitate senior government participation in policy development, implementation, and crisis-management. Government leadership cannot abrogate its responsibility by assigning tasks and then failing to provide oversight and firm direction. Bureaucratic weaknesses, alone, contribute to making such a system difficult to operate, if not unmanageable. Clearly defined goals must be established, time limits for achievement must be set, and a means of both co-ordination and decision-making must be functionally available.

Within the government structures of Canada, the United States, and the United Kingdom, organs currently exist to permit specific top-level decision-making, i.e. NSC in the USA; Cabinet Committees in Canada and Britain. *The Report of the Vice President's Task Force on Combatting Terrorism* included a recommendation for a new NSC position (with staff) to 'strengthen coordination of our national program.'[14] Admirable though the suggestion might appear, it is of little value unless the new position is given authoritative teeth and a very clear and practicable mandate. If it lacks a decision-making capability or the means of issuing firm directions it will simply function as another rubber-stamp office in the chain of command.

Similarly, the Cabinet Committees in Canada and the United Kingdom are capable of providing continuing and responsive oversight of counter-terrorism matters. Difficulty in penetrating the British governmental structure makes it impossible to do other than provide generalized observations. The system appears to work reasonably well, although the need to form the 'TIGER' apparatus in 1984[15] suggests that there is room for improvement. Within Canada, the McDonald Report pointed to the requirement for greater activity on the part of the Cabinet Committee on Security and Intelligence (CCSI). It is incumbent on the CCSI to provide definitive instructions and firm timetables to its supporting committee infrastructure. The latter, comprised of the Interdepartmental Committee on Security and Intelligence (ICSI) and its two reporting bodies, the Security Advisory Committee (SAC) and the Intelligence Advisory Committee (IAC), appears to be a satisfactory arrangement. The system has been improved by combining the domestic and foreign intelligence-assessment functions in the IAC, and by leaving the SAC free to advise on and develop security policy. The role of SAC has been further enhanced through the assumption of chairmanship by the Deputy Solicitor General.

*Crisis-management mechanisms*

The vast range of sophisticated resources available to the American

Government in terms of operations centres, communications, computers, and other technologically advanced equipments greatly facilitates the nation's crisis-management potential. Through the use of satellites and airborne and shipborne systems, command and control can be exercised from one location to sites around the world. The only adverse factor is the possibility of too stringent a control upon the initiative of subordinate facilities, or personnel by senior government leadership.

Under the circumstances it is invidious to make comparisons with similar arrangements in Canada and the United Kingdom. The two nations do not have equal global responsibilities and commitments, either with those of the United States or between themselves. The 1987 Report of the Senate Special Committee in Canada expressed concern about the Canadian counter-terrorism structure and crisis-management arrangements, particularly the junior department status of the Solicitor General. To the credit of the Canadian Government, an inter-departmental Task Force was quickly formed to report on the situation and to recommend improvements. Undoubtedly the Task Force will suggest means to strengthen the central co-ordinating role of the Solicitor General and to streamline the command, control, and communications procedures for policy and operational response to a terrorist threat or incident. Because of security restrictions it has not been possible to judge accurately the technical efficiency or practicality of British arrangements, especially such as are embodied in COBRA. The COBRA arrangement, however, is a sound and practicable method of co-ordinating government policy direction and the operational response of security forces. While designed for domestic use, the COBRA apparatus can also function in support of overseas requirements. It is a system which could have a workable application, with modifications, in other democratic nations.

Jurisdiction is one of the more vexatious problems of crisis management, particularly in North America. Within the United Kingdom the centrality of government tends to reduce the potential for frictions and overlap, although circumstances do arise when contention is present. The security communities particularly are prone to concerns about 'turf', but not to the extent witnessed in the United States. The United Kingdom has also developed a much smoother working relationship between the military and police, and a difference of opinion on responsibility for the maximum force role would be difficult to find. The United States has made moves to overcome some jurisdictional conflicts by expanding federal responsibility in relation to acts of terrorism. Through the introduction of new legislation, such as the Comprehensive Crime Control Act of 1984, and the amending of existing statutes, 'Current Federal law ... *is* generally effective in dealing with terrorist acts'.[16] Nonetheless, MOUs (Memorandums of Understanding) have been necessary to reduce overlapping jurisdictional responsibilities, and hostility continues to arise between and among federal, state, and local agencies in regard to jurisdictional issues.

A somewhat similar situation obtains in Canada, although not to the degree experienced by the nation's southern neighbour. The most obvious manifestations of jurisdictional dispute are undoubtedly related to federal–provincial matters. The fact that Canadian provinces have responsibility to administer the law should tend to reduce friction between law-enforcement agencies. Problems do occur, nonetheless, as a consequence of the Security Offences Act and the legislative recognition of federal responsibility for threats to the security of Canada and for Internationally Protected Persons and Premises. While local or provincial law-enforcement agencies may be first to respond to the scene of a terrorist incident, under the terms of the Security Offences Act the RCMP have primary responsibility for operational response and the subsequent investigation. The issue is the subject of continuing discussion and negotiation on a federal–provincial–municipal basis and MOUs are being prepared to achieve mutual working arrangements. Generally, a Joint Force Operation (JFO) would be established with the RCMP assuming the lead role.

## Resources and capabilities

### Policy

Consistency, clarity, and firmness are positive characteristics of particular importance in policy and policy development associated with response to the threat of terrorism. Generally, Canada, the United States, and the United Kingdom have been consistent, clear, and firm in regard to their policy positions of no concessions, international co-operation, and rule of law. With certain arguable exceptions, notably involved with the no concessions principle, the three nations maintained that posture through the 1970s and into the 1980s. Inherent with the rule of law, however, is the philosophy of use of force. It calls for a minimum application of force unless resort to the maximum cannot be avoided. In 1984 the United States departed from that philosophy by endorsing the conduct of pre-emptive strikes and reprisal raids against terrorists abroad. Implicit within the change in policy direction was the use of military force to carry out the actions. Terrorism, especially of a state-sponsored nature, was described as 'a weapon of unconventional war against democratic societies'.[17]

Terrorism is, of course, one of the methods of waging unconventional war, and there is no point in trying to deny that dimension. Nonetheless, two key points must be clearly understood and kept uppermost in mind where terrorism and response to terrorism are concerned. First, terrorism violates the laws of war. Second, it is important that liberal-democratic states do not over-react by suspending democracy and making a type of 'world war on terrorism'. Democratic nations have numerous legal and judicial control measures, and other sanctions (e.g. economic), available to them before having to resort to use of military force in response to terrorism. Those nations also have the obligation to avoid betraying their own democratic, legal, and moral values by using terror in the name of fighting terror. They are, as well, duty-bound to refrain from escalating terrorist conflict into a war which would be worse than the evil of terrorism that they are attempting to eradicate. As mentioned earlier, the American actions of 1985 and 1986 demonstrate a dangerous trend in the escalation of violence, threatening fundamentals of international law and democratic and constitutional principles. Once committed actively to a policy of pre-emptive and retaliatory strikes it is difficult for a nation to avoid having to repeat them, if only to retain credibility, and such actions could eventually lead to more serious international confrontations. The American raid on Libya placed severe strain on relations between western nations, a circumstance that could strain the fabric of the NATO Alliance if the policy of military retaliation in peace-time were to become the norm. Both the United States and its allies must seek more utilitarian and co-operative methods to combat terrorism within the accepted bounds of the rule of law.

Policy development in the three nations has not been marked by a smooth, uninterrupted evolution. Canada demonstrated a good beginning in the early 1970s, the government wisely ordering a special study of the nation's crisis-management capability (Dare Report). But a tendency to relax marked the following years until Canada faced incidents of domestic and international terrorism in the 1980s. The policy measures announced in 1986 indicated a more concerned attitude towards the threat of terrorism from the standpoint of the domestic environment. Nonetheless, while the government has given pronounced support to international co-operative agreements (e.g. UN Conventions and Summit Seven Declarations), Canadians still tend to view themselves as unlikely targets of international terrorism. American policy development was similarly of a mixed nature until the aftermath of the 1983 Beirut terrorist attacks. From that time the government focused increasing attention on the problem of terrorism, especially of the international and state-sponsored variety. Although beneficial changes were introduced in terms of improved physical security measures, special legislation, and the upgrading of anti-terrorist police and military resources, American policy moved in the direction of the quick-fix solution to terrorism. The experiences of other nations, e.g.

Israel, as well as America's own nightmare in Viet Nam, should have served as lessons that the suppression of terrorism demands long-term efforts and not merely the use of destructive military force.

To a considerable extent, British counter-terrorism policy development has been associated with the conflict in Ireland. But the need to react to a spill-over of terrorist attacks from across the Irish Sea into mainland Britain also helped to prepare the United Kingdom for the growth of the international threat. British policy development has been steady in its pursuit of solutions within the principle of the rule of law, and the desire to re-establish a state of normalcy in Northern Ireland. In that regard, the security forces have shown a commendable flexibility and adaptability in dealing with changing terrorist tactics and weapons. The government did err in the early stages of the Ulster unrest by seeking an immediate reduction in the violence through the use of internment. Similarly, the special-status provision for internees and prisoners was shown to be a mistake, and both policies were rescinded. Through the use of special inquiries and investigations, however, the British Government has managed to develop and to monitor policy in a manner that generally suited the needs of the situation. The Diplock court system, for example, although frequently subject to criticism (mainly in regard to use of a single judge), has proved to be a practical and feasible answer to terrorist intimidation while remaining within the parameters of the concept of the rule of law.

Because of the immediacy of the violence in Northern Ireland and the influence of international terrorist incidents in Britain combined with the proximity of those in Europe and the Middle East, the United Kingdom has had a more continuous awareness of the threat of modern terrorism than either Canada or the United States. The Irish dimension, in particular, has promoted the development of policy and policy measures; for the most part, they have been designed to thwart and to counter terrorist activity while treating the problem from a determined and long-range criminal justice position. Acts of international terrorism have been approached in much the same manner. Notwithstanding, Great Britain, as with other members of the European Community, failed to appreciate the long-term significance of Libyan involvement with terrorism, or the growth of US preoccupation with that nation as epitomizing state sponsorship of terrorist activity. Undoubtedly economic considerations played a large part in the maintenance of normal diplomatic and commercial relations between Britain and Libya until events in 1984. Certainly business matters appeared to have deterred the British Government from discouraging the continued existence of a large British expatriate community in Libya.

Britain displayed a marked lack of foresight in not at least demanding the immediate regularization of the diplomatic status of London-based members of the Libyan People's Bureau following its February 1984 take-over by a 'Committee of Revolutionary Students'.[18] While it was not possible to anticipate the tragedy of St James's Square, the activities of Gaddafi's hit-squads were well known. The increase of attacks against anti-Gaddafi dissidents in Britain during the month following the take-over should have stirred the British Government to prompt action. The eventual outcome was a frustrating stand-off, largely resolved by exchanging the occupants of the Libyan People's Bureau, including those persons suspected of the murder of WPC Fletcher, for the British-embassy staff in Tripoli. The only favourable comment that may be attached to the affair is that it served to generate international concern over the abuse of the privileges of the diplomatic bag for purposes of terrorism. On the other hand, despite the experiences of St James's Square and the later US military raid on Libya, Great Britain inexplicably continued many of its usual business relationships with Libya. The lack of more stringent sanctions against Libya on the part of the European Community, especially of an economic nature, merely serves to strengthen the American attitude toward use of military measures as a response to terrorist activity.

## Experience

This should be a major factor upon which nations rely for guidance and judgement in the development of counter-terrorism policy. Its use must include a global perspective to be of value, while taking into consideration the influences of each nation's *Envelope*. It must also be constantly updated, like intelligence, to ensure that a correct perspective is maintained. Canada benefited early from its domestic experience of terrorism associated with the FLQ, but lost that advantage by not heeding events in other nations until once again the victim of terrorist attacks in the 1980s. The nation was particularly slow to adopt the example of other countries in forming a special national hostage-rescue team, and equally dilatory in regard to modification of emergency legislation. The Canadian Armed Forces have shown little interest in counter-terrorism matters since the mid-1970s, although attacks on NATO facilities in Europe have prompted some improvements to the physical security of Canadian military bases overseas.

The United States has been guilty of failing to acknowledge past or current experience, which partially accounted for the Beirut disasters. In all fairness, the first suicide car-bomb (at the US embassy) was a new departure in the Lebanese conflict, but the lack of suitable access barriers and other physical protective measures cannot be excused in light of the circumstances in Beirut at the time. The history of events in Viet Nam, alone, should have provided warning of the need for adequate security precautions. Penetration of the US Marine perimeter by the second suicide vehicle-bomber speaks for itself without need to refer to the report of the Long Commission. Previous reference has been made to the American failure to observe the experience of other nations in regard to the government's choice of a policy of military retaliation in response to terrorist acts. Perhaps it is more correctly a matter of failing to assess those experiences in an objective and accurate manner. The United States elected to follow an Israeli-style retaliatory policy after the Shi'ite bombings in Lebanon. Yet the Israeli policies have done little more than keep the terrorists at bay, and Israel still experiences terrorist activities within the nation's borders. It is an aspect of the Israeli approach that the United States would be wise to consider.

The United Kingdom has had a broad range of experience with terrorism and the development of counter-terrorism policy over the past two decades. In that sense, other nations would do well to look to the course of events in the United Kingdom from 1969 to assess both the actions of the terrorists and those of the British Government and security forces. Lessons of value are available, both positive and negative in nature, for use in response to terrorist violence. The operations of the security forces are particularly instructive, and are discussed later in this chapter, as are legislation and relations with the media. Of equal significance has been the British Government's determination to adhere to the principle of the rule of law in opposing terrorism. Aside from actions such as internment, the government has not opted for short-term solutions to terrorist provocations. And even the policy of internment was only introduced following lengthy advocacy on the part of the government body at Stormont. The use of policies such as internment, special status, Diplock courts, supergrasses, and the reliance upon inquiries and investigations by officially appointed tribunals and committees provide rich sources of evaluative material. While not wholly or equally applicable to either Canada or the United States, they do offer many aspects of general guidance. Similarly, British complacency in regard to the pre-1969 situation in Northern Ireland is worthy of thoughtful reflection.

## Infrastructure

Earlier discussion of policy measures endorsed the lead ministry/agency concept, and emphasized the need for central co-ordination and direction. A need exists, however, to maintain a balance in response to the threat of terrorism; that is, to ensure the threat does not become either overblown or minimized, and especially from the perspective of one department or agency of government. Hence, it is even more important that central control is of a neutral nature. Terrorism is recognized as a criminal act in Canada, the United States, and the United Kingdom. Thus, the law-enforcement agencies/departments of government must have a major influence on the development of policy and policy measures in response to terrorism. Because terrorism has significant international implications, the foreign affairs departments must have a similar involvement. Also, because terrorism represents a threat to national security, and because Aid to the Civil Power or maximum-force options might be required, defence departments should share in the involvement. While other departments will also have specific inputs, all departments of government should be aware of the threat of terrorism and should introduce protective measures and develop their supportive responsibilities.

Security considerations must be of paramount importance, and one central body should have oversight powers. But, as with other elements which form the collective response to terrorism, security must not become the overriding factor. In the United States, on the other hand, the influence of the State Department appears to have become overwhelming. It is an understandable development in view of the fact that the majority of terrorist attacks have occurred against US facilities and personnel overseas. The result has been the elevation of terrorism to a form of warfare, instead of a more measured response encouraging use of a wide variety of resources. The Canadian structure appears reasonably suitable, given attention to the recommendations of the McDonald Report concerning more active participation by the Cabinet Committee. But more specific direction is needed to overcome bureaucratic inhibitions and stumbling-blocks.

Recognition and acceptance of the Solicitor General's responsibility for internal security in Canada must be firmly established. The Department should be viewed in much the same manner as the British Home Office or the Interior Ministries of European nations. Co-ordination of counter-terrorism planning, policy, and crisis management in Canada rests with the Solicitor General in terms of the lead-ministry role. A major co-ordinating function is exercised through the Security Advisory Committee (SAC), whose interdepartmental influence has been strengthened by the elevation of the chairmanship to the Deputy Solicitor General. Direction has also been improved by the formation of a counter-terrorism sub-committee of the SAC with membership at a senior working level. Similarly, combining the domestic and foreign intelligence assessment function under the Intelligence Advisory Committee (IAC) allows SAC the freedom to concentrate on development and monitoring of security policy. IAC, on the other hand, has benefited through its chairmanship under the Privy Council Office (PCO) Coordinator of Intelligence and Security.

Intelligence is a major primary resource in the combating of terrorism. The prerequisite for a successful counter-terrorism response is the highest calibre intelligence gathering, analysis, co-ordination, and dissemination. It is particularly important that co-ordination and co-operation be smooth, unhindered, and tightly linked among the security forces. Turf battles and rivalries have no place in achieving an effective counter-terrorism programme, especially at the operational level. It is also imperative that senior policy-makers are kept intimately informed of intelligence assessments and forecasts. The importance of the role of intelligence in counter-terrorism cannot be over-emphasized. Both HUMINT and technical means of intelligence gathering must be highly developed and given firm support and recognition at all policy and operational levels.

Canada, as with other nations, maintains a number of intelligence-gathering means and in particular the newly established Canadian Security Intelligence Service (CSIS). Criticisms following the 1985 attack on the Turkish embassy in Ottawa indicated problems in the collation, assessment, and distribution of intelligence material. Steps have been taken to improve the situation, but thought should be given to the McDonald recommendation for a central Bureau of Intelligence Assessments. The Report stressed the need for an ability to make long-range estimates and in conditions which would not place undue emphasis upon specific natures of intelligence, e.g. military oriented. Although CSIS has a principally domestic responsibility, it does have limited overseas functions. Thus, failing the establishment of the suggested Bureau of Intelligence Assessments, the CSIS operations should incorporate the broader activity of long-range evaluations. To achieve that goal, however, CSIS must recruit on a broad basis from qualified academic and professional sources. The 1985–6 Annual Report of the Security Intelligence Review Committee (which has oversight of CSIS) was not favourable in respect to the 'civilianization' of the Service.[19] It also displayed concern about the working relationship between CSIS and the RCMP associated with counter-terrorism activities, suggesting that overlapping occurred and that friction was present between the two organizations. CSIS has experienced the growing pains of a new organization, but it must make strenuous efforts to portray itself and to function as a civilian agency of government. Similarly, other departments and agencies of government must accept the role and place of CSIS and provide co-operation, as well as divorcing themselves from any previous CSIS-related tasks. It would probably be wiser for the Canadian Government to concentrate on the positive development of CSIS, including the long-range assessment role, than to attempt to introduce yet another intelligence organization into the infrastructure.

*The Report Of The Vice President's Task Force On Combatting*

*Terrorism* recommended changes to the US infrastructure which included an NSC co-ordinating position and a consolidated intelligence centre for dealing with terrorism. Certainly both measures would appear to have value, providing the NSC cell was given adequate functional authority. Currently, considerable friction exists between departments and agencies which inhibits the smooth flow of counter-terrorism policy development and implementation. The establishment of a central responsible body might have an ameliorative effect if provided with sufficient power to induce co-operation. The American bureaucratic structure is so large and unwieldy, however, that the cell may well exert little influence. American intelligence resources are such that a consolidated centre of terrorism-related functions would be beneficial. The centre would have to be staffed by personnel from various departments and agencies to ensure that a broad perspective is maintained and that proper input is received from all sources. The concept, nonetheless, is fraught with many bureaucratic obstacles which would require time and firm direction from senior government leadership to resolve.

The British infrastructure benefits from the centrality of the government system. It is also difficult to comment accurately upon the strengths and weaknesses of arrangements because of the closed nature of government operations. As stated earlier in this chapter, the need to initiate the TIGER concept indicated that a smooth working of intelligence-related matters was not present. Similar circumstances existed in Northern Ireland during the 1970s decade, but considerable improvements have been implemented as have been demonstrated in the increased success in counter-terrorism operations. The Brighton hotel bombing underlined some of the problems of co-ordination and control in Great Britain, and led to the TIGER function. It would appear that the difficulties are associated with bureaucratic fumbling and a degree of friction between law-enforcement agencies. The British COBRA cell for crisis-management operations, on the other hand, seems a very logical concept and particularly useful from the standpoint of its location within the Cabinet Office and close proximity to government leaders.

### Law-enforcement agencies

A major stumbling-block with law-enforcement personnel is their opinion that terrorism is merely another manifestation of crime. While terrorism should be approached from a criminal-justice position, and terrorists should be treated as criminals, it must be appreciated that terrorists do not function merely for personal gain or profit. In conjunction, law-enforcement agencies must be wary that their response to terrorism does not contribute to the achievement of the terrorists' goals. A co-operative attitude, both domestically and internationally, must be the hallmark of law-enforcement operations. Not only must that attitude be present within and between agencies, but it must extend outside the community and should be especially strong in terms of the military/police relationship. While police agencies need to strengthen their anti-terrorist resources, certain tasks may well be better left to military responsibility. A close bond should be present in regard to preparations for military support of police under conditions of Aid to the Civil Power.

Within the United Kingdom, the employment of maximum force in hostage-taking situations is the responsibility of the military. This has partially developed because police in Great Britain have a tradition of operating without weapons to the greatest extent possible. Posse Comitatus legislation precludes the American military from the domestic role (except for extraordinary circumstances), and it is a task which remains the purview of the police forces. Canada was ambivalent about the matter until 1986 when the government officially assigned responsibility to the RCMP. Because Canadian and American police forces are of the colonial model (i.e. armed), and the RCMP has historically had a paramilitary structure (although not functioning in that manner), it is not unreasonable that they should undertake the hostage-rescue role. Nonetheless, some distinct advantages obtain in the British preference for military tasking. The use of maximum force is inherently a military characteristic, whereas police employ minimum force and that approach is emphasized in their training and philosophy.

> Terrorist incidents involving the possible murder of hostages or widespread release of Nuclear, Biological, and Chemical material would demand ... the deadly application of maximum force. To attempt to modify a policeman's basic ethos for that purpose, however temporarily, could create a mortal danger to hostages and would-be rescuers alike, as well as represent an abdication of juridical ideals.[20]

The former head of the RCMP Security Service, John Starnes, commented following the Canadian announcement that

> the raison d'être of a soldier, his experience and his training seem naturally to fit the anti-terrorist role.... [The RCMP unit] will be using the weapons, equipment and tactics of the armed forces. If I had been around when they were making the decision, I would have argued very strongly for armed forces. The idea of assigning to a law enforcement officer a task which is essentially military in nature leaves me a bit uneasy.[21]

253

Mr Starnes's remarks would certainly receive favourable support from members of the British law-enforcement community. In conjunction, military forces are better prepared, and better suited to the conduct of such operations outside national borders.

The RUC has developed an impressive array of resources to combat the terrorist violence in Northern Ireland. Among various useful elements are the District Mobile Support Units (DMSUs), who often function in a paramilitary manner in addition to their intelligence-gathering duties. A danger associated with such units is their vulnerability to accusations of a shoot-to-kill attitude; the RUC has been accused of such a policy in the conduct of operations in recent years.[22] It is unlikely that such a sanction was ever endorsed, even on a restricted and highly classified basis. Given the murderous behaviour of PIRA and INLA members, however, it is not inconceivable that the use of lethal force was an understood policy in armed confrontations between security forces and terrorists. PIRA members only carry weapons when they intend to use them, and their use of weapons is an unequivocal shoot-to-kill policy. On occasions when PIRA are involved in a non-violent activity (e.g. a logistic operation) it is not the practice for them to carry weapons, so that if accosted by the security forces there can be no excuse for security forces to open fire. Maintaining the correct level of minimum force when dealing with ruthless, heavily armed, and experienced terrorists such as members of PIRA and INLA requires a fine balance of discipline, alertness, and operational proficiency on the part of security forces. It is an aspect which must be subject to thorough oversight at all policy and operational levels whenever countering terrorists. For anyone who viewed the television coverage of the brutal murder of the two British soldiers who inadvertently drove into the funeral cortege in Belfast in 1988, it should be possible to understand how members of security forces could individually and independently adopt a personal shoot-to-kill attitude. It is remarkable that the British security forces in Northern Ireland have been able to adhere to the regulations for opening fire only in self-defence when faced with the vicious subhuman calibre of persons who fill and support the ranks of the PIRA and INLA.

The development of the London Metropolitan Police anti-terrorist units, and the reconstruction of the RUC, offer much valuable guidance in the evolution of sound counter-terrorism forces. Both law-enforcement bodies have broad experience in terms of tactics, equipment, and intelligence-gathering requirements, as well as valuable knowledge of terrorist methods and operations. Law-enforcement agencies involved in counter-terrorism in other nations could benefit from a study of the experience of those two forces.

## Armed Forces

The essential role of the military in counter-terrorism operations is to provide a supportive back-up to the police. Military resources should never be considered as a major or first line of response to terrorist attacks in peacetime. The military role must be associated with Aid to the Civil Power and called upon only when law-enforcement agencies cannot cope or are strained beyond their limits. Such is not to say that the military should lightly treat its place as a counter-terrorism resource. To the contrary, the military should make serious efforts to ensure its readiness to carry out its emergency responsibilities, and should conduct close liaison and training with police forces to update and maintain high standards of performance in its role. Military commanders at all levels should be aware of the threat of terrorism, making certain that subordinates are well briefed and that security precautions are fully implemented.

The military can be used effectively for riot-control purposes, but only if suitably equipped and thoroughly trained. In that regard, reserve or part-time elements of military forces should not be employed in such duties. Situations such as prevail in the 'Bandit Country' of Ulster, where terrorist activities of the PIRA/INLA require a military-style response, are also suited to the armed forces; but always keeping in mind that it is in support of the police function and not warfare. In that regard, special forces such as the British SAS and US Delta Force are valuable for situations which require the surgical application of maximum force against terrorists, or for the gathering of intelligence. The use of military forces in the counter-terrorism role, especially in hostage-taking incidents, is particularly suited to overseas response. It is remarkable that the Canadian Armed Forces were so short-sighted as to not appreciate the benefits to be gained by accepting the hostage-rescue responsibility.

## Legislation

An important aspect of legislative response is assurance that it serves to counter the threat of terrorism while not making serious infringements upon civil rights and freedoms. Constitutionally-correct emergency legislation should meet that requirement, although it may abridge certain civil liberties on a temporary basis. Limitations placed on the life of such legislations, combined with requirements for government review and independent authoritative examination, represent other safeguards.

Canada has been tardy in the introduction of emergency legislation to replace the oppressive peacetime reliance on the War Measures Act.

The new Emergencies Act, however, provides safeguarded, comprehensive legislation to enable the Federal government to fulfil its constitutional responsibility for the safety and security of Canadians during national emergencies. Subject to the Canadian Charter of Rights and Freedoms and the Canadian Bill of Rights, the Act is consistent with the UN International Covenant on Civil and Political Rights. The Act was drafted in consultation with the provinces and contains appropriate safeguards for provincial interests. It also allows Parliament to review and, if necessary, revoke emergency powers introduced under the Act. In addition, it contains procedures to ensure that individuals who suffer loss or injury as a result of the application of the Act will be fairly compensated.

The United States has sought to avoid developing special anti-terrorism legislation by modifying current statutes or by including measures in crime-control laws. The United Kingdom has very specific anti-terrorism legislation which, although principally intended to cope with the Irish problem, has been expanded to include the threat of international terrorism. Nonetheless, the British Government is facing a challenge to the detention provisions of the Prevention of Terrorism Act (PTA) as a consequence of the decision of the European Court of Human Rights. As a signatory of the European Convention on Human Rights, Britain must change the law or seek special exemption within six months. The UK has also been subject to severe criticism over the 1988 decision to qualify the right to silence by allowing courts to draw such inferences as they think fit from an accused person's refusal to testify. While this may appear a regressive and repressive measure at first glance, it does not abolish the right to silence but gives the courts some discretion in judgement and helps to thwart terrorist groups who systematically train their members to exploit the right to silence as a means to block criminal investigations. The UK has, as well, taken two other important steps to counter terrorist activity: (1) introduced legislation to enable courts to convict those who handle terrorist funds, assets, and racketeering monies; and (2) introduced legislation requiring all candidates for local and national elective office in Northern Ireland to sign a declaration disavowing violence. By tightening legislation and legal loopholes, the government is demonstrating the resolve to defeat terrorism while remaining within the bounds of the rule of law.

## The Media

It is widely recognized that the media presents a difficult problem in framing a response to terrorism. A careful balance is required between freedom of the media and serving the cause of a terrorist group. The pubic must be well informed, but the aims of the terrorist must not be furthered in the process; nor should the operations of the security forces be endangered or compromised by media disclosures. The media must also take care not to assume the role of negotiator or arbiter between terrorists and the government or the security forces. The announced intention of the Canadian and American Governments to conduct discussions with senior media representatives is a positive measure. A better understanding of responsibilities on both sides would assist in reducing some of the problems. Similarly, government agencies should ensure that they have an adequate professional apparatus for dealing with the media and providing prompt, substantial information, and effective spokespersons. The media, on the other hand, must adopt the position that responsible reporting is the standard to be followed and not simply the achievement of a scoop.

The UK has recently introduced a ban on television and radio interviews with members of the Republican or Loyalist groups involved in Northern Ireland terrorism. The action drew adverse criticism from many sources, especially civil-rights agitators, but the criticism frequently appeared ill-informed or one-sided. Mention of a similar ban, operative since 1976, in the Irish Republic was absent in most articles which condemned the British action. The critics ignored the fact that terrorism thrives on what Mrs Thatcher describes as 'the oxygen of publicity'.[23] The PIRA, for instance, is known to use television appearances to gain an aura of legitimacy, to aid recruiting, and to obtain funding as well as to convey threats. Conor Cruise O'Brien, the Irish minister who imposed the 1976 ban in Eire, refused to accept the Provisional Sinn Fein as a legitimate political party and viewed it instead as a 'public-relations agency for a murder gang'.[24] As claimed by the British High Commissioner to Canada, perhaps the UK action is a not-so-drastic measure.[25]

### Comment

Modern terrorism is not 'an awesome threat, defying comprehension in terms of genesis and response.' Despite the characteristics of irrationality, the mind-numbing atrocities and the indiscriminate applications of violence, terrorism *can* be understood and opposed successfully. It must be constantly borne in mind that terrorism feeds on fear, weakness, uncertainty, and over-reaction. But through a careful scrutiny of terrorist motivations and goals, counter-terrorism policies may be developed in accordance with the rule of law to provide for effective measures of response. The use of such measures in a calm, determined, and persevering manner must eventually lead to the defeat of terrorist aggression.

The phenomenon of terrorism endangers the security and well-being of democratic nations. It is a danger which is particularly acute in relation to Third World states, where the overthrow of democratic institutions not only deprives citizens of their fundamental rights, freedoms, and dignity but also jeopardizes global stability. It is imperative that democratic nations recognize the long-term aims and goals of terrorism and respond by offering material assistance as well as by guidance through constitutionally correct behaviour when opposing the threat of terrorism.

Democratic nations have powerful resources and capabilities available to undertake the task of countering terrorism. The resources and capabilities, however, must be suitably prepared and appropriate for the task. The task is only appropriate if it reflects the democratic, moral, and legal principles inherent in democratic and constitutional ideals and adherence to the rule of law. In response to terrorism, it is of greater importance to demonstrate resolve, to function legitimately, and to achieve widespread consensus and support than to opt for quick-fix short-term gains.

# Addendum

The Report of the Senate Special Committee on Terrorism and the Public Safety issued in July 1987 was critical of the Canadian Government's counter-terrorism arrangements. Among other matters, the Report identified deficiencies associated with

> the organization and co-ordination of Federal departments and agencies having a role in counter-terrorism and crisis management; [and] co-ordination and co-operation between levels of government, particularly between the RCMP ... and provincial and municipal police forces....[1]

The Federal government viewed the Report seriously and established the interdepartmental Counter Terrorism Task Force in December 1987.

Functioning under the auspices of the Privy Council Office (PCO) and the Ministry of the Solicitor General, the Task Force was chaired by Major-General G.R. Cheriton (Ret'd). Membership comprised individuals seconded from Federal departments and agencies having a major counter-terrorism role, namely the RCMP, the Canadian Security Intelligence Service, Transport Canada, National Defence, the Communications Security Establishment, External Affairs, and the Ministry of the Solicitor General. The Task Force submitted an interim report to the Interdepartmental Committee on Security and Intelligence (ICSI) in April 1988 and was directed, as a major project, to prepare a National Counter-Terrorism Plan. 'In January 1989, the Plan was approved by ICSI and is being implemented on an administrative basis, pending Cabinet approval expected sometime this summer.'[2]

The National Counter-Terrorism Plan (NCTP) was the product of extensive consultation and negotiation among key Federal departments and agencies. A central feature of the NCTP is the National Security Coordination Centre (NSCC) located in the Ministry of the Solicitor General. Based on the former Security Planning and Co-ordination Directorate, the NSCC is responsible for the management of the national counter-terrorism programme and for co-ordination of government response to a terrorist threat or incident within Canada. In the event of a major threat or incident, the NSCC reconfigures to become the National Policy Centre, incorporating an operations centre, to provide policy decisions and advice to assist the police operational activities. The National Policy Centre, for example, facilitates such policy decisions as the deployment of the RCMP Special Emergency Response Team (SERT) should a terrorist incident involve a hostage-taking.[3]

The NCTP also makes provision for discussion and negotiation with provincial and municipal authorities 'leading ultimately to their integration into the Plan and its implementation'.[4] Provincial agreement and co-operation are essential to the concept and working of the NCTP, especially in the resolution of any jurisdictional controversies. One proposed means towards improving federal-provincial integration is an extension of the Federal government's Interdepartmental Terrorist Alert System (ITAS) to incorporate law-enforcement agencies at all levels across Canada.

A third feature of the NCTP is recognition of the need for formal, regular, training and exercises to test and refine Canada's counter-terrorism arrangements. The NSCC structure includes an Operations and Training section dedicated to the preparation, conduct, and assessment of individual and collective counter-terrorism training and exercises. In June 1989, a large-scale bilateral US–Canada counter-terrorism exercise was conducted which involved federal, state, provincial, and municipal governments and law-enforcement authorities. The exercise tested communications, policy, and operational decision-making procedures on an inter and intragovernmental basis, as well as reviewing international crisis management agreements.

On 7 April 1989, a Greyhound bus en route from Montreal to New York City was hijacked by a lone gunman as it departed from the Canadian city. Through an embarrassing combination of circumstances, the bus evaded police roadblocks and was not detected until it arrived in front of Canada's Parliament buildings in Ottawa late in the afternoon. Quickly surrounded by RCMP officers, who worked in conjunction with City of Ottawa Police to seal the Parliament Hill area, the bus and its passengers became the centre of media attention for several hours as police negotiated with the hijacker. The incident ended peacefully early in the evening when the hijacker surrendered and allowed his passengers to leave the vehicle.[5]

'In the aftermath ... several Senators ... began to wonder if the Federal government was better prepared to respond to a terrorist crisis than it had been ... in July 1987.'[6] Accordingly, the Second Special Committee of the Senate on Terrorism and Public Safety was established in May 1989. The purpose of the Committee was to 'review developments and progress and any response to the first Committee's recommendations over the past two years.'[7]

The Report of the Second Special Committee was submitted in June 1989 and reflected a positive approach to the government's efforts and the work of the Task Force. Nonetheless, the Committee cited reservations about specific matters, including 'the concern expressed in the first ... Report about the ability of the Department of the Solicitor General to effectively manage the government's response to a terrorist emergency'.[8] In keeping with a recommendation of the first Committee's Report, the Second Report 'persists in the belief that the proper location of this function ... is in the PCO' (Privy Council Office).[9] Lacking agreement for that recommendation, the Committee 'recommends that the Solicitor General be given clear statutory powers to be the *de jure* lead Ministry ... on counter-terrorism policy and planning'.[10] Further, while expressing satisfaction at the progress made by the RCMP SERT (and by the Ministry of Transport in the area of airport security), the Committee remains concerned about 'uncertainty over "who is in charge" during an incident.'[11]

The uncertainty arises from a perceived lack of clear operational command arrangements for response to security incidents as negotiated in bilateral agreements between the RCMP and several of the larger metropolitan police forces.

> The Committee feels that the RCMP – local police agreements, rather than clarifying the situation, have only papered over and may continue the confusion and 'turf wars' which the Committee witnessed two years ago.... The Committee strongly recommends that all RCMP – local police agreements contain a clause that clearly and unambiguously allows the RCMP, at its own discretion to exert 'operational command and primary responsibility' at any time in response to a terrorist incident, recognizing that the response will, in most cases, continue as a joint force operation.[12]

Despite the Committee's reservations, it is clear that the Canadian Government has 'responded effectively to a number of the [first] Committee's observations and recommendations'.[13] The NCTP and the establishment of the NSCC have enhanced the Federal counter-terrorism programme and offer a means to achieve continuing improvement. But certain major issues must be resolved (notably provincial co-operation and commitment and police operational command arrangements) if Canadian counter-terrorism policies and measures are to meet practical requirements.

# Notes

## 1 The threat

1 Lord Chalfont, 'Terrorism and International Security', *Terrorism, an International Journal* 5 (1982), p. 322.
2 Noel O'Sullivan, ed., *Terrorism, Ideology and Revolution* (Brighton: Harvester Press, 1986), p. 210.
3 ibid.
4 Neil C. Livingstone, *The War against Terrorism* (Lexington: D.C. Heath and Company, 1982), p. 2.
5 Harry Eckstein, *Internal War* (Westport: Greenwood Press, 1964), p. 81. See also Raymond Aron, *Peace and War* (London: Weidenfeld & Nicolson, 1966), p. 170.
6 *Daily Telegraph*, 10 December 1984.
7 ibid.
8 Interview with General George Grivas ('Dighenis'), Nicosia, Cyprus, November 1967.
9 G. Davidson Smith, 'A Positive Approach to Terrorism: The Case for an Elite Counter-Force in Canada', *Journal of the Royal United Services Institute* 129 (September 1984), p. 17. See also *U.S. News and World Report*, 9 January 1984, p. 20.
10 *The Times*, 21 April 1975.
11 G. Davidson Smith, 'Issue Group Terrorism: Animal Rights Militancy in Britain', *Terrorism, Violence, Insurgency Journal* 5 (Spring 1985), p. 44.
12 *Associated Press Wire Service*, 18 December 1985.
13 Ernest Evans, *Calling a Truce to Terror* (Westport: Greenwood Press Inc., 1979), p. 40.
14 ibid., pp. 28, 29.
15 Carlos Marighella, *Minimanual of the Urban Guerrilla* (Boulder: Paladin Press, 1978).
16 Yonah Alexander and Seymour Maxwell Finger, eds, *Terrorism: Interdisciplinary Perspectives* (New York: John Jay Press Limited, 1977), p. 50.
17 Smith, 'A Positive Approach', p. 19.
18 *Daily Telegraph*, 10 September 1985.
19 Louis Fourner, *F.L.Q. The Anatomy of an Underground Movement*, trans. Edward Baker (Toronto: NC Press Limited, 1984), p. 218.

20  Evans, *Calling a Truce*, p. 7.
21  James Adams, 'The Financing of Terror,' paper presented at the International Academic Conference on Terrorism, University of Aberdeen, April 1986, p. 8.
22  ibid., p. 19.
23  ibid., p. 20.
24  *Christian Science Monitor*, 22 May 1985.
25  Edgar O'Ballance, *Terror in Ireland* (Novato: Presidio Press, 1981), p. 263.
26  *Daily Telegraph*, 6 June 1986.
27  Michael McKinley, 'The Irish Republican Army and Terror International: An Inquiry into Material Aspects of the First Fifteen Years', paper presented at the International Academic Conference on Terrorism, University of Aberdeen, April 1986, p. 6.
28  *American Sentinel* 27 May 1985.
29  Adams, 'The Financing of Terror', p. 19. See also Walter Laqueur, ed., *The Terrorism Reader* (New York: Meridian Books, 1978), pp. 251–67.
30  Fournier, *F.L.Q.*, p. 14.
31  ibid., p. 44.
32  O'Sullivan, ed., *Terrorism*, p. 217.
33  ibid., p. 218.
34  Livingstone, *The War*, p. 60.
35  Yonah Alexander, 'Editor's Note', *Terrorism, an International Journal* 2 (1979).
36  'Prodded into Protests', *Economist*, 25–31 August 1984, p. 22.
37  *Sunday Times*, 30 June 1985.
38  *The Times*, 22 March 1984.
39  *Wall Street Journal*, 29 April 1986.
40  *The Listener*, 8 May 1986.
41  *Journal of Commerce*, 10 October 1985.
42  Smith, 'A Positive Approach', p. 20.
43  Defense Nuclear Agency, *Proceedings of the 10th Annual Symposium* (Springfield, Va.: n.p., 1985).
44  *U.S. News and World Report*, 5 December 1983.
45  O'Sullivan, ed., *Terrorism*, p. 215. See also Robert A. Friedlander, *Terrorism, Documents of International and Local Control*, vol. 2 (New York: Oceana Publications Inc., 1979).
46  *International Herald Tribune*, 7 May 1986.
47  ibid.
48  Claire Sterling, *The Terror Network* (London: Weidenfeld & Nicolson, 1981). See also Adams, 'The Financing of Terrorism', p. 21.
49  Maurice Tugwell, *On the Soviet Threat to NATO* (Fredericton, New Brunswick: Centre for Conflict Studies, n.p., 1984), pp. 56–9.
50  *Sunday Times*, 19 August 1984. See also Victor Suvorov, 'Spetsnaz: The Soviet Union's Special Forces', *Military Review* LXIV (March 1984), pp. 30–46.
51  Martha Crenshaw, *Revolutionary Terrorism* (Stanford: Hoover Institution Publication, 1978), p. 23.
52  ibid., p. 24.

53  ibid., p. 24.
54  Interview with Paul Wilkinson, University of Aberdeen, 12 February 1986.
55  United States Department of State, *Patterns of Global Terrorism: 1986* (Washington: Office of the Ambassador-at-Large for Counter-Terrorism, n.p., January 1988), p. 1.
56  Paul Wilkinson, ed., *British Perspectives on Terrorism* (London: George Allen & Unwin, 1981), p. 4.
57  *Maclean's*, 26 September 1988, p. 30.
58  'Ulster Survey', *Economist*, 2–8 June 1984, p. 40.
59  Livingstone, *The War*, p. 155.
60  John B. Wolf, *Fear of Fear* (New York: Plenum Press, 1981), p. 212. See also Evans, *Calling a Truce*, pp. 52–5.
61  Richard L. Clutterbuck, 'How Do We Explain Them?', *New Yorker* 54 (12 June 1978), p. 37.
62  Admiral James D. Watkins, 'Terrorism: An "Already Declared" War', *Wings of Gold* (Summer 1984), pp. 19–21.
63  *USA Today*, 30 December 1985.
64  *International Herald Tribune*, 17–18 May 1986. See also *Daily Telegraph*, 24 April 1986.
65  O'Sullivan, ed., *Terrorism*, p. 221.

## 2 General policy

1  *New York Times*, 7 March 1986.
2  Christopher Hewitt, *The Effectiveness of Anti-Terrorist Policies* (New York: University Press of American, Inc., 1984), p. xiv.
3  Richard Rose, 'Comparing Public Policy', *European Journal of Political Research* 1 (April 1973); pp. 67–94.
4  Cmnd. 9222, *Review of the Operation of the Northern Ireland (Emergency Provisions) Act 1978* by the Right Honourable Sir George Baker (London: HMSO, 1984), p. 9.
5  Rolf Tophoven, *GSG 9, German Response to Terrorism* (Koblenz: Bernard & Graefe Verlag, 1984), p. 11.
6  Richard Simeon, 'Studying Public Policy', *Canadian Journal of Political Science* IX (December 1976), p. 549.
7  Graham Allison, *Essence of Decision* (Boston: Little, Brown and Company, 1971).
8  Simeon, 'Studying', p. 549.
9  Neil C. Livingstone, *The War against Terrorism* (Lexington: D.C. Heath and Company, 1982), p. 250.
10  ibid.
11  Michael Kelly and Thomas Mitchell, 'The Study of Internal Conflict in Canada: Problems and Prospects', *Conflict Quarterly* II (Summer 1981), p. 10.
12  ibid.
13  ibid., p. 12.
14  W.L. White, R.H. Wagenberg, and R.C. Nelson, *Introduction to Canadian Government and Politics* (Toronto: Holt, Rinehart and Winston of Canada Ltd., 1977), p. 20.

15 Robert Bothwell, Ian Drummond, and John English, *Canadian Since 1945: Power, Politics, and Provincialism* (Toronto: University of Toronto Press, 1981), p. 388.
16 Louis Fournier, *F.L.Q. The Anatomy of an Underground Movement*, trans. Edward Baker (Toronto: NC Press Limited, 1984), p. 13.
17 ibid.
18 *Daily Telegraph*, 10 September 1984.
19 ibid., 11 March 1985.
20 *Ottawa Citizen*, 30 June 1984.
21 *Toronto Star*, 11 March 1986.
22 Ernest Evans, *Calling a Truce to Terror* (London: Greenwood Press, 1979), p. 132.
23 ibid., p. 130.
24 ibid.
25 Lester B. Hazen, 'Without Much Blood', *Military Review* LXII (September 1982), p. 58.
26 Walter Laqueur, *Terrorism* (Boston: Little, Brown and Co., 1977), p. 15.
27 James B. Motley, *U.S. Strategy to Counter Domestic Political Terrorism* (Washington: National Defence University Press, 1983), p. 21.
28 *N.Y. News*, 3 March 1985.
29 Motley, *U.S. Strategy*, p. 21.
30 ibid., p. 22.
31 ibid., p. 21.
32 *Milwaukee Sentinel*, 7 February 1985.
33 *A National Strategy to Reduce Crime* (New York: Avon Books, 1976).
34 Evans, *Calling a Truce*, p. 128.
35 Edward F. Mickolus, *Transnational Terrorism* (London: Aldwych Press, 1980), pp. 18–80.
36 Major Julian H. Burns, Jr., US Army, 'Tripoli to Teheran: Terrorism's Road Well-Travelled', *Joint Perspectives* (Fall 1981), pp. 42–53.
37 *Washington Post*, 2 March 1985.
38 ibid.
39 Paul Wilkinson, ed., *British Perspectives on Terrorism* (London: George Allen & Unwin, 1981), p. 1.
40 Richard Clutterbuck, *Britain in Agony* (Harmondsworth: Penguin Books Ltd., 1980), p. 21.
41 T.A. Critchley, *The Conquest of Violence* (London: Constable & Co. Ltd., 1970), p. 1.
42 ibid., pp. 141–76.
43 ibid., p. 177.
44 J.R. Thackrah, ed., *Contemporary Policing* (London: Sphere Reference, 1985), p. 145.
45 Edgar O'Ballance, *Terror in Ireland* (Novato: Presidio Press, 1981), p. 59.
46 Wilkinson, ed., *British Perspectives*, p. 4.
47 Desmond Hamill, *Pig in the Middle* (London: Methuen, 1985), p. 15.
48 *The Economist*, 18 January 1969, p. 15.
49 O'Ballance, *Terror*, p. 40.
50 Hamill, *Pig*, p. 12.

51 Wilkinson, ed., *British Perspectives*, p. 1.
52 O'Ballance, *Terror*, p. 100.
53 Paul Wilkinson, *Terrorism and the Liberal State* (London: The Macmillan Press, 1977), p. 16.
54 ibid., p. 5.
55 ibid., p. 17.
56 ibid.
57 *The Scottish Book of Common Prayer* (Edinburgh: Cambridge University Press, 1929), p. 310.
58 Yonah Alexander, ed., *International Terrorism: National, Regional and Global Perspectives*, 2 edn (New York: Praeger, 1980), pp. 4–27.
59 G. Davidson Smith, 'Counter-Terrorism: Third Force Viability' (Master's Essay, Nova University, 1980), pp. 191–202.
60 Interview with the *Toronto Star*, April 1985.
61 Smith, 'Counter-Terrorism', pp. 191–202.
62 Alexander, ed., *International Terrorism*, p. 22.
63 *Second Report of the Commission of Inquiry Concerning Certain Activities of the Royal Canadian Mounted Police* (Ottawa: Minister of Supply and Services Canada, 1981, hereinafter called *The McDonald Report*), p. 40.
64 *The Report of the Senate Special Committee on Terrorism and the Public Safety* (Ottawa: Minister of Supply and Services Canada, 1987).
65 ibid., p. 9.
66 *International Herald Tribune*, 14 March 1985.
67 Robert W. Taylor, 'Managing Terrorist Incidents', *The Bureaucrat* (Winter 1983–4), p. 53.
68 ibid., p. 54.
69 Motley, *U.S. Strategy*, p. 31.
70 *U.S. News and World Report*, 16 July 1984.
71 H.C. Debs., Vol. 832, cols. 743–52.
72 Wilkinson, ed., *British Perspectives*, p. 4.
73 Sir Robert Thompson, *Defeating Communist Insurgency* (London: Chatto & Windus Ltd., 1974), pp. 52, 54.
74 ibid., p. 52.
75 ibid., pp. 50–1.
76 Cmnd. 9222, *Review*, p. 14.
77 Benjamin Netanyahu, ed., *International Terrorism: Challenge and Response* (Jerusalem: The Jonathan Institute, 1980), p. 278.
78 Cmnd. 7009, *The Protection of Human Rights by Law in Northern Ireland* (London: HMSO, 1977).
79 Cmnd. 5847, *Report of a Committee to Consider, in the Context of Civil Liberties and Human Rights, Measures to Deal with Terrorism in Northern Ireland* (London: HMSO, 1975).
80 Netanyahu, ed., *International Terrorism*, pp. 280–1.
81 Wilkinson, ed., *British Perspectives*, p. 7.
82 ibid., p. 8.
83 Alexander, ed., *International Terrorism*, pp. 7, 9, 11, 12, 20.
84 ibid., p. 21.
85 Secretary of State George Shultz, 'Terrorism and the Modern World',

*Department of State Bulletin* (December, 1984), pp. 12–17.

86  Anthony C.E. Quainton, 'Terrorism: Do Something! But What?' Department of State Bulletin (September, 1979), pp. 60–4.

87  *Public Report of the Vice President's Task Force on Combatting Terrorism* (Washington: US Government Printing Office, 1986).

88  ibid., facing page.

89  ibid., p. 7.

90  ibid., facing page.

91  Cmnd. 7324, *Review of the Operations of the Prevention of Terrorism (Temporary Provisions) Acts 1974 and 1976* by the Right Honourable Lord Shackleton (London: HMSO, 1978), p. v.

92  Sir David McNee, *McNee's Law* (London: Collins, 1983), pp. 152-3.

93  Alexander, ed., *International Terrorism*, p. 10.

94  Wilkinson, ed., *British Perspectives*, p. 9.

95  *Report of the Crisis Management Study Group*, House of Commons, Canada, 15 October 1972.

96  ibid., p. 45.

97  Robin Bourne, 'Terrorist Incident Management and Jurisdictional Issues: A Canadian Perspective', *Terrorism, an International Journal* 1 (3 & 4, 1978), p. 309.

98  *The McDonald Report*, p. 82.

99  ibid., p. 84.

100  Jean-Francois Duchaine, *Report on the October Crisis of 1970* (Quebec: Ministry of Justice, 1981); Jean Keable *et al.*, *Report of the Commission of Inquiry into Police Operations within Quebec* (Quebec: Ministry of Justice, 1981).

101  *The McDonald Report*.

102  ibid., p. 70.

103  ibid., p. 45.

104  ibid.

105  CSIS Act, Part IV, Sections 57 and 61(1).

106  CSIS Act, Section 2, 'threats to the security of Canada'.

107  *Toronto Star*, 11 March 1986.

108  ibid.

109  Alexander, ed., *International Terrorism*, p. 12.

110  *Los Angeles Times*, 4 December 1983.

111  *Hamilton Spectator*, 11 March 1986.

112  The Emergencies Act.

113  Taylor, 'Managing Terrorist Incidents', p. 54.

114  ibid., p. 55.

115  ibid., p. 54.

116  Colonel Charlie A. Beckwith, USA (Ret.) and Donald Knox, *Delta Force* (Glasgow: William Collins Sons & Co., 1985), p. 190.

117  Lt. Col. John M. Oseth, 'Combatting Terrorism: The Dilemmas of a Decent Nation', *Parameters* XV (1985), pp. 65–76.

118  Motley, *U.S. Strategy*, p. 75.

119  Ray S. Cline, *The CIA Under Reagan, Bush, And Casey* (Washington: Acropolis Books Ltd., 1981), p. 302.

120  Oseth, 'Combatting Terrorism', p. 70.
121  Defense Nuclear Agency, *Proceedings of the 10th Annual Symposium* (Springfield, Va.: n.p., 1985), p. 90.
122  *U.S.A. Today*, 29 January 1985.
123  *Los Angeles Times*, 5 February 1985.
124  Wilkinson, ed., *British Perspectives*, pp. 112–13.
125  *Daily Telegraph*, 4 March 1985.
126  General Sir Edwin Bramall, 'The Place of the British Army in Public Order', paper delivered to the Royal Society for the Encouragement of Arts, Manufactures and Commerce, 6 February, 1980.
127  H.C. Debs., Vol. 833, col. 738.
128  H.C. Debs., Vol. 823, col. 317.
129  W.D. Flackes, *Northern Ireland: A Political Directory* (London: Ariel Books, British Broadcasting Corporation, 1983), p. 300.
130  *The Economist*, 2 June 1984, p. 40.
131  Cmnd. 7324, *Review*, p. vi.
132  Netanyahu, ed., *International Terrorism*, p. 281.
133  H.L. 101, H.C. 220, *Report of the Tribunal* by the Right Honourable Lord Widgery (London: HMSO, 1972).
134  Cmnd. 7497, *Report of the Committee of Inquiry into Police Interrogation Procedures in Northern Ireland* (London: HMSO, 1979).
135  William Regis Farrell, *The U.S. Government Response to Terrorism* (Boulder: Westview Press, Inc., 1982), p. 107.
136  *The McDonald Report*, p. 818.
137  ibid., p. 819.
138  ibid.
139  The Prevention of Terrorism (Temporary Provisions) Act 1976, Part II.
140  John F. Murphy, *Punishing International Terrorists* (Totowa: Rowman & Allenhead Publishers, 1985), p. 71.
141  *Daily Telegraph*, 15 July 1986.
142  Murphy, *Punishing*, p. 72.
143  *Daily Telegraph*, 30 September 1984.
144  Livingstone, *The War*, p. 159.
145  *New York Times*, 22 April 1984.
146  *Toronto Star*, 11 March 1986.
147  *International Herald Tribune*, 8 May 1986.
148  Jaffrey Z. Rubin and Nehemia Friedland, 'Theatre of Terror', *Psychology Today* (March 1986), p. 24.
149  ibid.

*Additional notes*

(1)  *Civil Aviation*. Three international conventions and one protocol exist to deal with air piracy or hijacking:

— *The Tokyo Convention* of 1969, originally proposed in 1963 by the International Civil Aviation Organization (ICAO). This provides for the return of aircraft after hijacking.
— *The Hague Convention* of 1970, which recognizes the need for

measures firmly based in national and international law against the illegal seizure of aircraft. It obliges the state in the territory of which the offender is found, if it does not extradite the offender, to submit the case to the competent authorities for the purposes of extradition, the principle of *aut dedere, aut judicare.*

— *The Montreal Convention* of 1971, which is concerned with the suppression of unlawful acts against the safety of civil aviation. This imposes the same obligations on signatories to take measures against those who commit other types of offence endangering aircraft, including acts of violence when an aircraft is in flight, the planting of bombs and other attempts at sabotage. It does break new ground, however, in extending its application, in some circumstances, when an aircraft is in service (as opposed to in flight) which includes both preflight preparation and until 24 hours after any landing.

The conventions do have limitations. They do not apply to acts done within the confines of airports, frequent targets of terrorists. Although they encourage extradition treaties, those treaties themselves allow for exceptions in the case of political offences.* The Montreal Convention, however, was extended by a Protocol in 1988. The Protocol includes terrorist acts against persons at international airports that are likely to cause serious injury or death, damage to facilities or aircraft not in service, or disruption of airport services if the act endangers airport safety.

\* See, for example, the extradition treaty between the United States and Canada which, in Article 4 thereof, allows for extradition not to be granted where the offence is of a 'political character'. Countries of all political persuasions are concerned with the difficult question as to whether or not to extradite some 'terrorists':

Although the Soviet Union and Eastern states have on a number of occasions proposed that extradition be obligatory in all cases, this approach has not been generally accepted. The West, for political reasons, is not prepared to return hijackers fleeing communist rule, and many developing states are not prepared to extradite members of certain national liberation movements. The principle thus attempts to separate the incidents themselves from their possible underlying political character and to place them in the context of universally-accepted international crimes. In this way a government may express sympathy for a hijacker's cause explicitly and by refusing to extradite him, while at the same time effectively may condemn the terrorist act itself by ensuring that the offender is prosecuted where he is found. J. Reiskind, 'International Conventions on Terrorism and Canadian Criminal Law', Canadian Council on International Law, *Proceedings of the Tenth Annual Conference,* Ottawa: 1981, pp. 68–9.

(2)   *United Nations Conventions*:

— *The International Convention on the Prevention and Punishment of Crimes against Internationally Protected Persons, including Diplomatic Agents, 1973.* The Convention includes provisions requiring either extradition of offenders or submission of the case to prosecuting authorities. States parties are required to assume jurisdictions over the specified offences against diplomats regardless of where in the world they were committed.

— *The International Convention against the Taking of Hostages, 1979.* This agreement obliges contracting states either to extradite any person charged with an act of hostage-taking, or to submit the case to prosecuting authorities, and to make the offence punishable by appropriate penalties.

(3) *United Nations Resolutions.* On 9 December 1985, the General Assembly adopted a resolution which unequivocally condemns as criminal all acts, methods, and practices of terrorism wherever and by whomever committed, including those which jeopardize friendly relations among states and their security. On 18 December 1985, the Security Council adopted, unanimously and without debate, Resolution 579 which condemned unequivocally all acts of hostage-taking and abduction, and called for the immediate safe release of all hostages and abducted persons wherever and by whomever they are being held. The Resolution, designed to avoid any attempt to define terrorism, appealed to all states who have not already done so to sign the relevant international agreements. It also urged the further development of international co-operation among states in devising and adopting effective measures which are in accordance with the rules of international law to facilitate the prevention, prosecution, and punishment of all acts of hostage-taking and abduction as manifestations of international terrorism. While such resolutions lack implementing procedures and are largely symbolic, they are important to the development of a consensus among all nations that terrorism is unacceptable international behaviour.

(4) *Summit Seven Agreements.* (Canada, United States, United Kingdom, France, West Germany, Italy, and Japan.) This group has issued six joint declarations of unity: Bonn, 1978; Venice, 1980; Ottawa, 1981; London, 1984; Tokyo, 1986; Toronto, 1988. The *Bonn* Declaration, for instance, called for member countries to terminate civilian airline service to any country failing to prosecute or extradite a hijacker. At the *Venice* Summit, they reaffirmed their determination to combat attacks on diplomatic and consular premises and personnel and to provide mutual assistance to that end. In *Ottawa* they expressed concern about the active support given to international terrorism through the supply of money and arms and the sanctuary and training offered to terrorists. Agreement was reached on the exchange of information, on the exploration of co-operative measures, and on the need for wider adherence to them. At the *London* Summit, the participants expressed concern at the ease with which terrorists moved across international boundaries and gained access to weapons, explosives, training, and finance, and particularly at the increasing involvement of states and governments in acts of terrorism, including the abuse of diplomatic immunity. The London Summit's declaration on international terrorism included specific proposals, such as closer co-ordination between police and security organizations and other authorities, especially

the exchange of information, intelligence, and technical knowledge and, as far as possible, co-operation over the expulsion from the participants' countries of known terrorists, including those of diplomatic status involved in terrorism. The *Tokyo* meeting included agreement to step up the exchange of information on terrorism and to improve extradition procedures. Also, a pledge was made to take action against countries sponsoring terrorism by refusing to sell them arms, limiting the size of their diplomatic mission, restricting travel by mission members, and tightening immigration requirements for their citizens. Libya was specifically named. The *Toronto* Summit included agreement that a hijacked aircraft should not be allowed to take off, except in certain circumstances, according to the ICAO Agreement.

(5) *European Convention on the Suppression of Terrorism, 1978.* This Convention complements existing extradition arrangements between the Council of Europe's twenty-one member states. It removed the traditional 'political offence' safeguard in extradition for crimes of hijacking or other offences against aircraft, serious attacks on internationally protected persons, kidnapping, taking of hostages, and offences involving the use of explosives or firearms if these endanger persons. It was signed by all members except Ireland and Malta, although in the wake of the Anglo-Irish Agreement, Ireland has stated its intent to do so.

(6) *Trevi Arrangements.* This was established in 1976 to facilitate practical discussion and exchanges of information and experience in countering terrorism in EEC countries. Regular meetings are held between Ministers, senior officials and working groups, especially involving law-enforcement representatives.

### 3 Decision-making and crisis-management machinery

1 Judy Torrance, 'The Response of Canadian Governments to Violence', *Canadian Journal of Political Science* 10 (September 1977) pp. 473–96.
2 ibid., p. 481.
3 See S.E. Finer, *Comparative Government* (London: Allen Lane The Penguin Press, 1970), p. 198. Also Ernest Evans, *Calling a Truce To Terror* (London: Greenwood Press, 1979), p. 128.
4 *Newsweek*, 21 November 1983.
5 T.A. Critchley, *The Conquest of Violence* (London: Constable & Co. Ltd., 1970).
6 ibid., p. 1.
7 ibid., p. 199.
8 ibid.
9 Edward Hyams, *Terrorists and Terrorism* (London: J.M. Dent & Sons Ltd., 1975), p. 43.
10 ibid.
11 R. MacGregor Dawson, rev. by Norman Ward, *The Government of Canada*, 5 ed. (Toronto: University of Toronto Press, 1970), p. 197.
12 ibid., p. 209.
13 Anthony H. Birch, *The British System of Government* (London: George

Allen & Unwin, 1980), p. 157.
14 *Second Report of the Commission of Inquiry Concerning Certain Activities of the Royal Canadian Mounted Police* (Ottawa: Minister of Supply and Services Canada, 1981), hereinafter called *The McDonald Report*.
15 *The Report of the Senate Special Committee on Terrorism and the Public Safety* (Ottawa: Minister of Supply and Services Canada, 1987), p. 55.
16 ibid., p. 53.
17 *Solicitor General Annual Report 1985–86* (Minister of Supply and Services Canada, 1987), p. 5.
18 Finer, *Comparative Government*, p. 193.
19 ibid., p. 209.
20 ibid., p. 224.
21 ibid., p. 257.
22 ibid., p. 250.
23 ibid.
24 ibid., p. 211.
25 ibid., p. 251.
26 Donald R. Whitnah, *Government Agencies* (Westport: Greenwood Press, 1983), p. 372.
27 ibid., p. 376.
28 William Regis Farrell, *The U.S. Government Response to Terrorism* (Boulder: Westview Press, Inc., 1982), p. 96.
29 ibid., p. 98.
30 Laurence Gonzales, 'The Targeting of America', *Playboy* (May, 1983), p. 9.
31 Farrell, *The U.S. Government Response*, p. 98.
32 ibid.
33 ibid., p. 88.
34 ibid., p. 36.
35 ibid.
36 James B. Motley, *U.S. Strategy to Counter Domestic Political Terrorism* (Washington: National Defense University Press, 1983), p. 35.
37 Farrell, *The U.S. Government Response*, p. 123.
38 ibid., p. 99.
39 ibid.
40 Defense Nuclear Agency, *Proceedings of the 10th Annual Symposium* (Springfield, Va., n.p., 1985), p. 77.
41 ibid.
42 ibid.
43 *Report of The Secretary of State's Advisory Panel on Overseas Security* (Washington: n.p., 1985), hereinafter known as *The Inman Report*.
44 ibid., p. 1.
45 ibid.
46 Farrell, *The U.S. Government Response*, p. 99.
47 ibid., p. 123.
48 Birch, *The British System*, p. 43.
49 Finer, *Comparative Government*, p. 149.
50 Birch, *The British System*, p. 44.
51 ibid., p. 45.

52 Finer, *Comparative Government*, p. 147.
53 Birch, *The British System*, p. 5.
54 Finer, *Comparative Government*, p. 146.
55 ibid., p. 147.
56 ibid., p. 148.
57 Birch, *The British System*, p. 21.
58 *Daily Telegraph*, 4 March 1986.
59 R.G.S. Brown and D.R. Steel, *The Administrative Process in Britain* (London: Methuen & Co. Ltd., 1979), p. 333.
60 ibid.
61 *The Times*, 30 April 1984; see also Peter Hennessy, *Cabinet* (Oxford: Basil Blackwell, 1986).
62 E.C.S. Wade and A.W. Bradley, *Constitutional and Administrative Law* (London: Longman, 1985), p. 550.
63 David Bonner, *Emergency Powers in Peacetime* (London: Sweet & Maxwell, 1985), p. 29.
64 ibid.
65 Christopher Andrew, *Secret Service* (London: Heinemann, 1985), p. 505.
66 ibid., p. 498.
67 ibid., p. 499.
68 M.R. Dare, 'The Enhancement of Crisis Handling Capability within the Canadian Federal Structure', Report to the Canadian House of Commons, 15 October 1972, p. 13.
69 CSIS Act, Part IV, s. 61.
70 Defense Nuclear Agency, *Proceedings*, p. 90.
71 ibid.
72 ibid., (original emphasis).
73 ibid., p. 83.
74 *U.S. News & World Report*, 7 February 1983.
75 Motley, *U.S. Strategy*, p. 56.
76 ibid., p. 57.
77 Tony Bunyan, *Political Police* (London: Julian Friedmann, 1976), p. 74.
78 ibid., p. 73.
79 Wade and Bradley, *Constitutional and Administrative Law*, p. 550.
80 Sir David McNee, *McNee's Law* (London: Collins, 1983), p. 166.
81 ibid., p. 161.
82 ibid., p. 154.
83 George Brock, Robin Lustig, Lawrence Marks, Robert Parker, and Patrick Seale, with Maureen McConville, *Siege* (London: Macmillan Ltd., 1980), p. 23.
84 ibid.
85 ibid.
86 ibid.
87 Paul Wilkinson, ed., *British Perspectives on Terrorism* (London: George Allen & Unwin, 1981), p. 113.
88 Tom Bowden, *Beyond the Limits of the Law* (Harmondsworth: Penguin Books, 1978), p. 233.
89 Richard Thackrah, ed., *Contemporary Policing* (London: Sphere Reference,

1985), p. 147.
90  ibid., p. 146.
91  ibid., p. 148.
92  ibid.
93  *Press and Journal*, 20 December 1985.
94  Bonner, *Emergency Powers*, p. 99.
95  Cmnd. 8803, *Review of the Operation of the Prevention of Terrorism (Temporary Provisions) Act 1976* by the Right Honourable Earl Jellicoe (London: HMSO, 1983).

## Additional note

(1)  A fundamental difficulty encountered in research on government policy is the profusion of differing names and titles associated with bureaucratic structures. (A problem compounded in the US system by the American predilection for acronyms and abbreviations.) Furthermore, 'students of government are often puzzled about the relationship between the organization within a government agency and the actual services it provides to the public. Moreover, the numerous executive and congressional reorganizational plans throughout [American] history have not resolved the puzzle.' (Whitnah, *Government Agencies*, p. 661)

The roles, functions, responsibilities, and authority of the bureaucratic components can be extremely confusing for the uninitiated. Some agencies have been created for regulatory purposes, some are subcomponents of a larger organization serving an operative function, others are of a purely administrative nature. All, in one manner or other, make or translate policy.

Within Canada and the United Kingdom, a number of national corporations exist, as in the airlines industry, which function as independent business entities. While the major Cabinet departments or ministries in the three countries are umbrella organizations, independent bodies also exist for purposes such as regulation, control, or administration. Generally, the Cabinet organizations are senior (and within which a hierarchy obtains, as well), but some of the subordinate components and independent bodies wield considerable influence.

Faced with a multitude and variety of names (e.g. departments, agencies, ministries, bureaux, commissions, corporations) which are complicated by the personal titles of ministers (with and without portfolio), secretaries (permanent, under, *et al.*), directors and ambassadors, the student can only be forewarned. One recommended solution is the use of a government telephone directory to determine the structural outline. Some government bodies do publish organizational charts which indicate their organization and relationship within the system. A sound functional knowledge of a government bureaucracy is an asset; it permits an insight to the loci of power, and enables an observer to appreciate various attempts at restructuring which often occur only for the purpose of increasing the power and influence of a given component. The ability to 'read' such activity is extremely important for an ambitious member of any civil service.

## 4 Resources and Capabilities

1 *News Release*, Solicitor General of Canada, 10 March 1986, p. 1.
2 ibid., p. 2.
3 ibid., p. 3.
4 ibid., p. 2.
5 *Baltimore Sun*, 23 September 1984.
6 *Richmond Times-Dispatch*, 18 July 1982.
7 *Los Angeles Times*, 4 August 1982.
8 *Harper's*, September 1982.
9 *New York Times*, 8 February 1984.
10 Oliver B. Revell, 'Responding to the Terrorist Threat, the Need for International Liaison and Cooperation', speech before the International Association of Chiefs of Police, 91 Annual Conference, 21 October 1984, Salt Lake City, Utah, p. 4.
11 *International Herald Tribune*, 8 May 1986.
12 ibid.
13 United Kingdom Staff College Precis, Number 4, paragraph 1.
14 ibid.
15 Sir David McNee, *McNee's Law* (London: Collins, 1983), p. 135.
16 *Daily Telegraph*, 15 July 1985.
17 ibid.
18 G. Davidson Smith, 'Political Violence in Animal Liberation', *Contemporary Review* 247 (July 1985), p. 27.
19 *Idem*, 'Counter-Terrorism: Third Force Viability' (Master's Essay, Nova University, 1980), p. 201.
20 Ibid., p. 199.
21 ibid., p. 191.
22 ibid., p. 195.
23 ibid., p. 194.
24 *News Release*, Solicitor General of Canada, 10 March 1986, pp. 3–8.
25 *NEWSCAN*, 8 (London: The Press Office, Canadian High Commission, 16 July 1986), p. 4.
26 *Public Report of the Vice President's Task Force on Combatting Terrorism* (Washington: US Government Printing Office, 1986), p. 7.
27 *Chicago Tribune*, 11 May 1986.
28 ibid.
29 ibid., 12 May 1984.
30 Honourable George P. Shultz, 'Terrorism and the Modern World', speech before the Park Avenue Synagogue, New York, N.W., 25 October 1984, p. 22.
31 ibid., p. 17.
32 See Netanyahu, Benjamin, ed. *Terrorism. How The West Can Win* (London: Weidenfeld and Nicolson, 1986).
33 See *Des Moines Register*, 20 May 1986.
34 *Washington Times*, 16 April 1984.
35 *Chicago Tribune*, 11 May 1986.
36 ibid., 12 May 1986.
37 ibid., 11 May 1986.

38 ibid., 13 May 1986.
39 See *International Herald Tribune*, 8 May 1986.
40 *Public Report of the Vice President's Task Force*, Facing Page.
41 ibid., p. 18.
42 ibid., p. 13.
43 ibid., p. 7.
44 Warren Christopher, *American Hostages in Iran: The Conduct of a Crisis* (New Haven: Yale University Press, 1985), p. 229.
45 *New York Times*, 21 April 1986.
46 *Atlanta Constitution*, 21 April 1986.
47 See *The Observer*, 20 April 1986.
48 Cmnd. 9222, *Review of the Operation of the Northern Ireland (Emergency Provisions) Act 1978* by The Right Honourable Sir George Baker (London: HMSO, 1984), p. 9.
49 Cmnd. 8803, *Review of the Operation of the Prevention of Terrorism (Temporary Provisions) Act 1976* by The Right Honourable Earl Jellicoe (London: MHSO, 1983), p. 9.
50 ibid., p. 27.
51 *Daily Telegraph*, 13 October 1984.
52 Cmnd. 8803, Jellicoe, *Review*, p. 4.
53 ibid., p. 217.
54 Kevin Boyle, Tom Hadden, and Paddy Hillyard, *Ten Years on in Northern Ireland* (London: The Cobden Trust, 1980).
55 ibid., p. 89.
56 ibid.
57 ibid.
58 ibid., p. 90.
59 W.D. Flackes, *Northern Ireland: A Political Directory*, (London: Ariel Books, BBC, 1983) p. 218.
60 ibid., p. 106.
61 Boyle *et al.*, *Ten Years on*, p. 93.
62 Cmnd. 5847, *Report of a Committee to Consider, in the Context of Civil Liberties and Human Rights, Measures to Deal with Terrorism in Northern Ireland* (London: HMSO, 1975).
63 ibid., p. 6.
64 Cmnd. 5185, *Report of the Commission to Consider Legal Procedures to Deal with Terrorist Activities in Northern Ireland* (London: HMSO, 1972), p. 5.
65 ibid., p. 3.
66 Boyle *et al.*, *Ten Years on*, p. 86.
67 ibid.
68 Cmnd. 4901, *Report of the Committee of Privy Counsellors Appointed to Consider Authorized Procedures for the Interrogation of Persons Suspected of Terrorism* (London: HMSO, 1972).
69 Cmnd. 7497, *Report of the Committee of Inquiry into Police Interrogations Procedures in Northern Ireland* (London: HMSO, 1979), p. iii.
70 ibid., p. 136.
71 ibid., p. 135.

72  Boyle *et al.*, *Ten Years on*, p. 40.
73  Cmnd. 5185, *Report of the Commission*, p. 30.
74  Cmnd. 9222, Baker, *Review*, p. 50.
75  Edgar O'Ballance, *Terror in Ireland* (Novato: Presidio Press, 1981), p. 143.
76  ibid.
77  Boyle *et al.*, *Ten Years on*, p. 24.
78  Cmnd. 4823, *Report of the Enquiry into Allegations against the Security Forces of Physical Brutality in Northern Ireland Arising out of Events on 9 August 1971* (London: HMSO, 1971).
79  ibid., p. 13.
80  Cmnd. 4901, *Report of the Committee*.
81  Flackes, *Northern Ireland*, p. 313.
82  O'Ballance, *Terror*, p. 153.
83  Flackes, *Northern Ireland*, p. 313.
84  O'Ballance, *Terror*, p. 150.
85  Paul Wilkinson, 'Northern Ireland: An Alternative to Terrorism', *Contemporary Affairs Briefing* 2 (February, 1986), p. 1.
86  ibid.
87  ibid.
88  ibid.
89  ibid., p. 3.
90  ibid. (original emphasis).
91  ibid., p. 4.
92  Cmnd. 9222, Baker, *Review*, p. 49.
93  Interview with Canadian Forces officers, National Defence Headquarters, Ottawa, 1982.
94  James B. Motley, *U.S. Strategy to Counter Domestic Political Terrorism* (Washington: National Defence University Press, 1983), p. 18.
95  ibid., p. 15.
96  See *FBI Analysis of Terrorist Incidents in the United States*, US Department of Justice, 1985.
97  *Daily Telegraph*, 9 June 1986.
98  Jay Mallin, *Terror and Urban Guerrillas: A Study of Tactics and Documents* (Corla Gables: University of Miami Press, 1971).
99  ibid., p. 60.
100  ibid., p. 65.
101  *Daily Telegraph*, 9 June 1986.
102  ibid.
103  ibid.
104  *Public Report of the Vice President's Task Force*, p. 17.
105  Claire Sterling, *The Terror Network* (London: Weidenfeld & Nicolson, 1981).
106  Frank Kitson, *Low Intensity Operations* (London: Faber & Faber Limited, 1971), p. 1.
107  James Callaghan, *A House Divided* (London: Collins, 1973), p. 133.
108  M.R. Dare, 'The Enhancement of Crisis Handling Capability within the Canadian Federal Structure', Report to the Canadian House of Commons,

15 October 1972, p. 11.

109 *Second Report of the Commission of Inquiry Concerning Certain Activities of the Royal Canadian Mounted Police* (Ottawa: Minister of Supply and Services Canada, 1981), hereinafter called *The McDonald Report*, p. 847.

110 ibid., p. 849.

111 ibid., p. 850 (original emphasis).

112 ibid., p. 852.

113 ibid.

114 ibid.

115 ibid., p. 854.

116 ibid., p. 853.

117 ibid., p. 855.

118 *The Report of the Senate Special Committee on Terrorism and the Public Safety* (Ottawa: Minister of Supply and Services Canada, 1987), p. 59.

119 S.E. Finer, *Comparative Government* (London: Allen Lane The Penguin Press, 1970), p. 188.

120 Colonel James B. Motley, 'Terrorist Warfare: A Reassessment', *Military Review* LXV (June, 1985), p. 49.

121 Robert W. Taylor, 'Managing Terrorist Incidents', *The Bureaucrat* (Winter 1983–4), p. 57.

122 *Public Report of the Vice President's Task Force*, p. 11.

123 Defense Nuclear Agency, *Proceedings of the 10th Annual Symposium* (Springfield, VA.: n.p., 1985), p. 77.

124 *Report of the Secretary of State's Advisory Panel on Overseas Security* (Washington: n.p., 1985), hereinafter known as *The Inman Report*, p. 47.

125 US Department of State, 'Combating International Terrorism', *Current Policy* No. 667 (Washington: Bureau of Public Affairs, n.p., March 1985), p. 4.

126 Defense Nuclear Agency, *Proceedings*, p. 77.

127 *Public Report of the Vice President's Task Force*, p. 23.

128 ibid., p. 12.

129 ibid., p. 33.

130 ibid.

131 *The Inman Report*, p. 48.

132 David Bonner, *Emergency Powers in Peacetime* (London: Sweet & Maxwell, 1985), p. 29.

133 *The Times*, 30 April 1984.

134 ibid.

135 ibid.

136 Bonner, *Emergency Powers*, p. 25.

137 E.C.S. Wade and A.W. Bradley, *Constitutional and Administrative Law* (London: Longman, 1985), p. 564.

138 *Sunday Telegraph*, 12 May 1985.

139 *Sunday Times*, 15 December 1985.

140 *Sunday Telegraph*, 12 May 1985.

141 Wade and Bradley, *Constitutional and Administrative Law*, p. 564.

142 Dare, 'The Enhancement', p. 12.

143 *Canadian Security Intelligence Service Act*, Part IV, section 61.
144 *Toronto Star*, 11 March 1986.
145 *Canadian Security Intelligence Service Act*, S.C. 1984, c. 21, p. 2, paragraph 2.
146 ibid., p. 10, paragraph 20(1).
147 ibid., p. 17, paragraph 34(1).
148 ibid., p. 25, paragraph 57.
149 ibid., p. 25, paragraph 59(2).
150 Christopher Dobson and Ronald Payne, *Terror! The West Fights Back* (London: PAPERMAC, 1982), p. 181. Also, US Department of Justice, *The FBI's Mission* (Washington, n.d.), p. 13.
151 Neil C. Livingstone, *The War against Terrorism* (Lexington: D.C. Heath & Company, 1982), p. 258.
152 Defense Nuclear Agency, *Proceedings*, p. 89.
153 *USA Today*, March 1984.
154 ibid.
155 Taylor, 'Managing Terrorist Incidents', p. 55.
156 ibid., p. 56.
157 *The Inman Report*, p. 57.
158 ibid., p. 5.
159 ibid., p. 51.
160 Tony Bunyan, *The Political Police* (London: Julian Friedmann Publishers Ltd., 1976), p. 74.
161 ibid.
162 Paul Wilkinson, ed., *British Perspectives on Terrorism* (London: George Allen & Unwin, 1981), p. 113.
163 *Daily Telegraph*, 29 April 1985.
164 Wilkinson, ed., *British Perspectives*, p. 115.
165 ibid., p. 116.
166 ibid., p. 117.
167 *Sunday Times*, 27 January 1985.
168 ibid.
169 *Sunday Times*, 14 October 1984.
170 ibid.
171 ibid.
172 *Daily Telegraph*, 23 October 1984.
173 ibid.
174 ibid.
175 *Sunday Times*, 27 January 1985.
176 Cmnd. 535, *Report of the Advisory Committee on Police in Northern Ireland* (Belfast: HMSO, 1969), p. 2.
177 ibid.
178 ibid., p. 13.
179 ibid.
180 ibid., p. 39.
181 ibid., p. 40.
182 ibid., p. 43.
183 Russell Murray, 'Killings in Northern Ireland 1969–1981', *Terrorism, an*

*International Journal* 7, Number 1 (1984), p. 14.

184  ibid.

185  ibid.

186  ibid.

187  *Chief Constable's Annual Report 1984*, presented to the Police Authority for Northern Ireland by J.C. Hermon, Chief Constable (Belfast: n.p., April, 1985), pp. 1, 29.

188  'Northern Ireland: An Anglo–Irish Dilemma?', *Conflict Studies*, Number 185 (London: The Institute for the Study of Conflict, 1986), p. 19 (original emphasis).

189  ibid.

190  *Defence 84* (Ottawa: Minister of Supply and Services Canada, 1985), p. 5.

191  ibid.

192  William Regis Farrell, *The U.S. Government Response to Terrorism* (Boulder: Westview Press, Inc., 1982), p. 101.

193  G. Davidson Smith, 'The Military in Aid of the Civil Power: Limits in a Democratic Society', *Canadian Defence Quarterly* 13 (Spring, 1984), p. 28.

194  Farrell, *U.S. Government Response*, p. 52.

195  *International Herald Tribune*, 17 July 1986.

196  Farrell, *U.S. Government Response*, p. 101.

197  ibid., p. 53.

198  *Chicago Tribune*, 11 May 1986.

199  ibid., 12 May 1986.

200  ibid.

201  ibid.

202  For an interesting and informative account, see Colonel Charlie A. Beckwith (Ret.) and Donald Knox, *Delta Force* (London: Arms & Armour Press, 1984).

203  *The Times*, 4 August 1986.

204  Farrell, *U.S. Government Response*, p. 64.

205  *The Times*, 4 August 1986.

206  ibid.

207  ibid.

208  ibid.

209  ibid.

210  ibid.

211  *International Herald Tribune*, 22–3 June 1985.

212  Jay Finegan, 'Terrorism,' *Air Force Times Magazine* (October, 1983), p. 16.

213  *The Times*, 4 August 1986.

214  Finer, *Comparative Government*, p. 136.

215  T.A. Critchley, *The Conquest of Violence* (London: Constable & Co. Ltd., 1970), pp. 95–176.

216  Michael Supperstone, *Brownlie's Law of Public Order and National Security*, 2 edn. (London: Butterworth, 1981), p. 210.

217  ibid.

218  General Sir Edwin Bramall, 'The Place of the British Army in Public

Order', paper delivered to the Royal Society for the Encouragement of Arts, Manufactures and Commerce, 6 February 1980, p. 7.

219 ibid., p. 5.
220 Bonner, *Emergency Powers*, p. 162.
221 ibid., p. 164.
222 *Press Release*, 'UDR – A Brief History', (Lisburn: n.p., October 1985).
223 ibid.
224 'Northern Ireland', *Conflict Studies* 185, p. 21.
225 *Press Release*, 'UDR – A Brief History', statement by the Secretary of State for Northern Ireland.
226 ibid.
227 *NEWSCAN*, 7 (London: The Press Office, Canadian High Commission, 5 November 1985), p. 2.
228 *The McDonald Report*, p. 913.
229 *NEWSCAN*, 7, p. 2.
230 Emergency Preparedness Canada, *Highlights of the Emergencies Act*.
231 *The Report of the Senate Committee*, p. 32.
232 Donald Macdonald, 'International and Domestic Measures against Terrorism', paper prepared by the Law and Government Division, Research Branch, Library of Parliament, Ottawa, 22 November 1985, p. 14.
233 ibid., p. 15.
234 *Daily Telegraph*, 12 July 1985.
235 *Public Report of the Vice President's Task Force*, p. 15.
236 Defense Nuclear Agency, *Proceedings*, p. 90.
237 *Public Report of the Vice President's Task Force*, p. 15.
238 ibid.
239 *International Herald Tribune*, 4 July 1985.
240 *Public Report of the Vice President's Task Force*, p. 16.
241 Wade and Bradley, *Constitutional and Administrative Law*, p. 556.
242 Bonner, *Emergency Powers*, p. 168.
243 ibid., p. 28.
244 ibid., p. 75.
245 ibid., p. 76.
246 ibid., p. 95.
247 Cmnd. 9222, Baker, *Review*, p. 4.
248 ibid., p. 14.
249 David Bonner, *Emergency Powers in Peacetime* (London: Sweet & Maxwell, 1985)
250 Bonner, *Emergency Powers*, p. 76.
251 Cmnd. 9222, Baker, *Review*, p. 5.
252 Flackes, *Northern Ireland*, p. 316.
253 Bonner, *Emergency Powers*, p. 104.
254 Cmnd.5185, *Report of the Commission*, p. 6.
255 Bonner, *Emergency Powers*, p. 106.
256 Wade and Bradley, *Constitutional and Administrative Law*, p. 560.
257 ibid., p. 562.
258 Cmnd. 8803, Jellicoe, *Review*, p. 1.

259  Background Brief, 'International Reaction to Terrorism', Foreign and Commonwealth Office, January 1986, p. 5.
260  Background Brief, 'International Terrorism: The European Response', Foreign and Commonwealth Office, June 1986, p. 4.
261  Background Brief, 'International Reaction,' p. 5.
262  ibid., p. 1.
263  Background Brief, 'International Terrorism,' p. 1.
264  ibid., p. 2.
265  ibid.
266  Ronald D. Crelinsten, 'Power and Meaning: Terrorism as a Struggle over Access to the Communication Structure', paper presented at the International Academic Conference on Terrorism, University of Aberdeen, April 1986.
267  Robin Bourne, 'Terrorism Incident Management in a Federal State', Emergency Planning Research Conference, Arnprior, Ontario, January 1979, p. 12.
268  ibid., pp. 13–14.
269  *News Release*, Solicitor General of Canada, 10 March 1986, p. 8.
270  ibid.
271  *International Herald Tribune*, 8 May 1986.
272  *Sunday Times*, 30 June 1985.
273  ibid.
274  ibid.
275  ibid.
276  ibid.
277  *Public Report of the Vice President's Task Force*, p. 19.
278  ibid.
279  ibid.
280  ibid.
281  ibid.
282  ibid.
283  ibid., p. 20.
284  ibid., p. 27.
285  Bonner, *Emergency Powers*, p. 77.
286  *Chief Constable's Annual Report 1984*, p. 22.
287  'Northern Ireland', *Conflict Studies* 185, p. 15.
288  ibid.
289  *Sunday Telegraph*, 2 September 1984.
290  ibid.
291  'Northern Ireland', *Conflict Studies* 185, p. 15.

**5 Concluding commentary**

1  Noel O'Sullivan, ed., *Terrorism, Ideology and Revolution: The Origins of Modern Political Violence* (Brighton: Wheatsheaf Books Ltd., 1986), p. 221.
2  *Chicago Tribune*, 11 May 1986.
3  ibid.

4  ibid.
5  ibid.
6  ibid., 12 May 1986.
7  ibid., 13 May 1986. For details of the *Achille Lauro* incident see *The Economist*, 12–18 October 1985; *International Herald Tribune*, 9 October 1985; *Daily Telegraph*, 12 October 1985; *International Herald Tribune*, 12–13 October 1985; *Sunday Times*, 13 October 1985; *New York Times*, 13 October 1985; *Daily Telegraph*, 13 October 1985; *International Herald Tribune*, 14 October 1985; ibid., 15 October 1985; ibid., 18 October 1985; ibid., 19 October 1985.
8  *Chicago Tribune*, 13 May 1986.
9  ibid.
10  ibid.
11  ibid. For details of the Libyan raid see *The Economist*, 19–25 April 1986; *Observer*, 20 April 1986; *Sunday Telegraph*, 20 April 1986; *Sunday Times*, 20 April 1986; *Daily Telegraph*, 14 through 19 April 1986.
12  *Sunday Times*, 4 December 1988.
13  *New York Times*, 19 November 1988.
14  *Public Report Of The Vice President's Task Force On Combatting Terrorism* (Washington: US Government Printing Office, 1986), p. 23.
15  *Daily Telegraph*, 23 October 1984.
16  Defense Nuclear Agency, *Proceedings of the 10th Annual Symposium* (Springfield, VA.: n.p., 1985), p. 90 (original emphasis).
17  *Los Angeles Times*, 15 April 1984.
18  Arthur J. Goldberg, 'The Murder in St. James's Square'. *Encounter* 63 (November, 1984), pp. 67–70.
19  Security Intelligence Review Committee, *Annual Report 1985–86* (Ottawa: Minister of Supply and Services Canada, 1986), p. 5.
20  G. Davidson Smith, 'A Positive Approach to Terrorism: The Case for an Elite Counter-Force in Canada,' *Journal of the Royal United Services Institute* 129 (September, 1984), p. 21.
21  *Ottawa Citizen*, 12 March 1986.
22  *Daily Telegraph*, 23 June 1984. See also Tom Hadden, 'Is It Murder To Shoot To Kill?' *New Society* (4 April, 1985), p. 11.
23  *New York Times*, 19 November 1988.
24  ibid.
25  *Globe and Mail*, 16 November 1988.

## Addendum

1  *Terrorism. The Report of the Second Special Committee of the Senate on Terrorism and Public Safety* (Ottawa: Minister of Supply and Services Canada, 1989), p. 3.
2  ibid., p. 4.
3  ibid., p. 14.
4  ibid., p. 4.
5  *Ottawa Citizen*, 8 April 1989.

## Notes

6 *The Report of the Second Special Committee,* p. 1.
7 ibid., p. 3.
8 ibid., p. 14.
9 ibid.
10 ibid., p. 15.
11 ibid., p. 19.
12 ibid., p. 24.
13 ibid., p. 4.

# Selected bibliography

## Books

Adams, James. *The Financing of Terror*. London: New English Library, 1986.

Adeniran, Tudne and Alexander, Yonah, eds. *International Violence*. New York: Praeger, 1983.

Alexander, Yonah, ed. *International Terrorism: National, Regional, and Global Perspectives*. 2 edn. New York: Praeger, 1980.

Alexander, Yonah and Finger, Seymour Maxwell, eds. *Terrorism: Interdisciplinary Perspectives*. New York: John Jay Press Limited, 1977.

Alexander, Yonah, Carlton, David, and Wilkinson, Paul, eds. *Terrorism: Theory and Practice*. Boulder: Westview Press, 1979.

Alexander, Yonah and Ebinger, Charles K., eds. *Political Terrorism and Energy: The Threat and Response*. New York: Praeger, 1982.

Alexander, Yonah and Meyers, Kenneth, eds. *Terrorism in Europe*. London: Croom Helm, 1982.

Alexander, Yonah and O'Day, Alan, eds. *Terrorism in Ireland*. London: Croom Helm, 1984.

Allison, Graham T. *Essence of Decision: Explaining the Cuban Missile Crisis*. Boston: Little, Brown and Company, 1971.

Andrew, Christopher. *Secret Service*. London: Heinemann, 1985.

Andrew, Christopher and Dilks, David, eds. *The Missing Dimension: Governments and Intelligence Communities in the Twentieth Century*. London: Macmillan, 1984.

Aron, Raymond. *Peace and War*. London: Weidenfeld & Nicolson, 1966.

Ascoli, David. *The Queen's Peace*. London: Hamish Hamilton, 1979.

Asprey, Robert B. *War in the Shadows*. 2 vols. New York: Doubleday and Co. Inc., 1975.

Aston, Clive C. *A Contemporary Crisis: Political Hostage-Taking and the Experience of Western Europe*. London: Greenwood Press, 1982.

Bamford, James. *The Puzzle Palace*. New York: Penguin Books, 1983.

Bassiouni, M. Cherif, ed. *International Terrorism and Political Crimes*. Springfield: Charles C. Thomas, 1975.

Beckwith, Colonel Charlie A., USA (Ret.) and Knox, Donald. *Delta Force*. Glasgow: William Collins Sons & Co., 1985.

Bell, J. Bowyer. *Transnational Terror*. Washington, DC: American Institute for Public Policy Research, 1975.

*Selected bibliography*

——*On Revolt*. London: Harvard University Press, 1976.
——*A Time of Terror*. New York: Basic Books, Inc., 1978.
——*The Secret Army*. Cambridge, Mass.: The MIT Press, 1980.
Beres, Louis Rene. *Terrorism and Global Security: The Nuclear Threat*. Boulder: Westview Press, 1979.
Birch, Anthony H. *The British System of Government*. 4th edn. London: George Allen & Unwin, 1980.
Blaufarb, Douglas S. *The Counterinsurgency Era: U.S. Doctrine and Performance*. London: The Free Press, Collier-Macmillan, 1977.
Bonner, David. *Emergency Powers in Peacetime*. London: Sweet & Maxwell, 1985.
Bothwell, Robert, Dummond, Ian, and English, John. *Canada Since 1945: Power, Politics, and Provincialism*. Toronto: University of Toronto Press, 1981.
Bowden, Tom. *The Breakdown of Public Security*. London: Sage Publications, 1977.
Boyle, Kevin, Hadden, Tom, and Hillyard, Paddy. *Ten Years on in Northern Ireland*. London: Cobden Trust, 1980.
Brock, George, Lustig, R., Marks, L., Parker, R., and Seale, P., with McConville, M. *Siege*. London: Macmillan, 1980.
Brown, R.G.S. and Steel, D.R. *The Administrative Process in Britain*. 2nd edn. London: Methuen & Co. Ltd., 1979.
Bunyan, Tony. *The Political Police in Britain*. London: Julian Friedmann Publishers, 1976.
Bunyard, R.S. *Police: Organization and Command*. Plymouth: Macdonald & Evans, Ltd., 1978.
Burton, Anthony. *Revolutionary Violence*. New York: Crane, Russak & Co., 1978.
Burton, Frank. *The Politics of Legitimacy*. London: Routledge & Kegan Paul, 1978.
Callaghan, James. *A House Divided*. London: Collins, 1973.
Campbell, Colin. *Governments Under Stress*. Toronto: University of Toronto Press, 1983.
Carlton, David, and Schaerf, Carlos, eds. *International Terrorism and World Security*. New York: John Wiley & Sons, 1975.
Christopher, Warren. *American Hostages in Iran: The Conduct of a Crisis*. New Haven: Yale University Press, 1985.
Cline, Ray S. *The CIA Under Reagan, Bush, and Casey*. Washington, DC: Acropolis Books Ltd., 1981.
Clutterbuck, Richard. *The Long, Long War*. London: Cassell, 1966.
——*Riot and Revolution in Singapore and Malaya, 1945–1963*. London: Faber & Faber Ltd., 1973.
——*Protest and the Urban Guerrilla*. London: Abelard-Schuman, 1973.
——*Living with Terrorism*. New York: Arlington House, 1976.
——*Guerrillas and Terrorists*. London: Faber & Faber, 1977.
——*Kidnap and Ransom: The Response*. London: Faber & Faber, 1978.
——*Britain in Agony*. Harmondsworth: Penguin, 1980.
Conquest, Robert. *The Great Terror*. New York: The Macmillan Co., 1968.
Coogan, Tim Pat. *The IRA*. London: Pall Mall Press, 1970.

Crelinsten, Ronald, Laberge, Altmejd, and Szabo, Denis. *Terrorism and Criminal Justice*. Toronto: Lexington Books, D.C. Heath and Company, 1978.

Crenshaw, Martha. *Revolutionary Terrorism*. Stanford: Hoover Institution Publication, 1978.

——*Terrorism, Legitimacy, and Power*. Middleton: Wesleyan University Press, 1983.

Critchley, T.A. *The Conquest of Violence*. London: Constable, 1970.

——*A History of Police in England and Wales*. Rev. edn. London: Constable, 1978.

Crozier, Brian. *The Rebels*. London: Chatto & Windus, 1960.

——*A Theory of Conflict*. London: Hamish Hamilton, 1974.

Dawson, R. MacGregor. Revised by Norman Ward. *The Government of Canada*. Toronto: University of Toronto Press, 1970.

Deacon, Richard. *'C' – A Biography of Sir Maurice Oldfield*. London: Futura Publications, 1985.

Deane-Drummond, A. *Riot-Control*. New York: Crane Russak, 1975.

Deutsch, Richard and Magowan, Vivien. *Northern Ireland Chronology of Events*. 3 vols. Belfast: Blackstaff Press, 1973, 1974, 1975.

de Vault, Carole, with Johnson, William. *The Informer*. Toronto: Fleet Books, 1982.

Dewar, Lt. Col. Michael. *The British Army in Northern Ireland*. London: Arms & Armour Press, 1985.

Dobson, Christopher and Payne, Ronald. *The Carlos Complex: A Study in Terror*. New York: Putnam, 1977.

——*The Terrorists*. New York: Facts on File, 1979.

——*Terror, The West Fights Back*. London: Macmillan, 1982.

——*War Without End*. London: Harrap Ltd., 1986.

Doerr, Audrey. *The Machinery of Government in Canada*. Toronto: Methuen, 1981.

Duffy, Maureen. *Men and Beasts. An Animal Rights Handbook*. London: Granada Publishing Ltd. 1984.

Eckstein, Harry. *Internal War*. Westport: Greenwood Press, 1964.

Elliot, John D. and Gibson, Leslie K. eds. *Contemporary Terrorism*. Gaithersburg: International Association of Chiefs of Police, 1978.

Elliot-Bateman, Michael, Ellis, John, and Bowden, Tom, eds. *Revolt To Revolution*. Manchester: Manchester University Press, 1974.

Emerson, Steven. *Secret Warriors*. New York: G.P. Putnam's Sons, 1988.

Evans, Ernest. *Calling A Truce to Terror*. Westport: Greenwood Press, 1979.

Evelegh, Robin. *Peace-Keeping in a Democratic Society*. London: C. Hurst & Co., 1978.

Fairbairn, Geoffrey. *Revolutionary Warfare and Communist Strategy*. London: Faber & Faber, 1958.

Falk, Stanley and Bauer, Theodore. *National Security Management: The National Security Structure*. Washington, DC: Industrial College of the Armed Forces, 1976.

Fanon, Frantz. *The Wretched of the Earth*. New York: Grove Press, 1965.

Farrell, William Regis. *The U.S. Government Response To Terrorism*. Boulder: Westview Press, 1982.

*Selected bibliography*

Finer, S.E. *Comparative Government*. London: Allen Lane, The Penguin Press, 1970.
Fisk, Robert. *The Point of No Return*. London: Andre Deutsch, 1975.
Flackes, W.D. *Northern Ireland: A Political Directory*. London: Ariel Books, The British Broadcasting Corporation, 1983.
Fournier, Louis. Translated by Edward Baxter. *F.L.Q. The Anatomy of an Underground Movement*. Toronto: NC Press Limited, 1984.
Freedman, Lawrence Zelic and Alexander, Yonah, eds. *Perspectives On Terrorism*. Wilmington: Scholarly Resources, Inc., 1983.
Friedlander, Robert A. *Terrorism, Documents of International and Local Control*. Dobbs Ferry, NY: Oceana Publications, Inc., 1979.
Gellner, John. *Bayonets in the Streets: Urban Guerrillas at Home and Abroad*. Don Mills: Collier-Macmillan, Canada, Ltd., 1974.
Geraghty, Tony. *WHO DARES WINS: The Story of the SAS, 1950–1980*. London: Arms & Armour Press, 1980.
Greene, Lt. Col. T.N., ed. *The Guerrilla and How to Fight Him*. New York: Frederick A. Praeger, 1962.
Greenspan, Edward L. *Martin's Annual Criminal Code, 1988*. Aurora, Ontario: Canada Law Book Inc., 1980.
Grivas, George. *Guerrilla Warfare*. London: Longman's Green, 1964.
Guevara, Che. *Guerrilla Warfare*. New York: Random, 1968.
Gutteridge, William, ed. *The New Terrorism*. London: Mansell Publishing, 1986.
Hacker, Frederick. *Crusaders, Criminals, Crazies: Terror and Terrorism in Our Time*. New York: W.W. Norton, 1976.
Halperin, Morton H. *Bureaucratic Politics and Foreign Policy*. Washington, DC: Brookings, 1974.
Hamill, Desmond. *Pig In The Middle*. London: Methuen, 1985.
Han, Henry Hyunwook, ed. *Terrorism, Political Violence, and World Order*. London: University Press of America, 1984.
Haycock, Ronald, ed. *Regular Armies and Insurgency*. London: Croom Helm, 1979.
Head, Richard G. and Rokke, Ervin J., eds. *American Defence Policy*. 3rd edn. London: The Johns Hopkins University Press, 1973.
Hennessy, Peter. *Cabinet*. Oxford: Basil Blackwell, 1986.
Herz, Martin F., ed. *Diplomats and Terrorists: What Works, What Doesn't*. Washington, DC: Institute for the Study of Diplomacy, Georgetown University, 1982.
Heskin, Ken. *Northern Ireland: A Psychological Analysis*. New York: Columbia Press, 1980.
Hewitt, Christopher. *The Effectiveness of Anti-Terrorist Policies*. New York: University Press of America, 1984.
Hull, Roger H. *The Irish Triangle*. Princeton: Princeton University Press, 1976.
Hyams, Edward. *A Dictionary of Modern Revolution*. London: Allen Lane, 1973.
——*Terrorists and Terrorism*. London: J.M. Dent & Sons, Ltd., 1975.
Jackson, Geoffrey. *Surviving The Long Night*. New York: Vanguard, 1974.
Janke, Peter. *Guerrilla and Terrorist Organizations: A World Directory and*

*Bibliography*. Brighton: The Harvester Press, 1983.

Jenkins, Brian. *International Terrorism: A New Mode of Conflict*. Los Angeles: Crescent Publications, 1975.

Johnson, Chalmers. *Revolutionary Change*. 2nd edn. London: Longman Group, 1983.

Kelly, Henry. *How Stormont Fell*. Dublin: Gill & Macmillan Ltd., 1972.

Kitson, Frank. *Low Intensity Operations*. London: Faber & Faber, 1977.

——*A Bunch of Five*. London: Faber & Faber, 1977.

Kobetz, Richard W. and Cooper, H.H.A. *Target Terrorism: Providing Protective Services*. Gaithersburg: International Association of Chiefs of Police, 1978.

Kupperman, Robert H. and Trent, Darrell, M. *Terrorism: Threat, Reality, and Response*. Stanford: Hoover Institution Press, 1979.

Laqueur, Walter. *Guerrilla: A Historical and Critical Study*. Boston: Little Brown, 1976.

——*Terrorism*. London: Weidenfeld & Nicholson, 1977.

——*The Terrorism Reader*. New York: The New American Library, Inc., 1978.

Leiden, Carl and Schmitt, Karl M. *The Politics of Violence*. Englewood Cliffs: Prentice-Hall, Inc., 1968.

Leigh, David. *The Frontiers of Secrecy*. London: Junction Books, 1980.

Leigh, L.A. *Police Powers in England and Wales*. London: Butterworths, 1975.

Livingston, Marious H., with Kress, Lee Bruce, and Wanek, Marie G., eds. *International Terrorism in the Contemporary World*. Westport: Greenwood Press, 1978.

Lodge, Juliet, ed. *Terrorism: A Challenge to the State*. Oxford: Martin Robertson, 1981.

Longford, Lord and McHardy, Anne. *Ulster*. London: Weidenfeld & Nicolson, 1981.

Loomis, Dan G. *Not Much Glory*. Toronto: Deneau Publishers, 1984.

Lowe, E. Nobels and Shargel, Harry D. *Legal and Other Aspects of Terrorism*. New York: Practicing Law Institute, 1979.

Macfarlane, Leslie. *Violence and the State*. London: Nelson & Sons, Ltd., 1974.

McNee, Sir David. *McNee's Law*. London: Collins, 1983.

Magee, John. *Northern Ireland: Crisis and Conflict*. London: Routledge & Kegan Paul, 1974.

Mallin, Jay. *Strategy for Conquest*. Coral Gables: University of Miami Press, 1970.

——*Terror and Urban Guerrillas: A Study of Tactics and Documents*. Coral Gables: University of Miami Press, 1971.

Marighella, Carlos. *Minimanual of the Urban Guerrilla*. Boulder: Paladin Press, 1978.

Mickolus, Edward F. *The Literature of Terrorism: A Selected Annotated Bibliography*. Westport: Greenwood Press, 1980.

——*Transnational Terrorism*. London: Aldwych Press, 1980.

Morf, Gustav. *Terror in Quebec*. Toronto: Clarke, Irwin, 1970.

Most, Johannes. *Military Science For Revolutionaries*. Cornville: Desert

Publications, 1978.

Murphy, John F. *The U.N. and the Control of International Violence.*
Manchester: Manchester University Press, 1983.

Netanyahu, Benjamin, ed. *International Terrorism: Challenge and Response.*
Jerusalem: The Jonathan Institute, 1980.

——*Terrorism: How The West Can Win.* London: Weidenfeld & Nicolson,
1986.

North, Richard. *The Animals Report.* Harmondsworth: Penguin Books Ltd.,
1983.

Norton, Augustus R. and Greenburg, Martin H. *International Terrorism: An
Annotated Bibliography and Research Guide.* Boulder: Westview Press,
1980.

O'Ballance, Edgar. *Terror In Ireland.* Novato, Calif.: Presidio Press, 1981.

O'Neill, Bard E., Heaton, William R., and Alberts, Donald J., eds. *Insurgency
in the Modern World.* Boulder: Westview Press, 1980.

O'Sullivan, Noel, ed. *Terrorism, Ideology and Revolution: The Origins of
Modern Political Violence.* Brighton: Wheatsheaf Books Ltd., 1986.

Parry, Albert. *Terrorism From Robespierre to Arafat.* New York: The
Vanguard Press, 1976.

Patrick, Derrick. *Fetch Felix.* London: Hamish Hamilton, 1981.

Pelletier, Gerard. *The October Crisis.* Toronto: McClellan & Stewart, 1971.

Pike, Douglas. *Viet Cong.* Cambridge: The MIT Press, 1966.

Powell, William. *The Anarchist Cookbook.* Secaucus: Lyle Stewart, 1971.

Rapoport, David C. *Assassination and Terrorism.* Toronto: The Canadian
Broadcasting System, 1971.

Rapoport, David C. and Alexander, Yonah. *The Morality of Terrorism.* New
York: Pergamon Press, 1982.

Richelson, Jeffrey T. *The U.S. Intelligence Community.* Cambridge, Mass.:
Ballinger Publishing Company, 1985.

Riddell, Patrick. *Fire Over Ulster.* London: Hamish Hamilton, 1970.

Roach, John and Thomaneck, Jurgen, eds. *Police and Public Order in
Europe.* London: Croom Helm, 1985.

Rose, Richard. *Governing Without Consensus.* London: Faber & Faber, 1971.

Schmid, Alex P. *Political Terrorism: A Research Guide to Concepts,
Theories, Data Bases, and Literature.* Amsterdam: North-Holland
Publishing Co., 1983.

Shaw, Jennifer, Gueritz, E.F., Younger, A.E., Gregory, F., and Palmer, J., eds.
*Ten Years of Terrorism.* New York: Crane, Russak and Co., 1979.

Sick, Garry. *ALL FALL DOWN: America's Tragic Encounter with Iran.* New
York: Random House, 1985.

Sloan, Steven. *Simulating Terrorism.* Norman, Okla.: University of Oklahoma
Press, 1981.

Smith, Myron J., Jr. *The Secret Wars: A Guide to Sources in English.* 3 vols.
Oxford: Clio Press Ltd., 1980.

Sobel, Lester A., ed. *Political Terrorism.* 2 vols. Oxford: Clio Press, Ltd.,
1975.

Stahl, Michael, ed. *The Politics of Terrorism.* New York: Marcel Dekker,
1979.

Sterling, Claire. *The Terror Network.* London: Weidenfeld & Nicolson, 1981.

Sun Tzu. Translated by Samuel B. Griffith. *The Art of War*. London: Oxford University Press, 1963.

Supperstone, Michael. *Brownlie's Law of Public Order and National Security*. 2nd edn. London: Butterworth, 1981.

Taber, Robert. *The War of the Flea*. London: Paladin, 1970.

Taylor, Peter. *Beating the Terrorists?* Harmondsworth: Penguin Books Ltd., 1980.

Thackrah, J.R., ed. *Contemporary Policing*. London: Sphere Reference, 1985.

Thompson, Sir Robert. *No Exit from Viet Nam*. London: Chatto & Windus, 1969.

——*Defeating Communist Insurgency*. London: Chatto & Windus, 1974.

Tomlinson, John. *Left, Right. The March of Political Extremism in Britain*. London: John Calder, 1981.

Tophoven, Rolf. *GSG-9: Anti-Terrorist Unit*. Berlin: Wehr & Wissen, 1977.

——*GSG-9. German Response to Terrorism*. Koblenz: Bernard & Graefe Verlag, 1984.

Townshend, Charles. *The British Campaign in Ireland, 1919–1921*. Oxford; Oxford University Press, 1975.

——*Political Violence in Ireland*. Oxford: Clarendon Press, 1983.

——*Britain's Civil Wars*. London: Faber & Faber, 1986.

Trinquier, Roger. *Modern Warfare*. New York: Praeger, 1964.

Truby, J. David. *How Terrorists Kill*. Boulder: Paladin Press, 1978.

Turner, Stansfield. *Secrecy and Diplomacy*. London: Sidgwick & Jackson, 1986.

Utley, T.E. *Lessons of Ulster*. London: J.M. Dent & Sons, 1975.

Van Den Haag, Ernest. *Political Violence and Civil Disobedience*. New York: Harper & Row, 1972.

Wade, E.C.S. and Bradley, A.W. *Constitutional and Administrative Law*. 10th edn. London: Longman, 1985.

Wallace, Martin. *British Government in Northern Ireland*. London: David & Charles Ltd., 1982.

Walter, E.V. *Terror and Resistance: A Study of Political Violence*. London: Oxford University Press, 1969.

Wardlaw, Grant. *Political Terrorism: Political Tactics and Counter Measures*. New York: Cambridge University Press, 1983.

Watson, Francis M. *Political Terrorism: The Threat and the Response*. Washington, DC: Robert B. Luce, 1976.

Watt, David, ed. *The Constitution of Northern Ireland. Problems and Prospects*. London: Heinemann, 1981.

Waugh, William L., Jr. *International Terrorism*. Salisbury, NC: Documentary Publications, 1982.

Whitnah, Donald R., ed. *Government Agencies*. Westport: Greenwood Press, 1983.

Wilkinson, Paul. *Political Terrorism*. London: The Macmillan Press, 1974.

——*The New Fascists*. London: Grant McIntyre Ltd., 1981.

——*Terrorism and the Liberal State*. Rev. edn. London: The Macmillan Press, 1986.

——ed. *British Perspectives on Terrorism*. London: George Allen & Unwin, 1981.

*Selected bibliography*

Wilkinson, Paul and Stewart, A.M., eds. *Contemporary Research on Terrorism*. Aberdeen: Aberdeen University Press, 1987.
Williams, David. *Keeping the Peace*. London: Hutchinson, 1967.
Wilson, James Q. *The Investigators: Managing FBI and Narcotics Agents*. New York: Basic Books, 1978.
——*American Government. Institutions and Politics*. Lexington: D.C. Heath & Co., 1980.
Wolf, John B. *Fear of Fear: A Survey of Terrorist Operations and Controls in Open Societies*. New York: Plenum Press, 1981.
Young, Oran R. *The Intermediaries. Third Parties in International Crises*. Princeton: Princeton University Press, 1967.


Articles, monographs, papers, proceedings

Andrew, Christopher. 'Whitehall, Washington and the Intelligence Services'. *International Affairs* 53 (July 1977): 390–404.
Barnett, R.W. 'The U.S. Navy's Role in Countering Maritime Terrorism'. *Terrorism, an International Journal* 6 (1983): 469–80.
Bassiouni, M. Cherif. 'Terrorism, Law Enforcement, and the Mass Media: Perspectives, Problems, Proposals'. *Journal of Criminal Law and Criminology* 72 (Spring 1981): 1–51.
Bourne, Robin. 'Terrorist Incident Management and Jurisdictional Issues: A Canadian Perspective'. *Terrorism, an International Journal* 1, Numbers 3 & 4 (1978): 307–13.
——'Terrorism Incident Management in a Federal State', paper presented at Emergency Planning Research Conference, Arnprior, Ontario, January 1979.
Bowden, Tom. 'Guarding the State: The Police Response to Crisis Politics in Europe'. *British Journal of Law and Society* 5 (Summer 1978): 69–88.
Bramall, General Sir Edwin. 'The Place of the British Army in Public Order', paper delivered to the Royal Society for the Encouragement of Arts, Manufactures and Commerce, 6 February 1980.
Burns, Major Julian H., Jr. 'Tripoli to Tehran: Terrorism's Road Well-Travelled'. *Joint Perspectives* (Fall 1981): 42–53.
Chalfont, Lord. 'Terrorism and International Security'. *Terrorism, an International Journal* 5 (1982): 309–23.
Charters, David. 'Intelligence and Psychological Warfare Operations in Northern Ireland'. *RUSI Journal* 122 (September 1977): 22–7.
——'Security Services in an Open Society', and 'The Changing Forms of Conflict in Northern Ireland', *Conflict Quarterly* I (Fall 1980): 8–14 and 32–8.
——'Organization, Selection and Training of National Response Teams – A Canadian Perspective', *Conflict Quarterly* I (Winter 1981): 26–30.
Cline, Ray S. 'Policy without Intelligence', *Foreign Policy* 17 (Winter 1974–5): 121–35.
Clissold, Stephen. 'Croat Separatism: Nationalism, Dissidence, and Terrorism', *Conflict Studies* 103 (1979).
Clutterbuck, Major-General Richard. 'A Third Force?' *The Army Quarterly and Defence Review* (October 1973): 22–8.

Cunningham, Cyril. 'International Interrogation Techniques', *RUSI Journal* 117 (September 1972): 31–4.

Defense Nuclear Agency. *Proceedings of the 10th Annual Symposium on the Role of Behavioural Science in Physical Security*. Springfield, Va.: n.p., April 1985.

Derrer, Lt. Cdr. Douglas S., USNR. 'Terrorism', *Proceedings*, Naval Review 1985 (May 1985): 190–203.

Dugard, John. 'International Terrorism: Problems of Definition', *International Affairs* 50 (January 1974): 67–81.

Easterbrook, Major-General Ernest F., US Army. 'Helicopter Operations in Algeria', *Army Aviation* 8 (January 1960): 13–14.

Finegan, Jay. 'Terrorism', *Air Force Times Magazine* (October 1983): 13–14, 16, 18, 20.

Franck, Thomas M. and Lockwood, Bert B., Jr. 'Preliminary Thoughts Toward an International Convention on Terrorism', *American Journal of International Law* 68 (January 1974): 69–90.

Frankel, Norman. 'Electoral Politics in a Divided Society', *Conflict Quarterly* (Spring 1984): 40–55.

Gale, General Sir Richard. 'Old Problem: New Setting', *RUSI Journal* 117 (March 1972): 43–6.

Garvin, Stephen. 'Northern Ireland: A Question of Identity', *RUSI Journal* 117 (March 1972): 40–2.

Goldberg, Arthur J. 'The Murder in St. James's Square', *Encounter* 63 (November 1984): 67–70.

Graham, Lt. Col. P.W. 'Low-level Civil/Military Coordination, Belfast 1970–73', *RUSI Journal* 119 (September 1974): 80–4.

Green, L.C. 'Aspects of Terrorism', *Terrorism, an International Journal* 5 (1982): 373–400.

Gunter, Michael M. 'The Armenian Terrorist Campaign against Turkey', *Orbis* 27 (Summer 1983): 447–77.

Hardman, J.B.S. 'Terrorism', *The Encyclopedia of the Social Sciences* XIV (1964).

Heclo, H. Hugh. 'Policy Analysis', *British Journal of Political Science* 2 (January 1972) 83–108.

Hennessy, Peter. 'The Quality of Cabinet Government in Britain', Paper delivered at the annual congress of the International Political Science Association, Paris, July 1985.

Hutchinson, S. 'The Police Role In Counter-Insurgency Operations', *RUSI Journal* CXIV (December 1969): 56–61.

Janke, Peter. 'Ulster: A Decade of Violence', *Conflict Studies* 108 (1979).

Jenkins, Brian Michael. 'The Study of Terrorism: Definitional Problems', *Rand Corporation Monograph*, P. 6564, December 1980.

——'Terrorism in the 1980s', *Rand Corporation Monograph*, P. 6586, February 1981.

——'Testimony before the Senate Governmental Affairs Committee, January 27, 1978', *Rand Corporation Monograph*, P. 6624, May 1981.

——'A Strategy for Combatting Terrorism', *Rand Corporation Report*, R-2714, December 1982.

——'New Modes of Conflict', *Orbis* 28 (Spring 1984): 5–16.

*Selected bibliography*

Kellen, Konrad. 'On Terrorists and Terrorism', *Rand Corporation Report*, N-1942-RC, December 1982.

Kelley, Michael, and Mitchell, Thomas. 'The Study of Internal Conflict in Canada: Problems and Prospects', *Conflict Quarterly* II (Summer 1981): 10–17.

Kyle, Keigh. 'Sunningdale and after: Britain, Ireland, and Ulster', *World Today* 31 (November 1975): 439–50.

Lavin, Marvin M. 'Intelligence Constraints of the 1970s and Domestic Terrorism: A Survey of Legal, Legislative, and Administrative Constraints', *Rand Corporation Report*, N-1902-DOJ, December 1982.

Little, Lieut. M.R. 'The Evolution and Future of Revolutionary Guerrilla Warfare and Terrorism', *RUSI Journal* 129 (June 1984): 33–8.

Macdonald, Donald. 'International and Domestic Measures Against Terrorism', Research paper prepared by the Law and Government Division, Research Branch, Library of Parliament, Ottawa, 22 November 1985.

McDowell, Michael. 'The British Initiative in Ulster', *Conflict Quarterly* I (Summer 1980): 35–9.

McIlheney, Colin J. 'Arbiters of Ulster's Destiny? The Military Role of the Protestant Paramilitaries in Northern Ireland', *Conflict Quarterly* V (Spring 1985): 33-9.

Maechling, Charles, Jr. 'Containing Terrorism', *Foreign Service Journal* (July/August 1984): 33-7.

Maksymchuck, S/Sgt A.F., OPP. 'Strategies in Crisis Management', *Royal Canadian Military Institute Year Book 1982*: 15–19, 45.

Mans, Rowland. 'Canada's Constitutional Crisis. Separatism and Subversion', *Conflict Studies* 98 (1978).

Motley, Colonel James B. 'Terrorist Warfare: A Reassessment', *Military Review* LXV (June 1985): 45–7.

Murray, Russell. 'Killings in Northern Ireland 1969-1981', *Terrorism, an International Journal* 7 (1984): 1–50.

Nelson, Sarah. 'From Soldiers to Politicians – and Back: Political Violence and the Protestant Paramilitaries of Northern Ireland', Collected Seminar Papers No. 30, *Political Violence*, University of London, Institute of Commonwealth Studies, 1982: 46–54.

'Northern Ireland: An Anglo–Irish Dilemma?', *Conflict Studies* 1985 (1986).

O'Ballance, Edgar. 'Policing by Consent', *Contemporary Review* 240 (April 1982): 188–92.

Ofri, Arie. 'Intelligence and Counterterrorism', *Orbis* 28 (Spring 1984): 41–52.

Oseth, Lt. Col. John M. 'Intelligence and Low-Intensity Conflict', *Naval War College Review* (November-December 1984): 19–36.

——'Combatting Terrorism: The Dilemmas of a Decent Nation', *Parameters* XV (1985): 65–76.

Perkins, Brigadier K. 'Soldiers or Policemen?', *The British Army Review* (December 1973): 7–10.

Quainton, Ambassador Anthony C.E. 'Terrorism: Do Something! But What?', *Department of State Bulletin* (September 1979): 60–4.

Reid, Edna F. 'An Analysis of Terrorism Literature: A Bibliometric and

Content Analysis Study', Ph.D. dissertation, University of Southern
Colifornia, 1983.
Reiner, Robert. 'Political Conflict and the British Police Tradition',
*Contemporary Review* 236 (April 1980): 191–200.
Rose, Richard. 'Comparing Public Policy', *European Journal of Political
Research* 1 (April 1973): 67–94.
Rutan, Gerard F. 'The Canadian Security Intelligence Service: Squaring the
Demands of National Security with Canadian Democracy', *Conflict
Quarterly* V (Fall 1985): 17–30.
Shultz, Secretary of State George. 'Terrorism and the Modern World',
*Department of State Bulletin* (December 1984): 12–17.
Sim, Joe and Thomas, Philip A. 'The Prevention of Terrorism Act:
Normalizing the Politics of Repression', *Journal of Law and Society* 10
(Summer 1983): 71–84.
Smith, G. Davidson, Lt.Col. (Ret). 'The Military in Aid of the Civil Power:
Limits in a Democratic Society', *Canadian Defence Quarterly* 13 (Spring
1984): 27–33.
——'A Positive Approach to Terrorism: The Case for an Elite Counter-Force
in Canada', *RUSI Journal* 129 (September 1984): 17–22.
——'Issue Group Terrorism: Animal Rights Militancy in Britain', *Terrorism
Violence Insurgency Journal* 5 (Spring 1985): 44–47.
——'Political Violence in Animal Liberation', *Contemporary Review* 247
(July 1985): 26–31.
——'The Liberal Democratic Response to Terrorism: a Comparative Study of
the Policies of Canada, the United States, and the United Kingdom', Ph.D.
dissertation, University of Aberdeen (Scotland), 1986.
——'Counter-Terrorism: The Administrative Response in the United
Kingdom', *Journal of Public Policy and Administration*, Vol. 2, No. 1
(Spring, 1987).
Starnes, John. 'Canadian Internal Security. The Need for a New Approach, a
New Organization', *Canadian Defence Quarterly* (Summer 1979): 21–6.
Suvorov, Victor. 'Spetsnaz: The Soviet Union's Special Forces', *Military
Review* LXIV (March 1984): 30–46.
Taylor, Robert W. 'Managing Terrorist Incidents', *The Bureaucrat* (Winter
1983–4): 53–8.
'Terrorism and the Liberal State: A Reasonable Response', *Police Studies* 4
(Fall 1981): 34–51.
'Terrorism: Why Business Is Now a Prime Target', *International
Management* 40 (August 1985): 20–6.
'The War against Terrorism', *Harvard International Review* VII (May/June
1985).
Thompson, Brigadier W.F.K. 'Northern Ireland to 1973', *Brassey's Annual*
1973: 60–80.
Torrance, Judy. 'The Response of Canadian Governments to Violence',
*Canadian Journal of Political Science* 10 (September 1977): 473–96.
Tugwell, Brigadier M.A.J. 'Revolutionary Propaganda and Possible
Counter-Measures', Study prepared for the Department of War Studies,
King's College, University of London, 1979.
'Ulster: Politics and Terrorism', *Conflict Studies* 36 (1973).

*Selected bibliography*

Walsh, Dermot P.J. 'Arrest and Interrogation: Northern Ireland 1981', *Journal of Law and Society* 9 (Summer 1982): 37–59.
Watkins, Admiral James D. 'Terrorism: An "Already Declared" War', *Wings of Gold* (Summer 1984): 19–21.
Wildhorn, Sorrel, Jenkins, Brian Michael, and Lavin, Marvin M. 'Intelligence Constraints of the 1970s and Domestic Terrorism: Effects on the Incidence, Investigation, and Prosecution of Terrorist Activity', *Rand Corporation Report*, N-1901-DOJ, December 1982.
Wilkinson, Paul. 'Three Questions on Terrorism', *Government and Opposition* 8 (Summer 1973): 290–312.
——'Terrorism: International Dimensions. Answering the Challenge', *Conflict Studies* 113 (1979).
——'The Provisional IRA: In the Wake of the 1981 Hunger Strike', *Government and Opposition* 17 (Spring 1982): 140–56.
——'How Do Democratic States Cope With Terrorism?', Ditchley Conference Report No. 5, 1984/5.
——'Northern Ireland: An Alternative to Terrorism', *Contemporary Affairs Briefing* 2 (February 1986).
Wolgang, Marvin E., ed. 'International Terrorism', *The Annals of the American Academy of Political and Social Science* 463 (September 1982).
Wright, Major Jeffrey W., US Army. 'Terrorism: A Mode of Warfare', *Military Review* LXIV (October 1984): 35–45.
Yoder, Amos. 'United Nations Resolutions against International Terrorism', *Terrorism, an International Journal* 6 (1983): 503–17.

**Official reports and documents**

*Canada*

Report to the Canadian House of Commons, 1972. *The Enhancement of Crisis Handling Capability Within The Federal Structure.*
Dare
*Canadian Human Rights Act.* 25–26 Elizabeth II, 14 July 1977. Amended 20=9–30–31–32 Elizabeth II, 30 March 1983.
*Second Report of the Commission of Inquiry Concerning Certain Activities of the Royal Canadian Mounted Police: Freedom and Security Under the Law.* 2 vols. 1981.
McDonald
*Report on the October Crisis of 1970 to the Government of Quebec.* 1981.
Duchaine
*Report of the Commission of Inquiry into Police Operations within Quebec to the Government of Quebec.* 1981.
Keable
*Contemporary International Terrorism and its Impact on Canada.* ORAE Report No. R100, 1988.
Kellett
*The Charter of Rights and Freedoms.* (Ottawa: Minister of Supply and Services Canada, 1982.)

Selected bibliography

*Access to Information Act, Privacy Act.* 29–30–31 Elizabeth II, 7 July 1982.
*Canadian Security Intelligence Service Act.* 32–33 Elizabeth II, 28 June, 1984.
*Annual Report 1985–86.* Security Intelligence Review Committee. (Ottawa: Minister of Supply and Services Canada, 1986.)
*The Report of the Senate Special Committee on Terrorism and the Public Safety.* 1987.

Kelly

*Terrorism. The Report of the Second Special Committee of the Senate on Terrorism and Public Safety.* 1989.
*Parliamentary Debates* (Hansard). House of Commons Official Reports, 1968–86.


United States

*Disorders and Terrorism: Report of the Task Force on Disorders and Terrorism.* National Advisory Committee on Criminal Justice Standards and Goals, 1976.
*Long Commission Report, 'Executive Summary'.* US Marine Corps Public Affairs Office, 1983.

Long

*Patterns of Global Terrorism: 1983–1987.* 5 vols. US Department of State, 1984, 1985, 1986, 1987, 1988.
*FBI Analysis of Terrorist Incidents in the United States.* 3 vols. US Department of Justice, 1983, 1984, 1985.
*Hearings Before The Subcommittee On Security And Terrorism Of The Committee On The Judiciary, United States Senate, 98th Congress, 1984.*
*State-Sponsored Terrorism.* Report prepared for the Subcommittee on Security and Terrorism, for the use of the Committee On The Judiciary, United States Senate, 1985.
*Lethal Terrorist Actions Against Americans, 1973–1985.* US Department of State, 1985.
*The Reality: An ASALA–RM Pamphlet on ASALA and the Current Internal Dispute.* Special Report. US Department of State, 1985.
*Report of The Secretary of State's Advisory Panel on Overseas Security.* US Department of State, 1985.
*Terrorist Attacks on U.S. Businesses Abroad.* US Department of State, 1986.
*Public Report of the Vice President's Task Force On Combatting Terrorism,* 1986.

Bush
or
Task Force

*Terrorist Group Profiles,* 1988.


United Kingdom

Cmnd. 3165. *Report by Mr. Roderick Bowen, Q.C., on Procedures for the Arrest, Interrogation and Detention of Suspected Terrorists in Aden,* 1966.
Bowen

## Selected bibliography

Cmd. 535. *Report of the Advisory Committee on Police in Northern Ireland*, 1969.

*Hunt*

Cmnd. 4154. *Downing Street Declaration*, 1969.

Cmnd. 4823. *Report of the Enquiry into Allegations Against the Security Forces of Physical Brutality in Northern Ireland Arising out of Events on 9 August*, 1971.

*Compton*

Cmnd. 4901. *Report of the Committee of Privy Counsellors Appointed to Consider Authorized Procedures for the Interrogation of Persons Suspected of Terrorism*, 1972.

*Parker*

Cmnd. 5185. *Report of the Commission to Consider Legal Procedures to Deal with Terrorist Activities in Northern Ireland*, 1972.

*Diplock*

Cmd. 566. *Violence and Civil Disturbances in Northern Ireland in 1969, Report of the Tribunal of Inquiry*, 1972.

*Scarman*

HL101/HC220. *Report of the Tribunal to Inquire into the Events on Sunday, 30 January, 1972, which led to the Loss of Life in Connection with the Procession in Londonderry on that Day*, by the Rt. Hon. Lord Widgery, OBE, TD, 1972.

*Widgery*

Cmnd. 5259. *Northern Ireland Constitutional Proposals*, 1973.

*Whitelaw*

Cmnd. 5627. *Report of the Law Enforcement Commission to the Secretary of State for Northern Ireland and the Minister of Justice of Ireland*, 1974.

Cmnd. 5847. *Report of a Committee to Consider, in the Context of Civil Liberties and Human Rights, Measures to Deal with Terrorism in Northern Ireland*, 1975.

*Gardiner*

Cmnd. 5919. *The Red Lion Square Disorders of 15 June, 1974*. Report of the Inquiry by the Rt. Hon. Lord Justice Scarman, OBE, 1975.

*Scarman*

Cmnd. 7009. *The Protection of Human Rights by Law in Northern Ireland*. Report of the Standing Advisory Commission on Human Rights, 1977.

*Feather–Rankin–Plant*

Cmnd. 7324. *Review of the Operation of the Prevention of Terrorism (Temporary Provisions) Acts 1974 and 1976*, by the Rt. Hon. Lord Shackleton, KG, OBE, 1978.

*Shackleton*

Cmnd. 7497. *Report of the Committee of Inquiry into Police Interrogation Procedures in Northern Ireland*, 1979.

*Bennett*

# Index

For Product Safety Concerns and Information please contact our EU
representative GPSR@taylorandfrancis.com
Taylor & Francis Verlag GmbH, Kaufingerstraße 24, 80331 München, Germany

www.ingramcontent.com/pod-product-compliance
Lightning Source LLC
Chambersburg PA
CBHW071837270326
41929CB00013B/2022